A STATE OF MIND

MY STORY

A STATE OF MIND

MY STORY

RAMTHA
The Adventure Begins

JZ KNIGHT

WARNER BOOKS

A Warner Communications Company

The events in this story are true. Names and physical characteristics of many individuals have been changed in order to protect their privacy.

Warner Books, Inc., 666 Fifth Avenue, New York, NY 10103

W A Warner Communications Company

Book Design by Nick Mazzella
Printed in the United States of America
First Printing: October 1987
10 9 8 7 6 5 4 3 2 1
Library of Congress Cataloging-in-Publication Data

Ramtha, the enlightened one.
  A state of mind, my story.

  I. Title.
PS3568.A475S7 1987   813'.54   87-16072

ISBN: 0-446-51405-5

*To my beloved husband, Jeff, and my sons,
Brandy and Chris Knight.*

ACKNOWLEDGMENTS

I wish to extend my deepest appreciation to Anne-Marie Bennstrom whose steadfast support enabled me to write this book. To my agent Ellen Levine and Nansey Neiman of Warner Books for their commitment to make *A State of Mind, My Story* a reality. Finally, to my mother, Helen Angley, who had the strength and tenacity of a great oak tree to allow this sapling to grow strong enough to endure the storms that often accompany just being alive.

CONTENTS

PROLOGUE xi

CHAPTER ONE: Meeting Ramtha 1

CHAPTER TWO: The Great White Structure 21

CHAPTER THREE: Reminiscences of Bootsie 33

CHAPTER FOUR: Judy 41

CHAPTER FIVE: My Big Red Balloon 53

CHAPTER SIX: Doesn't God Love June Bugs, Too? 58

CHAPTER SEVEN: Dreams, Sermons, and Grab Bags 71

CHAPTER EIGHT: "Faith Has Need of the Whole Truth" 82

CHAPTER NINE: Encounter: The UFO and Forgetfulness 91

CHAPTER TEN: Baby, I Love You 106

CHAPTER ELEVEN: Long Live the Queen 132

CHAPTER TWELVE: The Hope Is That We Live Again 156

CHAPTER THIRTEEN: The Death of the Rose and Lily 193

CHAPTER FOURTEEN: The Birth of a Mogul 205

CHAPTER FIFTEEN: The Ghost and Sarah Lee 225

CHAPTER SIXTEEN: The Promised Land 239

CHAPTER SEVENTEEN: If You Believed . . . 264

CHAPTER EIGHTEEN: An Abnormal Business Called Life 279

CHAPTER NINETEEN: The One 303

CHAPTER TWENTY: A Most Gentle Persuasion 318

CHAPTER TWENTY-ONE: Pork Chops, Pink Blouses, and
Penitence 352

CHAPTER TWENTY-TWO: Cowboy 377

CHAPTER TWENTY-THREE: No Regrets, My Love 402

CHAPTER TWENTY-FOUR: Hope, the Waking Dream 421

SELECTED READING 447

PROLOGUE

Following a recent interview, the reporter asked me "off the record" if I had recently had an IQ test. I replied that I had not had one since high school. He stated that he was curious because I was one of the most intelligent women that he had had the pleasure of talking to for some time. I was deeply flattered, but somewhat surprised. My formal education extended only to business college and the rest of my learning had come from experiencing life—the highest form of education there is.

Looking back, my life has resembled an uphill climb with many downhill detours. If there is truth in predestination, I certainly chose a life that imposed every conceivable hardship and obstacle. The purpose: to stretch myself to the limits and understand the reason of my being and to know God.

I remember my early childhood as one filled with innocent joy—that is until age four, when I was brutally raped.

I would bloom from an ugly duckling into a beautiful young woman, fighting to hold on to my virtue and struggling to gain a sense of self-respect. I would marry three times: the first time for need, which bore me two sons; the second for security and stability; and the third for love. In my lifetime, I would fight disease, prejudice, and loneliness. I created two corporations in cable TV and would become the first woman to rise to the top in the marketing end of the industry. During my lifetime, I experienced a UFO, a miraculous healing, and a visit from my closest friend the same evening that she died.

I've had the honor of meeting some of the most famous people in the world and a few have become dear friends. But the most important of all to me will always be Ramtha, the Enlightened One. For no one else in my life has remained so steadfast. He has taught me the meaning of the words "unconditional love," which has freed me to look back on my life and be able to say "I have no regrets."

There may always be unseeing entities who war for preeminence and glory. And yet, while the petty battles continue, Ramtha's love prevails and his knowledge has been embraced and shared by many. This is my life.

A STATE
OF MIND
MY STORY

Ramtha. Glittering light of an unearthly presence, illuminating, pulsating, a vision of perhaps the grandiose creative mind. The feeling of reality sweeping away the objective consciousness of the nuances of the real world. In what form does one express the experience of an encounter with an entity that modern-day life has yet to define? An emotional feeling grapples to express itself in common terms, but fails. Ramtha is in this subliminal sphere.

The experience defies the common bond of relative facts, for there are none. For me, this emotion, this vision, the experience of the enigma Ramtha, the Enlightened One, would become the most powerful reality in my life.

CHAPTER ONE

MEETING RAMTHA

The adventure began at a dinner party in Tacoma, Washington. It was one of those often-boring social gatherings of the professional elite at polite play. With a chilling February rain falling outside and the atmosphere in the restaurant warm and cheery, the conversation began to change as everyone swilled warmed brandy. I remembered clearly, while sipping my milk, the comment, "It's called pyramid power, and George just put a bottle of Blue Nun under one." Bored by the mundane chatter and gossip that always accompany these events, my thoughts had drifted to what to wear the following week for another round of much of the same.

"Pyramid power?" I said, suddenly awake. "What are we talking about? Excuse me, George, but what do you mean 'under one'?"

"Just that Marge brought home this book about the Great Pyramid—you know, the one in Egypt?" puffed George.

"But, what do a pyramid in Egypt and a bottle of Blue Nun have in common?" I asked.

"JZ, it's so exciting," gushed Marge. "They think that the Great Pyramid has a mysterious power that mummifies things—you know, like the mummies?"

George smiled at his wife with amusement. He plainly enjoyed Marge's childlike enthusiasm. "JZ, through extensive research, according to the book," he explained, "it is believed that the pyramid can dehydrate food, change milk into yogurt . . ."

"Oh, I see," I said, laughing. "So if it can do all of those things, why not try it on the wine? George, did you build the Great Pyramid just for this tiny little improvement in the wine?"

"Yeah, George, tell us what it can do for balls?" asked Tom, while peals of laughter roared from our table. "I mean, think of the possibilities for balls, George."

"C'mon, you creeps, pipe down," I whispered. "The people at the next table are starting to stare." I returned my astonished gaze to George. "Now, George, do you really believe this stuff?"

George finished off his brandy and signaled to the waitress for another round, though his cheeks and lips were already flushed to a bright apricot from the drink. The waitress took the order—three more hot toddies, two martinis, a gin and tonic, and milk on the rocks, my usual. Everyone lit up another cigarette. George took a deep draw and elegantly exhaled the smoke in the direction of the next table. He then leaned forward, eyes shifting to each of us, and began, again.

"I cannot say that it does or it doesn't, but shit, it's exciting. Who knows if something works unless they try? I just had a hell of a good time trying to make that damned pyramid to scale. Jesus, I was as precise with it as any crown I ever made." George was a dentist, talking to a table of dentists and their wives. "And I lined the thing up perfectly to true north so it would work. I've made four of those little bastards, and man are they nice. I put some fruit under one to see if I can dehydrate the stuff. If it works, shit, I'm headed for Angel Lake with a backpack lighter than hell."

I sat there staring into George's piggy eyes as my imagination began to run wild with countless innovations. Forget Angel Lake and backpacks filled with dehydrated food, you fool. How about a face cream with instant beauty? God, every woman in the world would love that.

I glanced over my shoulder at Jeremy, my husband, and saw his bright shining blue eyes dancing with amusement and fascination. He was silently entranced with this unusual conversation.

Gary, another doctor, renowned not so much for his less-than-brilliant practice as for his persistent womanizing, rarely missed our get-togethers, and his dates always added a little pepper to the otherwise bland evenings. But Gary being Gary, no matter who was with him, he still hawked the surrounding tables and bar for possible bedland conquests . . . and usually succeeded. Up to this point, Gary hadn't seemed to give a damn about our conversation. Now, he began to take interest in it.

"Where does one find this treasure of a book?" he purred.

I lit another cigarette, wondering if perhaps Gary was looking for the eternal hard-on.

"Oh, I'm sure in most any bookstore," Marge answered. "It's probably in that weirdo section, you know, with psychic stuff, UFOs. God, JZ, can you believe the garbage people read? Why, just last week my mother brought home one of those ghastly tabloids, the ones you get at the checkout counter. Well, of course, I would *never* read such trash. Really! A headline about hemorrhoids and—"

"Marge, just the bookstore, dear." George always had a way of handling his wife's delightful ramblings so as not to cause social embarrassment for himself. Marge resorted to her usual defense of being the pouty little child who has been chastised.

"Hemorrhoids Healed By Extraterrestrials, Survey Reveals. Detroit Sales Up as Asses Are Now in Full Swing," roared Gary. "My God, where in the hell do they get that stuff?"

"Probably from eavesdropping on conversations in restaurants like this one," I laughed.

Our evening broke up with Gary feeling warm primeval

urges toward his little darling and the need to fulfill them. The rest of us made promises to get together real soon, while the men, all with crack timing, pulled out their wallets to begin the ritual of paying the bill.

Driving home, I sat hypnotized by the windshield wipers and the persistent gentle rain. My mind kept returning to our conversation on pyramid power. Somehow I kept feeling that I should investigate this phenomenon for myself. My husband beside me was his usual quiet self—careful, methodical and prudent. He was an ethical man, a talented dentist who nurtured a compassion for his patients in their suffering of pain. I felt lucky, maybe even blessed, to be his wife and friend. Security affords one the privilege of feeling blessed.

We were happily greeted by our bulldog, Gus, whose guard dog potential left a lot to be desired. But his loving, patient nature made him another child of the family. With the sitter paid for her services, I began to make the rounds of the boys' bedroom upstairs while my husband showered.

I joined my husband in the bathroom to wash the paint off my face—all that beauty smeared off into cotton balls!— then retired to the bed. My husband came in smelling of soap, toothpaste, and fresh talc.

"Zebra, if you have time tomorrow, could you stop by a bookstore and see if you can pick that book up? I'd like to take a look at it."

"My precious mellow-yellow hubby, I didn't know that you were really listening to all that stuff. You surprise me. Could there possibly be more to you than filling, drilling, billing, and hunting season?" I asked teasingly.

"My sweet Zebra, there is so much more," he purred as he began to draw me close. "I'm feeling inspired to show you more of myself." The heat was on.

"Hmm . . . Well, I promise I'll find the book. I suppose we can get as crazy as everyone else. Darling, lights out for this one . . . okay?"

The early-morning sky was veined with stretches of deep heliotrope and gray clouds. A light silvery rain whispered at the windows. The dogwood gently scraped the walls from the breeze. The house was filled with deep lavender shadows that infused calm throughout the rooms. The silence was broken by the soft chatter and melodious laughter of Brandy and Chris awakening in their room. I woke up refreshed and energized, prepared for the usual hectic morning schedule of events: helping Brandy and Chris into their school attire, preparing breakfast, throwing my makeup and clothes on, letting the bulldog out, kissing my husband good-bye, preparing school lunches, and driving the boys to their nearby school. I returned home and had my usual orange juice. No coffee, thank you. My mother had long ago nipped that habit by telling me that if I drank coffee it would make my neck black. Odd how such novel statements in youth can have a lifelong effect. After a short interlude of peace and quiet, I quickly began to scour my house thoroughly. I'm known for my dust-free living. House cleaned, I drove to the nearest bookstore. I walked into the store, but was hesitant to ask the clerk for the pyramid section, so I set out to find it myself. My search was futile. I quietly inquired as to its whereabouts, only to find that there were numerous books available. Not wanting to show my ignorance—snobs never do that—and not wanting to ask the question "Which one tells you how to build a pyramid?" I purchased them all. The clerk asked, "You want all of these books?"

"Of course," I replied. "I'm doing . . . a . . . research paper . . ." then, clearing my throat, "Yes, on pyramids," I lied.

With a major investment in books, I hurried to the car and returned home. After dinner that evening, with the boys bathed, I found my husband hidden in his study, methodically examining each book. Later, I would be asked to fill his list of materials, which read like something the boys would need for arts and crafts at school: twenty sheets of white construction paper, cardboard posters, two rulers, and a compass. Also, I was to call the weather bureau and find out the degrees of true north. True north? Could there be any other north?

The items bought, true north determined—much to the

dismay of Canadian geese—everything was readied for the next chapter of the pyramid saga. My husband returned home from work the next day charged with excitement. He wolfed down dinner, fixed himself a hot toddy, and retired to his study. Before bedtime, he returned to the kitchen to announce with pride that he had "made one." I walked into the study to find an object sitting on his desk—a pyramid made of white paper. Beside it sat a compass. He gave me an in-depth description of how he made it. It did not look magical. I was dubious. Sensing this, my husband assured me that I should have an open mind and to think positive. Right. I retired to bed, alone, but feeling that all was secure since my husband was burning the midnight oil downstairs.

The following day was Friday, and we were scheduled to attend a dinner party at a friend's home. My husband's secretary called to relay a message that "the doctor wishes you to cancel your attendance at dinner this evening." I called and canceled with an outright lie. That evening I helped my husband in his creation of the pharaohs' pride. I wondered what all those mummies would think if they could see how easily their eternal resting place could be transformed into paper. And in place of the dazzling treasure encased in them, a piece of bologna now rested. Could we be altering history?

We worked feverishly into the night, my husband so intense that he became very irritated with my less-than-precise assistance. He always acted this way with me when I participated in anything he was doing. This attitude always left me feeling that he was a sexist at heart. He looked at me intently, grumbled, "What a waste it is for women not to have talent or genius!" and turned away.

What an attitude about women! I'm certain that at moments he believed women were devious and should be bred carefully for wifely duties. Oh, yes, attractive physical attributes should be encouraged for lovemaking, and strong backbones for housework. But never genius, never talent.

I listlessly stared at the paper cutouts on the table. "Jeremy, I know that I know very little, but I am really trying to help you, that's all. If you want me to just leave and go to bed, I will."

He looked at me, and his impatient face became suffused with pleasure and affection. "Of course you are, my Zebra. I think my perfectionist sense gets the best of me sometimes," he said, in that tone of apology that always touched me with its poignancy. "I appreciate your help. I'm sorry, forgive me." He stood up and kissed me with his velvety lips. "Now, beautiful madam, help me finish this one. Damn, this is exciting."

The heat in the study cooled down, and "Einstein" made a crucial decision. I was demoted from "assistant to Genius" to "delivery person of important experimental samples." Those all-important items included another piece of bologna, a bottle of cheap wine, a glass of milk, a bottle of aspirin, a beetle, sliced bananas, a dirty tennis shoe, a jar of my face cream (to be transformed into miracle salve to erase wrinkles), a thin slice of beef, and a piece of paper containing a prayer, for me. The items delivered to the laboratory, Einstein meticulously placed each item under the pharaohs' nightmares and then realigned each ancient tomb to true north. This handsome study that once smelled of leather, rich tobacco, old books, lemon oil polish, and firewood now reeked with the smell of glue, bologna, a mingling of face cream and old sneakers, cigarettes, cognac, and a hint of raw meat.

Saturday morning brought a shock to my organized household. The boys were watching cartoons in the family room, a trail of Oreo cookie crumbs leading to their campsite. The remains of cereal bowls, half-eaten peanut butter toast, and empty glasses of chocolate milk that the bulldog was now lapping up told me that they had breakfasted on the carpet. Walking into my kitchen, I was horrified to find every available space covered with those crisp white little tombs. Two on top of the refrigerator, three on the breakfast bar, one in the pantry, one on the stove, four above the cabinets, and one atop Gus's dried dog food. As I quickly checked the inside of the refrigerator and oven, the mad—I mean *mad*—scientist appeared. Wearing his robe and favorite house shoes that the bulldog had cut his teeth on, I noticed that my fantasy of dentist-turned-Einstein had, in fact, materialized.

His hair was standing on its ends, and there was a glint of intense hysteria in those blue eyes.

It was just too much. "What . . . in God's good name . . . *are you doing?*"

"Zebra, a man's gotta do what a man's gotta do. Could you hand me that piece of cheese on the counter, and then I want you to run to the store and pick up some more paper. . . . Oh, uh, not the white but some various colors, I think I've written it all down. Oh, and be a dear and make me some more coffee. And I have given orders to the boys —*no friends over.*"

"I just want to know one thing," I demanded. "Have you gone off your rocker? I mean, *look* at this place. Worse, look at you. I just can't believe all this is going on because of a stupid dinner conversation." I paused, shaking my head. "I don't know what in the hell you think you are going to accomplish here. Look around you, please, and just tell me how I am going to manage to cook in here, not to mention how I'm supposed to clean up afterwards. God knows what may happen if the kids slam the refrigerator door too damn hard and jar that . . . that . . . pyramid from true north to southwest. It might spoil whatever is under that thing and set mankind back at least ten thousand years."

At eye level with the apex of one of his pyramids, my husband sat at the kitchen table, staring at me with noble, controlled indignation. After all, what could a common knave know about anything?

"Zebra, I do apologize for the mess in the kitchen. And for my behavior. But, Zebra, I'm enjoying myself *immensely.* Can't you see that? I want you to share this with me and see just how exciting it can be. Please, Honey, be a little patient. My God, Zebra, what if it does work? I get excited just thinking about it. Tonight, let's sit down together and log all of the things that I, er, we have done on this project to date. I will—" His smooth reply was interrupted by an abrupt knocking on the back door.

Without saying anything, I went to the back door. I carefully peeked out the window to see who was there. It was Jamie from next door, a friend of Brandy and Chris's and a frequent guest at our home. Guarded, I opened the door just enough to squeeze my face through the crack. "Jamie, hi, what do you want?" Stupid question.

Trying to see in through my shifting legs, he replied, "I'm comin' over to watch TV with Brandy and Chris. Can I come in?" as he pressed against the door.

"No . . . uh . . . no, Jamie, you can't. Brandy and Chris are dreadfully sick. Uh . . . they're in bed, sick," I said, making the face of a sick kid and trying to close the door.

"Oh, that's all right, Mrs. Wilder, I've had all my shots. I'll just come in and cheer them up and—" I interrupted his invitation.

"Aren't you just the sweetest little Jamie, but they are going to the hospital and—"

He interrupted me—a rude thing for a child to do.

"Jumping thunderbolts, the hospital, wow, can I go in the ambulance? Please, please?"

I stared at him, amazed by the determination of an eight-year-old mind. A mind, no doubt, formed with the generous help of television. If that little kid got a good look at the kitchen and another good look at the good doctor, the neighborhood would come alive with utter pandemonium. Not to mention, of course, the gossip that would fly over the phone lines. I could see the PTA meetings, luncheons, professional dinners, Christmas balls, and the supermarket all becoming enthralled by such scandal.

"Jamie, come back in two weeks," I said, shutting the door. In my frenzy for security, I locked the door and lowered the blinds on its little window. Caught up in my anxiety, I hurried first into the kitchen and began drawing curtains, then closing shutters in one room after another. Night had descended upon our morning. The heightened sense of shame about the paranormal had set in.

Arriving back in the kitchen, I found Einstein observing me in dim light. "I just feel that it's best this way," I told him. "With the neighbors and all." I turned on the light above the table and then moved a writing lamp in from the study, sat it on the table, plugged it in, and turned it on. Einstein chuckled. I began to laugh with nervous release. Einstein changed back to my husband and gave me a big kiss and a hug. I was now committed. The kitchen became a top secret place. I was a partner in intrigue.

The pale Saturday afternoon sun passed into a mauve and glittering blue twilight. A white-faced moon slowly climbed through rosy-tinted mists. The fragrance of burning fruit-wood hung in the moist air. The delicious evening had come unnoticed. Our labor had been continuous, breaking only for hot dogs, chips, and Cokes for sustenance. With the boys put to bed, the bulldog fed with pyramid-power-packed dog food, and the phone off the hook, we proceeded into the evening. More pyramids were methodically constructed—blue, red, yellow, green, purple (adds power), and basic white ones. My kitchen was looking more like a wholesale warehouse than a kitchen, but it was worth it. We retired at three A.M. Exhausted.

Sunday morning began late. The bulldog was very upset at holding his usual morning constitution for so long. I had barely opened the door when he barged through my legs, throwing the door wide open, and disappeared behind a shrub. The morning came and went without even opening the Sunday paper. At noon, we all took a sandwich break. The boys were becoming irritable and fistfights broke out. Between shouted threats and name calling—"turkey breath"; "frog face"; "stupid turd"; "just try . . . I dare you, chicken liver"—I had come to the conclusion that prison life was not working for the inmates, whose only crime, after all, had been being born to crazed parents. Their parole came only when each had taken an oath that he would not even talk about the pyramids and our clandestine behavior. They were released to go over to their friends' houses and play.

Einstein and I were becoming giddy and downright silly. You can only do so many pyramids, and there are only so many things you can find to go under them. Maybe that is why all those mummies died so young—they laughed them-selves to death building their graves. At any rate, we began to laugh hysterically. In jest, I grabbed one of the rejects off the floor, held it over my head, and proclaimed, "Attention, attention please, you are now about to witness a miracle. We are about to place our new brain machine upon the willing victim, upon whom nature did not smile with great intelligence. Carefully we place the pyramid in the aligned position, encompassing the entire head and face. In moments, gentlemen, you will witness a truly magnificent transformation.''

I placed it on my head, and through peals of laughter from myself and Einstein, I mumbled, "I sure hope it works." After a few moments, I lifted the end of the pyramid just to eye level and, laughing so hard that tears were streaming from my eyes, I caught the glimmer of a bright light at the other end of my kitchen. The light was blurred by the tears, so I reached for a tissue and wiped the tears away. I blinked, and to my utter shock and amazement, there stood a giant man at the other end of my kitchen . . . just standing there, aglow.

This . . . thing . . . was made all of light, like golden glitter dropped through a ray of sunlight. His shoulders came to the top of the door, and it was as if the ceiling had disappeared to make room for his head. It was beautiful. His robe seemed to be of purple light, a dazzling display of color and crystal against this strangeness of immense human form. An illuminating white overlay formed the broad mantle of his shoulders. I could not make out if jewels and gold flashed upon his heavenly robe or if they were lights. These were the brightest lights and colors I had ever seen, and yet they were not harsh. His face . . . it was the most beautiful face I had ever seen . . . eyes that shone like ebony stones with copper flashes . . . skin, if that is what it was, the coloring of olive, bronze, illuminated, and a fine chiseled nose and a broad jawline and a smile that would rival any Hollywood star's. My eyes went glassy, like those of a sleepwalker. I could hear voices about me, but they were far away, like in a dream. The power to reason had fled my mind, and I felt pulled into the splendor of that unearthly magic. A blue light blazed and filled the room with an aura of innocence and holy peace that emanated from this stately form. A moment later—I don't know, maybe it was an *hour* later—I formed an utterance of words that must have come from a feeble innocence within my being. "You are so beautiful. Who are you?"

A smile so divine parted his lips to reveal glistening, immaculate teeth.

"I am Ramtha, the Enlightened One. I have come to help you over the ditch." The words were delivered in a most melodious manner.

My mind had been whirling up to that point, but the word "ditch"—ditch? what ditch?—caught my attention. I broke the gaze. I came out of the dreamstate and became of the earth again. Ditch? I quickly bent to see if the kitchen floor had fallen away. What other ditch could he mean? The floor was still under my chair, and the miracle cap had fallen off of my head. Stupid, stupid, stupid. Where had my good sense gone? What kind of crazy dream was I having, anyway? I started laughing nervously again, putting both hands to my head as if to clasp it together. Wake up, dummy, it's time to fix breakfast. Then I looked back in the direction of the "dream" and the "dream" was laughing, too. Suddenly this wasn't so funny anymore.

"Beloved woman, the greatest of things are achieved with a light heart," he continued. "It is the ditch of limitation and fear I will help you over. For you will, indeed, beloved woman, become a light unto the world. Know that you are greatly loved, for the Father in heaven knows of you and loves you, greatly, indeed."

Too stunned to feel frightened, I was without words, my mind unable to comprehend his message. I was mute as Ramtha continued to speak.

"Beloved woman, I desire you to know that you and your beloved family are in danger within this house. I desire you to be out of this place within five days in your counting and in number. Your children will dream a dream of that which is to come. Heed the dreams. Children are of the innocence to see many profound things, they are the prophets of a new age. I have prepared a great white structure for you as your new hovel. Indeed, there is a noble runner, entity, that will help you to find it. You will know who he is. Indeed, beloved woman, there are many changes coming.

Prepare yourself. Know that you are greatly loved. I am Ramtha, the Enlightened One." The lights went out. . . . The "dream" had gone.

As I sat there, numb, speechless, slowly everything that was normal began to become focused. A voice, faint and far away, was calling, "Zebra? Zebra, can you hear me?" Now, it was getting closer, more distinct.

I turned slowly in the direction of the voice. It was my husband. He got up and came over and put his arms around me, and I began to feel more real. I needed his warmth. After a few moments—I thought it was a few moments—I turned and looked into his eyes, searching to see if he had seen what I had seen. His eyes told me he had not.

"My God, Zebra, you're shaking. Don't move. I'll get you a wrap . . . and some tea." There was real concern in his voice. He returned shortly with a shawl and the hot tea. While I began to sip the nourishing liquid, my husband moved his chair in front of me and continued to soothe me.

I looked all around my kitchen. Everything was the way I had remembered it before the experience. A brilliant edge of sunlight shot through the white eyelet curtains, touching the table and floor like the tip of an illuminating sword. I gazed through the pulled curtains and embraced the silent beauty of low mauve clouds that shaded the dusky end-of-day sky. I shut my eyes for a moment and the vision vanished. Then I looked at my husband and I began to speak, feeling a bit less disconnected. "I . . . did you . . . see anything? Anything different . . . unusual . . . here in our kitchen?" I watched and waited intently for his reply. He hesitated, tenderness flooding his face.

"I don't know what went on in here, Zebra. I was laughing as much as you were, and then it was just as if you changed—"

"What do you mean that I changed?" I interrupted.

"It's hard to describe." Jeremy pondered, then shook his head. "You just looked like someone in shock. You were staring, and muttering things that didn't make any sense, and you looked, I don't know, like you were lit up, shining, like an angel. It was strange, Zebra, I felt like there was a rushing or a weird feeling, and that compass was going crazy. I felt funny—like in a dream, when you can't move? I want you to tell me what was going on. Do you feel you can? Just take your time, honey."

The emotion that flooded my being kept the memory of my vision alive, and I began to recount the event, pausing often to find the right words. I glanced over several times at the compass. Nothing was happening. I had an impulse to recant this whole thing and blame it on fatigue and exhaustion. Expecting my husband to disbelieve me, I fixed my eyes on the floor when I was done and awaited his comments.

"Zebra, I *know* that something went on," he said, and at his tone my discomfort quickened. "I did not see this vision and this Ramtha, but I do believe you. I believe you had a holy experience. Things like this have happened to people . . . really. I mean, I have never had anything like this happen . . . even when I watched my mother die." He paused, thinking. A slight tremor ran over his face. "Zebra, I think that the most important thing that we can do is not to be afraid. I know you have every right to be, but, Zebra, I feel that this has something to do with the will of God. It's good, Zebra, believe me. I just know it is. Trust me." He put his arms around me, gently rocking me. I held on tight. "Oh, my precious Zebra, I do love you, and it's going to be all right. Whoever this Ramtha is, I have a feeling he will be back and maybe we can find out what's going on. I feel so good about this, I really do."

I pulled myself away from him in unbelievable horror. "I can't believe you are saying this stuff: *You* feel good. Don't be scared. Shit I *am* scared. What the hell are you thinking? *You* didn't see that . . . that *thing,* remember? I did! *I don't want him to come back. Never! Never!*" I screamed with tears flowing down my face. He tried to take my trembling hand, but I pulled it away from him and covered my face with my hands. "I just want to go to bed and forget this nightmare ever happened, you hear me? I want to go to bed . . . now!"

I wheeled around, kicked the damn pyramid on the floor, and fled upstairs.

"It's *not* okay. Shut up, *please!*" I snapped. I tried to

regain my composure as I went to the boys' room to make sure they were all right. I was in such a daze, I'd forgotten they were outside playing. The only snoring coming from their room was that of the bulldog, who was not disturbed by my presence. Suddenly overcome by unusual exhaustion, I went to the bathroom to wash and prepare for bed. I stopped scrubbing my face and began to gaze at the reflection in the mirror. "Beloved woman, you will become a light unto the world." The thought was there, and soon was whispered lightly on my lips as if in wonderment at the woman in the mirror. The face was beautiful, yet it was the same old face I had seen a thousand times in the mirror, nothing changed. I washed the thought down the drain along with the remains of my makeup.

I quickly showered, refusing to think of anything but the soothing warm water and perfumed soap. I dressed for bed, noticing that my husband had not come up from downstairs. I started to go down and find out what he was doing and kiss him good night, but then I hesitated. There was something that I wanted to do in private. Pray. I always prayed to God for guidance and asked Him to protect our family, to help with my husband's practice. And I always gave thanks for the blessings in our family. I knelt down beside my bed, hands clasped, and I began, "Heavenly Father, I beseech your protection and love upon myself and my family. Father, I ask that you remove from my memory this odious experience and bring peace to my soul. Father, if I am wrong about this thing, I would ask that you send me a sign . . . something, that I would know that this is your will. Father, help me." I began to cry, and reached for some tissues on the nightstand to wipe the tears away. "Father, I'm so confused and scared. Please help me and restore me. This I humbly ask, Father, in the name of Jésus Christ, amen."

Feeling a bit better, for all my life God had answered my prayers, I got into bed. I remember hearing the boys come in and Jeremy telling them to be very quiet. Silver shadows lay across the room from the slivered crescent moon hanging in a purple sky. A branch gently scraped across the window, and the floor creaked beneath my bed. Normal.

Yes, everything was normal—and that, after all, is security. I quickly fell into a fast sleep, but during the night I was troubled by extraordinary dreams, a montage of ancient warriors, places, and events on a scale that equaled a Cecil B. de Mille production of *Ben Hur* and *The Ten Commandments*.

Monday morning came early, the alarm set for six A.M. I awoke feeling troubled by the dreams, but otherwise refreshed. I quickly dressed and went downstairs to tidy up and made breakfast and lunches for the boys. I pulled up the blinds on the windows and drew back the curtains. It was a fabulous day for February. The sun was not yet up, but the first rosy light of dawn was there to dispel the night, and the slight glimmer of frost on the window framed the beautiful quiet awakening of the day. A polished bowl of African violets sitting on the stiff linen tablecloth glimmered faintly with color. In an unseen tree, a robin sang his sweet notes into the new morning. It felt good to be alive. Looking around my kitchen, I saw that the pyramids were still there, but somehow they were not so ominous and imposing.

Lunch boxes filled with healthy goodies, breakfast ready, I proceeded upstairs. Someone was crying. I hurried to the boys' room to find that both of my children were sitting on Chris's bed, sobbing. "What are you both crying about, my precious li'l guys? Tell Mommy." I sat down and put my arms around them. "Shhhh, now, it's all right. Shhhh, Mommy is here. Tell me what's wrong."

Brandy began, "I . . . *hic* . . . dreamed that these hippies . . . *hic* . . . broke the back door down and shot my Dad dead. He was sitting a-at the table, and the one hippy shot my little brother." A cold chill ran up my spine. Chris stopped crying and repeated the same dream except, ". . . and I went to live with God, Mommy, in heaven." I sat there pretending everything was all right and comforted my dear children. My husband entered the room.

"Hey, guys and gal, what's going on? Start by giving me a big kiss." He grabbed them up in his arms, got them to smile, and received their kisses. "Now tell me what's wrong."

"No, don't. I mean, it was just a bad dream and they are going to be fine. Aren't you, guys?" I urged. Pulling some tissue out of my apron pocket, I wiped their eyes and had them blow their little noses. Then I proceeded to get them organized for school. My husband motioned for me and I left the boys' room. "Zebra," he whispered, "listen, I heard everything. Now, everything is going to be all right. I called the office and told them I would be late. I'll take the kids to school, and what I would like you to do for me is just go for a drive today. I want you to get out of the house for a while." I tried to interrupt him, but he was insistent and continued, "Just do this for me, okay?"

"Okay, but—"

"No buts, Zebra, that's an order. I'll call you later. Don't worry about dinner, I'll bring something home. Hey, I love you."

After they had gone, I let the bulldog in and then I locked up the house and checked my watch: nine-fifteen. I got in my car and started to warm up the engine. I kept trying to think of where I would go. The weather was wonderful. The sun was up, a faint mist was rising from the ground, and the air was cold and crisp. I would just drive around and maybe do a little shopping.

Driving through Lakewood, a lovely wealthy section with quaint little New England–style shops, I caught a glimpse of a gorgeous red sequined gown displayed in a window and decided to turn around and go back. I found a building with a circular drive and pulled in. Just then a voice, firm but gentle, said, "Stop here. Go inside and ask about a great white structure." Stunned, I turned off the car engine and began to look around for the source of the peculiar voice. There was no one in sight. I looked at the building that I was parked in front of. It appeared to be a house that had been tastefully converted into some sort of office building. I looked about the green doors. The sign read REAL ESTATE UNLIMITED. I hesitated, and the voice came again. "Ask of the entity Roy." Startled, I looked in the backseat. Nothing. I looked in the rearview mirror. Just me. Aggravated, I looked again in the mirror, checked my makeup, got out of the car, and walked into the reception area. It was very plain, the carpet looking as if it had come with the original house, the walls paneled in dark wood, a few sparse plants. And there was the heavy aroma of stale cigarette smoke. Losing my nerve, I turned around and was headed for the door when a woman behind a desk asked, "May I help you?"

Stopping, I turned to her and replied, "Yes . . . uh, is the entity Roy—" Crap! "I mean, is Roy in?"

Puzzled, she queried me, "Which one, Mr. Burnsides or Mr. Underhill. Both are named Roy."

Shit! Now you done it! Endeavoring to look cool and poised and not up the creek without a paddle, I purred, "Oh, my dear, I was referred to him, uh, them by a very, very wealthy friend who recommended that I specifically ask for Roy, the one who deals in large white structures . . . uh, buildings, oh, I mean houses, homes . . . large white ones." End of screwup.

"Of course, that must be Mr. Burnsides. May I ask your name and who referred you?" Very professional.

"Yes, tell him that Mrs. Wilder, wife of *Dr.* Wilder, is here to see him." Heavy emphasis on the word "doctor."

The attractive middle-aged secretary was writing down my name as she repeated it out loud, I suppose allowing me to correct it somehow.

"And Mrs. Wilder, who may I say referred you to Mr. Burnsides?" She looked up at me with a fixed red grin, waiting.

"Oh," I retorted, chuckling, "I *really* don't think Mr. Burnsides has had the privilege of meeting the voice—I mean our associate, who has a marvelous voice." Stupid.

Within a few moments, a man appeared. He was short, but firm and muscular. He moved with quiet and certain authority. His solid square face expressed strength and an enormous intelligence. He was balding, and possessed exquisite blue eyes that were quick and thoughtful. He was dressed quite casually, wearing a white shirt, tie, permapress slacks, and scuffed brown shoes. Only the plaid sport coat was missing. "Mrs. Wilder, I'm Roy Burnsides. Would you like to come into my office?"

"Certainly, Mr. Burnsides," I answered with formality. What airs I had learned.

He looked both charmed and amused. "Please, call me Roy."

"Very well, Roy." I followed him into his office and seated myself across from an enormous desk, the only items on it a large glass ashtray brimming over with old butts and ash, two pencils, a calendar, and a Styrofoam cup. The walls held maps of the greater Puget Sound area, well marked and well used. The office was small and stuffy. A light mantle of gray dust covered everything. Roy seated himself and asked, "Now, Mrs. Wilder, what can I help you with?"

I began to fumble and twist my wedding ring, thinking just how or what I was going to say to him. My neck was getting hot from my long thick hair, and I casually pulled it back. Oh, God! Here goes. "Roy, I am interested in looking at a great white house. It has to be large. And . . . white. The doctor and I need a large home to do an extensive amount of entertaining . . . you know." Well, it was a beginning.

"A large white house, eh?" He blinked his eyes several times and continued in his soft monotoned voice. "Any particular area? Any particular price range? When do you want to move in?"

I shifted in my seat, uncrossed my legs and recrossed them, pulled my skirt down over my knees. "I just love white houses, don't you?" He nodded. "They are so clean looking, just about anywhere you can find them, so wherever a large white house is for sale, and empty, and reasonable, we want to move in by Friday!"

The smiling nods had wilted into a look of controlled alarm. "You . . . want to move in by Friday . . . this Friday?"

"Yes, I always move forward quickly when I make up my mind. I admire decisiveness in anyone, don't you?" Sure, lady, was the expression. "And besides, we've been packed for some time, just waiting to find that . . . large white structure." Taking a deep breath, I exhaled the words, "I just know between us"—bat those big baby blues, honey—"that together we will find my dream home. So, now, how soon can we begin?" Bat, bat, smile.

Poor man, after that performance, I felt he would do anything now to find the means to my utter happiness. I watched him get up as if in a trance and utter, "Excuse me a moment," as he left the room. I was alone. The very thought that I was in this place, wanting to buy another house, pack up and be moved in by Friday, and lying, lying, lying was becoming somewhat detestable. Oh, God, I have to stop this nonsense. I must be going crazy. Now just stop this charade. Apologize to poor Roy, excuse yourself, and make up another blockbuster lie to add to the already growing list and get out of here. I got up, getting ready to leave, when Roy came bustling back into the office with a file full of papers. "Well, this is a bit unusual, but I do have some listings that you might want to look at. They are all local and we can leave right now and go see them. Does that sound decisive enough?"

I slowly sat down and smiled. "Oh, well, you are being decisive. I'm so impressed. And you want to leave *now?*" Keep it up, honey, you're doing just terrific.

"Shall we go, then?" he asked, putting on his gray coat. "My car is right outside."

"I'm ready. I can hardly wait!" I gushed.

CHAPTER TWO

THE GREAT WHITE STRUCTURE

Roy drove me around Lakewood in his yellow Cadillac. He was a very pleasant man to talk to. His manner was easy, and he had a smooth, relaxing voice. He could very easily have been a hypnotist—no doubt an asset in his work. He began to describe the first house that we were going to, the "dream" home built by a couple who had put a great deal of effort into it. Unfortunately, shortly after completion the couple was transferred to California and they put the house up for sale. They also had removed the front doors—antiques, he supposed—the porch and foyer chandeliers, and they'd never had the time to establish a yard. In spite of all these inadequacies, Roy felt that the house had "potential." He stressed the point that the house was in a quiet cul-de-sac, only one neighbor across the street. There was plenty of wooded area for even more privacy, and it was located very close to the best schools in

21

the Lakewood area. I was still feeling dubious about my "playacting"—a word that sounds so much better than just plain lying!

Roy continued to talk about real estate as we began to wind slowly into a quiet, beautiful neighborhood. We turned onto a street at the top of the hill, and Roy began, "Now if you look over to your right, second lot, you will see the first house. Remember about the doors, I've put up plywood to cover the entry."

A large two-story gray house came slowly into view. It looked more like a small Southern plantation house, with its large white columns and extended veranda. It was set deep on its spacious corner lot and it was painted gray . . . a pukey gray! There was not a sprig of grass to be found in the dandelion jungle of front grounds. Roy drove into the driveway in the rear of the house. Again, there was no lawn, no flowers, or bushes, just a plain concrete slab of a driveway and patio area. I just sat there looking at this unloved and uncared-for house. I did not get out of the car.

"Well, do you want to go in? It's empty, has been for about eight months now," he said, grasping the keys in his hand.

"I just don't think this is what I'm looking for, Roy. And it isn't even white." I was disappointed.

"All right. I have two more places to take you. They are presently occupied by the owners, but I've made arrangements with them and they are expecting us." He shook his head. "Boy, if someone wanted to put the time and money into a ready-built shell, this house could be a showplace. And, I do agree, it would look much better painted white."

I felt a tingle of feeling that gave me goose bumps. Roy drove us to the other appointments. They were both very nice but the feeling of "knowing what I want" wasn't there. Finally, Roy said, "Let's go back to the first house, and I want to take you inside. I just feel something about you and that house. I just think that you should see the inside as well. It's very close to where we are now. Do you have time to see it again?"

I checked my watch; it was 1:22 P.M. The boys would

be getting out of school at 2:15, and I would need to pick them up. I finally said yes and away we went. This time, however, I looked more intently at the outside as we drove up. I pictured the whole house painted white, a full luxurious lawn, immaculate gardens, and sparkling light fixtures on the outside. It felt great. Roy unlocked the back door and we walked into the laundry room. It was papered in a yellow design, and the floor was a white tile. Very cheery. We entered the kitchen. Everything was white—cabinets, floor, stove, refrigerator—and the room was brightly lit. The family room, adjacent to the kitchen, had pea green carpet, white walls, and an enormous fireplace made of brick to the ceiling. The room had sliding glass doors that opened onto the concrete patio out back. We went into the formal living room. Everything was white. The carpet was a thick white wool shag and the walls were painted white. Gorgeous bay windows faced the front yard. We then went into the formal entry. The floor was white, and the elegant spiral staircase was white wrought iron.

I was rapidly falling in love with this place. The dining room was laid out much like the living room, again all in white. We went up the thickly carpeted stairs. To the left was a guest room, then two smaller rooms, ideal for the boys' bedrooms. In the center of the hall was the main bathroom. It was very spacious. All white with gold fixtures. The master suite was very roomy and contained an enormous closet with the floor edged in cedar.

We returned downstairs to the family room, and Roy said, "Come to think of it, Mrs. Wilder, the only colors in this house other than white are the yellow wallpaper in the laundry room and this green carpet here in the family room." He was right. Just the outside needed to be painted. Roy seemed to be reading my mind. "And you can always paint the outside."

I started to feel wonderful things about this place. I think that I would have wanted it even if— Oh, my God, the boys' dream came rushing back to me. Suddenly I was filled with horror and anxiety. That vision—Ramtha or whatever his name was—that thing that I wanted to forget, I hadn't. Five days to leave . . . great white structure . . . the voice . . . "ask of the entity Roy" . . . "all is prepared." I began to respond to the possible truth of all these things, and as a result, I acted out of desperation.

"Roy, I know that this may seem strange to you, but is it possible to move into this house by Friday? It would be so very difficult to explain to you the reasons. Please, do try to understand. What do we need to do to get it . . . *now?*" My voice was filled with urgency and tinged with obvious stress.

"Well, first I have to call the owners. They're asking eighty-five thousand, and I don't think they will go any lower. Then, if an agreeable price can be established, you'll need to put some earnest money down. I suppose maybe you could rent the house from them until the loan closes. Is your husband moving in with you?" He slid that one in, and I was caught a little off guard.

"Of course my husband is moving in. . . . Oh, I see, you presumed from my urgency that I might be leaving my husband. No, no, that isn't the reason at all."

He smiled, maybe relieved. It was still uncommon in 1977 for a woman to buy her own home.

I asked Roy how much he would need for the earnest money agreement. I wrote him out a check and signed the agreement. Of course, he would have to contact my husband for his signature. My poor husband, little did he know that while he was extracting teeth, I had contracted for a house. It was the most expensive drive I had ever taken.

Roy returned me to my car, promising that he would call us at home that night after he had talked with the owners. I sped away to pick up the boys at school, then rushed home to call my husband's office. I told his receptionist that it was an emergency.

"Hello, Zebra, what's going on?"

"Dear, I bought the great white structure!" Anticipation was setting in and I began to chew my bottom lip.

Pause.

"Jeremy, are you there?"

"Yeah, I'm here."

"I said, I bought the great white structure. I went for

the drive as you suggested and . . ." I continued the story, blow by blow. He never said a word, and I was so caught up with myself that I never thought to ask him if he was still alive. ". . . so I gave Roy a check for the earnest money, signed the agreement—of course, you will have to sign also—and Roy will be calling you tonight at home. . . . Hello? . . . Jeremy?"

"Hello, I'm still here—I think. Zebra, that sounds just fine. Good girl. Listen, I've got to go. I'll see you when I get home."

"Jeremy, did you hear everything that I said?" I didn't believe my ears.

"Everything!"

"You mean to tell me you think I did the right thing? You haven't even seen this place. I mean, aren't you pissed off at me . . . after all there is quite a difference in buying underwear, not on sale, and buying a house, on sale?" I had to make sure he had heard me. It would make all the difference in what I made for dinner—something fabulous to ease the retribution I might be in for, or just my usual fare.

"Look, Zebra, I'm not pissed off at you. You did what you were supposed to do and it worked. Do me a favor, get ready to move by Friday. I'll see you later. Gotta go. Bye." Click.

I hung up the phone and stared at it, completely dumbfounded. I began to smile faintly, but not with amusement or relief. The clock in the hall chimed the hour. I fumbled a cigarette out of my purse and lit up. The hissing gray smoke spiraled into turbulent clouds in a stream of burning sunlight from the windows. My mind was a whirlwind. God! What was going on?

"My beloved woman, you have done well indeed!" He startled me. The cigarette dropped from my fingers and began to sizzle on the linoleum. "I am pleased! The great white structure you have chosen will be the beginning of many changes, for indeed, a great adventure awaits you. Now, beloved woman, you will be able to hear my words and, indeed, see my presence as no one else can. For I am Ramtha, the Enlightened One, the power that walks with you. Do not be in fear, for that which be I, be I of the I Am, and that be the I Am of God the Father, as you term it, indeed! There is, indeed, much for you to learn and, indeed, I will help you to unfold into greater knowingness, indeed, unto greater understanding. Speak to that which be your beloved husbandman as, indeed, I have spoken to you. There will come an hour in which, though he will not see me, he will speak to me. Indeed, beloved woman, his faith is strong. Know that you are loved!'' So spoke the beautiful being.

This was my second *seen* encounter with Ramtha. He had just appeared in front of me in the kitchen. The same illuminating light was on him, just as it was the first time. I was not afraid this time, but I was stunned by the things he had said. I had been touched by a holy light. One would certainly expect me to react differently, but somehow, the light of his presence brought a peace that I had never experienced in my life, and with that, I became more calm and centered. This is not to say that I didn't have a thousand questions. I was still puzzled, unsure of it all, dazzled by his beauty and the light that seemed to exude from his presence and its altogether unearthly and uncommon existence. It and he were a mystery, and still even today I marvel at his very existence just as I marvel at the total concept of God. There was a strength that accompanied him that would begin, at that second meeting, to flow into me. It certainly gave me the tenacity to flow with the changes. My stewardship with Ramtha and his teachings had begun.

I stood there, gazing at him, feeling an ardent love within me and joy that I had never doubted the beneficence of God, who must be responsible for this angel and his message. I wondered if I could ask this Ramtha a question. Before I could form the question and make my mouth respond, his face became even more glowing as a breathtaking smile came over his face and his eyes sparkled. "Indeed, beloved woman, you may ask, indeed!''

My mouth flew open. *He read my mind,* I thought. *How did he do that?*

"Indeed, beloved entity, I know what you know. For desire I that you should be in knowledge of that that which you are be that which be God. . . . All is. That which be I, be God. . . . All is. Unto this understanding that I have given you, the only difference between you, beloved woman, and I, Ramtha, the Enlightened One, is that I, indeed, know that I am God and you do not know that you also be God. For then, that which know I, indeed, be All that I am for know I All. The All that I am in, indeed, is the All that you are in . . . thus all that you know, indeed, beloved entity, I know," said the All in All.

I did not understand all of the "indeed" stuff or most of what he said to me, but I *felt* like I did. And one thing had become clear—he could read my thoughts. There was just one little thing that had crept up from the back of my mind! Who was he? Where did he come from? How come I didn't remember his name in the Bible, the Who's Who of the divine elite? Good heavens! Why was he there with me? Why me? That stung me. Suddenly I felt a surge of unworthiness—ugly, crude, and clumsy.

"Beloved woman, I will not tell you all but I shall tell you this: I was and am the Great Ram. I lived a life that was thirty-five thousand years ago according to the Julian calendar as you know and understand your time. I was a great warrior and, indeed, as it was known then. I conquered two thirds of the known world. I became enlightened as to the unknown God of my ancient peoples and, indeed, in the sixty-third year of my march, I ascended. Indeed, beloved woman, that be all that I will teach you about that which be I. For it is not I that you need to know, indeed, but rather you that you need, indeed, to know and love, for you are the greatest mystery unto yourself. I will help you to understand these things. Go and prepare for your journey to your new hovel, indeed, make great haste. I love you grandly."

Still speechless, I looked at Ramtha, my eyes glazed with his words, his light, and this strong and compelling feeling of familiarity. I swallowed dryly, and asked in a tight, dwindled voice, "Sir . . . uh, did you speak this way before? I mean, in English?"

His exotic black eyes widened and danced with copper light. "This be your common speech, is it not?"

I moistened my lips, nodded, but did not speak.

"Understand you other common speech, beloved woman?"

I shrank visibly. "No."

"If speak I unto you that which you do not understand, would you understand?"

"That's true!" I whispered. "I wouldn't. But did you speak English before . . . before coming here . . . on earth?"

"There be not the utterances of sounds in verbiages of words where I come from, but rather, beloved, that which speaks in emotions, thoughts. Words be a great limitation and that which is a crippler of expansive truth. I hear you, learn I from you this common speech, that you may understand my message to you. Indeed! I am Ramtha, the Enlightened One." He left—or rather, he disappeared. The light was gone.

The days that followed, needless to say, were filled with so many things that had to be done, and yet we accomplished them all with amazing speed and organization. The rental of the house was approved until final closing. I checked the boys out of their school and entered them in the nearby elementary school. Chris was in the second grade and Brandy was in the fourth. They were very unhappy about being uprooted and leaving all their friends, but I instilled in them the joy of starting at a new school and the opportunity to make new friends. I also excited them about the new house, with their new bedrooms and the places outside that they could play. They were very enthusiastic about the woods.

My husband's normal workweek was Monday through Thursday, Friday being a regular day off. Unfortunately, the moving company could not move our furniture until the following Monday, so only our clothes and essentials were moved on Friday. It was critical to be out of our old house by Friday evening, when the supposed nightmare would become a reality. On Friday, my husband was irritable. I knew his reaction was due to the same fear that was building within all of us. He was very curt with the boys, often needlessly hurting their feelings. But Friday evening, we were situated in the great white structure. Since there were no chairs in the kitchen, I put some TV dinners in the oven and we feasted on the hearth by the fireplace. There were no beds, so we all slept in the formal living room on a bearskin that my husband had shot some years before we met. Brandy's pillow was the bear's head. It was a very tranquil and quiet house. Feeling secure at last, we all fell fast asleep.

The following morning, Saturday, the sun came streaming in through the large bay window. Birds were singing cheerfully in the wild bushes and brambles, while a dog barked faintly in the distance. I prepared juice, eggs, toast, and coffee, but the boys only ate half of their meal for they were in a hurry to go outside and explore. I tidied up the kitchen, then sat down beside my husband on the hearth to have some hot tea. Jeremy was contemplative.

"Well," I asked, "what do you think? Do you feel good about what we have done here? I know it will take some work to get this place fixed up, but I think we'll have a great time doing it. And besides, it will look much different once we get our furniture moved in."

Pursing his lips, he gently sat his cup back onto the saucer, got up, and went over to the sliding glass doors, staring outside. He looked worried. Without turning to look at me, he said, "We've gotta go back. Back to the house. I feel we need to get the rest of our things. Zebra, I have to know if someone broke in. I just have to know. We'll use the El Camino to load our things."

"But the El Camino can't possibly hold everything we need to take. And besides, it will take us days to move that way."

"We can get what we need and work all day and night if we have to. Then the movers can pick up the rest on Monday. C'mon, let's get the boys and go before it gets much later." He was right.

The El Camino only had two front seats, and the four of us managed to squeeze in for the ride back to the old house! We arrived, parked the car, and my husband told me to stay in the car with the boys. I was getting worried. I glanced around the neighborhood, and there was no one out and about, only the voices and laughter of children far down the street. The boys were quiet. I saw my husband stop and stare at the back door for a moment. As he opened the door, it swung out to reveal that the window had been shattered and part of the curtain was hanging out. My heart started pounding. Brandy gasped and drew nearer. Chris's little heart was beating faster than mine as I held him tighter. It seemed like hours passed before my husband returned.

"Zebra, no one's in the house, but it's had the hell tore out of it. Someone has ransacked it and torn the place apart. You better come in and leave the boys in the car." Brandy and Chris began to cry. "Listen, guys, I want you to act like men. Nothing is going to hurt you or your mother. Just stay in the car and don't get out. Do you hear me? We will be back in a few moments."

I looked at my little boys and felt I wanted to cry with them. I couldn't be feeling everything they were feeling, for only they had dreamed the dream, but apparently their nightmare had come true. I didn't want to leave them in that car alone, but I felt I had to.

I got out of the car and shut the door. I stooped down and looked at their little faces. Both had wet eyelashes and a deep flush to their skin. "I want you to lock the doors and roll up the windows and don't open the door until I come back . . . okay? I love you both so much. Now do as I ask."

As I entered the battered door into the kitchen, I saw that every cabinet was open and dishes lay broken on the counters below. The whole room had been gone through. Every room, in fact, had been turned upside down. My husband came down the stairs with grocery sacks filled with various items from upstairs. "Those Goddamn hippies, those sons of bitches, they've torn the hell out of this place, those bastards, those dope-smoking bastards. I wish I could get my hands on those mothers. I'd blow their fucking heads off. Here, take this bag out to the car. Let's get the hell out of this place. Shit, I can't believe this really happened to our home."

I was so dulled by what had happened to my once happy and beautiful home, I could only reply, "I'm thankful that we were gone." I turned to take the bag out to the car, but my husband took hold of my arm. His face was very sad. "Zebra, forgive me for cursing. I lost my head. There was a part of me that did not want to believe this would happen, and yet it did. I can't tell you how thankful I am to God and Ramtha. I know it's crazy, but we were saved. Most people never know something like this is going to happen; it just does. Shit, no one tells them. But someone *did* tell us. Why? Was it God's will? Zebra, I'm scared as hell to find out why. C'mon, let's get loaded up and leave this place. It just doesn't seem like home anymore." He tenderly kissed me and held me close for some moments.

He was right. Why were we saved from this nightmare? I would ask the same question many times over the next few days. As we drove away, I turned to watch my home, my past, glide away into greenish shadows. I thought: How naive I am. How little I have truly known about the deviousness of the human soul! I really don't know anything, nothing at all about the cruelties of desperate men. Desperate men who haunt the dreams of innocents. Such men had torn apart our home. For what? Yes, it was true, I thought. I could not forgive cruelty.

Brandy suddenly wrapped his arms around my neck, and Chris found peace in my lap. I glanced over at Jeremy. He gave me a malevolent look. Then he turned his eyes back to the road and continued to drive us to the great white house, where wickedness did not lurk.

By Sunday night, we had moved the rest of our belongings, except for the heavy furniture which was moved on Monday by the moving company. I was exhausted but the excitement of arranging the new house kept me going. I wanted to create the feeling of home again. By Tuesday, we were situated and comfortable. The house looked beautiful. By the following Thursday, I had some time in the early afternoon to myself. I fixed a cup of hot tea and went to the family room and sat down in my comfortable chair. The chair sat next to the sliding glass doors and the view was very pleasant. Even though there was not a yard, the back lot was filled with vine maples, slender alders and flowering dog-wood trees. Early spring buds were already on the trees and robins were flying to and fro singing quite merrily. A mellow sun flooded the little forest with golden light, while a pale mist flowed through the purple shadows of its branches. The faded crimson and yellow of autumn leaves lay rotting, while fresh green sprigs pushed their way through to new life. There was such extraordinary beauty in the little forest out-side my window. I felt so blessed and happy to be a part of it all. Blessed. The thought stuck in my mind, waiting for an explanation. I became caught up in the imagery of Ramtha and all that had happened in recent weeks. Why had it hap-pened to me? In the days and the years that followed, many people would ask me that same question. Why me?

CHAPTER THREE

REMINISCENCES OF BOOTSIE

As I sat in my new home, a week's worth of settling in behind me, I looked back on my life's experiences, searching for a way to make sense of these experiences with Ramtha. I knew only one thing for sure— that I could not continue to accept him unless I knew why he was in my life. Why me? So I needed to go back in my life to my beginning, my birth . . . maybe even before I was born. Perhaps, through the reliving of my life, I would come across something that might answer my question. Visions began to flow forth, beginning with my parents. Bits and pieces of information that I had gleaned from family members concerning my parents, their background, and the conditions that I was born into.

My mother, Helen Printes Hart, left home at the age of thirteen. She wasn't a runaway; she left with the consent of her mother and stepfather. As a child, Mother had always worked, along with her other sisters, in the fields of the family farm, often trudging behind the plow, driving the mules for many long hours. Because of her farm duties, her education suffered, and she was only able to acquire an eighth-grade education. This was certainly not uncommon in large families of the 1920s.

Mother decided to leave her family and home because of an unfortunate incident with her stepfather. He had promised her earlier in the year that if she would work rather than attend school, when the crops were sold in autumn he would buy her a new winter coat. She had outgrown the only one she owned, and was in desperate need of one before the winter set in. So she worked the fields from spring until fall. She drove the mules, plowed the fields, planted the seed, hoed the weeds, and did the final harvesting. Enough work to test any man's endurance, let alone a thirteen-year-old girl's. When sale of the harvest was completed, her stepfather took the extra money and purchased himself a new and expensive silver saddle. My poor mother froze that winter.

Mother was a beautiful woman in her youth. Of her sisters and one brother, she was the only one to inherit the looks and coloring of the Hall side of the family—the side referred to as the "English blood." She had thick blond hair, violet blue eyes, and a peaches-and-cream complexion. The rest were stamped with the features and coloring of the Indian blood in their line—dark, handsome, and exotic.

Mother found a job cooking in a kitchen, and there she met a handsome older man, whom she married. Together they had two sons, Victor and Marion. It was a short-lived marriage due to her overbearing mother-in-law, who thought that her son had married beneath him. Inexperienced and young, Mother was intimidated by her mother-in-law into giving up her two sons after the divorce, so they could have the opportunity for a more enriched and fulfilling life. They went to live with their grandmother. Mother would never know the joy of sharing their lives, nor would she ever know them as grown men.

Times were hard in those days. The country was still in the midst of the Depression. The only work to be found was in the cotton fields of East Texas. My beautiful, young, and lonely mother became a cotton picker. There, in the cotton fields, she met my father, Charles Hampton. He was a handsome cuss who loved liquor and women, in that order. They were married, and Mother, who was very much in love with him, had hopes, like any young woman, that fortune and happiness would shine upon their lives. Almost immediately, Mother became pregnant. But her condition did not deter her from continuing to work. Every day, she would work from the first light of morning until dusk, on her knees, dragging a long and heavy cotton sack behind her as she picked the cotton.

The laborers and their families all lived in shanties—shacks loosely constructed of wood, without insulation, each with a porch and two rooms, one for cooking and the other for sleeping. The only heat was from a woodburning stove in the kitchen. These pathetic shacks did not have running water, electricity, central heating, or indoor toilets. But to many, like Mother, it was their only home, and they were thankful for it.

Every payday, my father would take the week's earnings and go on a drinking binge with his good ol' buddies. Mother would not see him for days on end. She had gotten into the habit of hiding some of her wages just to keep the family from going hungry. She delivered her first child in the cotton field by herself. Mother named her Bootsie Hampton. The day after the delivery, mother packed up the daily ration of food, Bootsie, and herself and headed out to the cotton fields. There was no such thing as "sick leave" in the fields, and Mother couldn't afford to lose one day's wages. Their very survival rested on Mother's shoulders.

When Bootsie was two, Mother found she was pregnant again. Ignorance, poverty, and alcoholism, blended together, do not create an ideal mind for careful family planning. She delivered another girl, Wanda Zoe Hampton. My father decided he wanted to return to New Mexico to see if he could get hired on to work the fields there. Packing up their few belongings, they hitchhiked over one thousand miles to Dexter, New Mexico, where both of my parents were hired on by a local grower to do irrigation and planting. A small shack was provided for their home. Father soon fell back into his old habits and would disappear for long periods of time, leaving my mother to care for the children and to carry out the backbreaking work of the farm.

One afternoon in late May, Mother was bathing little Wanda in a washtub on the table in the shack. She had dressed Bootsie up in a new clean blue dress, and given her her a bag of marbles to play with while she finished bathing Wanda. It was payday, and Mother was going into town to buy her groceries. She did not own a car. She and the girls would have to walk to town and walk back, carrying heavy bags of food.

As she worked, a car drove up outside and a man fell out of it. The car then sped away. It was my father, and as usual, he was drunk. He got up and staggered to the door, paused, and lit up a Camel cigarette. He removed a fifth of Jim Beam whiskey from the back pocket of his khaki pants. He fumbled the cap off and took a long hard drink, and after returning his prize to its usual holding place, he wiped the yellow drool from the corners of his mouth. After a long drag on the cigarette, he barged through the door. Weaving from side to side, he demanded, "Whut the hell iz goin' on here?" Mother continued to bathe Wanda and did not answer him.

Infuriated that my mother wouldn't reply, he charged toward her and hit the table, nearly knocking his daughter and the tub onto the floor. "Ya bitch, ya ol' whore. Goddamn it, ya bedder answer me when I ask ya sump'n," he shouted, slurring his words.

"Charlie, why do ya call me all them bad thangs? I don't deserve 'em. You're all likkered up, Charlie, it's that likker tha makes ya say them thangs. An where ya been—oh, never mind. I know where ya been . . . makes no difference anyhow." She looked back at little Wanda, who had been gripping tightly the rim of the tub.

Father pulled himself upright and lunged at Mother, shouting more obscenities at her. He hit her on the side of the head and nearly knocked her to the floor. Little Wanda started screaming while Bootsie backed into a corner, rigid with fright.

"Ya ol' whore. Ya ol' cocksucking bitch. Ya don't ask me wheres I've been. It ain't none of ya fucking business, ya ol' hole. Goddamn you, I work hard fur my money . . .

ya hear? . . . an there ain't no ol' whore gonna tell me whut in the hell ta do." He stood there staring at her, waiting for her to make a wrong move. "Ya know . . . I oughta just kill ya. I oughta just kill ya . . . and those li'l whores of yourn."

"Charlie, for the sake of Jesus Christ, don't go a-say'n' thangs like that 'bout yer children. Them's yer own flesh 'n' blood."

He grabbed her by the hair and began to kick her hard around the lower body and legs. He hurled a series of blows to her face and head. Blood was streaming from Mother's ears and nose. She retaliated by sending some blows of her own, fighting for her life. Little Wanda stood up in the middle of the tub and began to scream and cry for her mother. Bootsie ran from her hiding place and tried to kick her father in an effort to protect her mother. He wheeled around, grabbed Bootsie's arm, and flung her against the wall, where she fell to the floor. "Run, Bootsie," Mother yelled. "Get out of here. He's gonna hurt ya bad . . . run."

Bootsie, whose arm had been badly hurt, pulled her little self up and began to run. Father caught her and lifted her up to eye level. What this helpless little child of three thought and felt about her father in that moment would never be known. "I wanna tell ya somethin' 'bout yuz an ya mother. Yur a li'l whore. Ya even smell like a whore. An I knowz ya ain't mine cuz yur mother over thar is a two-bit whore. Hell, ever'one knows it."

My mother jumped up and tried to get Bootsie away from her tormentor. He held her off and turned for the door, with Mother screaming, "Don't hurt her, Charlie, she's jest a baby, in tha name of God, Charlie, put her down. I'd do anythang ya ask, but don't hurt her." In panic, she ran to a cabinet and reached for a coffee tin on a shelf. Wiping the blood from her nose, she went on, "Look, Charlie, money, lotsa money. I been a-sav'n' it fer a real fine present fer ya. Here . . . here, go 'n' buy ya someth'n' real nice fer yourself." In desperation she held the money up in an effort to get him to forget about Bootsie. It worked. He grabbed the money out of her hand and tried to count it. He was too drunk. "Why, you ol' bitch, ya been a-hold'n' out on me. I oughta—"

Bootsie quickly scooped up the bag of marbles from the floor, left Wanda screaming in the tub, and fled outside. She stumbled on the porch and fell facedown in the dirt. When she got up, her clean little dress was covered in dirt, and her once-clean face was smeared with mud, tears, and snot. Wolf, the family dog, ran to greet her, but her little body was still hurting and her mind was too troubled to play. She walked a few steps, then turned to glance one last time at her home, her ears ringing with the cursing and rage that was still going on inside. With Wolf dancing merrily around her, she turned and began to walk toward the reservoir, soft tears flowing down her muddy cheeks and into her mouth.

She was still holding the little bag of marbles—her only toys—when she squatted down by the water's edge, staring at her own reflection in the water. She had gotten all dirty and she knew that would upset her mother. Refusing to look anymore at the dirty little girl in the water, she took out her marbles, one by one, until she found her favorite—the blue and red one. She put the sack of remaining marbles down so she could admire her favorite, but forgot to pull the strings to reclose the sack, and the marbles started running down the bank and into the water. In futile desperation, she tried to reach into the water to rescue them. As she reached, she lost her balance and fell into the water.

The current that carried the water out of the reservoir, through an aqueduct, and into the irrigation ditches was very swift. Even if this three-year-old knew how to swim, the eddies would have pulled her to the bottom and held her there while the current swept her away through the aqueduct. Wolf started barking wildly. He ran back and forth frantically along the bank, trying to find his friend. He leaped into the water, but the current carried him to the far side of the reservoir.

Hearing a slam, Wolf turned and ran to the house. Charlie had gotten his money, and a few more blows in for good measure, and was now leaving. He went to the farm road and began hitching a ride into town for some more good times. The dog was barking at him, trying to get his attention, but good ol' Charlie had more important things to do than play with the dog. Wolf followed him only a few steps, then turned and ran to the reservoir again. Sniffing, he finally sat down on his haunches and began to howl. By some primeval instinct, the dog knew that his friend was gone forever.

While consoling and drying Wanda, Mother suddenly heard the dog's howl and sensed that something was wrong. The dog had never acted that way before. She ran outside, calling for Bootsie, and Wolf ran up to her and started to moan. She ran around the house calling and searching. The dog jumped at her and began to bark.

"Where is she, Wolf? Find my li'l baby. Show me, where's my baby, where's Bootsie?" The dog took off and ran to the spot. Mother followed. Coming to the bank, she saw the bag and what remained of the marbles. There were the marks on the bank where the little girl had fallen into the water. It was evident what had happened. Mother began to wail, running frantically around the reservoir. Another worker heard Mother's hysterics and knew that something was wrong. He quickly rounded up the other farmhands and their families.

The search for Bootsie continued into the night, but she was not found. The next day a fireman, who had been helping in the rescue effort, went two miles further down, following the irrigation ditch. There was the little girl, Bootsie, face up with eyes open as the clear water flowed over her. The swift current had taken her past a tree, and there her body was snagged by an underwater branch.

Two days later, Bootsie Hampton was buried in the Dexter cemetery. The funeral expenses were paid for by all those who had come to love and respect my mother. They had become very familiar with her desperation. All the money that she had saved had gone down the road with a man who had more important things to do with it. He would not know for nearly two more months about the tragic death of his daughter, about the funeral, or that his wife was again four months pregnant. He had gone with some good ol' boys over to Texas to have a good time.

Bootsie was the sister that I never knew. I came to learn of her brief life by overhearing bits of a conversation between my mother and my sister, Wanda. The vivid description of

Bootsie's demise was told by my mother in tones of pain and sorrow that even I, as young as I was, understood. My mother gave birth to three sons before my birth, and one after me. A total of nine children, one deceased and eight living. Bootsie became an important part of the puzzle of my life. I did not fully understand why until much later on.

CHAPTER FOUR

JUDY

It was an unusual March day in Dexter, New Mexico. The March winds did not blow, allowing the day to become warm and cheery. It had been twelve years since Bootsie's death, and in that time little had changed. My brothers, Charles Jr., Gayle, and Donnie, had been born, and my sister, Wanda, was now thirteen. The family had moved into the country outside Dexter, into a better house, but my parents still worked the land of other farmers. Beside the house ran a long road that led to the closest city, Roswell. Alfalfa fields framed the house. In front was parked an old green Dodge, the license plate reading, "New Mexico. The Land of Enchantment. 1946."

The front door slammed, and a woman emerged, assertively making her way to the hood of the car. She opened it, and expertly tended to the carburetor. The mechanic was my mother. She was dressed in an attractive floral print maternity dress, certainly not what one would wear to work on a car. She continued to work, muttering to herself in obvious frustration.

"Women weren't made to do such work. That ol' cornball"—my father—"ain't never around when he's needed. I've always worked like a man . . . guess I always will." Finished, she slammed the hood down and proceeded to get into the car, pump the accelerator, and turn the key. Success! It started, and away she drove, down that long road to Roswell. When she arrived at St. Mary's Hospital, she got out and began to adjust her dress and pat her hair, but her face suddenly contorted with pain. Mother was well advanced in her labor. Soon the pain passed and she quickly shuffled into the hospital. At 12:02 A.M., March the sixteenth, 1946, Mother delivered a baby girl. She named her Judith Darlene Hampton. Judith—a name she got from the Bible. The name of a holy and mystical woman. I had finally arrived.

Two weeks later, my mother placed me in a makeshift crib in the front yard, by the water pump. I was entertained by the rooster and chickens, scratching, pecking, and clucking around me on the ground. From the fields came the sounds of the workers at their labor, sometimes laughing, sometimes moaning. Suddenly, Mother returned with an old Yaqui Indian woman, and the chickens scattered. The Indian woman wore a bandanna tied in the back and long dangling earrings. Mother stood for a moment, her hands on her hips, looking down at me. Then she removed her sunbonnet and wiped her forehead with her sleeve. The Indian woman picked me up and stared at me intently.

"Helen, this li'l girl of yourn will see what no one else sees . . . her destiny . . . important."

"Well, I liked ta died with the delivery. None of ma uthers gave me that bad a time. Lord be Jesus, I even had ta fix the damn fuel pump on the ol' car just ta get ta the hospital," she said chuckling.

The Indian woman smiled through alert and wise eyes, handed me back to Mother, and quietly left. Mother seated herself on the front porch and began to nurse me.

"The good Lord, I know, don't burden me with more'n

I can bear." She sighed resignedly. "My life is what it was supposed to be. My li'l girl, I hope that I'll live ta see whut your life is suppose ta be . . . the Lord a-willin', I will."

Two years later, the family moved to Rockwall, in East Texas. My mother had gotten work on a farm owned by Ozzie and Hazel Eubanks. As usual, my father was absent, spending most of his time drinking and carousing. It was another step downward, in terms of the living accommodations. The only available house was a shack situated on a T road crossing that lined the fields. The closest neighbors were a mile away. The shack had the usual appointments— porch, kitchen, sleeping area, with an additional room large enough for a sleeping cot. There was a broken-down tractor sitting in front, and an outdoor toilet in back. The sight of all of this did not deter my mother. She had become used to this gypsy life-style and immediately began moving in.

The first order was to Wanda, Gayle, and Charles to begin scrubbing walls, ceiling, floors, and the stove. She brought up a large washtub, filled it full of water from the pump, and began washing the bedding. Donnie was put in charge of watching my baby brother, Loy, and myself. By evening, the coal oil lamp was burning on the eating bench. Mother was washing the dishes from the evening meal and admiring the curtains she had made out of flour sacks. There were no kitchen cabinets, so she rescued the orange crates that we used to move and nailed them above the stove and sink. By then Loy and I had already had our baths and were asleep in the back room together. Donnie and Gayle were playing in the front yard, catching fireflies. Wanda and Charles had hitchhiked into nearby Rockwall, to go honky-tonkin'.

Morning came at four-thirty. Mother prepared pancakes, bacon, biscuits, and gravy for breakfast and set the bench, ready to serve.

"C'mon, you kids, git up. Git up, ya hear? Food a-gitten cold. Donnie, boy, git up an git your baby sister an bruther in here. Wanda, girl, git up!"

Everyone got up, took turns washing and going outside to the toilet, and returned to the table. Everyone but Wanda.

"Wanda Zoe, *git up!*" Mother said, getting flustered.

"I'm too tired, Momma. I feel sick," Wanda moaned, putting the pillow over her head.

Mother went back to the kitchen, reached into a crate, and pulled out a box of baking soda. She spooned some into a glass and pumped it full of water. Then she returned to where Wanda was lying. "Here, git up an drink this," Momma ordered.

Wanda moved the pillow back and glanced up at her mother. "Whut is it? What's it for?"

"I want ya to gargle it. It'll get tha whiskey off yur breath before ya go ta school."

Wanda reluctantly got up and took the glass. Everyone in the kitchen began to snicker—including me, although I didn't know what was so funny.

Mother prepared herself to go to work, while the rest got themselves ready for school. She put on her kneepads, an apron, her durable steel-toed boots, and then her homemade bonnet. She had Donnie carry the food buckets, keeping me beside him, while she picked up Loy and walked to the fields a half a mile away. Donnie dropped off the buckets under the cotton wagon and joined his brothers and sister for the long walk to the main highway, to catch the school bus into Rockwall.

Mother, along with the other workers, was on her knees, picking cotton row by row from the cool of the early morning until the heat of midday. I played happily around the sack she dragged behind her. Sometimes, I would sit right down on it and hope she wouldn't notice, but the moment she would ease forward, she felt the weight and without turning around would scold me to get off. Other times, I would hear singing coming from the other workers and I would sneak over to the row next to them and listen to their songs. At noon, all of the workers took a lunch break and made for the shade of the cotton wagons. There, they pulled out fried chicken, potato salad, some fresh fruit, and the biscuits and jelly left over from breakfast. It was very much like a feast, with everyone sharing what they brought with everyone else. They were relieved to be out of the searing heat of high noon.

The meal was more a reward for the morning's labor than the mere quieting of hunger. The men compared their total weight of cotton picked, but my mother, despite being a woman, beat them all. A lot of teasing went on about that, but Mom could hold her own. Eventually they grew to love and respect her for her strength and endurance.

The women recanted the activities of their children, complained of the heat and their undue miseries, but always with the humor and courage that enabled them to endure it all.

The feast finished, the women repacked the leftovers—nothing was thrown out—while the men lit up their hand-rolled cigarettes made of Bull Durham tobacco. One old Negro gentleman took out his corncob pipe and packed it full of an aromatic cherry-blend tobacco, then lit it up with a stick match he struck off the heel of his boot. I loved the smell of his pipe. It was sweet and inviting to little noses.

All of the children gathered around, sitting real still, and waited for him to blow a smoke ring over each of our heads. Then he proclaimed, "Seez? Now all ya young'uns are real li'l angels. Da good Lord luvz ya all. If'n ya be real good an mind ya folks, ol' Bugs'll give ya another one tomorra." We all jumped with glee and promised to be extra good to our parents and mind them well. With the promise extracted, he went to his cooler and pulled out an ice-cold bottle of Dr. Pepper for each of us. That was a big treat for all of us. We would never have had one but for this wonderful and kind soul. I soon came to love him.

My mother came and retrieved me and my Dr. Pepper and sat me on the edge of the wagon. She began to brush my snow white, baby fine hair. Then, she pulled a piece of yellow satin ribbon from her apron and tied a bow around my hair. Mother then pulled over another child and proceeded to do the same thing, only this time she tied a red ribbon in her hair. I clutched my pop bottle and began to suck on it, observing the procedure. A gentle breeze came up and blew the ribbon off my head, which caused me to pout. Seeing this Mother said, "Child . . . now don't go a pout'n . . . yuz got purty hair but ther's not enuff on yur head ta hold tha ribbon . . . I'll tie it back on snugg'r." She repaired the damage and soon the remains of my big crocodile tears evaporated in the breeze.

Over the next two years, the events of this difficult but wonderful day, so close and warm in my memory, were repeated as our family settled happily into our new life in East Texas.

Wanda grew into a beautiful young woman with flawless olive skin, emerald green eyes, and perfect white teeth, her crown a glory of deep auburn hair. She was a natural beauty whose only bit of added color was the red lipstick she wore. With her hourglass figure and long, gorgeous legs, Wanda could easily have achieved fame as one of the most beautiful women in the world, but the environment in which she was raised kept her from realizing her own dreams. I do not, in any way, place the blame upon my mother but, rather, on the conditions of the times. Our family lacked the kind of traditions that support scholastic and social achievements. Mother herself did not come from a family that instilled such traditions. Traditions were luxuries in those times; it was difficult enough just to survive.

Wanda was also deeply affected by our father's alcoholism, which robbed us all of his love and support. She had to endure the drunken rages that he vented on her mother, as well as the personal torment of being called "li'l whore, fucking li'l bitch, no good fer nuth'n' pig." When his buddies were around, he'd shout, "C'mon out her, Wanda Zoe, I wanna show sum good ol' boys of mine whut your daddy can stud, let 'em hava look." This obvious distortion of fatherly love created a wounded, wild woman whose only desire for a long time would be to have "a good time"—the only way she knew to handle the insecurity, pain, anger, and shame she harbored within her. Her only friend, a beautiful girl named Dorothy, came from an identical environment. Their appearance was so similar, they were often mistaken for sisters—a belief they encouraged. Their bond of friendship would take them on many adventures in the years to come.

Wanda and Dorothy finally ran away from home together when I was four years old. Much later in my life, Wanda told me the story of the dreadful evening that had prompted her leaving. One night, Wanda and Dorothy went honky-tonkin' in Rockwall and ran into my father. He had been sitting at a table, surrounded by his drinking buddies. He was sot drunk and broke. Apparently, he had been trying his damnedest to "borrow" money from the establishment's other customers but to no avail. Good ol' Charlie's credit was bad; he never paid back his debts. But now, heaven had sent the answer—his beautiful daughter. He dragged my sister over to his table of ne'er-do-well friends, shouting about her "virtues." There, the shrewd old rooster put on an act of being the proud and loving father. This was to get Wanda and Dorothy to sit down at the table. With a wicked glimmer in his eyes, he blatantly offered the services of his voluptuous daughter and equally tempting friend to his tantalized and vulgar friends. The price? A bottle of Johnny Walker Red Label whiskey, of course.

With this final thrust of the dagger into her soul, my sister became enraged and released all her suppressed anger. Wanda was the best fistfighter in the family. She could easily clean the plow of her brothers and often did. She battered the old sucker with a series of blows that broke his nose and blackened his eyes. Not one person in the entire place came to his rescue. Maybe they were afraid to intervene, but perhaps they felt that he deserved what he was getting. Her two long legs towered above the bloody mess of a man on the floor. She waited for him to move, preparing to deliver a final swift kick. "You . . . sorry . . . ol' son-of-a-bitch. If you weren't my own father, I'd slit your fuckin' throat," she hissed. "God damn you, you're a sorry man, Charles Hampton. You've shamed me an my brothers, an you've treated my poor ol' mother like a dog. I hate you, you son-of-a-bitch. An I wanna tell you sumthin'. If you just try an go back home to get any money from that saint of a woman, I'll hunt you down, you scum . . . an *I will kill you.*" She thrust a kick into his side just to make sure he was listening. "Do you hear me? I'll kill you!"

Wanda wheeled around, her eyes surveying everyone

in the room. The band had stopped playing "Your Cheatin' Heart," and no one made a move or a sound. "I want to make something clear to the rest of you sons-of-bitches," she continued. "I'll blow your fuckin' heads off if any of you *ever* give this bastard a ride to my momma's house. *Do you hear me?*" Most, staring with fright, nodded their heads, while others simply kept their eyes focused to the floor in obvious shame.

Wanda quickly picked up her small handbag and made for the door, Dorothy hot on her heels. She paused, tears pouring from those beautiful wild eyes, peered around the room, and then said to the man sprawled on the floor, wallowing in his own spit and blood, "I wanna forget all you yellow-bellied, spineless white trash . . . all of you whores. Where in hell are *your* kids? Shit, take a good Goddamn look at me an remember what you're lookin' at, cuz your own kids are gonna grow up just like me. Cuz you ain't fuckin' any better than that bastard on the floor. An you"—pointing her finger at our father—"you ain't my father no more. You've caused me misery all my life. Hell, you were give'n me whiskey when most kids were drinkin' milk . . . you've ruined me, Charles Hampton, an I'll never forgive you for it. One day, old man, *you're going to get all you deserve an* then I hope to hell you suffer as much as me an my poor mother have. See here old man, I damned sure mean what I said. Leave my mother alone." Done saying her piece, she and Dorothy left for good.

I would not see my "fairy princess" sister for a long time to come. In her adventures, she traveled extensively, mostly hitchhiking rides along the way. She won the prestigious title of Miss Wool of Texas, was beloved and wooed by a notorious gangster, did some modeling, beat the hell out of a motorcycle gang member and out of his "mother" for good measure. She had an affair with a respectable businessman but declined his offer to marry her. She insisted on raising her illegitimate son without the help of the child's father. She worked in bars, for the excitement and the good pay. She experienced a vision of Jesus Christ that caused a dramatic improvement in her language and, for a time, her life-style. She sent the article and picture of herself as Miss Wool of Texas to Mother, who, upon its receipt, proudly showed it to all the workers and her employers. It became my mother's most treasured possession.

I was four years old now and out of diapers but still, on occasion, had "accidents." My attire was the usual gray striped coveralls. Being that they were a one-piece outfit, it was an arduous task to unsnap the snaps, pull out my arms, and pull them down to expose my bottom. And often there were more important things to do such as play a game of marbles, which is what often led to the accidents. One of those accidents caused an incident that would influence my later life.

I was playing with my marbles on the ground, while my baby brother, Loy, in diapers, was playing in the dirt next to me. Two of my older brothers came tearing into view, dragging a furry animal they had apparently trapped. Mother sprang up from her cotton-picking knees. "I told you boys I'd whop your butts if'n you brought them thangs around! An I mean ta do just that." Not wanting to be a part of the carnage that followed, I drifted away, having an accident on the way. I shamefully sneaked back toward our shanty, climbed onto the porch, and made my way inside. I rummaged around until I found some clean panties, then went through the process of removing the evidence.

Clean panties on and the evidence stashed under a mattress, I heard someone in the back room. I quietly sneaked to the room to see the source of the noise. There, fully dressed in his khaki shirt and pants, lay my uncle Harrison. He was my father's older brother. He was drunk. Opening his glazed eyes in my direction, he leered at me. He scratched his crotch and then began to fondle himself. "Well, if'n it ain't li'l Judy girl." I smiled, noticing the yellow spit drooling from the corners of his mouth. "Well, c'mon over here an let me take a look at ya." He fumbled the button loose on his fly and began taking his pants off. I hesitated, feeling a fear growing inside of me. I had seen him drunk before with my daddy, but I had never been alone with him and he was scaring me.

"I said c'mon, you little bitch," he snarled, leaping toward me. My eyes were welling up with tears and there was no one around to help . . . not even my guardian, Donnie. He was getting a thrashing from Mommy down the road in the fields. In a moment, my uncle grabbed me by the arm, pulled my panties off, and forced me onto him. I struggled to get away but was overpowered by my tormentor. He pulled down his shorts with one hand, revealing his organ. He reeked with the stench of dung and urine. I did not know what he was doing. He split my legs, spread them apart, and lifted me slightly in the air. He brought me down hard on top of him and I began to scream with terror.

"So, ya wanna know whut I'm go'n ta do, ya li'l bitch?" he asked, as he tried to force himself into me. He was too drunk and I was too small. I was paralyzed with fear. In a final thrust of disappointment, he got up and hurled me against the wall. "Whore! You sucking li'l whore! Bitch!" He wobbled and then fell back onto the cot. I picked myself up and ran out of the house, holding myself with pain. I stumbled and fell off the porch into the dirt. Hurting even more from the fall, I just sat for a few moments, naked, dirty, and snotty, squalling in futile desperation and fear. But no one heard my crying. I was alone. Getting up, I ran the best I could toward the cotton field. Mother had already dispensed punishment to my brothers and was back at her work. I ran up to face my mother, but stumbled over the dried cotton stalks and fell in front of her.

"Whut is it, Judy girl? Hows come you ain't got ya clothes on? Honey, whut's ya been a-cryin' fer?" Her voice was a blend of harshness and compassion. It was, after all, a bit trying to have to baby-sit all the kids and work hard at the same time.

"My pee-pee . . . [sniff] . . . my pee-pee hurts real bad, Momma."

"Yeah, well, it's probably just one of 'em rashes from peein' your britches. Mercy goodness, child, go on back up thar und'r the wagon an wait fer ya momma, hear? An I want ya ta see ta Loy till I git thar . . . go on, now." She resumed her picking.

I walked pitifully back to the wagon and found my little brother merrily playing with the marbles. No one noticed my nudity. I kept casting my eyes in the direction of the shanty with a feeling of looming mistrust. I rubbed myself, trying to remove the throbbing pain.

Later that same evening, after supper, Mother was preparing to bathe Loy and me. She began to lather my body when the lye in the soap began to sting and burn me. I began to cry and point to my private area. Mother stopped and examined me closely, then, without saying a word, she reached for a can in the crate and pulled it out. It was the cure-all powder—baking soda. She shook a large amount into her hand and began to rub my tender little area with it. It was, indeed, a healing balm. She gently washed my face and hair, careful not to disturb or wash away the powder. I was wrapped in a towel and sat in front of the cookstove to warm up. As Mother proceeded to wash Loy, I began to recount the miserable event to my mother, who listened quietly, continuing Loy's bath. Then, without saying anything, she left the room with Loy still in the tub. In a moment she returned, wiping her hands on her apron. "Judy girl, thar ain't been nobody in that back room." After studying me for a moment, she continued, "Your uncle Harrison ain't been round fer a long time now. Yuz gonna be all right. Ya just had a accident." She returned to Loy, who had been having a joyful time rubbing the soap through his hair and slapping the bubbles on the water with glee.

That was that. Mother did not know that Harrison had sneaked into our home, knowing everyone was in the field, to sleep one off before returning to his own wife and children. He had removed any evidence of himself and of what he did to me. I do not know where he hid my panties, but if my mother had found them, she would have only surmised they were a part of my own shameful stash of "accidents."

I don't remember ever seeing my dreadful uncle again, nor do I know if he remembered the disgusting act he had perpetrated upon me. The event left a deep and ugly scar that would later cause me to mistrust all men. I owned a terrible secret—one that destroyed my innocence, my open love and trust for others, and for many years to come ruined my self-respect. After the birth of my first son, Brandy, I would hear the "pitiful" news of "poor ol' uncle Harrison's painful demise." I gloated with a smug feeling of delicious revenge. Oh, how sweet it is.

CHAPTER FIVE

MY BIG
RED BALLOON

A few months later, on a Saturday morning, Mother dressed herself in her best pair of slacks and shirt and readied herself to make the five-mile walk into Rockwall to purchase groceries.

"Yer daddy snuck in here last week and stole off with the car. We ain't got no car, child, an I can't take you young'uns ta town with me. I wont ya ta stay here an watch Loy Gene fer me . . . here, take this brush an brush yer straggly hair." She tossed me the brush from her brown bag and walked purposefully out the door. I followed behind her for a little way. There she went, out across the plowed field. I watched her fade in the distance with heat waves distorting my vision. I strained my eyes harder but she had disappeared. Tears filled my eyes as I took the brush and began to straighten out the rat's nest atop my head. With my siblings gone— Gayle had joined the army, Charles the navy, and Donnie was off somewhere with his friends—I was all alone except for my darling baby brother.

We managed to entertain ourselves the rest of the day, with me keeping a careful eye on the field, hoping to see my mother returning. Suddenly a figure, far off in the distance, began emerging. It was Mother. I ran toward her and Loy toddled the best he could to keep up. There she was at last, lugging two heavy bags of food for over five miles of plowed fields. Once in the house, she pulled out a loaf of bread, opened it, and took out a little treasure. It was a red balloon. I tied the bread back up as she asked and waited as she began to fill the balloon with her tired breath. I was elated. I had never seen a balloon, or anything quite so beautiful. Mother tied the end with a piece of twine and gave it to me. I was overjoyed. She then pulled out a red plastic car and gave it to Loy. He immediately dropped to his hands and knees and began pushing the car around the linoleum floor, making engine noises with his mouth.

I took my prize outside and held it up to examine its mysteries more closely. I looked at the sun through it and found that the sun and everything else had turned a glorious rose color. It was magic. I began to toss the balloon lightly into the air, then catch it again. I was ecstatic with my new toy. Suddenly, a wind came up and caught my balloon. With lighter-than-air grace it floated beyond my reach. I frantically ran after it but it had gone far beyond my reach, dancing lightly like a magical elf across the fields of freedom. I stumbled and fell over a large clump of dirt, and when I tried to get up I only fell on my haunches again. I wept, bitterly. There I sat in the field, dwarfed by the poverty of my hopeless surroundings.

Some nights later, as Mother, Loy, and I were eating a supper of salt pork and biscuits, washed down with iced tea, a car pulled up outside. The car door slammed, and Mother, chewing, put down her biscuit and waited, her eyes on the door. A man appeared. It was ol' Charlie, drunk and holding a .22 rifle in his hands. Mother didn't move.

"I came fer some money, Helen. I need some money," he muttered, standing at the screen door.

"Ya don't need no money, ya need yer liquor. An I ain't a-givin' ya nuthin'. Go own . . . git outta here an leave us alone." She did not get up from the table.

Enraged, he threw open the screen and rushed in threateningly. "I said gimme some money, Helen!"

"Charlie Hampton, ya used ta pick more cotton than a whole truckload of workers. Now ya drink that much."

"If'n ya don't gimme some money, I'll just take it," he snarled, raising his rifle to his hip.

Mother coolly stood, walked over to a crate, and pulled out a butcher knife. Charlie lurched toward her. Loy and I remained seated and silent. We had experienced this many times before. "Ya just try, Charlie Hampton. I'll knock ya upside the face till you is cuckoo. Then I'll cut yer chicken throat," she retorted.

He took a step forward.

"C'mon, I want ya ta try me." Mother took on an ominous air that was steadfast and fearless. It was an unequal match. Charlie glared at her drunkenly.

Mother continued, "Charlie Hampton, ya make a choice right here'n now. It's gonna either be yer family or yer liquor."

"Gimme some money."

"Choose!" She was holding her ground.

"I'll take the liquor."

"Then ya back yerself outta here." As she raised the butcher knife, he stood rigid.

"I said *back outta here!*" Her intimidating manner made her seem more like a looming terror than a small woman. Charlie realized in that moment that his life was in peril and slowly began to back out the door, close it, and return to his car. The door slammed and off sped ol' Charlie, running for his life.

Mother closed the door and calmly sat back down to resume her supper. "Ma life is choppin' cotton, pickin' it, an waitin' fer it ta come up agin. I can't hardly wait fer it all ta git over with." She began to serve us one of her homemade fruit pies. We all ate quietly.

Mother rose to a larger-than-life stature that night.

Through strife and hardship she had become a seasoned warrior and had successfully defeated her hated oppressor. Charlie Hampton never returned to our shanty. I would only have the pleasure of his company two more times in my life.

Mother had gotten her old car back by finding it one day parked outside a bar in town. She hot-wired it and drove it back home. Mother had had enough of the fields, and of the memories. She made the decision to pack us all up and start a new life for us all. It was a sad time. We were packed into the car, saying our forever farewells. All the workers gathered around, some weeping, as Mother gave them clothes she had made out of cotton sacks, along with some cookies she had made the night before.

An old Negro woman who always sang so beautifully in the fields said to my mother in a voice choked with emotion, "We'z gonna miss you, Mizz Helen. You'z done so much fer us all. We thank ya . . . thank ya. God bless ya an yer young'uns."

Children without shoes and underpants joined the others on the cotton piles in the wagons to watch the crowded farewells.

"As long as the sun rises ever' mornin' an sets ever' night, the day in between will be beautiful," Mother said poetically. "The sun is the gold of life, an hard work never hurt nobody."

"Helen, we ain't never gonna fergit ya," wept an old woman. At that moment my favorite old man with the pipe appeared around the corner of the car and, with a twinkling grin on his face, held up two Dr. Peppers. I rolled the window down the rest of the way, and he handed me the pops. "You be my good li'l angel. When the good Lord gives me the okay, I'z gonna blow you'unz a halo. Makes no difference where ya is, ya git it. Be good ta ya mother." He rubbed Loy's hair and gave me a pinch on the cheek. Then he disappeared into the crowd. Tears began to roll off my cheeks and drop, one by one, onto my Dr. Pepper bottle.

Mother started the engine, and with a final farewell we began to roll on down the long road. I pushed my face against the window, watching those beautiful souls until they were out of sight. I wondered if my balloon was still out there somewhere. Maybe it had just kept on going, far away . . . away from me and that field.

Our shanty and those fields now lie at the bottom of a great body of water. A dam was built there some years ago. All that remain are the memories.

CHAPTER SIX

DOESN'T GOD LOVE JUNE BUGS, TOO?

We were now living in Artesia, New Mexico. Mother had found two jobs. One was working as a waitress in a drugstore in town. She would get up at four, fix breakfast to leave on the stove for us, and walk three miles to be at work by five. She liked this job, and because of her unique personality, she developed her own clientele. They were loyal to her, and if her section was filled, they would wait until one of her booths became available. She made fair wages, but she made generous tips. Of course, it helped that she was single and pretty.

With her shift over, she would repeat the three-mile walk back home. When she finished a full day's housework, she would iron a fresh uniform and prepare to go to her next job—the six-to-eleven shift at a hamburger stand just across a vacant lot from where we lived.

The stand was owned by a dear old couple who were

deeply religious. Loy and I would occasionally stroll over to the stand and pretend to be customers. To our delight, the old couple would often give us bubble gum.

Home consisted of a three-room apartment, one of six located in a long building that looked like an army barracks. There was only one tree and no grass. Grass was a luxury for rich folks.

Our apartment was located at the very end. It had a front and back door with high porches, an actual living room—very tiny, of course—a bedroom, and a large kitchen with running water and a gas stove, which I marveled at since you didn't have to chop wood to put in it. Just turn the knob, hold a match to the burner, and presto! instant fire.

My older brother Donnie had joined the navy, but Gayle had come back from the Korean War and had established quite a reputation about town. He was a handsome man who was a notorious womanizer. He loved to drink and have a good time, and made a point of dressing very nicely. He always wore a Stetson hat, Western shirts, a tooled Western belt with a large buckle, and Wrangler jeans starched and pressed to a meticulous crease on both legs. His handsome Western boots always sported a spit shine. The picture he presented was of a man sensuous and tough, tantalizing to any female, young or old.

What a hunk he was, with loads of dark brown curly hair, oiled with Vaseline Hair Tonic, hazel eyes, rimmed with thick brown lashes, a pug nose, for that innocent look, a wide mouth revealing pearl white teeth. He stood six feet tall with a long muscular torso and well developed legs, slightly bowed for effect. Gayle was employed with a road-construction company and was a crack dozer and blade man. I adored him. The few times I saw him, he always called me Sissy—short for sister—and brought me some little toy or would give me a dime. But his absences from us were extensive. His manhood demanded he do more invigorating things with his time.

Charles was even more of a rarity to me. All I remember about him at this time is that he, too, was great looking, with hair a bit lighter than Gayle's dark brown. His personality was somewhat different from the rest, however. He didn't drink, he worked hard, and he spent most of his free time on the rivers catching "the big ones." He was slow to anger, but when fired up he could outfight anyone. He was renowned in the family and around the bars as "a lean, mean fighting machine, fast as lightning." But most of my life, he would remain a mystery to me.

Wanda had married into a close-knit family of pure Spanish blood. Her husband, Billy, looked more like a movie star than a husband. They were living in Los Angeles with her son, Markey, from a previous, tragic romance, and their son, Sudsy, who had been born with a hole in his heart. The little boy underwent a twelve-hour heart operation when he was only a couple of months old. He would have to have another operation when he was about twelve and would die on the operating table.

They tried to have a happy home, but Billy was intensely loyal to his "other family," who felt that Billy had married below himself. Mother would receive about two letters a week, which often contained pictures of her beloved grandchildren. She longed to see them all.

Donnie loved his seaman's existence and the big guns that he fired. He was nicknamed Deadeye Donnie. We would get letters from him about his adventures, and I would make Mother read and reread them, while I stared in wonderment at the pictures he would send. I had never seen the ocean, or a ship. It was all so foreign and magical to me. Often Mother would bake some goodies and send them to him, her way of saying, "I love and miss you." I had never heard Mother tell me or anyone else in words that she loved them. In fact, I didn't know there was such a word, which of course gives credence to the saying "What you don't know won't hurt you." Come to think of it, I don't ever remember getting kissed or hugged by Mother, so I didn't know about missing that either.

My closest playmate was my younger brother, Loy. I was five years old and Loy was three. He was a beautiful child with thick black hair, deep-set hazel eyes rimmed with long thick lashes, and gorgeous skin with a dash of freckles across his pug nose. He was Mother's pride and joy, her last baby.

Since I was not in school at that time—something I knew nothing about—Loy and I would spend our days playing and entertaining one another. We knew no such animal as a baby-sitter. Our store-bought toys were few, but the ones provided by nature were many. Our favorites were June bugs. These large metallic-green bugs were beautiful and harmless. We would tie thread around them, under their wings, and then extend a generous length, sort of a makeshift leash. The June bugs would fly around, sort of like small helicopters—definitely more exciting than plastic ones. With those, you had to do all the flying with your hands and arms. Then we would find some sticks and straddle them—they were horses, don't you know—tie the bugs' strings to the top of the sticks, and we would ride many dusty trails together. What fun we had.

At the trail's end, we would park our stick horses by the back door, untie the June bugs—who were probably exhausted and harrowed to say the least—and find a bush that we could tie them to for the night. We always left plenty of string for them just in case they wanted to play by themselves, so it was not uncommon some mornings to find the strings wrapped tightly around some helpless bush—not to mention, of course, the shocking plight of the bugs. One morning I ran out to retrieve my bug and found that the poor creature had hung himself. I wasn't certain if it had been an accident or if he just couldn't face those endless dusty trails one more day. At any rate, I sought out the June bug cemetery, the Forest Lawn of famous June bugs who had come to their demise heroically in the service of their owner—me. I laid him to rest. Grief over, I hastened to find another willing recruit.

On a lazy warm summer day, Loy and I were playing out by the back porch. Loy parked his stick horse and ran up the steps to use the bathroom. In the meantime, my activities had been interrupted by a large booger that was plugging up my breathing. I fingered the slimy thing out and then stuck it to the underside of the porch. Suddenly I was startled by a man rounding the corner of the house. Thinking I had been caught picking boogers and wiping them on something, I felt the heat of a deep blush reddening my face. Then I recognized this intruder. It was ol' Charlie, and he was intoxicated. He wore a soiled white shirt and khaki pants sitting low on his hips and held in place by a skinny belt. He reeked of booze.

"Well, ya must be ma li'l Judy." He stooped down, wobbling a bit. His eyes were bloodshot, their lids heavy.

"And I know who you are too," I said as I squinted my eyes and recoiled from the stench of his breath. He pulled a gift-wrapped box and a candy cane from behind him and handed them to me.

"Here, this is fer ya. I bot a present fer ma li'l girl."

I put the candy cane immediately in my mouth and began to suck on it as I watched him open the box with his nicotine-stained fingers. It was a green-and-white striped dress.

He held the dress high for a moment and then he gave it to me. He was so proud of the dress, and pleased with himself for making such a generous gesture. He was trying to ask forgiveness in his own way.

"I know'd ya like green-'n'-white stripes," he said, smiling.

"Uh-huh," I answered, checking over my prize.

"An here's a brand-new shiny dime fer ya."

I took the dime without saying anything. An old, broken-down car full of men pulled around the corner and stopped, stirring up lots of dust. The driver honked the horn. "C'mon, Charlie, gotta go. We're a-waitin'," they yelled.

Good ol' Charlie patted me on the head, stroked my hair, and without a word turned around and walked toward the car, a pint of Jim Beam stuck in his back pocket. He removed it from the pocket and took a swig as he weaved toward the car. He got in and drove off. When Loy came back out, I handed him the candy cane and put the new dress on. Carefully setting the new dime on the porch Loy and I resumed riding our stick horses down the tree-lined street.

* * *

Later that afternoon, Loy and I ventured into the large open courtyard of a motel that was directly in front of our barracks. It had no paving, just the usual dirt covered with dead elm leaves. While we were galloping our stick horses around the area, a pretty blond-headed girl came out of one of the doors and sat down on her porch. She was dressed in a pink taffeta dress with a pink satin sash around her waist, patent-leather shoes, and a pink satin ribbon tied into a bow in her hair. She was sipping tea. I looked and waved. I had never seen such lavish clothes on a kid my age. She looked more like the doll I had seen at the drugstore, lying with a bored expression in a box wrapped in plastic.

Seeing me in my new—but by now dirty—dress, my hair stringy, and my feet bare must have made her want to puke. She made a face like she had just been given a tablespoon of pink Pepto-Bismol. It would have matched her dress.

"Ughhh. My mommy says I can't play with you," she stated smugly.

"Why?" I said innocently.

"Because," she retorted.

"Because why?" I insisted.

"Because you're dirty and my mommy says not to touch you," she answered in an I'm-better-than-you-are voice.

"Not to touch me?"

"Yes, my mommy says that you're poor white trash," she said, sticking her dumb nose in the air.

I pursed my lips and scooped up a wad of dirt and let her have it good. God, I'm such a good shot, I thought. I'll just give her another one, except this time I'll add some spit to add texture and glue. I fired it off. Splat! Right in the puss! She jumped up, spilling her tea over her dress and breaking the cup on the porch. She let out a miserable wail and started bawling for her mommy. Good grief! You would have thought I had boxed her ears or something, the way she was squalling. What a sissy-snot! Her mother appeared at the door. "What's going on here?" she demanded.

"She called me trash and says you won't let her touch me," I retorted smartly, my hands on my hips in defiance.

Her mother now got a good look at her little doll's dress

and that stupid little face. One eye was glued together by the spitball, and the other had the remains scattered among her eyelashes. And boy, was she bawling!

"You *are* trash . . . filthy trash. Just filthy poor trash. Get out of here! Get away before I whop your dirty little butt good!" She retrieved her crying wimp and disappeared behind a slammed door.

I broke into tears, grabbed Loy's hand, and ran back to our apartment. Mom was home, changing into a clean uniform for the evening.

"Momma, why are we trash?" I pouted.

"What in tha world are you talking about, Judy?"

"This girl's momma said I was poor white trash and that she couldn't touch me."

Mom finished dressing and marched out of the back door with Loy and me in tow. She asked me where the woman lived, and I pointed to the apartment where the fight had taken place. Momma marched up to the front door and began to yell.

"Jolene Foster, you git your cotton-pickin' ass out here."

Mother waited. Oh Lord, was she pissed. And when she was, she took on a brute masculine air. I cowered behind her. Mrs. Foster came out, dressed in a robe and with curlers in her hair. Mother continued, "Of course I know why you is dressed with a robe on in the daytime. When I finish with you, I'm a-comin' in after your boyfriend, ya ol' whore!"

Stupid woman, she scurried out the door toward Mother in an effort to hush her loud voice. Helen the Ominous— aka Mom—didn't even acknowledge her feeble attempt to shush her up. Instead, Mom slapped her hard. I swear I thought I saw some rollers fly from the stupid creature's head. Then, quick as a fly, Mom drove a left hook right to the kisser that knocked the already silly-with-stars woman right off the porch. She landed hard on the ground, sprawled in a most indecent manner.

Mother towered over her victim and began, "Nobody calls my children trash . . . especially a trash prostitute the likes of you!"

Choking, Mrs. Foster replied in a near whisper, "I'm not going to fight you. It's against my religious beliefs."

"Religious beliefs, eh? Ya sorry thang, the good Lord done forgot about ya. Ya bedd'r get a-prayin' hard, cuz I ain't through with ya." Whereupon Mom the Hun grabbed Mrs. Foster's broom off the porch and proceeded to clean her plow. She got the bewildered Mrs. Foster over the hood of a nearby car and beat her silly. More rollers were flying. I was staring in wide-eyed amazement. I knew one thing— Mom would permanently remove the word "trash" from the woman's vocabulary.

Cars began to stop, their occupants gawking in utter disbelief. This was a most unusual roadside attraction. A few onlookers moved in closer and began to applaud. Mother then left her limp and bleeding victim on the hood and, true to her word, marched inside, stalking her next prey—the boyfriend. Everyone waited with bated breath, including myself. Soon there was a loud crashing sound, then another, and then the screams of a man—or at least I think it was a man. Mother had taken care of the boyfriend too. She reappeared, blood all over her white uniform, muttering something about who really was poor white trash. She grabbed my hand and marched back home, leaving bloody carnage in our wake.

"Ain't nobody gonna gimme no lip without me a-buttonin' it up fer 'em." Mother had saved the day and our dignity but good!

A few days later, on Saturday, Mother bought Loy and me a new pair of shoes and each a new outfit. She told us that Mr. and Mrs. Andrews, the old couple who owned the hamburger stand, had asked if they could take us to church on Sunday. We weren't sure what church was, so Mother gave us a little lesson on manners and emphasized that we should not talk. And when it was time to pray, she told us, we were to keep our eyes closed tight with heads bowed. I asked why we were to do this, and she said that would give the good Lord time to look us over. If the good Lord liked what He saw, He and God, who was His father, would smile upon us. But, we were *not to look up*.

The following morning, Mother helped us with our baths and getting dressed. The night before she had rolled my hair into tight pin curls, and was now removing the pins one by one. She took the brush and began to brush my hair in a creative fury, causing static electricity that began to snap, crackle, and pop each time she pulled the brush through my hair. The more she tried to make it behave, the worse it got. Feeling a bit defeated by it all, she put the brush down and just patted the wild stuff. I did not get to look in the mirror. At that moment, Loy walked into the room and stopped short. His eyes widened and his face revealed horrible fright.

"What are *you* staring at?" I demanded to know. "Egads, you look as if ya'd seen the boogerman or somethin'." I studied his strange expression for a moment and slowly began to suspect that *I* was the boogerman. I jumped up and shoved him out of my way and ran to the bathroom. I leaped upon the toilet, leaned over the sink, and glared into the mirror. The reflection revealed an electrocuted child who had probably stuck her finger in an electrical socket. My usual "limp" mop was now standing, frizzed all over my head. Even my bangs were standing at attention. I tried to touch the stuff, but I got short circuited. The stuff was *alive* and obviously *pissed off!*

Mother came in and retrieved me and the mess, to hurry us off on our adventure. She pretended not to notice my "do." I had come to a stark realization that morning. Mother could forget any ideas she might have had about being a beautician. And I made a secret pact with myself that I would never again let her mess with my hair.

Before leaving, I ran outside and untied my June bug. I put him in my handkerchief, string and all, and placed him in my dress pocket. I wanted him to meet God, too.

Mr. and Mrs. Andrews were waiting out in the car, and Mother shuffled us out the door and into the waiting car. She gave Loy and me each a quarter. I thought it was a payoff for the hair job. Loy gleefully stashed his in his pocket.

"Now, y'all be good an remember whut I said 'bout keepin' your eyes closed an all. An the quarter is fer God. Just put it in the offerin' plate when it's passed ta ya." She smiled.

"Offerin' plate?" I asked. "Ya mean we gotta pay for the good Lord's and His father's supper?" Mrs. Andrews turned slowly in my direction to reveal a nervous little smile, while Mr. Andrews looked at me with a curious jolt. His eyes, already magnified by his thick glasses, bulged terribly. He was staring at my hair. The wild electrified stuff was clinging to the felt lining of the ceiling of the car. He stared, with mouth falling open in a state of shock. A very similar reaction to that of my brother's. Realizing his impolite reaction, he smiled a little and started the engine. Momma waved good-bye and we left.

Loy had removed the quarter from his pocket and began to fumble with it. Then with a "psssst" he leaned over and whispered in my ear, "Sure hope this is gonna be a good show. Just better be worth a quarter. Do ya think we'll get some Cokes an candy bars?" I just shrugged my shoulder.

Presently we arrived for "the services." I got out, and the wind blew a little as we walked up the steps to the doors. My hair responded with its own repertoire of unnatural sounds. I entered the doors and began walking down the aisle with Mrs. Andrews, my hair snapping and crackling all the way. Mrs. Andrews glared at the hissing mess in wonderment.

Quietly seated, Loy and I were perfect angels in quiet reverence. The pastor walked up to the pulpit. His name was Brother Phillips, and he was the son of the Andrewses. He began to preach on "sinners" and "hellfire" and "burning alive" for the "just deserving." My eyes widened in disbelief. Loy and I glanced at each other, scared as hell! Then I glanced over to see what Mrs. Andrews was doing. Well, she just sat there, clutching her Bible and nodding sweetly. I heard someone yell, "Amen, praise tha Lord." I jolted and turned in the direction of the voice. Everyone was nodding, some were wiping tears from their eyes. I guess they were scared to death like me. Brother Phillips broke off and asked everyone to bow their heads in prayer. This was our cue. After hearing all about what God could do if he didn't like you, I closed my eyes tight, hoping he would look at Loy and me and like us.

While the prayer rambled on, people all over would moan and shout, but I didn't peek. That was why I didn't notice that my June bug had crawled out. Seeing his freedom, he took a deep breath and took flight. The string uncoiled, but the end stayed snagged in the handkerchief in my pocket. All of a sudden I heard a terrible scream and the stomping of feet, backed up with a choir of amens. It grew to an awful roar, but I just figured it was another crazed person "filled with the glory of God."

Well, it turns out that "the glory of God" was my June bug, and it had "anointed" a little old lady sitting behind us by flying into her hair and getting stuck to her hair spray. He was trying to get out when the woman felt something moving in her hair. Raising her hand to feel around, her finger came upon the bug who immediately mistook the finger as freedom. The old lady jumped up and started screaming in fright, while the June bug, free again, started flying around her head, wrapping the string round and round her face. Her jumping and shouting was not at all uncommon during Sunday services, so no one responded. They just kept hollering, "Amen, sister, amen."

Finally the preacher, thinking she was overdoing it a bit, opened his eyes and beheld a shocking sight. There, the fourth pew over to the left, danced poor Sister Sue. She had knocked over an old gent sitting next to her, who lay stunned on the floor. She had popped a few buttons on her blouse, and a saggy boob was weaving to and fro beneath her slip. Her head was wound in white thread, which left only enough line for the June bug to hover at eye level. Brother Phillips, rushing down from the pulpit, caught his foot in the carpet and landed smack on his holy puss. Everyone stopped amenin' it and opened their eyes in utter amazement. Everyone, of course, but Loy and I. We were hoping—real hard—that God was liking us . . . a lot!

Ol' Brother Phillips got up and ran to Sister Sue's rescue. There sure was a lot of commotion going on behind us. We didn't dare take a look. He grabbed the June bug and began to unravel the thread from around Sister Sue's face. Then he followed the thread right over my shoulder and into my pocket. He shook my shoulder, and I opened my eyes to see if I was liked. Loy opened his at that moment and asked, "Is it time ta buy somethin' for God an his kid to eat?'' reaching in his pocket to get the quarter. The June bug crawled out of the preacher's hand and flew in between me and Mrs. Andrews. She reacted by fainting right there on the spot. I grabbed my June bug and began to scold it for killing poor Mrs. Andrews and chasing God off. Mr. Andrews leaped up to help his wife, while everyone gasped in the pews. Sister Sue was escorted pathetically out of the church, and Brother Phillips "escorted" Loy, me, and the June bug out of the church, too.

We were severely chastised for our behavior. June bugs, we learned, were not permitted in God's house.

"Just wait till I tell my Momma you yelled at us," Loy threatened. "She'll clean your pl—" I slapped my hand over his big fat mouth.

"Doesn't God love June bugs too?" I asked, as my hair began to sing again. Brother Phillips just stood there trying to find the words to answer me with. At that moment, Mr. Andrews appeared at the door, holding up poor Mrs. Andrews, who was fanning herself with her handkerchief.

"Wow, you're *not* dead, Mizz Andrews!" I said as I ran over to her, leaving Loy to "guard" the good pastor.

"No, child . . . not yet, anyways," she moaned, clutching her Good Book even tighter and resuming her fanning.

I pulled out my June bug and held it up to her, and proclaimed, "My June bug is real sorry fer scaring you. He's really very nice an . . ." I was rambling on about his virtues when he took flight once more. The poor lady gasped, and Mr. Andrews grabbed the string. The bug buzzed around his head, bewildering him even further. I dashed forward and seized the string, while he yelled at me to let it go. I hesitated. I looked back at Loy, then the preacher, back to the victims, and then to my beloved bug. I untied him and gave him his freedom.

Mr. Andrews escorted us quickly to the car. Loy hesitated a moment, turned and looked at the preacher, and stated, "God's a mean ol' sucker. We didn't even git a small candy bar. Heck, I'm not gonna come back here!" Mr. Andrews sighed and off we sped.

Later that evening we told "our story" to Mother, who listened quietly. When we were finished, she got up from the table, went to the bathroom, and closed the door. A moment later, roars of laughter billowed through the door. I just looked at Loy and we shrugged our shoulders, wondering what was so funny.

CHAPTER SEVEN

DREAMS, SERMONS, AND GRAB BAGS

Zora Neale Hurston once stated, "There is something about poverty that smells like death. Dead dreams dropping off the heart like leaves in a dry season and rotting around the feet." Mother was our sole provider. She loathed those "lazy thangs" that were on welfare, and her diligent efforts alone kept food on the table, a roof over our heads, and shoes on our feet.

We had never celebrated Christmas—or any other traditional holiday—in the commercial sense of the word. Never in my short life did we have a Christmas tree adorned with colored lights and festive ornaments, with mysterious papered and bowed boxes beneath it. Nor did I don the guise of a ghost, witch, goblin, or monster and canvass the neighborhood for a trick-or-treat handout. These lavish celebrations were part of a society we did not belong to. They *were* the stuff of Mother's dreams and hopes for us, but alas, the daily drudge of keeping one's nose to the grindstone never permitted such frivolity. Fortunately, Loy and I did not know that we were missing anything, nor did we realize that there was a better life than the one we were living, so we were never filled with a sense of self-pity and shame. Innocence allows the absence of shame.

Mother's dreams of a better life for Loy and me were becoming more urgent by the end of summer of 1951. She knew that in the fall she would have to enroll me in a public school to begin my formal education. There, exposed to class distinctions, lacking the things that I had not missed—an adequate wardrobe for a little girl rather than hand-me-downs from my older brothers, shoes for everyday wear, school supplies—our position would become all too obvious to me. I would be introduced to holidays at school that would end in a disappointing follow-through at home. All of these dreams and dreads spoke silently to my mother daily.

To a single woman in the 1950s who was uneducated, divorced, and had children, the road to prosperity was narrow indeed. The solution often took the form of another marriage. Though such a choice often nullifies the dream of personal achievement and the possibility to control one's destiny, in effect selling oneself short for the long-term gain, Mother, under mounting frustration, must have decided on this option as so many women do when they find every other door shut to them.

Mother's other two marriages had only brought her misery. This time, she would seek different qualifications in a husband. This time, it would be a marriage of convenience rather than of love. She would find a respectable, kind, gentle, compassionate, supportive man who would take care of her and her children. After all she had been through, it would be worth it.

The dream was on the verge of coming true. Mother's popularity with her customers at both jobs was immense. The fact that she was a beautiful woman certainly didn't hurt. One customer, a divorcé, was a well-to-do businessman who had taken an instant liking to Mother. His name was Bill Angley. He owned the sporting goods store in town and was an upstanding citizen in the community. Bill was a shrewd businessman who found it very difficult to be humble because of his prosperity. His wealth had earned him many friends, who always laughed at his jokes and ignored his many faults. At sixty years old, he was well preserved, tall, well rounded in the girth, and always well dressed. He had been married before and had fathered two handsome daughters.

Bill and his former wife had owned several furniture companies together. Both were egomaniacal, stingy with their money, and fought incessantly for control of their financial enterprises as well as of the family—a bitter dispute that finally caused the marriage to collapse. The daughters took their mother's side in the divorce and she was awarded their custody. Bill was deeply disappointed in his daughters and resented them for the rest of his life. Fatherhood had left him bitter. Children were annoying, offensive, and painfully galling. Girls in particular.

Bill was quite taken with Mother. He thought her simplicity, attractiveness, and hard-working attitude were the very traits all women should have. Mother began to respond to his wooing and flattery. Her moods showed a noticeable change from resignation to a cheerfulness that was quite becoming. She smiled more, laughed more, and in general felt better about herself. It was a wonderful sight to see her so gay, though at first I didn't know the catalyst. I was about to learn.

Late one afternoon, Mother was busying herself in the kitchen preparing supper with greater than usual intensity. Earlier she had washed and ironed some clothes that she wanted us to wear that evening at mealtime. They were our best things. She began to tell us about a guest she had invited over for supper, and she stressed the need for us to be quiet and courteous. At the appropriate hour, a man came to the door, and we were introduced. He shook Loy's hand approvingly, and rather ignored me. Mother said that we should call him "Daddy Bill."

The four of us sat down to supper, with Bill and Mother chatting as if Loy and I were invisible. It was my custom to just reach for whatever I wanted on the table, sort of a help-yourself habit. When I helped myself to the mashed potatoes, Bill delivered a quick and severe slap on my arm.

"Mind your manners. Don't reach," he said with authority.

"But I'm hungry," I said, peering at the ruthless Bill.

"You mind your new Daddy Bill. He's only doing what's best for you," she said, and she turned to Loy. "Lloyd Gene, I'm going to be a-packin' your clothes in the mornin' becuz you are a-goin' with us on our honeymoon."

She had failed to mention me going along.

"Can't I go too?"

Without looking up from her plate she replied, "No, Judy girl. Daddy Bill is gonna teach Lloyd Gene some athletics. You're to stay with tha widow lady." She then glanced up at me and continued, "You gotta learn ta do somethin' with that straggly hair of yourn. And when we come back, we're movin' into a real house."

Everyone else continued to eat, but I had lost my appetite. I felt the obvious exclusion and thought it was because of my straggly hair that I was being left behind. I also felt that this intruder into our lives did not like me, that he wished I was not a part of Mother's life. Later on, I would discover that Bill had tried to convince Mother to give me away before their marriage. He did not like little girls, and felt that happiness could be achieved only in their absence. Mother had insisted that I remain, and so I did. But the resentfulness he showed toward me in the years that followed was his way of excluding me from his life and pretending I didn't even exist. His prize forever would be Loy. He would be the son he had never had.

In the weeks of my family's absence, I spent much of my time with the widow lady and Mrs. Andrews, both religious women whose dutiful endeavors to live the Good Word occupied most of their time. As a result, I was indoctrinated into the ways of God and Jesus Christ. They read me stories from the Bible, and every Sunday I went to church with the both of them, listening to the fierce sermons of the preacher. These were very much in contrast to the sublime, low-keyed tales I was hearing at Bible school that summer.

On Wednesday evenings there was often a guest revivalist who would raise the roof with his harrowing tales of a "sinner's woes." One evening, after such a sermon, a little girl from my Bible class remarked to me, "I've been a-prayin' real hard for you, because your mother's a sinner." I was dumbfounded, and asked her why she thought that Mother was a sinner. She sighed, "Because she doesn't go to church."

When my family returned, I was promptly enrolled in the first grade at a new and wealthy elementary school. Hermosa Elementary School. While I was struggling with the three Rs, not being sufficiently prepared for all of this, Daddy Bill and Mother busied themselves with our new house. Bill had taken it upon himself to pick out all the furniture. The house was very attractive, with its two bedrooms, living room, dining room, kitchen, and one bathroom. Oh, I forgot to mention that there was one other room, a small niche that had been a home office. A small cutout window into the hall, where the phone sat, was its only source of light. This, Bill decided, would be my room. The other, more spacious one, with two windows and a walk-in closet, would be Loy's. Mother, however, disagreed with this scheme. She felt it only right that I should have the larger one, being that I was the oldest and that I was a girl. Bill puffed himself up with anger at Mother's outrageous disobedience. It had dented his ego. But Mother won out. Not without compromise, however. Bill decorated my room with dark brown curtains and matching bedspread, the opposite of a little girl's dreams of pinks, yellows, lace, and dreamy bright walls. Loy inherited the niche, which fit only a bed and a small chest of drawers. Nonetheless, this house was a castle to Loy and me.

In school I displayed an intense desire to learn. I wanted so much to be able to read and read well. In the beginning, I suffered so much from the ostracism and snubs of my classmates that learning was difficult. I felt outclassed and outdressed by everyone. It was not uncommon to hear other children yell, "Hey, boy," because of my dirty overalls, stringy hair, and freckled face. I was kicked by the boys and called "ugly duck" and once, on Easter, a girl in my class came to school sporting her new Easter attire, complete with black patent-leather shoes and a new Toni Perm in her golden locks. I thought she looked beautiful and rushed up to tell her so, but all I got for my compliments was her spit on my pants and, "You're ugly." I stood there staring at her, and then retorted, "Someday, Amy Watts, I am going to be the most beautiful girl in this stupid town." She just glared, while her entourage of friends snickered. All this cruelty deeply affected my sense of security in the classroom, making me afraid to have to read, write, or do blackboard work in front of this dangerous mob.

Social alienation led me to hope more for the existence of God, whose love, I had been told, was all-encompassing. At times on the playground, when things got tough, I would wander away and find a place to myself, look up at the clouds, and ask, "God, are you up there, sitting on a cloud, watching me? I know you are. I love you, God. You are my friend. Do you love me? Have I been a good girl? I have, you know, because when they slap me on the cheek, I do just as you say, and I turn the other one. Boy, it's hard not to punch their lights out." Then I would remember what the preacher had once said to a naughty boy at church. He told him Solomon had said, "Man is wicked from his birth and evil from his youth." There just had to be *some* good kids around. A gentle gust of wind would brush my hair and face. Just feeling the wind made me feel better, and somehow gave me the courage to return to my classroom when the bell rang. "Help me be a better kid, God. Gotta go. Amen."

At home, my dark and gloomy boudoir had become my refuge. Often Loy would join me, complaining of claustrophobia from his dark den. Bill and Mother were always doing something around the house. Both loved gardening, and much of their free time was spent creating a flower paradise, where they sat and sipped iced tea in the evening. I retreated from these activities because of the coolness I felt from Bill. Though he was my stepfather, for the most part he lacked the slightest inclination to treat me with charity or kindness or gentleness of thought. To me, it was as if he had been born without—what shall I call it?—without humanity. But I had learned to "honor thy father and thy mother," and tried to carry out their wishes regardless of my own.

"Judy, you come out here an be sociable," Mother would bark.

"I'm busy, Momma." I was drawing pictures of Moses, Noah in the Flood, and other biblical scenes that I would paste on felt and tack to a large display board, just like the ones in Bible school. I was doing all this for an important lesson I was scheduled to deliver to the neighborhood children.

"So, when Moses parted the Red Sea, it was because God loved him. And He was ticked off at the Egyptians," I would tell them.

"How could God make the water separate?" quipped one child as he picked his nose.

"God can do anything."

"But we have to ask Him, right?" asked another.

"Right. You talk to Him. The Bible says, 'Ask and you shall receive.' "

"Can God give my daddy some money for a new car?"

"Well, maybe he should ask a lot harder," I said with confidence.

"Oh, yeah? My daddy says there is no such thing as God!" the brat snarled back.

"Your daddy is wrong. God is my friend. God loves me. And God loves you, too—even your daddy," I replied smugly.

At this point, a larger kid, named Sammy, came sauntering up to my little "Bible meetin'."

"I think you're full of it. I don't think God loves anybody . . . and I don't believe He's your stupid friend. And I don't believe you talk to Him, stupid face," Sammy said.

"Oh, yes I do." I rose up and put on my usual defensive glare, my fists resting on my hips.

"Oh, no you don't! You're full of shit."

This was too much. I was going to fight like King David and smear the creep! I lunged toward him and landed a right hook under his nose. I continued to preach, while beating the snot out of him.

"Don't you give me your lip or I'll button it up for you."
Smack. "You don't know what you're talking about . . . you
stupid sinner, creep. God loves you." Smack, kick. "God
loves you."

To the other children, this was high drama and induced
giggles and jokes among the gathering crowd. Violence was
the way of settling all affairs, as far as they were concerned.
For me, too, when it came to questioning the validity of God.

After making my point to Sammy, I moved my Bible
class further down the street, and the faithful followed. Echoes
of Sammy's bawling grew fainter as he ran home.

Over the next five years my reputation among my classmates improved. Mother spent many days sewing wonderful
stylish dresses that were more in keeping with the clothing
of my peers. I wore six starched petticoats underneath these
designer originals, which made me look like I was wearing
a tutu rather than excessive undergarments. I wore matching
anklets with an assortment of brown-and-white saddle oxfords. I hated those ugly suckers! I had learned to roll and
style my own hair with good taste. And my marks were
improving. By the age of ten I had a new confidence in
myself, and reveled in my new popularity in school.

One morning my sixth-grade teacher, Mrs. Tyner, announced that she wished for the girls to remain in the classroom, while she excused the boys to go outside for their play
period. When the last one, Jake Harper—my heartthrob—
left, Mrs. Tyner had the girls follow her into the girls' rest
room. Attached to the wall beside the sinks was a peculiar
machine that had not been there yesterday.

After a pause, as she waited for us to shut up, Mrs.
Tyner began, "Young ladies, I wanted to personally inform
you that we have installed this machine for your use. Accidents do occur, from time to time, so to help you in those
'times of need,' this machine is ready for your convenience.
It requires a nickel. That will be all. You may join the boys
for the rest of the play period." At that, we quickly filed out
to the playground, and I began to speculate with my friends
Pam, Cheryl, and Ellen what that was all about, what the
machine was for.

"Gads, I bet I know what it is," said Pam.

"What?" we all asked.

"Of course, don't ya see. It's a grab-bag machine. It's got grab bags in it just like the ones at the school carnival. Wow! Whatta neat idea!" Pam was jubilant. So was I. What a nice thing for the school to do for us kids. Put a machine in the rest room that has bags of toys, just for us.

"Ya think there's one in the boys' rest room, too?" asked Cheryl.

"Who cares? Let's go get one."

"Yeah, we can use our milk money," I said. With that, we ran back into the building and into the girls' rest room, heading straight for the grab-bag dispenser. Pam bullied her way to be first. She inserted her nickel and twisted the knob. Plunk, the machine delivered her grab bag full of toys and surprises. A neat return for a nickel investment. Without stopping to see what was in her bag, the rest of us repeated the ritual. By then Pam was finished tearing apart the bag, the cotton, and the surrounding tissue, looking for her prize. We all did the same . . . and came up with zilch!

"I can't believe this. We got gypped," Pam said, finishing off the last bit of cotton.

Cheryl, looking bewildered at her worthless bag of cotton, said, "I think we better show this to Mrs. Tyner and she'll get our nickels back. She probably doesn't even know there aren't any toys in these bags."

"Yeah, I'll bet she'll do something about it, too. Let's go show her this stuff." That was MY bright idea.

So, away we went back to the classroom to find Mrs. Tyner. The bell rang signaling the end of recess, and everyone returned to the room. In we barged, the Justice Committee, evidence in tow to present to Mrs. Tyner. To her horror, we began to put in front of her the shredded, mangled debris of the fraudulent grab bags. One boy, Robin Whittey, snatched the one from Ellen's hand and began to slap Clovis Harding over the head with it.

Mrs. Tyner jumped to her feet. "Robin Whittey, put that . . . that *thing* on my desk, now! The rest of you sit down and *be quiet.*" We stood there frozen in our tracks. This attempt on the school's part to gyp little kids out of their nickels had obviously made Mrs. Tyner very angry. She was beet red!

"Ladies," she whispered, "this is not what it appears to be. I think it would be much wiser to have your mothers explain this most unfortunate incident to you. Now, I will write a note for you to take home. Things will be much clearer in the morning."

"But Mrs. Tyner, don't we even get our nickels back?" I wanted to know. "If these aren't grab bags, what are they?"

"I'm sorry, I cannot refund your nickels to you. That would be against school policy. *Please* understand," she pleaded.

Not wanting to be put off, I weighed the evidence and then had a brilliant realization. "Oh, now I get it, Mrs. Tyner. These are bandages just in case you get hurt real bad." She was not overjoyed with my persistent genius.

"My dear, they are called Kotex. I'm certain your mother will explain it all to you." She began to write feverishly a note to each of our mothers. She then folded them neatly and wrote "PERSONAL" on the outside. "Now, take these home with you and kindly return to your seats."

I returned home from school that day and delivered the note to Mother. I waited while she read it, preparing to be enlightened on the meaning of "Kotex." Without saying a word, she tore the note up and told me to go do my homework and clean my room. I felt cheated.

In those days, sex education was not part of the school curriculum. The birds 'n' bees was left up to hardy parents to muddle through, since it was considered a sign of ill breeding to talk of such matters in public. It was as if everyone were sexless. Since Mother was mute on the subject, I continued on through the sixth grade and into the seventh grade ignorant of just what a Kotex was. In the eighth grade I was shocked when I got home one day to find blood all over my panties. I thought I was dying, like people did on *Dr. Kildare*. Crying, I phoned my mother, who then worked part-time for Bill in the store. She told me I was not dying but "menstruating." She came home and handed me a brown paper bag and in it contained a box that read, "KOTEX."

"Here, put one of these on. Change them daily until you stop menstruating." She went about preparing supper and that was that. So, this was a Kotex. But why was I bleeding? It beat me. All I knew was that I felt very ashamed to have to wear one and hated to hear that word, "menstruating." Oh, it was such an odious word and only MY mother ever said it. Only later, through discussions with my friends on this most intimate matter, would I learn it meant "now you can have babies." I rather liked their term for this monthly dark side of womanhood. They called it a "period." But I would never experience the unraveling of the mystery of sex with my mother. I was on my own in that department.

CHAPTER EIGHT

"FAITH HAS NEED OF THE WHOLE TRUTH"

With my "coming of age" at thirteen, I was now considered a teenager. My appearance had changed somewhat. I was rather thin, and my hair was much longer—but not so stringy because of my new expertise with coiffure design. I still possessed a tomboyish air and was endowed with great athletic abilities and quick reflexes. All I lacked was polished beauty, but I was getting there.

I had also taught myself to twirl the baton and practiced daily. One Sunday morning I was dutifully rehearsing my routine in the backyard for the junior high school majorette tryouts that would be held the following Wednesday. The radio in the kitchen was playing "Onward Christian Soldiers," and I stepped high to the military rhythm around the weeping willow tree. I paraded in and out of the wash hanging on the clothesline, and into the greenhouse, challenging my tight twirl amid the hanging geranium baskets. The music stopped and Mother's voice rang out.

"Judy, you a-goin' to church or not? Come in here an dress so's ya won't be late, ya hear?"

"Okay . . . be there in a minute."

Mother was baking a pecan pie . . . decadent little thing. "Oh, Lord, this kitchen needs washin' down," she said as I came in.

"Uh-huh . . . guess it does," I answered, sneaking a pecan off the pie.

"Look at you, girl. When are ya plannin' on becomin' more ladylike? Just look at that hair. Go'n do somethin' with it."

"Momma, I *do* do something with it. It's the *style* . . . *see?*" showing her as I whirled around for a 360-degree exposure. "Momma, I got me twelve jackrabbits yesterday. I can outshoot Loy. I did some *fine* shootin'."

"Lord have mercy, I don't know whut caused me ta have all ma babies. I shoulda quit yer father a long time before I did," she said, shaking her head as she placed the pie on the windowsill to cool.

"Yes, Momma." I had heard this before and had stopped feeling bad about my birth some time ago.

"Just look at your nose. It's just so turned up. I don't know whut to do about that. It's a Hampton nose, I reckon."

"Well, Ma, that's purty strange, since your nose looks a lot like mine." I pinched her pug nose on the end. "I reckon ya can't blame everything on the Hamptons. Besides, my nose gives me something to hang on to around here." Laughing, I led myself out of the kitchen by my nose.

"That's enough sass outta you now," she said sharply. "I gotta teach her who's tha boss 'round here." She grinned to herself and then laughed at my foolishness.

I went to my bedroom—though a bit dark, it was a neat place. I pulled the brown curtains back and rays of bright morning sun filled the room. The warm light danced on the walls and the many pictures of movie stars I had cut from magazines. My favorite was directly above my bed—Richard Chamberlain, aka Dr. Kildare. The floor was strewn with

Levis, dirty socks, tennis shoes, my homework, and some
Coca-Cola cups saved as mementos from various Saturday
matinees. I went over to the mirror and took a look at myself.
What I saw made me wince. After all, I was a far cry from
the picture of Candice Bergen, who was just about my age.
Turning to a dramatic profile shot, I studied my nose and
my best angle. . . . Hmmm, not too bad. But head-on, forget
it. I pulled my bangs up to check out my high forehead.
Mother said it was a sign of great intelligence. I insisted it
was a genetic flaw. I kept all those brains covered up with
ample bangs. It looked better. I began brushing my hair with
determined strokes, when Mother rang again.

"I want ya ta clean Lloyd Gene's room an iron a pair of
his Levis. He's got baseball practice this evenin'."

I stuck my tongue out at myself in the mirror. "Yes,
Momma, I'll clean the invalid's bed and iron the invalid's
pants. We mustn't tire tha precious thang . . . not ta mention
he might pull a hamstring tuckin' the sheets in. Oh, what
horrors that might bring upon us all!" In a flurry, I slapped
the ironing board into place, plugged in the iron, and ran to
Loy's room, where I picked up his dirty laundry, straightened his bed, kicked several pairs of shoes under the bed,
and threw the stuff on his dresser into the first drawer, which
now held a bounty of "presumed stolen or lost" items. Then
I returned to the waiting ironing board, flung a pair of "precious" jeans to the board, doused them with water and steamed
away.

Finished with the labor of slaves, I ran back to my closet
and pulled out a pink ruffled dress with matching sash and
threw it over my head. I grabbed ten thousand petticoats
from off the closet floor and pulled them up under the dress,
all the while wondering when I was going to start wearing
straight skirts like everyone else I knew. Instead, I always
looked like some stupid, overgrown Kewpie doll in ruffled
garb. I put on my Sunday-go-ta-meetin' white anklets, which
I despised, and proceeded to search for my white patent flats,
thinking, I'm the only *child* in my Sunday school class. I
would give *anything* if Momma would buy me some of those
squashed-heel pumps. I billowed around, not able to see
much for the flair of my dress. Finally finding my shoes, I

toed them onto my feet. I plopped my straw hat on my head, bent over and strapped my roller skates to my flats, grabbed my Bible, and rolled out the door and down the sidewalk to some neighbors two blocks away. They took me to and from church, sort of "carin' for the flock." I was the flock.

The smell of fragrant rose bushes, fresh-cut lawns, and warm morning sun bathed my senses as I skated along the street. My mind reviewed the questions that I had written down and intended to ask my Sunday school teacher, Sister Effy Bell. As my knowledge of "the Word" had increased, I found there were some very peculiar events in the Bible that vexed me. I needed to have them clarified by someone who knew what she was talking about, and today seemed as good a time as any to resolve these nagging inaccuracies.

The sign read, "The Lord Watches Over Artesia." It greeted everyone who came to church and even those "lost souls" that didn't. It was very large and loomed on the corner lot where the church was built. The church was situated near a cross section of streets that led to various honky-tonk bars a block or so down from "Salvation." I'm certain that the guilt produced by that sign only made passersby have a few more belts to wash away its dreadful memory. The bar business was brisk in that neighborhood.

I unsnapped my skates and rushed to my classroom, parking my wheels outside the door. I seated myself in prayerful meditation. Just then the door opened and in breezed Karla Easystreet—we called her Easy for short. I glared with righteous green eyes at her outfit. There she was—all fifty-two pounds sleeked into a *tight* skirt, her form-fitting jacket exposing unnaturally *large* mountains that were not there last Sunday. A pillbox hat sat atop a French roll. To my horror, I saw that she wore hose with *black seams* running all the way down to her naked heels that were cranked up on the spiked heels of her "spring-a-laters." Good God, all that was missing were the scarlet lips, a cigarette holder, and a black poodle with a diamond-studded collar. She took delicate steps to an empty chair—probably because the skirt squeezed her knees into immobility. I turned around to give her one of those saintly, "poor-tainted-little-soul" looks as she struggled to cross her legs. Tommy ("the Lewd") Cox was giving her a different sort of look. God, was *HE FRESH*! I turned back around and glanced at my anklets and flats and modestly pulled them back under my chair. "Out of sight, out of mind."

Sister Effy Bell entered and walked to the felt board to begin another picture story. Her overall appearance changed little from Sunday to Sunday. Her thinning gray hair was always worn in a tight bun, and cat-eyed pink plastic glasses sat on her hooked nose. Her neck was framed by a Pilgrim's collar attached to a 1930s blue floral silk dress that hung unevenly. She wore support hose and black laced shoes. This skinny-as-a-rail, sweet, God-fearing woman always smelled of lavender. I opened my Bible to review my list of questions, then raised my hand.

"Sister Judy. My, my, questions already. The Lord does work in mysterious ways," cooed Sister Effy Bell.

"Praise the Lord for His mysterious ways—and 'mystery' is exactly what my questions are about, Sister Effy Bell. I know the light of the Lord shines upon you so you may clear away my darkness." Very poetic, I was. The others were impressed as well, for a chorus of amens rang out all around me.

Sister Effy Bell smiled, sat down near me, and opened her Bible in her lap. " 'Unto whomsoever much is given, of him shall be much required.' Luke 12:48. 'Am I my brother's keeper?' Genesis 4:9," she said as books opened and a rustle of pages filled the room. The ignorant searching for the verses. They would be tested later.

"Praise the Lord. Ah, Sister Effy Bell"—glancing at my notes—"ah, were you aware of the two contradictory stories in the Book of Genesis? First"—clearing my throat—"how could there have been light before the sun was even made? And secondly, ah, I'm curious as to who exactly Cain married." I glanced up from my notes and saw a bit of a frown on Sister Effy Bell's face as she fingered the lines in the Book of Genesis. She paused, and looked at me for a moment, chewing on her bottom lip.

"Child, you must trust in the Word of God . . . and in His mysterious ways."

I was not to be divinely put off. I continued my quest.

"Now, about Lot and his daughters . . . how could God give the consent and even encourage Lot to rape his own daughters? And Abraham giving Sara, his own wife, away to a king to save his hide—I mean to save his life. And Esau defrauding his dear father, Jacob. These are horrible crimes, but in the Bible, God doesn't even *do* anything about them. It's almost like He *approved* them somehow."

There were gasps, then a hush, then the flying open of pages, then another hush from the astounded around me—who were finding the verses and reading this stuff on their own, probably for the first time. Sister Effy Bell's face turned from chalk white to a deep crimson. She squirmed in her chair.

"I'm sure you must have read it all wrong. . . ."

I flew to the verses and began to recite them, with heavy emphasis on the "outrages." She stood up and interrupted me.

"Be ye as a little child a—"

I interrupted *her*. "I am a little child, and it still means the same thing. Are Lot, Abraham, Jacob, and Sara sinners? Did they go to hell?" I wanted to know. After all, these were God's words, and since He was the author, and I wanted to please the Man, it was important to understand just what sinners got saved and which ones He let off scot-free. I must have made my point, as she sat there as if paralyzed and mute.

My "ask and ye shall be given" had given me nothing except a growing agitation. I continued my interrogation.

"Moving right along to the New Testament . . ." I glanced around me as if to instruct the others. "Both Matthew and Luke have traced Jesus in a family tree back to King David. Oh, yeah, I almost forgot about King David. Well, the commandment 'Thou shalt not kill'—did it apply to King David? He did a lot of killin', ya know. Anyway, back to Matthew and Luke. Matthew traced, according to the Bible, twenty-eight generations between King David and Jesus, as compared to Luke's forty-three. And look here"—showing her the comparison of the ancestral names—"hardly any of these names match up in their lists. How could Matthew *and* Luke represent the true Word of God?"

Well, I had done it then. The enraged Sister Effy jumped
to her feet, clutching her Bible tight, and yelled, " 'Oh thou
of little faith, wherefore didst thou doubt?' Matthew 14:31.
'For by grace are ye saved through faith; and that not of
yourselves: it is the gift of God.' Ephesians 2:8." Then she
just stood there in a pious glare.

I felt my shoulders slump in desperation. I looked out
the window for a moment while I closed my Bible. I glanced
down to my lap, pulled a hankie out of my dress pocket,
and began to twist it. I felt the shocked stares of everyone
around me burning holes into me. Then I looked back up
and replied in a soft tone, "Sister Effy Bell, faith has need
of the whole truth to be believable. I yearn to believe in God,
to obey His commandments, to be as those who listened to
the Sermon on the Mount. But all I have to go on, to know
that God exist, is His written Word . . . this, this book is all
I have to go on, to say for sure that He is real. You keep
talkin' faith, have faith, but Sister Effy, this book is an illogical
belief of things that happened that don't add up. It is hard
to have faith in contradictions."

The bell rang, ending Sister Effy's ordeal. It was time
for everyone to assemble in the church for the morning sermon. I went and took my place in the third pew, oblivious
to the kissing and hugging and soft chattering as everyone
came in. I was lost in a state of confusion and despair. Things
came to order when the organ music began and everyone
rose to sing the hymns. At the conclusion of the music,
Brother Phillips came to the podium and began his sermon.
Although I usually paid close attention to Brother Phillips's
words, I was too lost in troubling thoughts to listen. I was
jarred awake by the whispering going on around me and
realized that the sermon had come to a halt. Everyone had
turned around and was peering into the back of the church.
I turned too. To my surprise, there walking into the church
was my half brother Marion, who was next to the oldest,
and my sister-in-law Tommy. Tommy always came to church;
she was deeply religious. But my brother . . . *never!* He felt
this was all fairy-tale stuff followed by a lot of hypocrites.

Now, Marion had always wanted Tommy to wear a bit
of makeup like most women. Though she was a natural beauty,

he liked the effect of lipstick now and then. But she wouldn't dare wear the stuff; our church considered makeup a sin. "A woman who paints herself up is the devil in disguise, trying to tempt the hearts of honest men," we were told. On the other hand, Tommy had been trying to "save" my brother and get him to church before the Day of Judgment came— like tomorrow, for instance. They apparently had compromised. She was willing to sin a little bit by wearing the palest peach lipstick ever made, if he would come to church just this one time. So, the die was cast.

I smiled at them both. I was very proud to see my brother, and I thought Tommy looked gorgeous. I waved and signaled to her that I thought she looked great. I turned back around and noticed that Brother Phillips was staring at them intently.

"Could we please stop for a moment?" he roared. "I see that Sister Tommy has joined us this morning. Get thee behind me, Satan, for blessed is the man that endureth temptation, hallelujah, Jeesssus, hallelujah," he bellowed forth.

I was mortified. My face burned and stung with embarrassment. I slowly turned to look in their direction. My brother's face was flushed with contempt and my dear sweet Tommy's color had drained to a deathly pallor.

"Dearest child of God, it is a sin to paint your face for the evil of Satan. It is a sin to tempt the flesh. You must pray for forgiveness from the Lord Jeesssus. . . . Come, come to the altar of forgiveness. Let us pray for your soul, here 'n' now." He held his hand out to her, waiting for her to come forward. She stood up, tears streaming down her face, and began walking to the altar, on the way smearing the lipstick off with her hand. She knelt down to the altar and Brother Phillips thrust his hand hard upon her head and began his lamentations.

"Sister Tommy, you will now ask God, through the Lord Jesus, to forgive you. The rest of us will bow our heads in forgiveness for your sin." The preacher and congregation all began to chant, "Oh, precious Jesus, bring forward the sinner from damnation. Help her, Lord, that she may repent and be saved from eternal damnation. . . . Repent! Hallelujah! Praise the Lord."

I couldn't join in. I turned to see what my brother was

doing while this hideous and humiliating act was being performed on his beloved wife. The pew where he had sat was empty. He had left. I looked at that poor woman on her knees, bawling and pleading for forgiveness. For what? Because she wore lipstick, of all things. While the fury of the congregation rose to a frenzied uproar, I began to wonder, Were they pleading for her soul to the same God that had sanctioned and even blessed Lot for raping his own flesh and blood? Who had blessed Abraham for letting an Egyptian king seduce his wife, Sara, just to save his own hide? The same God that chose David to be a king and let David use his sword to murder God's own children? Why were they not sinners for all of their atrocities? But my poor sister-in-law was a sinner because she wore a little lipstick? Crap! I had had enough! I stood up, took a long glance at the fanatical mess around me. I wanted to remember this moment. I had a strong feeling that such moments bring wisdom, that they give you the kind of truth that frees you from ignorance.

Loudly I declared, "I love my own good God. The God of my soul would not judge his own child like this. . . . I no longer belong here. It is finished." With that I turned and walked out. And I never looked back in regret.

Though I had left the church and its religious dogma, I never left God, nor did I forget the simple teachings of Jesus Christ. His message was that God and the Kingdom of Heaven were within all of us, and that to love all would be to love God. Jesus was and is a living light within my life this very day. I endeavor to judge no one for what they believe or don't believe. Like Jesus, I have chosen rather to love all. I am one less persecutor of righteous indignation—and a lot fewer suffer because I'm not.

Some years later, while visiting Mother, I inquired as to Brother Phillips's whereabouts.

"Oh, well, Judy, ya know that Mizz Phillips died of cancers. And Brother Phillips, he went plum crazy—crazy as an ol' bull in a peach orchard. God rest his soul."

"He will."

CHAPTER NINE

ENCOUNTER: THE UFO AND FORGETFULNESS

Tuesday evening, I went through the dry cleaning, searching for my turquoise blue felt poodle-dog skirt. It was my favorite thing to wear for special school days, and I was very excited and nervous about tomorrow. I would be trying out for the prestigious position of Artesia Junior High majorette. I wanted to look "groovy" for all the congrats I would be receiving after I won.

Everything assembled, I ran my bathwater and put tons of bubble bath in and proceeded to lather myself with the suds. How positively *fabulous* I felt in this dreamy bubble cloud. Everything was perfect, right down to the elegant pink ribbon I used to tie up my silky curls. . . . Well, almost every-thing. As I began to run the washrag (God, why couldn't we have sea sponge?) over my legs, I noticed that the soap had pasted down the hair into slobby curls. Holy Moses, I never realized the stuff was *that* long . . . and curly, too. I wondered if anyone had ever noticed the bush growing on my legs before. I visioned myself at tryouts . . . whirling, twirling, throwing the baton high and catching it behind my back while everyone swooned with sheer envy . . . and then threw up when they saw the hair on my legs doing a jive all on its own.

That did it. I rose up out of my blissful bath and leaned over the sink to open the medicine cabinet. There it was. The Gillette razor—"for that clean shave when the game's over." Well, the clean shave was needed before the game even started. Of course, I had never shaved *anything* in my life. Well, it couldn't be all *that* difficult, so I popped in a new blade, grabbed the shaving brush and cup, and gently oozed myself back into the bath.

With my right leg lathered, I began to stroke with the razor. I felt a slight sting, but no blood. I examined the job . . . hmmmm, like silk. I continued, now with more confidence and speed . . . still tingling, maybe a little stinging. Then I sliced off part of my knee. Crap! I started to panic in my fluff. I jumped up again to the medicine cabinet and frantically searched for a Band-Aid. Not one in the whole stupid cabinet. I slammed the door. "God, you could die with a medicine chest like that!" That's when I noticed that the bubbles had turned a deep shade of pink. I jumped out and grabbed a towel, and realized to my horror that both legs were pouring blood. That's when I called for help.

"What the . . . ? Mercy goodness, girl, what have ya gone an done to yourself? Lordy, lordy, you're gonna make a purty sight tamorra," Mother said, shaking her head.

About that time Loy heard all the hollering and came to investigate. He started laughing and teasing me something awful.

"I'm gonna kill ya, creep!" I yelled. Mother disappeared, and I hobbled shamefully to my room, where Mother met me with a box of Band-Aids.

"Momma, why weren't these in the medicine cabinet?"

"Cuz I had 'em put up . . . in a safe place," she answered, as she pasted big bandages over the nicks.

"Momma, don't put those big ugly ones all over my legs. Don't ya have some smaller ones that are less conspicuous?

And Momma, why do ya need to hide the Band-Aids in a safe place? Ya think a thief is gonna steal 'em or somethin'?''

"I wanna know I *have* some case I ever need 'em."

"Great idea, Mom. I'll know never to waste my time lookin' for 'em again. I'll just bleed to death!"

I never did get to understand why she hid those things.

With the wounded taken care of, Mother left and I looked down pitifully at my legs. How awful they looked. Crap! I had missed the whole left side of my left leg . . . the normal side. Great, just great!

The next morning I got all dolled up—pulled my hair back into a ponytail with a white silk scarf tied around it, put some spit curls in front of my ears, and snuck into Mother's room to douse my face with powder, pinch my cheeks for that "blushed" look, Vaseline my eyebrows, and dab on some cherry red lipstick. I put on my new white cashmere sweater, poodle skirt, bobby socks, and saddle oxfords, then dashed Lily of the Valley over my neck—all to Santo and Johnny's "Sleep Walk" and "Peggy Sue" playing on my record player. God, what a chick! I thought as I looked one last time in the mirror. I surveyed my legs. The skirt came well past the knees, and between that and my bobby socks only two small Band-Aids showed.

Walking down the school halls with my friends, I got a few wolf whistles. Some I pretended I didn't hear, but for a few I turned around, pretending to be mad, and yelled, "Fresh," or "Cool it, Gator Face."

When third period came, I changed into my shorts and majorette boots, squeezed my cheeks for more blush, and went to the gym. The jury sat at a long table. The band was assembled, and so were the girls who would try out. I watched as Kelly Moore did her routine. She was a freshman, kind of pretty, and had *big boobs*. She also was very talented— with guys and with the baton. Then came Pamela Sue Boyls. She was really beautiful. Streaked blond hair, teal blue eyes, thick black lashes, gorgeous toasted brown skin, big boobs (again), and beautiful legs. When she finished, she came over to me and glanced down at *my* legs.

"Oh, Jude, what happened to your legs?" she asked.

"Oh, these legs . . . ah, my legs. I practiced so late yesterday, and the mosquitos just ate me up. Don't ya just hate 'em?"

"It's soooo sad, you poor thing! I can't believe this would happen to you." She turned to walk away and then said, laughing, "Hey, try Nair. I use it all the time."

I was next. I performed my routine perfectly. What I lacked in some departments (boobs), I made up for in talent. I got a lot of yells and whistles when it was over. Now came the waiting. We were all told that by that afternoon, the announcement would be made. We all got dressed and went on to our classes. During my fifth-period English class the announcement came over the loudspeaker. ". . . and the five are: Kelly Moore, freshman; Pamela Sue Boyls, eighth grade; Janet Miller, eighth grade; Barbara Downs, eighth grade; and"—I held my breath—"Judy Hampton, eighth grade. Congratulations to all of you." I jumped up with joy and everyone in the class was clapping. Wow! I was in the groove! I had worked hard for the honor, and I felt great about myself. I couldn't wait until school was out to go and get my majorette uniform.

When the bell rang, I ran to put my books in my locker, checked my face in the mirror, and headed off to the band office. As soon as I walked through the door, the other girls that had made it started screaming and jumping around in a sort of victory frenzy. I screamed with them.

Mr. Buzz—that's what we all called him because of his buzzed flat top—appeared at the door. He was one of the neatest teachers I ever had. He had been a sergeant in the army and it showed. His band won consistently every year at competitions. He was enormously funny, which helped him blend well with young people. And he had a great respect for women.

"Ladies, I see by your responses that you're real upset at being chosen," he said, laughing, his hands on his hips.

"Yeah, Mr. Buzz, we're really depressed," I said in mock despair. Everyone was joking and laughing.

"Ladies, you all performed excellently. You showed a great deal of showmanship and precision. And I'd like to add that you are the best-looking group of majorettes I have seen in a long time. But before we start assigning uniforms, I would like to take up a collection"—he began reaching into his back pocket and pulling out his billfold—"to buy"—he was holding back a laugh—"an electric razor for Judy." He held up a twenty-dollar bill between his fingers. With that, peals of laughter rang out.

"That's just swell, you guys," I replied, blushing.

"Seriously, Judy, you've got great legs, kid, take care of them. Now, your head majorette will be Kelly Moore; she's the freshman of the group. Kelly, it will be your responsibility to organize the troops and help prepare your routines. And remember, believe in yourselves, and your dreams. You're the best, and when you know you're the best, you will succeed in this life. Never think of failing because when you do, you're gonna fail. *Don't be failures. Be winners!* You kids got that?"

"Yeah, Mr. Buzz." In unison.

After our uniforms had been assigned, Kelly asked if we could all spend Friday night at her house and begin to work out our routines. It would be "the majorettes' slumber party." I was so excited I could hardly wait for Friday night.

I walked home from school, entered the house, and immediately noticed that something was missing. The television. A plant had replaced it in the living room. I ran into the kitchen and then to the backyard to find Momma. She was digging up a flower bed.

"Momma, you'll *never* guess what happened today."

"I tell ya, the grubs are a-eatin' my begonias up. Them's the nastiest li'l thangs. . . . No, whut happ'n at school?" She continued stalking the invader grubs.

"Your daughter—me—got chosen to be a majorette. Isn't it terrific? I'm sooooo proud."

"That's nice, Judy, real nice," she said, getting up and wiping the sweat off her brow. "Whew! Lord, I'm gonna need a bath. Now, I wants ya ta go clean ya room; it's a filthy mess. And I want ya to clean Loy Gene's room an clean up the kitchen for supper. Go on, git with it."

I felt bruised that she hadn't reacted with more joy—as

if it wasn't a big deal to her or to anyone. I had tried so hard to make my mother and Daddy Bill proud of me, but they were so wrapped up in Loy Gene's baseball that it was all they talked about. Daddy Bill pitched to Loy every evening, coached him, and talked incessantly about his abilities at the supper table. Daddy Bill *NEVER* talked to me. Never watched me practice my baton, never inquired about my grades. Never attended my parent-teacher conferences at school. Sometimes I think Mother kept her interest in me low-key in order to keep peace in the family.

"Momma, Kelly Moore is the head majorette and she's having a slumber party over at her house Friday night so us girls can start practicing together. Can I please go, please?"

She looked shocked. "Kelly Moore? Surely you're joshin' me. The only thangs she can twirl are them tits of hers."

"Momma, please. Why do you say that stuff? She's a nice girl and she's great with the baton." Now I was shocked.

"Don't go a-pleasin' me. That ol' thang is nuts. She's boy crazy. Why, all she thanks about's whuts in a pair of Levis. I've seen her 'round, why she's always a-gawkin' with tha guys. She's a wild ol' thang just like her momma. There's a lotta talk 'bout them two."

"Momma, how can you say all that stuff? Where do ya get off—"

She raised her hand to slap me. "Don't ya go bein' smart mouthed with me er I'll slap some sense into ya head."

I felt my eyes begin to sting with hot tears. Mother could be so cruel at times, so hard. Why couldn't she be like other mothers—soft, gently loving, and supportive? I never invited any of my friends to stay the night or to come over. I was afraid of what they would think of her . . . and of me.

Seeing my tears coming on, she dropped her hand, then continued. "I'm a straight-talkin' gal. I speak whut's on ma mind. I've seen that ol' Kelly with ma own eyes. I know whut she's all 'bout. Ya just a silly li'l girl that don't know nuthin. Now, you can go over thar Friday night, but if'n there's any boys hangin' round, gal, I'll whop ya all the way home. I'm not gonna have ya knocked up, no sir." She walked over to the wheelbarrow and began rolling it toward the back gate.

I stood there for a moment and watched her. I didn't know what she meant about being "knocked up"—unless she thought someone was going to beat me up. But one thing was for sure, I could not stay there if boys did come over, because Momma always kept her word.

My spirits lifted a little and I started to go in the house, when suddenly I remembered the television.

"Momma, where's the TV?" I shouted. Her head popped up on the other side of the gate.

"Ain't no more TV," she shouted.

"Why? Where did it go?"

"Aw, it blew a tube or somethin', an your Daddy Bill had it hauled off. He figgers Loy Gene watches too much TV, wants him to do better in school. I sa'pose it's for the best. Anyhows, I sure will miss ol' no-nuts." Her head disappeared.

Old no-nuts was Lucille Ball. Mother was a faithful fan of hers. She was the only one I ever saw that could make Mother laugh so hard. What a shame. Loy and I were going to miss Saturday morning cartoons. I wondered if Bill got rid of it because it would cost money to have the thing fixed (he was stingy), or if he really wanted Loy to study more. Probably both.

Feeling sad about the TV, I walked into the house and up to my bedroom. There, I got the shock of my life. When I opened the door I thought I was in the wrong room. There was a beautiful new cream-colored bedspread on the bed. Pink, peach, and blue satin throw pillows adorned it, with my Lady Alexander wedding doll sitting on top of them. Embroidered lace curtains had been hung elegantly. My nightstand had a pale green frosted lamp with matching satin shade, and there were two more lamps on the dresser. And the dresser! There on top of a lace doily sat a pink brush and comb set with matching hand mirror, all inlaid with gold. Next to them lay a blue spray bottle of My Love cologne, a white compact with powder puff, a long brown pencil with a gold tip, two tubes of lipstick, an eyelash curler, a tube of mascara, and a small bottle filled with brown liquid and a painting brush beside it. There was a fingernail set with pale pink polish. I stood there inspecting each item, my mouth open. I had never had any makeup of my own. I picked up one of the lipsticks and rolled up a luscious pink color. I quickly put it on. It looked fabulous!

Gazing in the mirror at my "hot lips," I noticed a box I had overlooked—a Lady Schick electric razor. Out the door I ran to find Momma. She was in the kitchen washing her hands. I ran up and put my arms around her and just squeezed her.

"What's that fer? Lord, girl, you're a-sprayin' water all over the kitchen," she said, trying to hide a smile.

"I don't care. I'll clean it up. Momma, I love you . . ya li'l bugger. My room looks groovy, Momma. Terrific!" I cried. "I love you so much, Momma . . . and the makeup. Wow! Momma, how did you know what all ta buy?" I was still squeezing her to death.

"Let go of ma self, you're a-suffocatin' me an don't go a callin' me no bugger. Lands goodness. Mizz Simmons at tha drugstore, bless her soul, shez the best ol' woman . . . well, she picked all tha makeup out an what have ya. Well, I tell ya, Judy, I knew ya was a-goin' to make majorette cuz I dreamed it. My dreams always foretell me thangs. All my life they have." She thought for a moment. A smile came, and her cheeks flushed slightly. She said gently, "So, I saw ya marchin' 'round in this here dream. An ya was real beautiful. Well, all ma kids turned out that way, but I was beginnin' ta think that ya was gonna stay real plain somehow, different from the rest. But in the dream you was real beautiful. So I just went ta the drugstore, cuz I felt that the dream told me to help ya that way." She turned and pulled a dish towel from off the stove and said, "So I wunt ya ta practice puttin' the stuff on," as she dried her hands on the dish towel. "Go on now, git ta work. I've got supper to put on the table."

I thought about what she had said about the dream of me. It was not a strange thing to hear in our family. Mother's dreams did come true, and her "suspicions" were in reality a very active psychic ability that she used all of the time. She may not have been an educated woman, but in my opinion, her broad common sense and her ability to know about things before they happened gave her a unique intelligence that unfortunately cannot be taught in school. The sweet things that she had bought for me were her way of telling me that she loved me—something she never voiced.

Loy came in from playing with his friends, and asked about the missing television. He got the same reply I had. Groaning, he threw his mitt onto the couch. "Heck, it's gonna get borin' around here," he complained. "I jest wish we could have more fun like other kids. Now what are we gonna do . . . sit around an play dominoes while Daddy Bill an Momma drink their stupid wine? That should be real fun, huh?"

I suddenly felt sorry for my little brother. Trying to cheer him up, I told him the good news.

"Hey, guess what? I'm a majorette now. Neat, huh?"

His face lit up. "Cool . . . that's cool," he said sweetly. "Atta way to go, sis."

Friday finally rolled around. After school I quickly did my chores and Momma drove me over to Kelly's house.

"Remember whut I said," Mother reminded me as we pulled up to the driveway. "No boys an no gallivantin' 'round, ya hear? If'n anythang strange happ'ns, ya call Mizz Cole an she'll tell me an I'll come after ya." A phone was something else that Daddy Bill didn't approve of.

"Momma, nothing is going to happen, I promise. Bye, see ya tomorrow. I'll just walk home, okay?" I said as I got out of the car.

Momma drove off, and I shuffled up to the door with my things in tow. I knocked on the door. Music was coming from inside. It was Elvis singing, "Jailhouse Rock." Kelly came to the door dressed in very tight short-shorts and a baggy blue sweatshirt. Her face was red and sweaty and her chest was heaving with short breaths. The rest of the girls were already there, dancing, eating pimento cheese sandwiches that Mrs. Moore had prepared, and drinking Cokes. I joined right in. Mrs. Moore came out and introduced herself as Mrs. Hentington. I blushed.

"Hey, it's cool, my mom just got married again. Didn't ya, Mom?" Kelly said, putting her arm around her mother's neck and kissing her on the cheek. "I tried to get her to play the field a li'l longer, have some fun, get a li'l hip . . . but ol' Jack nailed 'er, huh, Mom? Ya didn't stand a chance—hey, he's got some money, honey." Mrs. Hentington gave her daughter a kidding shove. At that moment Elvis started singing "Fools rush in where angels fear to tread," and Kelly started singing right along, pointing her finger at her mother, who pulled away and went shaking her head back to the kitchen.

"Your mom's neat, Kelly. Did your stepfather knock her up?" I turned in shock. I couldn't believe that Janet Miller had asked such a peculiar question. I didn't know what it meant, but it sounded dirty. I thought for sure that Kelly would let her have it.

"Are you kiddin'? Shit, she wouldn't have another brat. She's got me . . . ha, ha." She plopped down on the couch, took a long sucking drink from the Coke bottle, and then fingered the mouth of the bottle. "They were screwing all the time anyway, so why not make it legal?" We all looked at one another. Janet was getting this naughty look on her face, Pam giggled, and Kay, the proper prude, started chewing on her already gnawed fingernail stubs. I kept looking over my shoulder, waiting for her mother to walk in any minute.

"How do you know they're screwing all the time? What ya do, hide under the bed and listen?" That was Janet's question, not mine. But I was glad she asked.

"Man, it's easy. Her douche bag is always wet every morning in the bathroom, hanging on the bathroom door . . . drip, drip. And tha moans—God, I get hot just thinking about it." She sighed as she flopped her head back on the couch pillows.

"Yeah, I caught my parents 'doin' it' one afternoon," Janet said mischievously. "I kept hearing this thumping noise. I just walked in to see what was going on. I'll never forget the look on their faces . . . wow!"

"Neat! I bet you got your ass whipped," Kelly said. "What did they say they were doing?"

"You're not gonna believe this shit, but he said that he was rubbin' her down cuz she was feelin' poorly. God! He must of thought I was stupid or somethin'." Janet folded one leg underneath the other and took a bite out of her sandwich.

I couldn't resist. "Hey, what's a douche bag?"

Everyone stopped laughing and stared at me in utter disbelief. Then they all broke up laughing again and started pointing at me. Janet shoved me and fell into my lap, laughing her bloody head off. Pam had both hands covering her face, heaving with mirth, and even Kay, the prude, wasn't being so prudish. She sat there with eyes wide and mouth open, nostrils flaring in and out, and not making a sound. God was she weird! They *all* were! Then Kelly leaned forward and tried to speak through the laughter.

"Hampton, come on, you gotta be kiddin'. You don't know what a *douche bag* is? Oh, my God, what a virgin. Hampton you *are* a virgin, *aren't* ya?"

I could feel my face burning with embarrassment. I had *never* been with friends that talked this way. I had never thought about my mother and Daddy Bill . . . doin' it. I felt like some kid from Mars. I didn't *know* any of this stuff.

"Hampton, look at me. Read my lips. D-o-u-c-h-e b-a-g. C'mon I'll show ya one, follow me." She got up, and everyone else did, and we followed her down the hall to the bathroom. I looked over my shoulder again, expecting her mother any moment. We all squeezed into the bathroom, and there hanging on the door was a red bag with a long tube and an obscene spray attachment on the end. Everyone started giggling. It looked like a hot-water bottle to me. Kelly took it down, squatted, and mimicked the workings of the infamous thing. I got embarrassed again. Demonstration over, Kelly quizzed me if Momma had one. I didn't answer. I had never seen a thing like this in our bathroom, or anywhere else. Come to think of it, it was probably stashed with the Band-Aids in Mother's safe hiding place.

The rest of the evening was spent working on our new routines in Kelly's front yard while occasional carloads of guys drove slowly by, scoping everything out. Kelly would stop and go over to hang on their windows and talk to them. A blue and white Chevy Impala circled the blocks a couple of times with two guys in it. Kelly was getting hot, she said.

"I'm *crazy* over Dennis Harper. Oh God, he sends me. I'd give my bod if he would come around again and just stop. Oh, he's the *sexiest* man alive."

"Who is he?" asked Janet.

"Where have you turds been? He's a junior in high school, plays football, and every girl would die to go out with him. They say he's got 'Roman fingers.' "

I was worried that they would stop and come in, and then Mother would find out. Mother was right about one thing. Kelly *was* a little boy crazy and, I must admit, a little loose. We started to practice once more, when here came that blue and white Impala again with Roman Fingers at the wheel. He slowly came to the curb, and Kelly dropped her baton and made for the car, pulling down her shorts in back as she walked. Janet did the same thing . . . definitely a gutsy priss. Kay, Pam, and I went back over to the porch and sat down.

"My dad would kill me if that was me out there," Pam said. "Kelly and Janet sure know a lot about stuff . . . ya know . . . stuff."

"Sure do. I can't believe Kelly's mother lets her talk so ugly. Do you guys date yet?" I asked.

"Are ya kiddin'?" Pam replied. "Daddy said I couldn't until I got into high school . . . and even then he wants ta meet 'em first. My parents are real strict." Kay had been thumping the porch floor between her legs with her baton tip, staring down at the ground, listening.

"Kay, how 'bout you?"

She just shook her head. "I want to *be* somebody someday. I just study a lot." She did, too. She was a straight A student. A little on the plain side, but she had a lot of brains.

Suddenly, I heard Janet say my name, and I looked over to the car. Kelly had turned around and was looking at me, then turned back, saying something and shaking her head. Dennis was looking over the steering wheel at me. I heard a laugh. They then drove off, and the girls came walking over, whispering and giggling.

"Hey, Jude, guess who thinks you're hot?" Janet said, raising her eyebrows.

"Shut up, creep!" sneered Kelly.

"Look who's talking. I think you're just a little green cuz ol' Roman Fingers, stud of Artesia High, is hip on Hampton and not you, babe! Guess he likes virgins."

Kelly was fuming. I was a little mad myself. I didn't like the way he had been looking at me, and I didn't find older guys interesting. It all made me sick.

"Shut up, forget it. I'm not interested!" I huffed, feeling guilty and dirty.

It got dark, so we went inside. Mr. and Mrs. Hentington were sitting hugging one another, watching TV. I pretended not to notice. We went into Kelly's bedroom. It was very nice. Tons of Coke cups piled high in the corners, a lot of school stuff on the walls, along with some pictures of Elvis, Fabian, and Chuck Berry. Her bed was a twin pushed up against the wall with a window directly above it. There was another window on another wall, and the wall where her dresser was was connected to her parents' room. Hmmm, maybe that's how she knew so much about her parents' intimacy—thin walls! We played records, painted our fingernails, rolled our hair, and mostly gossiped . . . about boys. Then Kelly got a great idea. She decided we should develop a silent finger code so we could talk to each other in class and no one would know what we were talking about. Terrific idea. It took us hours to learn to interpret the sign language she devised, but we all caught on and soon began to gossip in sign language.

The record player was playing Bobby Darin's latest hit, and Janet was standing next to the far window, leaning up against the wall, lip-syncing the words. Suddenly, the whole side of her face lit up with an eerie red glow. For a moment I thought that Roman Fingers had snuck up to the house and turned a red light on to scare us. . . . What a creep! But then Janet turned and looked out the window. "God, that's *weird!*"

We all jumped up and ran to the window. I got there first. I could not believe what I saw.

"That thang gives me the heebie-jeebies. What *is* that?" Janet asked.

It was about one-thirty in the morning, and the crescent

moon was sitting low off to the west. The house two lots away from Kelly's, across the vacant lot, had a huge orange ball twice the size of the house suspended about a hundred feet above the rooftop. It was so bloody orange that everything, even the house further down, was bathed in an eerie orange glow. I just kept staring at it, trying to make out what it was. It didn't make a sound; it just hung there, suspended in midair. I thought it looked like a planet of some sort for it seemed to have craters all over it. Then, all of a sudden, blinding flashes started coming off of it. I panicked and ran from the window to the bed. I started praying. The thought came to me that the world had ended. In Revelation, it says that in the last days the moon will turn to blood and that Jesus will already have come in the Holy Rapture in the sky, and all of the pure in heart that had been saved would go to heaven. Those left would endure the punishment of God. I thought this was "the moon turned to blood" over the neighbors' housetop.

"What are you doing? Are you nuts?" Kelly demanded. The strange red light flowed over her face, making her look like a gargoyle.

"I'm praying for us. Don't you know what has happened? Jesus has come and left us *all* behind." I was crying. "Oh Father, don't leave us behind, we are only children. Make this go away. Come back for us, please."

At that moment, flashes started coming through the window above the bed I was on. I heard someone cry, "I'm scared . . . help us!" Then someone climbed under the bed to hide. I kept my head buried under a stuffed toy . . . sobbing.

"Hey, you guys, it's gone," cried Janet. "The thing is gone."

We all ran to the window. Everything was normal again. The pale moonlight now lit up the houses, and there were only twinkling stars in the night sky. I was filled with relief. I don't remember anything else that happened that night. Not when we went to bed, or if we even did. I don't remember any discussion . . . nothing. It was like a blank spot in my memory, and apparently in everyone else's, too. The next morning I was awakened by a fly crawling on my eye-lashes. I opened my eyes just in time to see Kelly walk in the door with a tray of orange juice for everyone.

"C'mon, you guys. My mom is fixing breakfast. Come and help, okay?"

We slowly got up, washed, and went to the kitchen, chattering away about the normal stuff. Kelly's mom remarked that we had been perfect guests, since she didn't hear a peep out of us all night.

"Cool, huh, Mom? We learned to talk with our fingers, see?" Kelly demonstrated and we interpreted. We had a great breakfast, cleaned up the kitchen, got dressed and went outside to work on our routines. It was a warm and sunny day.

When I got home, Momma asked, "Well, anythang excitin' happen?"

"Nope." I never told her about the guys in the cars, or about Roman Fingers. "Nope, just worked on the routines."

Perhaps you're feeling that I am acting a bit blasé about what happened that night. You might even be thinking that I'm holding out about what really happened. Or maybe you're thinking I just made this one up. Wrong! All of us at that slumber party experienced the strange event. No, I'm not holding out on you, at least not intentionally. And if you think that we were rather nonchalant the following morning, well, you're right. You see, my friends and I didn't remember it. It was as if it hadn't happened. I would not recall this incident for four more years. Sorry, you'll just have to stay tuned to this channel for a few more chapters to find out what really did happen.

CHAPTER TEN

BABY, I LOVE YOU

At seventeen, my metamorphosis from the ugly duckling into the beautiful swan was complete. I now wore makeup I expertly applied so that the natural apricot color of my cheeks glowed through. My large azure green eyes and thick pale lashes were accented with light mascara, becoming bright and alive. My turned-up nose was generously dashed with freckles, reflecting an inward innocence. My hair was lightened to a pear blond—the Marilyn Monroe look—a beautiful color that was not hard or cheap but was rather dazzling. My bust had bloomed into a size thirty-six above an hourglass twenty-inch waist.

Though many commented that I looked like a calendar girl, others occasionally gave me sly smiles that seemed to hold me guilty of some mysterious wickedness. By nature, I would cast off the compliments and would become guilty in my heart, feeling saddened by the slanderous whispers.

I suspected that they were quite correct. I was ugly. I would look at myself in the mirror and would not see the vivid beauty, color or contour. I only saw distortion and ugliness. Little did I know that it was the distortion and ugliness of others seen through their envy. I was simply too innocent, too naive to see through the malice of my peers and to know that I possessed a magical combination of sexy-babe, virginal tomboy looks that created quite a stir. I never truly understood what all of the fuss was about. I mistook my "difference" as being, well, shockingly ugly. To escape my pain, I spent much of my free time riding my horse. Wild and free, and alone.

My horse's name was Slim. He was a beautiful chestnut and was my friend. I had loved horses ever since my stick-horse days, when I would play long hours in Mother's flower house, pretending I had a ranch with lots of horses on it. It was a dream that I loved, and I knew that when I grew up I was going to marry a rancher and have a lot of horses all my own. Lately, though, I had been having some real dreams that puzzled me. I kept dreaming I was riding this beautiful gelding in a park—a gorgeous place, but it was in a city. And there were people walking up and down the walkways, all dressed oddly. The women wore bonnets and long dresses, while the men wore top hats and long frock coats. Open carriages were drawn by magnificent teams of horses, the women riding in them carrying parasols. And in the dream, I knew everyone. I even knew the name of the horse I rode—Redskin. But I rode him sidesaddle, in a long black dress. Someone would call out, "Lily," and I would turn to see who it was. Then I would wake up. I always felt like I was waking up from a sleep, and that the dream . . . was just yesterday. Strange.

I remember asking Momma about the dream. She just looked at me, then replied, "Oh, that's probably who ya were back then . . . before." I thought maybe she hadn't heard me, so I asked her to tell me what she meant by "before." She hesitated, then said, "Look out yonder at the grass. It's a-dying. But it's gonna come back again in the spring. You see, Judy, the good Lord made ever'thang, an ever'thang has its season ta grow. When winter comes, well, it'll die, but it'll live again in the spring. It's born again. What ya dreamin' could be yer life in another spring, long time ago." Somehow, a part of me understood what she was trying to say, but yet another part of myself just got confused, so I just dropped it. A human trait we all possess.

A slight hot wind blew over the golden desert, tossing the sparse trees and rustling the tumbleweed. The pale sky brightened into a deeper violet blue as the lowering brass sun hung over the far horizon. Orange and white puffed clouds sailed rapidly, casting moving shadows over the purple sagebush. As I rode Slim, the smell of his sweet lather and the oiled leather saddle filled the wind around me. His hooves struck up the saffron dust, glittering in the light and coming to rest in my hair and dusting my lashes.

Suddenly, Slim spooked a jackrabbit. I halted and pulled out my .22, took careful aim, and shot him. With the rabbit tied to my saddle horn, I rode with the wind back to the boarding barn, where I groomed Slim, gave him his grain, and, leaving him with a hug and a pat, headed for home.

I came in breathless and happy. The smells of fried chicken and mashed potatoes and cigar smoke lurked familiarly in the house. I knew I was late, so I went straight to the kitchen to say I was sorry for being late and to brag somewhat on my rabbit. Mom and Daddy Bill were playing dominoes on the kitchen table.

"Hi. I'm sorry I'm late, but I got one jackrabbit today. I'm going to give it to Loy." I walked out to the back porch to put the rabbit away. Mom watched with a little admiration and a wee bit of envy.

"You an your tight Levis," she said when I came back. "Why, Levis is downright dangerous for both sexes. Lord have mercy, it seems like I'd just look at a pair of men's Levis and I'd get pregnant." Then she took a sip of her Mogen David wine and Daddy Bill took a puff of his Havana cigar.

"Oh, Momma," I sighed. "For a long time after I heard Charles's wife say something like that to you, I didn't look at men's Levis because I thought that it would happen to me." I stood over the sink washing my hands, and realized I still wasn't sure what *did* make you that way.

I was about to open the refrigerator door, when Momma said, "You watch yourself, li'l girl. Ya know that men just use ya. They git what they want, knock ya up, an leave ya with the mess. Lord, they is selfish an mean. I don't want ya bein' no tramp fer the pleasin' of no man."

I slammed the refrigerator door and wheeled around, feeling degraded somehow because of men and their natural urges.

"I'm no tramp. Never, ever say that to me again, for that is something I will never be." I felt my face burning. Daddy Bill didn't say a word. I suppose *he* thought that I already was one. Girls are tramps. Men are saints!

"Yeah, well, I'm not a-sayin' ya are, but I'll be a-watchin'." She took a puff off of Bill's cigar and looked at him. She blew the acrid blue smoke over to me and said with some exasperation, "Go an wash. Ya face is red an dirty. Your hair is messed up an filled with dirt. Go do somethin' with yourself."

I just rolled my eyes and sighed. "Yes, Momma, I know. Did Suzanne call?"

"No, but Shirley did. Wants ya to call her back. And don't be on that phone all night."

I walked back through the house and stopped to look into the hall mirror. My face looked like it had been in a dust storm, and my rioting hair had lost its sheen. "Why couldn't I be born with some looks, like my sister?" I sighed. Feeling depressed just looking at myself, I turned and went to the little window into Loy's dark den that held the phone. God, was I glad Momma had talked Daddy Bill into letting us have a phone. I'm certain she must have had to compromise in some way for this absolute necessity.

"Shirley?" I asked.

"Jude, listen, can ya talk? I've gotta tell ya somethin' you're not gonna believe," she whispered.

I glanced out into the hallway and around into the living room. Coast was clear. "Yeah, what's happened? Get grounded again?" I whispered.

"No, creepo. But listen ta *this*. Guy got three hard-ons last night. His Levis were a-risin' and sittin' all last night. My God, it was so neat," she gushed.

I really didn't know what she was talking about, as usual, but I dared not even hint at my stupidity. It wasn't cool. Everyone who was *anyone* was definitely in the know—whether they knew or not. "Really? Neat. Definitely neat-o. I bet that felt great, huh?" That sounded convincing.

"Really . . . can you believe he's such a raunchy stud?"

"No. I really can't. Wow! Hey, what did ya do?" I asked, trying to laugh it off, checking to make sure that Momma wasn't in the living room eavesdropping.

"What? Honey pie, I just enjoyed the ride," she answered with a demure voice.

"Oh, me too. I had a great ride. I just got back from riding Slim, and I nailed a jack with the first crack. Neat, huh?" I responded, eager to share my own good news.

"Oh," she said in flat tone.

"Hey, Shirl, that's really terrific, I'm glad you're finally gettin' somewhere with Guy. Let's talk some more tomorrow at school. Love ya. Bye."

"Yeah, sure. Bye."

I hung up and went quietly to my room and closed my door. The wind had come up and a strong gale caused the spruce to rake across my windows. The house creaked. I glanced at the assortment of makeup on my dresser. Bobby pin, combs, "rats" barrettes, ribbons, and cans of hair spray everywhere. The walls were covered with plastic Coke cups saved from every Coke date. I then looked over at the orange and white pom-poms and the assortment of batons standing in the corner. And finally at my Bible on the nightstand. I put a stack of 45s on the record player and turned it on. The Everly Brothers started to sing "Cathy's Clown." I loved the Everly Brothers. Then I lay down on the bed, thinking about my conversation with Shirley. She had been a cheerleader since the eighth grade, and Guy Roberts, a sophomore, would come to our junior high games just to see her. I knew that they "petted" a lot—she told everybody that—but I had never heard her say more than how "hot" she would get.

And as far as I knew, "going all the way" was something no one I knew ever did.

Now "Blue Bayou" was playing. God, I loved Roy Orbison's voice. I heard Loy come home, Daddy Bill greeting him with questions about his baseball game. I got up, fluffed my hair, sucked in my cheeks (Audrey Hepburn, who else?), and quietly opened my door.

"Loy?" I whispered.

"Hey, Jude, Momma says you got another jack."

"It's out on the back porch." Loy started to go and see it, but I gently grabbed his arm, gesturing for him to come into my room. He sensed my mischief—and my seriousness.

My little brother, now fifteen, was a hunk. Even my girlfriends had secret crushes on him.

"Hey, what's up?" he asked, smiling.

I sat down on the side of my bed. I was trying to put my question into words that wouldn't sound dumb. "Loy, what's a hard-on?" I whispered.

He choked and fell into my bed, staring at me. "A what?"

"A hard-on. My friend Shirley—you know Shirley— well, she called me tonight and said that Guy got three hard-ons last night. I don't want to sound stupid or anything, but what does that mean, three hard-ons?"

Loy sat up next to me on the bed. He hesitated for a moment, then said, "You mean that a guy . . . any guy that you've gone out with . . . like Kerry Butts, that you went with for a while . . . you mean to tell me he didn't take you down?"

"Take me down? All Kerry Butts wanted to do was marry me. I just couldn't see calling myself 'Mrs. Butts.' What do you mean?"

"Well, ya know, make it with ya. . . . Go all the way."

"Loy, I'm gonna tell ya somethin'. I don't know what that means. I've never really had a discussion about, you know, sex an' stuff, not even with my girlfriends . . . just stuff like 'pett'n' or 'hot' you know, junk like that, but usually it always embarrassed me . . . real bad . . . but I just feel like . . . like maybe you could . . . uh, help me ta know some stuff." I kept my eyes glued to the floor. "And no, Loy, I've never done anything. Kissed, but not that 'Frenchy' stuff. I don't want to be a tramp . . . and if I ever get married . . . I want my husband ta know that I was a good girl." I reached for my Bible and opened it to Matthew. "Look here, Jesus said, 'Blessed are the pure in heart: for they shall see God.' I have this feeling that doing stuff—goin' all the way—would keep me from seeing God. Dumb, huh?"

Loy took the Bible, closed it, and put it back on the nightstand. He put his arm around me.

"Jude, I got a news flash for ya. You are the sexiest babe in this whole town. I mean, even my friends start pantin' when you're around. Any guy would. Man, you're beautiful. C'mon, who do you think is such a good girl, anyway?"

"My friends—except for maybe Shirley."

"Shirley? What about Sara, Pam, Cheryl, and Suzanne? They've all done it."

I was shocked—but also curious. Suzanne? Never!

"They have?"

"Sure."

"Hmmm . . . have you done it, Loy?"

"Sure!" shrugging casually.

"You're a liar."

"Hey, no I'm not. I've done it."

"When? I don't believe ya."

"Seventh grade."

"Where? Who?"

Loy cleared his throat. "On the rock slab in the vacant lot."

I just stared at him. This was too much. On the concrete slab . . . in a vacant lot . . . surrounded by houses.

"That's just the way guys are."

"What about girls, Mr. Experience?" I retorted.

"Hey, there's the pigs an' there's the girls who only do it sometimes."

I was mesmerized. What was the difference? "Have you ever gotten anybody knocked up?"

He straightened up with authority. "No, I always use a rubber." He was clearly gilding the lily of experience.

"A rubber?"

"Sure. Remember the time at the baseball game when you came around the corner and saw me and Tom blowin' up balloons? Blowing up balloons, at a baseball game? Well, babe, those weren't balloons. Those were rubbers."

"Where did ya get'm?"

"At the fillin' station, in the john."

"Like Kotex machines in the girls' bathrooms?"

"Yeah, well, for girls it's different, ya know."

"Yeah, I remember when I went to Momma and told her I thought I was gonna die—"

"What?"

"Oh, 'cause there was some blood on my panties and I had real bad pains. I thought I was gonna die. She said, 'Silly girl, you ain't gonna die, ya just menstruating,' but she forgot to tell me what that was."

Tijuana Brass was playing "El Toro" on the record player. Loy continued.

"Well, ya gotta ask some girl about that. I can only tell ya about hard-ons and rubbers and stuff like that." Hmm, Mr. Experience wasn't so experienced after all.

"So, what is a hard-on then?"

"Well, yeah, uh . . . a hard-on is when a guy's thing, you know, gets big?" He cleared his throat again.

I was trying to picture what he was saying. "How big does it get?"

"Oh, a real stud gets to 'bout six and a half or seven inches, and—"

"Seven inches! You mean seven inches long?" trying to calculate an infinite weenie.

"Yeah."

"Do they come any smaller, like maybe four inches, say?"

"Four inches, he ain't a stud. He's a li'l pecker."

"So how do you know all this about studs an' peckers?"

" 'Cause I've seen 'em," Loy answered matter-of-factly.

"You've seen 'em?"

"Sure. When we take showers after practice, we always look at each other's thing and compare."

"Oh! What a creep! You are so *weird*. That's awful." Loy

was laughing and really enjoying this shocking version of show-and-tell. I started twisting a curl of my hair around and around, contemplating the nastiness of it all.

"See, Jude, the studs, when they're soft, hang long an' loose." (Oh, my G-O-D.) He was laughing, "The peckers take showers behind the doors!" He was rolling on the bed with laughter. I just sat there.

"Oh, Loy, my stars. . . . Tell me more about my friends."

"Hey, they've just been around the bush a few times."

"Oh, Loy Gene!" I put both of my hands to my head in shocked disbelief.

"I can't believe ya don't know about this stuff, lookin' like ya do an' all."

"I wanna be a good girl . . . always. I still don't see how a guy with a hard-on *that* big can get it in. That scares me ta death. Loy, do you think if a girl uses a Tampax, she will still be a virgin?" He stared at me. I think I was getting to be a little too much for him.

"I don't know about that stuff, Jude. You gotta ask a girl or somethin'."

At that moment Momma called, "Food's on the table, you two."

I took hold of his arm and squeezed. "Promise . . . swear that you won't breathe a word of this to anyone. Promise?"

"I promise. They wouldn't believe a word of it anyway."

I got up and went to the mirror and put more lipstick on.

"Hey, Jude, why do you wear all that stuff on your face?" Loy asked.

"Well, gorgeous puss, some people like you are just born beautiful." I was teasing him a little, but I also felt sad about myself for having to wear any of it.

"I think you're beautiful."

I looked over at him. He was so sweet. I wished that I felt beautiful. "You're my little brother, that's why you think that."

"Mike Phipps thinks you're beautiful."

I whirled around with excitement. "Did he tell you that?"

"Sure. He tells everybody that. He's got a big crush on

you. Look at you. God, who wouldn't? Someday, Sis, that won't be news to ya."

"What else did he tell you? What-all have you heard?" I pressed, wanting to know everything.

"Ah-hah! So you like him too."

"It's just that he's a great football player . . . and I've seen him around . . . and he's going steady with someone . . . that's all."

"And you like him too," he insisted.

"Well, he is cute," I admitted, feeling slightly embarrassed.

"And he's a stud—at least that's what everyone says. I've never taken a shower with him, so I haven't checked it out for sure."

"Oh, Loy, you're crude, terrible. Forget it, I don't want to talk about this anymore." I turned my back on him and pretended to be interested in some dumb thing on my dresser.

"Okay. You said the jack was on the back porch?" he said as he got up to go to the door.

"Yeah."

"Does Phipps know you can shoot so well?"

"Don't be weird. I've never been with him or anyone else when I went hunting. And I don't want him to know, ya hear? It's not ladylike, so just shut up about it, okay?"

The next day, my girlfriends and I were gabbing between classes about a slumber party we were planning for Friday night.

"So, I'll bring my records, chips, and makeup, and you can bring some oatmeal cookies. Don't forget to bring your diaries," I said. About that time I saw Mike Phipps walking toward us with some other hunks. My friends just sort of wandered off. Mike had dark brown hair, innocent brown eyes, a broad jaw, and he always wore his football jacket. I looked up, smiling.

"So, can a sophomore like me ask a junior like you to go out on a date? Like, after school? We'll go get a Coke." He leaned one hand on the locker. God, he was sexy.

"Uh . . . I'm . . . I can't. I'm going to ride my horse

today. I haven't ridden him in a few days . . . sorry." Crap! I must be sounding like some stupid nerd!

"Oh, yeah? Out by the rodeo grounds?" He was smiling and staring at me. I just locked my eyes onto the torn edge of my history book.

"Yeah. . . . I mean no. Sometimes I ride that far." I was talking like an idiot. I looked back up at him. He licked his lips and smiled. His friends were in a huddle, sneaking glances in our direction.

"Little brother is right, you're beautiful. See ya later." He smiled and went back to his pack. As they walked away, I heard one of them yell, "Wow, Mother, what a woman!"

I was standing there as if I had been turned into a pillar of salt like Lot's wife. I felt my knees shake and go weak. I came to my senses and left before I wet my pants.

Later that day, as I was riding my horse in the open country, with jackrabbits running all around me, I just couldn't concentrate on shooting. I got off my horse and slouched under a tree while Slim nibbled at some nearby bushes. A breeze came up loaded with the sweet smells of nearby thickets and sage. I closed my eyes and allowed events to float by me in a dreamy vision. Soon Mike's face came into view—his mouth with its pixie turned-up corners, his eyes that twinkled. Mmmm, I felt my heart start to pound in my ears. He made me feel like no other boy ever had.

But Loy had called him a stud, and from what that meant, I did not want to have this stupid feeling. Studs were for other girls like Shirl, not for me. I opened my eyes and turned my head to check on Slim. To my surprise there was Mike Phipps, squatting beside me. I thought it was my daydream carried a little too far.

"Hi," he said, smiling.

"Where did you come from?" I was a good hunter with sharp hearing, but I hadn't heard him walk up. "How long have you been here?"

He stood up, looked down at his boots, and said, "For a while. I saw you from the highway, and then you just disappeared behind the hill. So I just walked up to see if I could find you, and I did. I wasn't trying to spy on ya or anythin'."

"What *were* you doing, then?" I snapped, feeling as if I had been caught at something.

"Hey, you were just a beautiful sight, sitting underneath the tree, the wind blowing your hair. Anyway, I come out here a lot and hunt rabbits."

"That's funny, I don't ever remember seeing you out here." I hadn't, either. This was a little suspicious.

I stood up, brushed off my Levis, and looked back at him through my hair as the wind blew it across my face. I didn't know he hunted, but then I didn't really know anything about him.

"Judy, has anyone ever told you that . . . man, you're like a dream girl? God, you're beautiful." He got a serious look on his face, and my heart started pounding so loud I thought he could hear it. I changed the subject.

"You hunt . . . jackrabbits?"

"Yeah. I've got my .22 in the car. Ever hunted before?"

"That's not really a thing a girl does." I frowned innocently to cover up my lie.

"Hey, would you like to come with me? It'll be fun."

I turned and looked at my horse. My gun and holster couldn't be seen from this side. I didn't know what to do.

"I like your horse," Mike said. "Ya look great on him. If you want to ride him back and put him up, I can meet ya at the stables."

I thought a minute . . . and decided to do it.

"Okay, ya sure ya don't mind? It'll take a little while."

"Hey, it's worth the wait. I'll meet you over at the stables."

He turned and disappeared over the hill. I mounted Slim and rode across to the rodeo grounds, feeling nervous the whole way. I met him there and he helped me feed my horse while I groomed him down. I got into his car and away we went. I was hoping that hunting jacks, not "parking," was what he had in mind. Finally we pulled over to a lonely stretch of road. This was the test. When he got out and opened the trunk, I got out to make sure he wasn't pulling out a blanket instead of a .22. To my relief, he took out a beautiful Remington automatic.

We started walking and scared up a jack and Mike pulled

the gun up, fired, and missed. I shook my head a little bit.

"Wanna try? I'll help you. It's real easy."

I hesitated.

"I promise you won't get hurt. I wouldn't let anything hurt ya."

"Oh, okay."

He gave me the gun and then put his arms around me to help support it. "See that beer bottle over there? Now look down the barrel at that little sight . . . put the sight on the bottle . . . and then gently squeeze the trigger." He released his hold on the gun and I fired. I hit the bottle right in the middle.

"Hey, first time a bull's-eye! Let's try another. There's a Coors can to your right. See if ya can hit it." He put his arm around me again. "Now, lay your cheek down gently . . . line up the sight . . . and squeeze the trigger again."

Bam! Another direct hit. Mike looked a little startled. "Have you ever done this before?"

"Well . . ."

"Wait a minute." Mike arranged a line of rocks, found some more bottles and cans, and propped them up on the rocks. "Can you shoot those on your own?"

I was getting excited by the challenge, forgetting this might scare him away. "How fast?"

He laughed. "As fast as you can pull the trigger on my automatic."

I fired away in rapid succession. I didn't miss a lick.

Mike started laughing out loud. "Why didn't you tell me you could shoot as good as that? Why did you tell me you didn't shoot at all?"

"Well, it's not very ladylike and all." That was sincere.

"Tha hell it's not!" He threw a bottle in the air. *Blam!* He stood there, the wind blowing his hair, a look of absolute pride on his face. "Damn, you're better than anyone I know. What a woman. Did ya think I wouldn't like it or somethin' cuz ya can shoot a gun? I knew you were different from the rest of the girls. They don't know *anything* what a guy really likes. But you . . . I mean, you're beautiful, and being able to shoot a gun doesn't take away from that." He walked up and took the gun out of my hand and put both hands around my face. I started to feel weak again. "Woman, you are some piece of work. You're the kind of woman I've dreamed of. Since the first day I ever laid my eyes on you, I wanted to hold ya like this." He put his arms around me and rested his head on mine. God, he smelled so good. It felt wonderful to have his arms around me. I thought I was going to melt. He pulled me toward him and kissed me tenderly. With full-blown teenage passion, my first affair was about to begin.

Over the next month we went to a few movies, and we went hunting after school. I always managed to avoid compromising situations. Then one night after a show, we went for a drive out close to where we usually hunted. Mike pulled his parents' Cadillac off the road into a desolate area. He parked, and turned up the radio a little. "The Wolf Man Jack" out of Oklahoma City was the DJ and he played "Only the Lonely," by Roy Orbison. It was a lovers' song. Mike put his arms around me and pulled me close to him. I lay there in his arms, the full moon shining on my face, while he stroked my hair ever so gently.

"Baby, you're so beautiful. I wish you could see how ya look tonight with the moonlight shining on your face." He bent over and kissed me . . . then again. The heavy breathing started. Then the petting. I reached up and kissed him on the neck and then on the ear. He whispered, "Let's go get in the backseat, baby."

I pulled away a little. "Why?"

"It would be better. I don't like cramming ya up between me and the steering wheel." He paused and looked into my eyes. "Baby, I have fallen so much in love with you. I can't seem to eat, or sleep, or play football without thinking about you . . . wanting you. 'Ya know the way I feel tonight.' " He was whispering Roy Orbison's words into my ear.

I didn't know what love was all about. My sister, Wanda, had once told me it was just "a state of mind," that it really didn't exist. I thought about that while looking into his beautiful face. Maybe I did love him, maybe Wanda had been wrong. "I love you, too, Mike, but what if we just have a crush on one another, and we just *think* we love each other?" He put his hand over my mouth.

"Baby, I know the difference. This is no crush. Come."

With that he moved me aside and rolled over into the back-seat. "Come with me, baby, please let me hold you and show you what love is."

I got up and put one leg over the seat, and then bumped my head on the roof of the car. I hiked myself on over and fell right on top of Mr. Wonderful. He started laughing. He pulled me close and started to stroke my hair while Henry Mancini played "Moon River." Then he rolled me under him. I looked up at him in the soft light. We started kissing again, and he began to move his hand down onto my leg and slowly up under my skirt. I bolted up and pulled my skirt down. He waited, then unbuttoned his shirt and gently pulled my face to his chest. I loved the smell of him.

"Don't worry, baby, I'm not going to hurt you. I love you. I want you to know how much." I relaxed a little and he began to start up my skirt again.

"God, you're wearing one of those girdles." He pulled back a little, smiling. "Baby, you don't need to wear a girdle. Some girls, yeah, but not you."

I felt so embarrassed. Girdles were such ugly things.

"Hey, relax. I know what to do."

I started to feel like I was just another girl to add to his collection. Slowly Mike pulled the girdle down and removed my shoes. I quickly pulled my skirt down again and squeezed my eyes closed. "Mike, I'm really scared."

"Baby, your heart's beating so fast," he murmured as he began to unbutton his Levis. I opened my eyes and sat up.

"I can't . . . I can't. I've never done this before. I don't want to . . . please, I'm sorry." I turned my head in shame and stared out the window into the night. I felt uncontrollable tears spill over my cheeks. Mike tried to turn my face around by my chin, but I wouldn't budge. God, why was this happening to me, us? Why couldn't we just go on having fun? Why did we have to do this?

"Baby, please, look at me." He turned my face around and a big tear rolled onto his hand.

"Baby, haven't you ever . . . gone all the way with some-one? I hate to ask you that. I get mad thinking that you might have. Baby, don't ya know what we're doing?"

I thought about the experience with Uncle Harrison and I got sick. Maybe I wasn't a virgin. Maybe he had robbed me of that. I couldn't think about that.

"Mike, I'm scared . . . scared of everything. I've never felt like this with anyone before, and it scares me. I guess I look like I know it all, but I don't! I'm weird! Please, don't tell anyone about this, not even your friends."

He moved close to my face and gently wiped away my tears. "Baby, I didn't know you were a virgin. It was stupid that I thought you weren't. But don't ya see, I'm proud ya are. It makes me love you more. Yeah, the guys kid me. They think we're foolin' around but they'd give anything to be in my shoes. Terry says it makes him cream in his pants just looking at you. I told him that I would kill him if he ever said that to me again. I love you. You're mine, baby, and it's no one's business what we do."

I started to cry. "I'm sorry, Mike. I just can't."

"Hey, it's okay. I understand. Don't worry."

Mike drove me home, and when we arrived I opened the door quietly, afraid that Mother would hear me and ask questions. Everything was quiet. I tiptoed to my room and looked at myself in the mirror. What a mess. I started to cry softly. I couldn't stay inside. I left my room and went out to the backyard. Everything looked magical in the moonlight. I sat under the willow tree and looked up at the stars in the sky.

"Oh, Father, forgive me please for what I almost did. I know that it's wrong, but I can't help these feelings. Make them go away. I don't want to be a tramp. Please help me." Tears were flowing like a river down my face. A gentle night breeze came up and rustled the leaves as if in answer. A train whistle blew mournfully in the distance. I wondered where it was going.

The next morning I walked onto the school campus and saw Mike standing by a tree, waiting for me. I pretended I didn't see him and turned in another direction, but he had seen me and came up beside me.

"How's my woman? You look real nice."

I turned and looked at him. The early-morning light

shone on his face. He looked so good. It was a crisp autumn morning, and I watched his breath take form in the air. "Mike, did you tell anybody?"

"What? Tell anybody that we got hot last night? That I wanted to make love to you but we didn't and you're still my virgin?" I thought he sounded exasperated.

"But did you?"

"Baby, I told you it's nobody's business but ours, okay? Please, believe me. Not every guy is a jerk!"

We started to walk again, and he put his arm around me. Later that day, Suzanne, Janet, and Cheryl were talking with me in front of my locker as I was getting my books out for the next class.

"Jude, you've been actin' a little weird lately. What's wrong? You and Mike have a fight?" Suzanne asked.

"Nothing . . ." I rushed off to class, leaving my friends to just look at one another.

At noon, Mike and I sat together in the cafeteria.

"C'mon, baby, please don't be so sad," he pleaded.

I started to cry. "I can't help it. I feel so dirty. I don't want to be a tramp." I dropped my fork and hid my head in my hands.

"Listen, you're my dream girl. You're innocent, you're beautiful, you go hunting with me. That doesn't make you a tramp."

I looked up at him. "Mike, if anybody found out how far we did go, they'd make me out to be some sort of a pig, don't ya see?"

"No one would ever make you out to be a pig. I'd kill 'em." He beat his fist on the table. "Did your mom say anything last night?"

"No. I didn't see her last night. But she's always suspecting I'm laying with somebody. Once, when I went down to the river, with Cheryl and Suzanne, she found sand in my underwear and accused me of laying with somebody. It was awful. She said I was a liar when I told her the truth. Oh, God, I feel so dirty."

"Hey, just stay cool. Remember, we didn't *do* anything."

"Then why do I feel like we did?"

He sighed and then smiled. "Because we both wanted to. I still do, baby. Hey, I love you . . . dream girl . . . *my* dream girl."

It was a Saturday afternoon, and the girls and I were sitting in Janet's car at the A&W, sipping Cokes and eating french fries. We all had our hair in huge rollers. I had two juice cans in mine, full makeup, and was wearing shrink-to-fit Levis with a striped shirt and socks to match. I had my usual place in the backseat. The conversation got into full swing about boys.

"Well, Gene and I did it so much, we both went dry." That was Janet, also known as "the Nymph."

I turned and gazed out the window.

"Do you think ya'll get married?" Cheryl casually inquired.

"For what? Shit, I just don't want ta get pregnant. Sometimes he forgets to use his thing, ya know?"

"Hampton, come clean, have you and Mike done it?" Suzanne turned her head around, waiting.

"No, ya dumb turd, we haven't." What nerve!

"Really? God, he's so neat. What a bod! How do you keep your hands off him?" I glared at Suzanne. Janet lit up a cigarette.

"Suzanne, you *better* keep your hands off him. I think you're a piss ant. Shit, Janet, can you blow that crap somewhere else?"

"Oh, come on, Hampton, what's the matter with you? You're such a prude," Janet barked.

I turned to Janet and let her have it. "You call me a prude one more time and I'll knock your ugly puss right off your block!"

Janet was silent for a moment, shocked by my uncustomary outburst. Finally she retorted, "One thing is for certain. When Hampton finally does do it, we're gonna have *such* a slumber party, with all the delicious details."

I punched her arm good-naturedly, and called her "douche bag."

"All right, who farted?" Cheryl demanded. Everyone

bailed out of the car and started laughing hysterically. Janet was choking on her cigarette smoke, and we all pointed our fingers at one another.

"C'mon, you ladies, let's haul ass outta here."

Janet revved up the car and we took off, a carload of boys trailing behind.

Later that night, all four of us were sitting with our dates, holding hands and eating popcorn at the movie theater. Our ratted bouffant hairdos (transformed by the juice cans and rollers) made the screen nearly invisible for those unfortunate people sitting behind us.

Mike kissed me tenderly and squeezed my hand. At that moment a grape sucker came flying from nowhere and landed right on my cheek. It just stuck there. I thought someone had slapped me. Everyone started laughing so hard, the theater manager came and threatened to kick us out if we didn't shut up. Mike slowly peeled the sucker off my face, holding back a laugh. Then he proceeded to lick my face.

"God, you taste good!"

Mike's house was only a block from campus. We often went over there to eat at lunchtime. Both his parents worked during the day, so there was never anyone around at noon. One day as we sat on the lawn studying, Mike got up suddenly and went into the house. He called me to come in. He took me into his bedroom and started to kiss me. I responded, and he gently led me to his bed. Struggling, I looked at my watch and gasped. "We'd better return to school before the bell rings." A good excuse.

A week or so later, Mike and I were leaning up against a tree. He was trying to hug me. I couldn't respond.

"Baby, come on, what's wrong? Why are you so sad?" He put his hand on my cheek.

"Guess I'm not very happy. I feel like I'm a bore."

He glanced around and watched the new girl in town walk by. She was definitely sexy.

"Well, why are you so unhappy? You're more beautiful when you're happy."

I hesitated for a moment, then came out with it. "Mike, I think we should break up, at least for a while anyway."

"Break up? What are you talking about?"

"I just think it would be better if you went out with some other girls for a while. Ya need to be with someone you can . . . uh, have some fun with."

Mike was stunned. "Baby, I don't want to break up. I don't want to have fun with other girls . . . can't you get it through that . . . dense, pretty head, that I LOVE YOU . . . I WANT YOU?"

"But we're getting too serious and—"

"Too serious? What's too serious? I said I love you. Don't you think that's all right?"

"I love you, too . . . maybe too much. Look around, Mike. You can have any girl here. Someone who isn't screwed up, like me."

He looked around the campus, then turned back to me. "This is about going all the way, isn't it?"

"But don't you think that's what you need? And there are girls who will do that with you. I can't."

Mike slammed his fist into the tree. "But I don't need to go all the way with somebody else."

"Look, I don't want you to hate me and not respect me. I've heard that when guys break up with girls, they talk about what tramps they are. I don't want you to ever feel that way about me . . . ever!"

He lifted his head and stared at me. "That'll never happen."

"Please, go and find Paula, that new girl. I saw the way you looked at her. Everyone says she's sexy. I know she'll go all the way with you."

Mike began to look a little desperate. I was pushing him away, something I would regret later. He started laughing sarcastically.

"Oh, so you think Paula will go all the way with me, huh? And you also say I should do it? Who do you think you are? I don't want to do it with Paula. I don't love anyone but you. Damn it, can't you understand that?"

"And can't you understand that I *don't want to go all the way!*"

Mike jammed his fist into the tree again. He glared at me in confusion and anger. I turned and walked away toward the school. But before I even reached the building I realized how I had messed things up. I didn't want to leave him. But when I stopped and turned around, he was gone.

Later that day, Cheryl, Janet, and Suzanne came rushing up to my locker. Suzanne started talking.

"What happened with you and Mike? Everyone is saying you guys broke up."

Cheryl added, "Yeah, are you crazy?"

"What am I supposed to be crazy about?"

"You *did* it, didn't you, Hampton? C'mon, you and Phipps did it."

"Wrong, Janet, dear." I couldn't hold it back. "I just think we were getting too serious."

"But . . . what's wrong with that? He's the neatest guy in this friggin' school."

"I don't want to talk about it, okay?"

"Fine. But I think you should have your head examined."

I shrugged and tried to brush it off. Suzanne, the relentless, started up again.

"Listen, Hampton, I just hope you know what you're doing, because when he finds another girl and all of a sudden you don't have him anymore, crap, I sure hope you feel that you did the right thing. Any girl who gets her dirty li'l paws on him is not going to let him go. I really think you're stupid!"

I slammed my locker hard and glared at her. "Bug off! It's none of your business!" With that, I walked away and out of the school. The girls followed.

I was walking toward Janet's car when Suzanne yelled, "Hey, Jude, wait!"

I stopped with tears in my eyes. "What, gonna tell me I'm stupid again?"

"Hey, are you in love with Mike Phipps? I mean, do you really love him?"

I paused for a moment, wiped my face, then for the first time put together what was really bothering me. "What do you mean, am I really in love with Mike Phipps? Love is only a state of mind."

She looked startled. "A state of mind? Where did you get that from?"

"I don't know. But I think sometimes you just convince yourself that that's what you're supposed ta feel. But it's really not there."

"God, I've never heard anybody call love a state of mind. It's just something you *feel* . . . isn't it?"

"Not feel, think."

"Well, maybe you shouldn't think so much."

I looked over at the other girls and I think they thought I had lost my marbles.

"You know what I really think?" Suzanne asked.

"What?"

"I think you have a state of mind full of shit!"

The following Saturday afternoon, looking our usual rolled-up selves, we were out draggin' Main Street. "Stop here!" I demanded.

Janet braked the car and peeled rubber into the grocery store parking lot. I got out and went in. I returned shortly with a big bag of bubble gum that I started throwing around to all the girls. Janet was smoking.

"If you don't put that weed out, I'm getting out and walking."

"Okay, Hampton, cool your jets. You're such a bossy ass!"

Suzanne rolled down the window and waved the smoke out.

"Please, roll up the window," I yelled. "It's blowing my hair loose from the cans!"

We all started stuffing as much bubble gum as possible into our mouths. We blew bubbles as big as our faces. Janet began to drag race with a car full of guys. Cheryl began to roll up her hair with an old sock. The others started pulling their socks off and doing the same. We must have made an impression on the carload of guys, with our man-eating bubbles and hair full of socks. They sped off. Janet yelled after them, "Want some more, come on back!"

"Well, I think it's so sad about you and Mike," said

Cheryl, checking out her one long fingernail. "I really do, Hampton. That guy loves you so much."

"I told ya, it's just a state of mind for him too," I said, trying to convince myself.

"Where in tha shit do you get that crap? It's love, that's all!"

"Hampton, God, you need to get laid . . . and by Phipps, too. Then you wouldn't be givin' us that state-of-mind shit. What are you going to do?" asked Janet while she honked the horn at some guy.

"I don't know."

"If someone asks you for a date, will you go?" Cheryl asked.

"I don't know. Nobody's called yet."

"Nobody's gonna ask her for a date. Because all the guys dig Phipps, and they think she's his girl," Suzanne said.

"So, what are you gonna feel when you see him with somebody else?" Cheryl was looking straight at me. Janet chucked her pink blob and lit up a cigarette.

That question was burning a hole in my mind. I had told him to do it, to find someone else, but the thought began to hurt. Why was I hurting, if this was just in my mind?

"I don't know that either. Hey, you guys, I want to go home."

As we turned onto my street, Janet yelled, "Oh, shit!" Mike's car was parked in front of my house. My heart started to pound. We drove up, and Janet honked and everyone waved. I got out of the car, and the girls drove away blasting the horn. I just walked past him up to the porch.

"Baby, I want to talk. Please, can we talk?"

"I don't want to talk to you, not now!" I slammed the door in his face, ran to the back door and out to the flower house, where I tried to hide among the flowers . . . shaking. Mike came and stood in the door of the flower house. I squeezed my eyes closed as if to make him go away. He walked over to me and squatted down among the flowers.

"Baby, I don't want to break up. Please open your beautiful eyes. Don't shut me out of your life." He leaned forward and kissed me on the side of the face. I opened my eyes. He looked like something out of a dream, a beautiful dream.

"Who did you go out with last weekend?"

He looked surprised. "Me? Nobody."

"That's not what I heard." I was lying.

"What did you hear?"

"I heard you were out with somebody," I lied again.

"Who?" as he moved a little closer.

"It doesn't make any difference."

"Who told you that?"

"I can't say. I don't want to get anybody in trouble."

"That's a Goddamn lie."

I got up and walked to the other side of the flower house, trying to ignore him.

"Stop walking away from me. Don't play this stupid game with my feelings. I want to know who told you that."

"So what would you do? Knock their block off?"

"Yeah, I'll knock their block off."

"Big jock."

"Hey, when I'm not with you, all I do is shoot jackrabbit, play pool, and work hard at football. Ask Terry, he'll tell you."

"Sure, Terry would tell me black's white for you." I started to walk away, but he grabbed me by both shoulders.

"Baby, you're killing me inside. I haven't been able to sleep or anything. I'm hurting, real bad."

I broke away from him and ran out of the flower house. Mike ran after me and tackled me onto the ground. I slugged him. "You bastard."

Mike held my arms down. He was very strong. "You're not going to call me a bastard."

"Yes, I will. Bastard!"

I started to kick him, and when that didn't do the trick I started to scream.

"Judy, stop it."

"No, I hate you, Mike Phipps. I wish I had never met you. I don't want to see you again. *Ever!*"

Mike got a wrestling hold on me and finally pinned me down. I wanted to kill him.

"You don't hate me. You love me. You know you do. And I know, too. That's why you're all hung up, baby. You just won't admit it."

That did it. I started screaming even louder, broke free, and scrambled away. "I hate you . . . you . . . bastard! You don't know what you're talking about. You just think you love me. It's just that you can't have me."

He rose to his feet and stood over me, his head low. "You're right. Go inside, little girl. You're free. The bastard's not going to bother you anymore. What I want is a real woman, not a little girl. I made a mistake."

He brushed off his jacket and walked through the back gate and out to his car in front. I heard the car start and drive away. I lay there, alone. I started to cry.

"Oh, God, please help me. I don't hate Mike, I hate myself. Just me. What's wrong with me?" I laid my head on the ground and sobbed. When I opened my eyes again, there was Mike standing by the tree, smiling compassionately. "You gonna say you're sorry?"

All I could think of was my mascara running through my makeup. I quickly tried to brush it away. I got up to go inside.

"Don't go inside. Come with me and let me buy you a Coke."

"No way can I go like this." He seemed to understand.

"Okay, five minutes."

I smiled and ran into the house. I ran into my room, and tried to do a full makeup job in five minutes. Mike came in and leaned against the door, watching me.

"Good God, Hampton, no wonder you're not happy. What time do you have to get up to do all this every morning?"

I started to laugh, then sputtered, "Well, Mike. I wasn't born gorgeous like you."

"Wrong again. You were born gorgeous. It's just that I know it and you don't."

I stopped applying my makeup. "Mike, did you think about taking out someone else?"

"I thought about it . . . for a minute. But I didn't, because I didn't want to. And if I had, some guy would think the coast was clear and ask you out. Then I knew we'd never get back together." He took me around the shoulders. "C'mon, you're already beautiful, and I'm thirsty."

The next night, after the movies, we got a quick Coke at the drive-in and left. We parked in the same place as before. We started kissing and began to pet. It felt so good to be with Mike. The windows began to steam up.

"Baby, you're so good. Are you all right?"

"Yeah, I just don't want this night to end. I do love you, Mike. Maybe I always will."

"Oh, baby, don't ever worry. I would never hurt you." I watched him as he began to unbutton my blouse. He gently pulled it off from around my shoulders. Then the bra. When it fell to the floor, I just sat there, the light of the moon pouring in through the steamy window. Mike looked at me.

"God, baby, you're more beautiful than I pictured you in my dreams. I want to love you. I want to make love to you." He kissed me, and together we lay down in the seat. I loved him all the way.

"Baby, now we are one person. One life."

CHAPTER ELEVEN

LONG LIVE THE QUEEN

It was Friday night and the slumber party was in full swing at Suzanne's house. Cookies and empty glasses were scattered everywhere. The grandfather clock chimed midnight. Everyone, their hair in socks, rollers, juice cans, and pin curls, sat around gabbing about what else? Boys.

"All I can say is once you get into it, there's nothing like it," Janet said as she painted a finger and held it out to examine it.

Cheryl, who was usually quiet, asked an important question. "Yeah, great, but how do ya tell 'em to wear a rubber? God, I mean, it's so embarrassing."

"Hey, whenever I think about all those moves, like taking your pants off, struggling with a bra with a combination lock, I just bust out laughing," giggled Suzanne, who was the good girl of the group.

I picked up a cookie and started to gnaw on it.

"Well, Hampton, what do you do with Phipps? And if you give me that shit about state-of-mind screwing, I'm going to puke!" demanded Janet.

I swallowed my cookie. I couldn't quite bring myself to express my feelings, but I tried.

Evading the question, I turned to Cheryl and asked, "Listen, what did *you* feel like after you first did it?"

The room became silent. You could have heard a cookie crumb drop off of Janet's lips. I guess they never really heard me ask that question before.

"I don't know. I guess I was afraid that everyone would talk, you know, and I was afraid I'd get pregnant. My parents would get Tim on statutory rape. It would be all over the papers. More guys would ask me out because they would think that I put out. Crud like that."

"How do you feel, now?"

"You mean with Billy?"

"Yeah." I started to chew on my bottom lip.

"I don't know. I love him, that's all."

"But did it make you feel like a tramp, dirty?"

"Hey, why are you ask'n these questions? Hampton, did you and Mike go all the way? Is this what this is all about?"

"No. Don't be stupid," I snapped.

Cheryl stared at me for a moment, then continued. "Look, when you love somebody, you want more of them. What I think you need is to just do it. Then you'll see whether Mike really loves you or not."

"You mean just pop in the backseat and wham, bam, thank you ma'am?"

"Well, that's as good a place as any, considering what we're up against privacy-wise. Jude, look, how are you gonna find out any of this stuff if you don't try it? But one word of advice: Please don't wear a girdle. It stops the heat." Cheryl was serious, but everyone else started laughing again.

The next morning, we were all still asleep when Suzanne's mother, Joe Ella, came to wake us up. Joe Ella was the neatest mother I'd ever met. She had the craziest personality and, in fact, acted like one of us. I loved going over to Suzanne's house. It was like a second home to me.

"Okay all of you crazies, it's time for breakfast. My, my, don't we all look breathtaking this morning. So ya'll have boyfriends, huh? It's a good thing they don't see ya this morning!"

One by one, dreading the light of day, we got up and staggered to the bathroom. Janet was sitting on the john, smoking, while the rest of us washed, moaned, and cursed in the bathroom mirror.

"Shit! I've got my period!"

"One more month without worry," laughed Cheryl.

"God I slept good," yawned Suzanne.

"Yeah, me too. I had such peaceful dreams about Light 'n God and stuff," I said, as I tried to unglue the mascara from ten of my eyelashes.

"Hampton, you're sort of religious, huh? That's probably what's wrong. You think it's a sin or somethin' to fool around," said Cheryl.

"Well, I love God, but I don't think I'm religious or anything, 'cause if I was, I sure wouldn't be hanging around you creeps!"

I grabbed a spare toilet paper roll and threw it at Cheryl. Then I proceeded to remove the socks and juice cans from my hair.

Christmas of 1964 was a wonderful one. For the past few years, Momma hadn't put up a Christmas tree because "Daddy Bill and I just didn't want to bother with it this year." Those were such sad times for me. But this year she had "managed" to put one up.

Mike's parents were always in the holiday spirit. Their house looked so lovely and festive. While Mrs. Phipps busied herself making Christmas cookies, Mike had been doing a lot of shopping, and he would tease me about what each fat box held. I loved it. Christmas Eve, we gathered at their house, had roasted chestnuts, some special "brew" that Mr. Phipps made for us, and we sang—if a little off key—all our favorite Christmas carols.

When the hour came to open all the gifts, Mike went to the tree and pulled out not one, but *four* beautifully wrapped gifts and handed them to me. But before I began, he gave me a Christmas card. It was the most beautiful card I had ever seen. You had to look through a little hole, and a three-dimensional winter scene came to life. On it, Mike had written how much he loved me and how he would forever. I started to cry as he helped me unwrap my gifts—a blue bowling ball with my name engraved on it, a hand-tooled bag to hold the ball, then a Western belt with my name on the back. The smallest gift of all was a delicate gold chain necklace with a miniature diamond engagement ring. I was stunned, and very happy. Mike said it was an "engaged-to-be-engaged" necklace. As he put it around my neck and fastened the clasp, he kissed me and said, "Merry Christmas, baby . . . this one's for keeps."

By this time I had already started applying to college and was worried where my relationship with Mike was going to lead. I was a senior and he was a junior. He was certain to get a football scholarship to some college, but I didn't know what would happen to us in the interim after I graduated and he was left behind to finish high school. I had always wanted to get married and have children, but as the first Hampton to finish high school, I was determined to get a college education. I did not want to "have" to get married. I wanted to stop the pattern of ignorance in my family and achieve something. To me, that meant getting a college degree. But what would that mean for Mike and me? Would it be best for our relationship to end when I graduated? That way Mike, too, would be free to pursue his own dreams. I had to make myself believe that if what we had was really true love, if God meant for us to be together, it would be so. Still, I worried that Mike might find someone else if I left town. What if, after going all the way with him, he ended up hating me? Would I become just another pig? The thought terrified me. Oh God, I prayed, don't let it be that way. I had to trust that what we shared, no matter the outcome of our lives, would always seem sweet and innocent. If it didn't, I knew that my first few steps into intimacy would always be associated with shame and guilt.

Five months later, my family was around the table eating supper. As usual, Daddy Bill had little to say, while Momma tried to generate some mealtime conversation. I had received a letter and couldn't wait to share my good news.

"I've got a surprise for everyone. I got accepted at Texas State University—here's the letter."

"Loy Gene, pass me the potatoes," Daddy Bill said.

"Did ya, now?" Momma said rather sadly. Only Loy got excited.

"Yes. Isn't that great?" I answered.

"Well . . ." Mom started, but she didn't go on.

"Momma, I *can* go to college, can't I?" She offered me more candied yams and I refused.

"Why no, as a matter of fact, you can't. We're not rich folks that can squander money on a girl's education."

Daddy Bill put his forkful of ham in his mouth while he watched me.

"But if I got a job while I was going to school, couldn't you help me a little bit? Lots of kids do that," I pleaded, sensing my dream was about to crumble.

"I can't help ya. I got the store ta run. This man's sick with the diabetes. Lord goodness, child, all my money goes for his medical expenses."

"But Loy is going to college, isn't he?"

"Well, he'll get a scholarship. Lord goodness, he can pick what college he wants ta go to since baseball is a-gettin' him thar. You ain't good at nothin'."

"Yeah, I ain't good at nothin'."

I left the table, hearing Daddy Bill say, "Helen, girls are a waste of a good education. She'll just run off with some ol' boy, have a bunch of kids."

I ran to my room and put on my 45s. The first record to play was "It's Judy's Turn to Cry" and that was my cue. I did just that for the rest of the night.

The following day, Mike and I walked out of the Annual Club meeting. They were nominating the Annual Queen and King. I leaned up against the wall, feeling very depressed, but I was trying not to let Mike know what was wrong. Suddenly, the principal came out the door, beaming.

"May I be the first to offer my congratulations to you, Judy, for being selected this year's Annual Queen?"

"Mr. Price, please, I don't want to be the Annual Queen. Give it to someone else."

Mike and Mr. Price were stunned.

"Why did you say that?" Mike whispered.

I ignored him.

"Mr. Price, there are so many more qualified girls in my class. I don't deserve it, honest I don't."

"Judy, this is highly unusual. Don't you *want* the title?"

Mike spoke up quickly. "Yeah, she just doesn't feel good today."

My only answer was to walk down the hall to the exit door. Mike followed me and put his arm across the door, blocking my way.

"Hey, you're the Annual Queen. That's an honor—just like when you won Most Beautiful this year. Come to think of it, you didn't want that either. Baby, what's with you? What's gone wrong?"

"I just don't feel I should be Annual Queen."

"Funny. A lot of other people think you should."

"Look, Annual Queen is someone who represents the school, who is beautiful, dedicated. Someone who is taking those assets on to college." My eyes were filling up with tears.

"Yeah . . . well?"

"Well, I'm not those things. I'm not going to college."

"Baby, what do you mean, you're not going to college? You're doing great in school."

"I'm just not going, that's all." I turned my head away and watched a couple leaning against a tree.

"Baby, are you pregnant?"

"No, I'm not pregnant."

Mike turned my head back slowly. His face was so tender. "Look, it's okay . . . I love you."

"Mike, that's not it. Not it at all. My parents don't have the money for me to go to college. My stepfather thinks I'm not worth it, anyway." I started to cry in anger, and out of a hopeless, bitter feeling about my future.

"Come on, baby. You can work and put yourself through school, show your stepfather he's wrong about you."

"You'd love that, wouldn't you?"

"Love what?"

"You'd love to have me off at some school while you play the big super jock here at school. So you can get to screw that big-ass Paula." I was taking out my anger on Mike, but I couldn't stop myself.

Mike was floored. He stared into my eyes, searching for some reason for what I was saying. "Damn it, Judy, what are you doing? What is wrong with you?"

"I don't know. I don't know anything anymore. And don't swear at me."

"Well, baby, what you're saying is even cruder than what I said."

I didn't say anything.

"Hey, the real reason you don't want to go to college is because I'm not graduating yet, right? Isn't that it?"

"It's true I don't want to leave you, but I do want to go. Mike, I really wanted to be a lawyer, to become somebody. Now, I'm nobody."

"Hey, I thought you wanted to get married and have babies."

"Yeah, I do, but I also want to have an education. I don't want to end up like my mother and the rest of my family. They're so unhappy. I want to be somebody!"

"Baby, we both can be somebody. Can't we be somebody together?"

"How? You'll want to play football at college. How can you play football, get an education, and have a wife and kids all at the same time?"

"Hey, it's been done before. But first I have to finish high school."

"Yeah, sure . . . so you can be the super jock here while I'm gone. You'll end up with Paula or somebody in six months. I know it. You're a man. That's how men are."

Mike exploded. "You're crazy. You're acting like a first-class bitch!"

I exploded too.

"You bastard! Nobody calls me a bitch! Not even you!"

"I just did! And it's the truth. You've hurt me for the last time!"

Hearing that, I pulled off his high school ring and threw it down the marble hall. "It's better to do this now. It's over . . . over!"

"You're right, you don't deserve to be Annual Queen." He calmly walked over, picked his ring up off the floor, and disappeared down the hall.

The following morning, I brought my prom gown to school for the inauguration of the Annual Court. My friends helped me get dressed in the rest room. They didn't have much to say except that I looked beautiful and that it was "so damn sad" about Mike and me.

The entire student body was assembled in the auditorium as the Annual Court waited to march in. I was hesitant to leave the rest room because Mike was part of the Court, too. The gown I was wearing, a beautiful powder pink satin jeweled with crystal flowers, was the one I had been saving to wear to the prom with Mike.

I finally came out. Mike was dressed in a white sport coat with a pink carnation. He looked at me with sad, angry eyes.

When the ceremony began, the Court preceded the Annual King and Queen. Then we paraded down the aisle under a spotlight while some wonderful melody played. Everyone started to applaud. The student body president was waiting on the stage to do the honors. When I was crowned, the president gave me a kiss, which was greeted by a lot of hooting from the audience. Apparently when the president kissed me, Mike, who was also on the stage, had glared angrily. I walked back down the aisle and it was over.

The next day, in my home ec class, I was making a lemon meringue pie and thinking about how Mike had called me a bitch. While I whipped the meringue, I also fancied that he was telling everybody that I was "easy." I whipped both the meringue and myself into a frenzy. At that moment, Mike appeared at the door in the hallway. He just stood there, giving me a hard look, then disappeared. I slapped the meringue onto the pie and then had a thought: I'm going to throw this sucker in his face! I would be avenged!

The bell rang for lunch and I hitched a ride home with Caris Hensley. He asked for a bite but I replied that I was saving it for Mike. "Lucky guy," was his comment. I asked if he could pick me up in thirty minutes and take me back to school. He happily agreed.

I arrived at school and was a bit shocked! Everybody was waiting for me. Apparently, someone in my class had revealed my plan to throw the pie at Mike. They all started crowding around me asking if I was really going to do it. I was dumbfounded and asked how they all knew. "The whole school knows," I was told.

Not everyone knew.

Mike and his friend Terry rounded a corner and stopped short. Everyone in the crowd watched him. The bell rang for school to commence, but no one was going into the building. Finally, Mike and Terry started walking to the door. Now was my chance. I walked up to him in the hall. Everyone was trying to squeeze in behind me to watch.

"What are you doing?" he asked. "What's going on?"

"Mike Phipps, no one calls me a bitch and gets away with it!" I brought the pie around and *splat!* Right in his puss! I quickly turned to walk away, when he lunged at me. Tommy, a huge football player, grabbed Mike. "C'mon, Mike, don't hurt her. She's hurt already, man, can't you see that?" About that time, my prissy Spanish teacher came barging out of his classroom door and demanded to know what was going on. Seeing Mike being held like that, he figured Mike was trying to beat me up or something.

"Mr. Phipps, young men don't hit young women. Don't ever lay a hand on a woman again, at least not in my school."

Poor Mike!

When Mr. Price appeared he ordered everyone back to class, and Mike and me to his office. I went upstairs and sat down in the waiting room. Mike came in and had to sit beside me.

I turned to look at him. There were pieces of meringue in his ear. I was starting to feel so bad about my stupidity. I wanted to cry out to him and tell him how much I hurt and how much I loved him. I wanted to say that I was sorry, but my bruised ego wouldn't let me. This whole miserable thing was my fault. I deserved to suffer. From that day forward, I certainly would.

Mr. Price asked us to come into his office. He looked at us and struggled to keep from laughing.

"I don't think I want to know the whole story. However, I do want to point out this: Mike, you and Judy have represented this school with dignity. I feel you both owe one another an apology for whatever caused this. Then both of you can return to school and continue to set that good example. You're excused."

We both left. Mike went his own way without saying anything to me. I slowly went down the stairs hearing the janitors complain about the behavior of today's children.

Three days later I walked into the hall. Everyone was milling around, getting ready to go to class. I spotted my friends. They were involved in a heated discussion, and Janet was pointing to a classroom door.

"Hi, what are you guys whispering about?" I asked.

"Hampton, do ya love me? Cuz if ya do, you won't go by that door," said Janet, not showing her normal cool.

I turned around to look. "Why not?"

"Oh, shit!" Cheryl said. "This is so damn sad. I gotta leave." She turned and walked quickly to the rest room.

Janet took a deep breath. "Because Mike is in there with somebody."

"Who?"

"Cathy." The real cute girl that Mike had broken up with to go with me.

"What are they doing?" I was afraid to hear the answer.

"They're . . . well, word is that they're getting back together. Oh, shit, I'm so sad about this mess. I loved you and Phipps. I always hoped I could find someone and be like you guys. Shit, I'm so sorry, Jude."

I felt numb. I walked slowly over to the door and looked in.

Mike and Cathy were sitting at two desks that they had pulled together. Mike was holding her hands. They both looked up and saw me standing there, then quickly resumed their intimate conversation. I turned without a word and walked out of the school.

I went to my best friend, Slim, and saddled him. I rode wild and fast, outrunning the wind. I wanted to leave my world behind—school, hurts, fights, slumber parties, going all the way, Momma, Daddy Bill, and Mike. I kept riding far out into the country. Most of all, I wanted to lose me! A jackrabbit jumped up and started running. I pulled out my .22, aimed, and fired. I missed. The lucky little creature scampered away. I dismounted, and fell to the ground, sobbing about my miserable life. And that's where I stayed all night.

About first light, I took Slim's reins and started walking. I watched the sun fill the horizon with a blaze of color. The mountains far in the distance were shrouded in purple mist. A mockingbird in the tree above began to greet the morning with his cheery melody, while others flew from the thickets nearby. Though I was a part of the morning majesty, I felt like a fugitive with a troubled soul. I wanted to pray. I wanted to ask God to help me. But I couldn't find the words. There were none.

As much as I wanted to stay there forever, I returned home to find my mother in a tizzy. I told her about breaking up with Mike and explained why I had run away. She cooled down and answered, "It's for the best."

The few days before the prom were very lonely for me, and I avoided everyone as much as I could. Dean Hall, a classmate I had known since the sixth grade, found out I didn't have a date to the prom. He asked, I accepted. But I soon was sorry I had agreed to go.

While dancing with Dean, I spotted Mike and Cathy dancing like a tender, married couple. I asked Dean if I could take a break and went over to Cheryl at the punch bowl.

"I've never been drunk before."

"Well, ya won't accomplish that here," she said, taking a sip of the punch. "Hey, Hampton. I'm with Robin and you're with Dean. Let's go get drunk. You know, have some real fun. Those two guys will take care of us."

I turned around and saw Mike kiss Cathy. I decided that Cheryl's idea was a good one.

Dean was driving a rusted green van that didn't have any side windows—perfect for getting snockered in. No one could see in. Robin and Dean were all for it. They drove us home to change out of our gowns, while they went and loaded up with the goods. Cheryl and I changed into our Levis, sweat shirts, and tennis shoes. She wore her "letter sweater" that had all the letters she had won in music. We left our hair the way it was for the prom: ratted, sprayed, piled high on our heads, sprayed, pinned, and sprayed a few more times so it wouldn't move. We looked like Mae West in jeans.

When Momma asked what we were doing. I told her I was going to get drunk. Expecting retribution for my boldness, I stepped back a step. She replied, "Make it a good one, cuz ya sure is gonna feel it in the mornin'." A car honked outside, so I kissed her good-bye and Cheryl and I went off to an unforgettable adventure.

Dean and Robin sat up in front, driving to somewhere (I never remembered where), while Cheryl and I in back inspected the goods. There were several quarts of booze: scotch, gin, vodka, and whiskey. There was a bag full of lemons and limes, and a saltshaker, and four cups. Robin turned around and threw us a bottle of red cherries.

"Here, I bought these just for you guys—since you don't have any . . . ha, ha."

Cheryl and I looked at each other. I called him a creep! Cheryl called him a "mutherfuck'nsonofabitchassthatwas square." God, could that girl say what was on her mind.

Cheryl unscrewed the bottle of scotch. "Now, let's try this. What you do is take a swig of this booze while you're holding your lemon. Then, when you swallow it, you suck on the lemon. It makes the taste go away."

Robin turned around to watch as I took the bottle in my hand and downed a huge gulp. Yuck, it was the worst thing I had ever tasted. My face contorted and my throat burned. Cheryl quickly handed me the lemon and took the bottle. I sat there sucking the guts out of the lemon, watching Cheryl chugalug that bat piss like a pro.

Still sucking the rind on the lemon, I said in a hoarse voice, "The stuff burns. Is that all there is to this? . . . When do I get drunk?"

Robin and Dean were making wisecracks and laughing to themselves. I had the feeling they were so happy because they figured they would end up in the sack with us. At least, they hoped. Things turned out much differently.

"Yeah, well, the burnin' will stop and you will be drunk," Cheryl said with a tone of experience.

"Okay, let's do another," I said.

For two girls who didn't drink, we managed to do away with two quarts of scotch and most of the vodka. Needless to say, the following account is hearsay. I can't remember a thing that happened.

"We don't d-d-d-drink ana we don't chew—uh, screw —ana we don't go witha boys that dooo . . ." According to witnesses, we sang this little number in unison.

We continued to toast various individuals: a few aunts and uncles; Billy, Cheryl's fiancé, who was away at college; and Mike, who was away with Cathy. We laughed and drank while the radio blared.

I raised another bottle in toast. "Screw Mike Phipps and screw football."

"Yeah . . . screw Phipps . . . he's more foot than ballssssssss," echoed Cheryl.

We took more swigs and devoured more lemons.

"Sheee-it!" Cheryl moaned. "I think I must have heartburn or somethin'. I don't feeeeel so good."

"You're suppose ta feel good," I reportedly said.

Dean glanced back and said, "I think they're drunk."

"Let's go over to the A&W and get somethin' ta eat," Robin said in an exasperated tone.

According to a reliable source, I suddenly held my stomach and began to roll my eyes. It must have been because Dean tried to do a wheelie at a light, but only burned out and did a 360 in the parking lot of the A&W.

"Oh, my starssss . . ." *Splat!* I had upchucked all over Cheryl.

"Hampton, you puked on my letter sweater."

"Sorry . . . oomph." I'm sorry to say I repeated the hideous act.

"Hampton, you puked in my hair." Unfortunately for Cheryl, she had worn a little hairpiece. In my state of drunkenness, I reached over, pulled the hairpiece off, and slung it, full of vomit, across the van and hit Robin on the side of his face.

"Oh, my God. I don't believe you did that, Hampton." Poor Robin.

"It's Phipps," Cheryl yelled bitterly. "It's all Phipps's fault."

A car pulled up beside the aromatic van. Two boys in front got out and went around to open the door of the van.

"Jesus Christ, it's like a horror movie in there. Who puked?" It was suave Jake.

"Sarah Bernhardt, you butthole," I shrieked.

"Funny. Hampton, is that you?" he asked, provoking me even more.

I picked up the vomit-covered hair piece and slung it at him. He ducked.

Another car load of guys pulled up. "Has anybody seen Hampton?"

"Yeah . . . she's in here . . . drunk out of her rabbit-assed mind. The Puke Queen is in here," hissed Jake, no longer so suave.

Cheryl started yelling, "It's Phipps. He drove her to drink. Hampton never smoked and never drank, and now look what Phipps has turned her into."

At that point, I stuck my head out of the back door to see what was going on. "How sad, how crappin' sad," was all I could say.

Cheryl retrieved her hairpiece from the front seat. "See, he made her puke in my hair. Men!"

With that, we both started to cry.

Dean and Robin decided it was time to get us home. They stuffed Cheryl and me back inside the van, dodging to avoid the upchucks. On the way to my house, Cheryl and I lay side by side, and with each sway of the van we would pour our guts out.

The van pulled up in front of my house at about nine-thirty in the morning. The sun was shining bright.

I crawled to the window, looking like Lady Macbeth after walking ninety miles of bad road. My hair was matted with puke, there was vomit all over Cheryl's letter sweater, which

I somehow was now wearing. I attempted to climb out of the van, but was so drunk that I fell down to the curb and started to dry-heave. Dean tried to find a dry place to grab me so he could help me up. "But Hampton," he groaned, "I don't want to touch you. . . ."

"Shit on you, Dean . . . ya butthole."

Just then Dean heard Cheryl moan, so he left me on the curb, climbed into his van, and drove off.

I simply could not get up. I crawled from the curb, trying to make it to my front door. I looked up. "The shittin' sun is out. What is it doing up so late?"

Mrs. Cole, our next-door neighbor, opened the window and called, "Judy, are you all right?"

"The shitty sun is out."

I think she understood. "Yes, it usually is this time of day."

I continued my quest for the front porch. The door opened, and out came my brothers, Loy and Gayle.

"Sis, is that you? Naw, it couldn't be. That's just a drunk-ard," Gayle said mockingly.

"Shit on you," I threatened.

"Well, Gayle," Loy laughed, "I think you had better help me."

Loy and Gayle moved toward me, but they stopped short and nearly fell dead with the smell.

"Shit on you both," I shouted. "I don't need your cotton-pickin' help."

Loy and Gayle cracked up laughing, and Loy hollered into the house, "Momma, come out here. You gotta see your beautiful, sweet-talkin' daughter."

Momma came to the door dressed in her robe. "Lord have mercy . . . is this the girl who walked outta the house last night with the beautiful hair smellin' like a flower?"

"The shitty sun is out!" I said, the record stuck in the same old groove.

"Yep. Like clockwork. It's just a timely old thang . . . been a-happenin' for years this way." That was Momma in one of her more poetic moments.

Loy went to help me up again, while he held his nose.

Gayle started to laugh, "Now you come on inside and I'll fix you somethin' the real drunkards drink. They mix beer, milk, and eggs together. Now how does that sound?"

I started dry-heaving again, so Loy picked me up and carried me into my bedroom, where he laid me on the bed. "Maybe we'll just throw this bedspread away," he said.

"Shit on you," I said, hissing the same old tune.

I started to fall asleep while Loy smiled down at me. "I hate Mike Phipps," I heard him say.

I vaguely remember talking to Cheryl on the phone a few times that day about her letter sweater—Momma had to have it dry-cleaned twice—and about how I was having trouble getting all the vomit out of my hair. I loved Cheryl. She had been a great friend.

A few days later we had Senior Day—the last time we would be students at Artesia High School. In the auditorium, each of us was presented to the student body and then we walked our last walk down the aisle. It was a very emotional day.

As I walked up the aisle on the way out the door, I turned and saw Mike. He was sitting in the juniors' section next to Cathy. He looked up and smiled and gave me the thumbs-up sign. I smiled at him with tears in my eyes and walked out of the building . . . forever.

All my friends wanted to go to a nearby reservoir and swim for the rest of the afternoon. I didn't feel in the mood, so I went home, changed, and walked back up to the school's football field. I wandered around, my mind flooded with memories of football games, twirling my baton, the pep squad, the crowds, the Bulldog football team, the victories, and Mike. All this was over for me. I sat down on a bench with my head in my hands. Suddenly, I heard someone call my name.

"Hey, Hampton, is that you?"

I looked up to see Kelly Moore. She was home from college and was visiting her alma mater.

"Hi. God, I haven't seen you in ages. Do ya like college?" I asked, hooding my eyes from the sun with my hand.

"It's the greatest. Especially rush week. And guys . . .

whew, Hampton, you wouldn't believe the men. God, talk about a good time? College is where it's at."

"I'll bet. What are you majoring in?"

"Oh, I started out with a major in business, but I might change to physiology. Everyone changes their majors," she said, very carefree.

"But once you change your major, doesn't it take longer to get through school?"

"Yeah, but who wants to stop going to college? I mean, I could go for being a professional student. College is where the action is."

"Won't your parents get a little upset? I mean, costing so much and all?"

"Hell, they don't care. It's no skin off of Jack's ass. He's not paying the bills, my real dad is. He left me a lot of money in a trust, just for my little ol' education. So I'm gonna take my time and have a ball."

Kelly continued to brag about her conquests with guys, while I sat there wishing I had the chance to go to college. I knew I wouldn't just "have a ball." I knew what I wanted to study. Some people had all the breaks in life.

My thoughts were interrupted abruptly. For a moment my vision faded, and inside my head there was a flash of bright light, a red glow, Janet doing sign language. Then I was walking into this light. I was in a tunnel . . . strange noises . . . a whirling sound . . . and then a hum. A voice, far away, calling my name. I walked into the light. I blended with it. Flash! A fly on my eyelashes and Kelly serving orange juice. The vision drifted away, and Kelly's voice became audible once again.

"Hampton, did you hear me? Is something wrong? Hampton, are you okay?"

I sat there frozen, trying desperately to recall a hazy moment from the past. Then I remembered! The slumber party at Kelly's house, when I was in eighth grade. Why hadn't I remembered before today? I looked up at Kelly, who was examining me curiously.

"Kelly, do you remember that slumber party we had at your house the week we all made cheerleader? Remember, we came over to practice our routines and stayed the night?"

"Hmmm, a little. What a dumb thing to remember. That was ages ago."

"I know it was, but . . . I just now remembered it, and also something that I never remembered before." I continued to remind her of what went on that night: the lights, the red thing above the neighbor's house. And I asked her why we never talked about it the next morning, or ever mentioned it afterward. "It just doesn't make any sense that we didn't talk about something that weird. It is as if we weren't *supposed* to remember it."

She didn't comment. She just stood there twisting her class ring around on her finger.

"Kelly, do you know what I'm talking about?" I demanded.

She started looking around nervously.

"Kelly?"

"Hampton, just drop it, okay?" she snapped.

"Why? Why should I drop it? It did happen. Why didn't we remember it?" Her behavior seemed very strange to me.

"I don't want to talk about it anymore. I gotta go. See ya."

With that, she walked swiftly back to her car and drove off, leaving me to puzzle over my own questions. Something *did* happen to us that night, and something or someone made us forget it. Maybe we made our own selves forget it. But a part of my mind, the deep subconscious part, had held on to the experience, perhaps because my conscious mind wouldn't accept it. But why me? I didn't have any answers. Whom could I talk to that wouldn't think I was off my rocker—or worse, who would try to convince me I hadn't seen anything at all? Rummaging through my mind, I thought of Mr. Stanhope, the science teacher at school. Of course. I considered Mr. Stanhope a brilliant teacher. Maybe he might be able to explain this experience.

I walked briskly over to the science building. It was only two-thirty, and students were still drifting in and out of the building. I walked up to Mr. Stanhope's door and knocked. "The door is open," he called out. I walked in to see Mr. Stanhope behind his desk, leaning back in his chair, reviewing a paper while he munched on a bag of peanuts. He was so engrossed in his paper that he didn't even look up to see who I was. I was so nervous that I didn't know how to start out this conversation, or how to interrupt him. So I began with this little number: "What do you think of the world population crisis?"

He immediately dropped his papers back onto his desk and looked up at me, surprised. "You mean, am I for it or against it?"

I smiled.

"Overpopulation could easily be cured if everyone became celibate for five years." He chuckled and finished chewing his peanut. "Miss Hampton, what can I do for you this afternoon? Come to think of it, why aren't you out there with the other seniors celebrating your graduation?"

"Well, I needed to talk to someone who might have some answers . . . to something I need to understand . . . and I thought that maybe . . . if you had the time . . . you could help me."

He studied me for a moment. "Young ladies don't usually come to a science teacher for help."

"Oh, no, it's nothing like that. It has to do with an explanation. A scientific explanation." I was obviously nervous.

"Then I apologize for being presumptuous. Here, have a seat, and I'll see if I can be of some assistance."

I began tentatively, but as the eighth-grade experience came back to me, my account began to flow. Mr. Stanhope listened quietly with apparent interest. When I finished, I felt as though I had been rambling on for hours and I began apologizing. He merely raised his hand to tell me it was all right. I sat there waiting, not knowing what to expect from him. Fearing ridicule, I began to sweat. Mr. Stanhope got up and walked over to the window.

"I had a roommate at college who was drafted by NASA to work on the military applications of science and mathematics. I think that it was a move spurred by political interest. For whatever reasons, he had a keen interest, even back in college, in the existence of bogies."

"Bogies?"

"Bogies . . . uh, unidentified flying objects. UFOs. 'Bogies' was the term my friend used for them. I became very familiar with this phenomenon through the research he did on the subject. At that time, he suspected these UFOs were of vital concern to the CIA and the Air Force. That was back in the early fifties, when a rash of sightings caused some people to fear UFOs were hostile, a threat to our national security. I know there were some penetrations of our airspace by aircraft from the Communist bloc that were hushed up, and I think the government's silence about that helped to feed the public's imagination. There have probably been over a million reported sightings, but the Air Force has dismissed them as merely weather balloons, the aurora borealis, experimental aircraft, or pranks. The official investigation done by the Air Force called Project Blue Book has been officially closed down due to lack of progress in proving once and for all that UFOs exist. However, there are a lot of people out there that still believe these craft contain extraterrestrial life. Some people with psychiatric delusions think the extraterrestrials are here to redeem mankind."

I was fascinated by what Mr. Stanhope told me, but he hadn't said a word about my own experience. Maybe he didn't believe there were such things as UFOs, or that I saw one.

"What about you, Mr. Stanhope? Do you believe they exist?"

He walked back to his desk and sat down. "I'm only a science teacher, but I'm a scientist at heart. Perhaps I haven't explained the methods of science as well as I should have to my students. For the most part, they just want to get through the authorized textbook material. I also probably haven't always taught what Einstein professed: that the cosmic religious feeling is the strongest and noblest motive for scientific research.

"I find it difficult to pursue scientific purpose and facts with an active imagination when what I do every day is reiterate established theories that my students are required to learn. Also, I must admit I am skeptical about any doctrine that is not supported by empirical data."

"So, Mr. Stanhope, are you saying that you are skeptical about the existence of UFOs, and maybe even about my experience?" I felt a hot flush on my face and a tingling of disappointment.

"I am in no way saying that this didn't happen to you, but on the other hand, I have no way of proving it did." He began fidgeting with his yellow legal pad. I was beginning to think I had made a mistake in pouring all of this out to him. I felt angry at myself for being so foolish. He must have detected this.

"Miss Hampton, I don't want you to think that I think you made this all up." He took a deep breath, hesitated, and continued. "Let me clarify. As a scientist, I need proof of the experience in order to help you—and me—to understand it. I can't disprove it either, but without sufficient evidence, I can only conclude that what you witnessed is undefinable and therefore may be only illusionary."

"But Mr. Stanhope, I *did* see this thing. It *did* happen." I felt a desperate urgency to prove my sanity.

"Do you have any proof?" he asked smoothly.

"Not proof, but the others with me saw it. I wasn't the only one."

"All right, do they have any proof? Say, a piece of the object, or a photograph of it?"

I was wilting with the realization that without the things he was asking, I could not support my claim. "No, nothing like that."

"Then without such tangible evidence, it remains merely a hypothesis. Of course, Miss Hampton, that's the skeptical scientist in me speaking. There also resides within me a romantic side. A part of me is enticed and even believes in such things as UFOs, and perhaps is even a little envious of your apparent contact with one. That aspect of my nature does believe you. It sounds very much like some of the reports my friend at school investigated—memory loss, flashing lights, the craft seeming to defy gravity. Tell me, are you familiar with the Book of Ezekiel in the Bible?"

I was feeling a little better about where this conversation was heading, but I was thrown a bit by Mr. Stanhope's question. I thought it odd. Scientists have always been denounced by fundamentalists, but here was a teacher of science familiar enough with the Bible to ask me a question about it. Fascinating.

"Ezekiel?" I lit up. "No one that I ever knew could interpret Ezekiel. You mean you can?"

"Only with my own interpretation, of course. Ezekiel's 'wheel within a wheel' was a machine, a UFO. And perhaps the 'angel' was an extraterrestrial. I feel Ezekiel described the angel as bearing a resemblance to the faces of animals, because he lacked knowledge of high technology. In fact, he may have been seeing some kind of space suit. At least that's how UFO buffs explain it. They argue a definite similarity between 'the wheel' and modern-day sightings and claim that Ezekiel either possessed a rare genius for the macabre, or with his broad and uneducated description he did, in fact, have an encounter."

I imagined Ezekiel trying to figure a way to tell his friends and family about his experience. I could relate to his dilemma.

"Mr. Stanhope," I asked, "do you believe in God?" I must have caught him off guard; his face reddened a little. He took a deep breath, put down the pencil he had been rolling between his thumb and forefinger, and leaned back in his chair with his hands behind his head.

"Miss Hampton, I've always recoiled from discussing religion in mixed company. One never knows whom one may offend." He paused, looking at me. "Would you think me offensive if I asked you the same question?"

"Excuse me, Mr. Stanhope, I didn't mean to put you on the spot."

"Have I put you on the spot?"

"Well, no, you haven't. Not at all. It's just that I have learned a lot from you, and I would like to hear more of your own theories . . . I guess about what you think God is."

"Personally, I think every scientist feels that there exists a great intelligence at work in nature and the cosmos. But if you are asking me if I believe in the God of fundamentalist religion, no. The fundamentalist interpretation of the Bible is wildly inconsistent with the evolutionary process. Every major religion on earth contradicts each other vying for position of supreme truth. Prophecies that could admit to lots of possible interpretations, fragments of supposed miracles that were never documented. Why hasn't God spoken to anyone today? Many fundamentalists still believe and teach that the world is only six thousand years old, while science knows that it's *billions* of years old. Miss Hampton, I'm not endeavoring to dissuade anyone from their own personal beliefs, but as to my own . . . ? Well, it's comprised of the testament to the preeminence of a greater mind: nature itself."

"I tried getting answers to some of those contradictions myself," I told him.

"What answer did you get?"

"I was humiliated for asking, for daring to test God's words. I never got the answers and I never went back to church. I still believe in God and in Jesus Christ. If everyone could really live according to the brilliant simplicity of the Sermon on the Mount, I think we all would get along together—even science and religion could be compatible."

"You left out politics," Mr. Stanhope laughed. "I must admit, I can't remember having a more invigorating discussion with a student. I haven't been able to help you understand your experience, I'm sure, but perhaps just knowing that others have had similar experiences may give you some comfort. By the way, I wish you had pursued science more intently. I believe your natural curiosity suits you for it. Ah well, college will offer much broader opportunities for study than high school."

I felt disappointed that he had said that. If only I could have such an opportunity. I noticed that he was starting to assemble some papers on his desk and felt that it was time to go.

"Mr. Stanhope, it's been a pleasure talking with you. You've helped me more than you know."

I left the room and walked home, resigned to the fact that my experience was something that I couldn't explain. Yet one thing was certain: I wasn't the only one to have had such a strange experience. That comforted me somewhat. Maybe one day I would understand the full significance of what happened the night of the slumber party, but for now I needed to decide what I would do with my life.

In the weeks that followed, I saw Mike only one more time. He and Terry were sitting on his front porch watching the VJ Day Rodeo Parade that passed in front of his house. I had won the title of VJ Day Rodeo Queen, and I rode Slim at the head of the parade, next to the governor of New Mexico on his beautiful buckskin stud. As I rode past, I simply smiled, and Mike returned the favor. Mike and Cathy continued their relationship throughout their senior year. Mike won a football scholarship from the University of Arkansas and played for the Arkansas Razorbacks. Cathy attended the same college. They were soon married, and last I heard they had three children. Mike is the head football coach for Artesia High School.

I have often thought how different our lives might have been if I had been able to express my feelings rather than repress them. If I had possessed enough confidence in Mike to tell him of the horrors I had experienced with my uncle, and of the deep resentment of men that my mother had passed on to me, maybe he would have had a clearer understanding of the anger I so readily displayed. But unfortunately, I never opened up, even when he tried to help me.

I suppose Mother was right when she said it was "for the best." We are both happy in our own separate lives. I guess I did love him for enriching my life with tenderness, compassion, and friendship, but I don't think I was in love with him, because I didn't love myself enough to give completely of myself.

I enjoyed writing this chapter. It brought back many emotions and allowed me to better understand why I pulled the rug out from under myself. Also, I never got to apologize to Mike for my behavior with his class ring, or for the ominous lemon meringue pie, so after twenty-three years of a guilty conscience, please, Mike, accept my apology.

CHAPTER TWELVE

THE HOPE IS
THAT WE LIVE AGAIN

I had made up my mind that I was going to get some kind of an education. I just wasn't sure how I would make this miracle happen. A friend of mine, a sophomore at Texas Tech University, was going back to Lubbock, Texas, in August, and I pleaded with Mother to make me a small loan just so I could get there, find a job, and get a hole-in-the-wall to live in. Needless to say, there was a bit of fighting about investing in such a high-risk venture. Finally, she loaned me $145 and said that that was it. Loy was on my side and promised that he would help however he could. I packed up my things, and on the day of departure I got a less than enthusiastic sendoff.

The day I arrived in Lubbock, I spotted an ad for a one-room apartment near the campus. I walked to the address and inquired. Amazingly, the owners—a mother and daughter by the name of White—immediately recognized me as

"Helen's girl, Judy." I had asked God to help me and it seemed He did. You see, the mother, Mrs. Ivy White, was a cousin to my father. The Whites were delighted that I was family and said I could have a discount on the rent. The young Miss White also knew the manager of the nearby Safeway quite well. They were having an affair, so she really did have an in. I paid one month's rent, moved my things, and when I was settled, Miss White drove me to Safeway and personally introduced me to the manager, who hired me as a grocery checker.

The job was only part-time, but that, I told them, would be perfect, if I could manage to find a school. The university was definitely out, though; the tuition was too high. The store manager and Miss White recommended the Lubbock Business College. It was within walking distance of home and Safeway.

The following day I walked over to the business college. I told them how desperately I wanted to go to school and that, if necessary, I would be willing to work at the school to help out with my tuition. A deal was struck. I would be at work by 7:00 A.M. and work until classes started at 9:00. When classes were finished, I would work in the office in the afternoon. Weekends I would work at Safeway for eight hours each day, and again on Tuesday and Thursday night. Somewhere in between all this I would study.

By the end of the first week I had lost ten pounds but gained two roommates, who went to a nearby beauty school. Candy was a doll, and Susan was a dainty little thing who, though she looked more like an elf than a human, possessed a classical beauty. It was quite an ordeal getting dressed in our tiny apartment, with clothes hanging in every available space. Taking a shower was also interesting. You had to remove several pairs of hose, panties, and bras from a make-shift clothesline in the shower, and then replace the under-garments when you were done. Due to our financial situations, whenever one of us was taken out to dinner, she would order as much as she could and bring home the leftovers in a doggie bag. With all my money fed into my education, there were plenty of days I went hungry.

"So, Candy Pooh, who is it tonight?" I asked while preparing a paper for tomorrow's exam.

"Some nice dude with a credit card. I told him I wanted Chinese," replied Candy as she patted her hair.

"Hey, I forgot to tell you," Susan said. "I've got a date with a good-looking lawyer. What should we have for dinner?"

"Prime ribs," I said, licking my chops as I went into the bathroom to get my Safeway uniform. "Listen, you dolls, I've gotta get to work. Have a great time, and don't forget about dinner."

I came home that night exhausted. I didn't know if I had enough energy to do my homework. Candy and Susan arrived within moments of one another, doggie bags in their hands.

"God, I'm starved. What have you got? Open it up," I said, feeling invigorated by the smell of food.

Candy opened her bag. "I ordered two extra dishes and said I just wanted to think of him later when I was eatin' the leftovers at home."

"And I got his prime rib as well as mine. The potatoes looked kinda soggy, so I left them. He said I must have a horse for a dog." Susan laughed.

I grabbed a plate and started wolfing down the leftovers. "God, you guys, this is great. This is my first real meal in maybe a week. Are you going out again? Like tomorrow night?"

"Saturday night, I'll squeeze for dinner." To cheer me up, she changed the subject. "Look at your hair, Jude. You really need a touch-up. Let me do a little homework on you." Candy started measuring out bottles of bleach and gathered some old newspaper to put on the floor. Candy and Susan started the bleach job. Some time later, they proceeded to rinse the bleach out of my hair. When Candy started to dry it, the hair started breaking off in her hand. She had left the bleach on too long.

"Oh my God, Jude, your hair broke off. It looks awful. Oh, shit, I'm so sorry."

I ran a comb through my tangled hair. I looked at the

comb. It was full of hair. I just smiled and threw up my hands. "My hair is just like my life. All broken up!"

Walking to school early one foggy morning a few weeks later, I was feeling unbelievably tired. I was carrying an armload of books and, thinking I couldn't make it across the street, I leaned up against the traffic light and tried to breathe deeply. I started crying. I looked up into the fog. "God, I love you so much. Why don't you help me to go to school? Help me, I feel like I'm just dying." The light changed, but I was too weak to move. I dropped my books and clung to the post. It was no use. Slowly I crumpled to the wet street. I remembered nothing else.

"Miss Hampton, how are you feeling? . . . Miss Hampton, can you hear me?" asked Dr. Weston.

I opened my eyes and tried to focus them. Slowly the face of a man came into view. He was wearing a green gown. I tried to swallow, but had a little difficulty; my mouth was very dry.

"Uh, can I have a drink of water please?" I said as I began to look around. I realized that I was in a hospital room. Why? Then I remembered feeling sick at the street crossing. I must have fainted. Dr. Weston handed me a glass of water with a straw, and I drank almost all of it. "I think I must have the flu or something."

The good doctor looked at me rather suspiciously. "No, I don't think you have the flu. You are a very sick young woman. When was the last time you had a decent dinner?"

"Well, I've been trying to watch my figure," I lied.

"Then I think you're taking it a little too seriously. You are suffering from mild malnutrition," he said as he pulled up a chair and sat down beside my bed.

"You're kidding . . . malnutrition?" I stared down at him in disbelief.

"That's right. Your stomach is distended and your blood count is dangerously low." He flipped through my chart.

"Oh, well, I've been working really hard and—"

"Where?" he interrupted me.

"I work at the Safeway near my school, and I work at

my business college to help pay for my education. A lot of kids do that."

"What are you studying at business college?"

"I want to be a lawyer someday," I said, feeling as if that would never happen.

He looked puzzled. "A lawyer? I didn't know that you could study for that in business college."

"I figure if I can learn to be a legal secretary or a businesswoman, then I can afford to go to night school to get my master's degree and . . ." Dream on.

"Ah, I see. So in other words, you don't have the money for your education, and that's why you have the two jobs." He sat there shaking his head and pursing his lips.

Hmmm, I didn't think that was so strange. "That's right. Didn't you once want to be a doctor?" I reminded him. "And now you are a doctor, aren't you?"

"Yes, I like taking care of people, and yes, I am a doctor. I'm doing my internship here," he said, smiling. He certainly had a pleasant enough attitude.

"Uh, Doctor, I don't have any money to pay you or the hospital for this conversation. I really can't stay here." I was beginning to think of how much all this might cost.

"Well, I'll tell you what. You're going to get a bill for this, and it's going to be a pretty good one. If you can't pay it, don't worry about it. The important thing is that we get you healthy again."

"But, that's not very fair to you."

"There are a lot of people who come in here and can't pay for their care. That's what taxes are for. So you just relax about it. One day you'll be paying a lot of taxes yourself." He laughed and so did I.

"Tell me, did you ever wonder whether you'd ever become a doctor?"

"Of course. With so much to learn, there were times when I wanted to say, 'Hell, it's not worth it.' "

"But you didn't give up?"

"No, I didn't. And someday you'll accomplish your dream. But for now, I want you to get better. And that means I want you to go home. You do have a family to take care of you?" He closed the chart.

"Yeah, but . . ." I felt so disappointed.

"You need to go home and be with people who love you. You're very sick. Maybe you don't think you are, but you are. It would be impossible for you to continue the way you've been going, with work, school, and trying to survive."

I started shaking my head and began to cry. I just couldn't give up. If I left now, I would lose everything I had worked for. I didn't want to go home defeated and lonely. All my friends were away at school, and my mother was working at the store and taking care of my stepfather day and night. He had had a leg removed and was now in a wheelchair. The thought of it all, the failure, was unbearable. Dr. Weston, sensing the depth of my depression, got up, put his hand on mine, and leaned over very close.

"I understand what you're feeling, but nothing, not even becoming a lawyer, is worth jeopardizing your health. You will never make it if you starve to death."

I just nodded.

Relieved by my nod, he continued, "Anyway, who wants to look at a skinny lawyer?"

I started laughing in spite of my misery.

"Now, Miss Hampton, if you could have anything you wanted from the best restaurant in Lubbock, what would it be?"

I was having a bit of difficulty thinking about food when my future had gone down the drain. "Oh, uh, I guess I would order a big T-bone . . . mmm, some mashed potatoes with gravy, a roll, and a gallon of milk." Suddenly, it started to sound good.

"That's it then. And if you don't mind, I'll join you. Then I want you out of here and home. Is it a deal?"

"I don't really want to go home but . . . I guess I don't have a choice."

"Good girl. I'll be right back with your entrée, madame."

I watched the door slowly close behind him, then turned over on my side and stared at the wristband with my name on it. I began to wonder why this was happening to me at all. Why had God not answered my prayers? God helps those who help themselves . . . and I obviously had done more than I could. What was God's will for me? What was I supposed to learn from all this—how to starve in three easy lessons? And what was I to gain from going back home? Oh, God, I asked, why haven't you helped me? What have I done wrong?

The dinner was wonderful—though I wasn't able to eat very much—and Dr. Weston was charming company. I knew he was going to be very successful, because he really did care about people. He had done a good job with me.

The good doctor took the tray and left me with orders to go to sleep. I did. But after a while I was awakened by a woman's laughter—not loud, but soft, muted. I thought maybe it was a nurse, but the smell . . . it was like a thousand flowers in bloom on a summer's eve. It was heavenly. I turned around and was stunned by what I saw. There, floating in front of the lavatory mirror, was a woman—the most beautiful woman I had ever seen—glowing with a light that seemed to fill the room . . . an unearthly kind of a light. She was looking at herself in the mirror and giggling. Her gleaming snow white hair had been pulled into a roll in back and came high off her forehead, spilling in deep waves on either side of her temples. She had thick eyebrows that arched rather high and ice blue eyes that twinkled like stars. Her nose was small and perfect and her teeth glowed pearly white. Her skin was golden. She was draped in a turquoise blue gown of some unbelievable fabric that seemed to have a life all its own.

But there was only half of her. From the waist down she melted into a mist. I looked at her beauty and had a strange feeling that I knew her. I also knew somehow that she was overjoyed with her own beauty. I sat up in the hospital bed and said, "You're so beautiful . . . who are you?"

Quietly she turned around, smiled a brilliant, familiar smile, and started floating over to my bed. I panicked and slid back down onto my bed. This was very strange. Although there seemed to be only half of her, I distinctly heard the swishing noise that nylons make when you walk. I heard a voice in my head say, "Judy, I've come to say good-bye. I'm so happy." Suddenly I knew that she was going to kiss me on the cheek. I don't know how I knew it, I just did. I remember turning away and throwing my right hand up, as if to say no. I heard the swishing sound stop and felt something very warm touch my hand—something that felt very much like a kiss. Whatever it was, I was terrified. Then I heard the swishing sound become faint, as if it were leaving. I turned slowly and there she was again, floating out the door. She smiled a very familiar smile and just evaporated into thin air, taking the smell of perfume with her.

I lay there dumbfounded, shaking like a leaf. I couldn't believe what I had just seen. Suddenly I remembered my hand and inspected it carefully, looking for traces of pink lipstick. There weren't any, although I knew I had felt her kiss my hand. Then I began to think about how familiar this thing had seemed. I had the feeling I knew who—or what —it was. Chills ran up and down my spine. Goose bumps were breaking out all over my body. Did I dream this? Did I dream that smell? I had never dreamed anything like this before—and I couldn't remember ever dreaming about a smell. At that moment, the door began to open slowly. I froze! I thought it was coming back. When a nurse peeked in, I slumped in relief, my heart pounding.

"Oh, I didn't mean to frighten you. You look like you've seen a ghost." Little did she know. She came over to me and commented that I looked chilled.

"Nurse, did you by any chance see, uh, anyone unusual—I mean a woman, very beautiful—in the hall just now?"

She tucked my blankets in. "No, just the usual employees. The nurse's station is right down the hall, so I know who's here and who isn't. Not much goes on during my night shift. Sometimes I wish it would. It gets a little boring. There now, do you feel warmer? Can I get you anything?"

"No, thank you, this feels much better."

"Get some sleep." She smiled and silently left.

I didn't sleep much. Troubled by my dreams, I kept waking up and looking at the mirror.

The next morning, after donating urine and blood, taking two shots, and swallowing some pills, I decided to call

Momma. She needed to know what had happened to me. I would then call Mrs. White and see if she would notify my school and Safeway and pick up my paycheck. There was a· pay phone a little ways down the hall. When I first got up, my head began to swim a little, but eventually I made my way to the pay phone down the hall. I had the operator dial, since the call was to be "collect." She said the number had been disconnected, so I had her call Mrs. Cole. We got through. Mrs. Cole accepted the call and then went to get Momma. I waited.

"Well, hello thar, Judy girl. I'm real glad you called. How's thangs goin' over thar for ya?"

"I'm in a hospital . . . nothing to worry about. Just seems I haven't been eating right. Anyway, not to worry, Momma, but the doctor says I have to come home."

"What's wrong?"

"I just told you. I'm run down . . . been working too hard, I guess."

"Oh, I see. You just come on home then. But Judy, I want ta tell ya somethin'." I had this funny feeling that I knew what she was going to say.

"What?"

"Well, I'll just come right out with it. Suzanne passed away last night in her mother's arms. I don't know all tha details, but seems she might have had a brain tumor or somethin' like that. Anyway, I wanted ta tell ya. I know'd how much you loved her."

In a way, I didn't believe what she had said. It just couldn't be true. Yet at the same time I had known it all along. The beautiful woman in my room last night had seemed so familiar because that woman was Suzanne.

"Judy, are ya there?"

"Yeah, I am. Momma, I knew she died. She appeared in my room last night. I didn't recognize her at first, with the light, the smell, the white hair. But when she smiled, I knew that was Suzanne's smile. She kissed my hand. I heard this voice in my head say good-bye, and that she was really happy. Momma, I know it sounds crazy, but I didn't dream it."

Momma hesitated, but she never said what she was

thinking. "Well, darlin', you come on home. I'll send ya a bus ticket. Your brothers is here."

A few days later as the bus pulled out of the station and passed through Lubbock, I looked back at the campus of Texas Tech University. It was so beautiful. The leaves of the trees were golden and were falling gently to the ground. Students walking, sitting, riding bicycles everywhere . . . how fortunate they were. The scene passed out of view and out of my mind.

My mind kept turning back to Suzanne and how miraculous her vision was. But why was her hair snow white, her eyes a different color? Isn't this dumb, I told myself. I mean really, to be wondering why a ghost had changed her hair and eye color. I remembered how once we had bleached her hair. She loved it, but her mother was furious. She took Suzanne to the beauty shop and had it dyed back to her natural color. . . . Wait a minute! I remembered how she had cried . . . and said she had always dreamed of having hair the color of mine!

I sat there shaken by my realization. It must be that once we die, we are transfigured in the afterlife, somehow glorified. Maybe transfiguration is all about how we see ourselves, how we want to look. That was why Suzanne was giggling in the mirror! That explained her eyes, too. She once had a crush on a guy just because she loved his ice blue eyes. "I wish I had eyes that color," she'd told me. That must be what the Bible means when it says we are transformed in a moment. It doesn't mean just that we live after death, but that we change our whole appearance, the way we longed to do in life. I felt a cold rush go up my spine. I was so happy for Suzanne. She was at last free to be as she wanted to be. And she had come back to share her happiness with me.

A slumber party during our senior year suddenly came to mind. We had made a pact: whoever kicked the can first would come back and let the others know if there were slumber parties in heaven. . . . Cold chills again! My eyes started burning with hot tears. Suzanne had kept her promise. Something I had forgotten all about . . . but she hadn't. Life did exist after death and seemingly a more joyful one. Suzanne was at peace in a magnificent, serene way that I did not know. I wondered if she was looking into the face of God or just getting ready for a heavenly slumber party. I leaned my face against the bus window and started laughing and crying at the same time. I wished in my soul that I could be with her, so great was my love and my grief.

Some nights later I was sitting around the supper table with Momma, Loy, and Gayle. Daddy Bill was already in bed. As I picked away at my food, feeling depressed and out of it, I heard the conversation at the table begin to change.

"Well, sir," Momma said, "in my dreams I can always tell who's fixin' ta die in the family . . . an so far it's always happened." She picked up her napkin and wiped her hands.

"Hell," Gayle added, "I dreamed the smoke was a-pourin' outta the barn up thar and next day the dang thang caught on fire."

"But Suzanne wasn't a dream," I told them. "She was actually in my room." I was a little put out that everyone seemed to think I had dreamed this.

"I know, I know what you're a-sayin'," Momma reassured me. "I feel a presence with me most of ma life. I don't know what it is, but of course faith is one thang I never faulted on, no sir."

Loy looked around the table and then at me. "I never told anybody this, but one night after a baseball practice, I was feelin' really low and some kind of cool hand pressed me on my brow. It made me feel better. It was when I was lying down in my room there. I mean, I know it was real."

Momma adjusted her glasses, sat her elbow on the table, and took a fork of food with the other hand. "We've had a lot of them thangs in my family. Wanda says she sees some kind of powerful figure in her kitchen from time ta time. The figure told her not to cuss people out so much. But ya know Wanda, she did anyway for a long time. An when her son Sudsy died, a bright light came into her room just like Suzanne came into Judy's room."

"Ya know, a lotta people are seein' them UFOs around this territory," Gayle put in. "I seen two of them dudes myself . . . big suckers. Remember that football game where seven thousand people saw one of them thangs over in East

Texas? Papers were full of it. Then the Air Force said it was nothin' but a weather balloon. That's crap! Ain't no weather balloon look like that. I mean, that sucker was lit up real bright and it flashed on and off." I stared at Gayle. Hmmm, this sounded very familiar—at least, that's what poor Ezekiel and I would think.

"Well, the mysteries of the universe is gettin' stronger an stronger," Momma answered. "Even them astronauts say there's a hole or somethin' at the North Pole. So maybe they're comin' from that hole." She sat there studying what she'd said, and so did I.

"Yeah, I heard about them flittin' and flyin'; they say one of them carried a man off for three days and he come back in a telephone booth. A lumberman working up in Williams, Arizona. The government put him through so many dadgum tests with lie detectors and all and he was tellin' tha truth. They say they're experimental military things, but I don't believe it," Loy said, reaching for the pumpkin pie.

I remembered what Mr. Stanhope had said about the Air Force investigations. And I remembered a quote from a book I read at school—something like, "the army is a nation within the nation: it is a vice of our time." I wondered if that author had had a similar experience.

"Gayle," Momma said, interrupting my thoughts, "go take Daddy Bill some coffee an a piece of that pie."

"That's okay, Momma, I'll do it. Then I think I'll call it a night. I'm really tired." Listlessly I got up and left the table.

The next morning, Momma asked me to pull some weeds in the front yard. She said it was good therapy, the sunshine would cheer me up. While I was working, a car pulled up at the curb. It was Caris Hensley, a boy I knew from high school. I didn't go over to talk. I just stayed where I was.

"Oh, hi, Caris."

"Hi, Judy. I'm surprised to see you home from school," he said, his arm wrapped around the steering wheel.

"Yeah, I'm home for a while."

"Tough, eh?"

"Not really, I did real well. I got mostly A's."

"Then why ain't you still in school?"

"Oh, I sort of got real sick so I took a break." God, some people are the nosiest!

"Hey, cut your hair?"

"Yeah, too much."

"You always had such beautiful hair, but this looks cute."

"Thanks." I was hoping he would drive off.

"And I always loved your nose . . . looked like a ski jump ta me."

I smiled. "Caris, did you ever go back to school after you dropped out?"

"Na, my daddy needed my help down at the fillin' station."

"Don't you think that's a cop-out?"

"No, you know my daddy didn't have no money."

"C'mon, Caris. I know what you were doing. You had that hot car, so if you worked at the fillin' station, you could keep it gassed up and pretty so you could go out and party, huh?"

"Yeah, that's about it." He hung his head a little. I think I shamed him into the truth.

"Hey, I'm a dropout too. So?"

"God, I thought you'd be back at Princeton or someplace like that!" He was genuinely surprised.

"Princeton? Where did you hear about Princeton?"

"Well, it's one of them hip colleges. I always thought you'd marry somebody like a senator or maybe even a president."

I started laughing. "A president? Oh, my you've been smelling that gas too much."

"Well, why not? You're as pretty as Jackie Kennedy."

I shook my head. Where did people get this stuff? "So, you thought I'd marry a senator?"

"Yeah, I always thought you'd end up living in Philadelphia or Paris or somewheres like that."

"Hardly. Lubbock, Texas, is a little far from Philadelphia or Paris." At that moment, I even felt sad about not going to Philadelphia.

"Hey, you like root beer?"

"I hate root beer . . . any kind of beer!"

"Well, ya gotta like Cokes."

"Yeah."

"Then would ya let me buy ya a Coke?"

I wasn't interested in going anywhere . . . but, stupidly, I went anyway.

We were cruising along with the windows open and the Beatles singing on the radio when we drove past Mike Phipps's house.

"Did you ever hear from Mike Phipps when you were away at school?"

"No, I never did." Why did he have to bring up Mike?

"He was a great football player."

"Yeah, he was a great football player." What else could I say?

"Do ya still like ta dance? I used to love to watch you dance."

"I haven't done it in a while. I dunno if I do or not."

"Would you like to go dancin' with me sometime?"

I did not want to go anywhere with him or anyone like him. All he knew was how to have a good time. I didn't feel like kicking my heels up with someone who couldn't give a damn about his education. Not my style!

"No, I don't think so. I have other things to do with my spare time, Caris, but thanks anyway."

"How about the football game on Friday night?" Jesus, I thought, this guy doesn't give up. I gave him one of those stares that says, "Can't you take a hint, buster?"

"Hey, are you sure you didn't hear from Mike Phipps?"

Give me a break, sucker. "I'm sure."

"Whatever happened to you guys, anyway?"

I braced myself, trying to remember I was a lady, and answered through my teeth. "We just broke up. It was for the best."

"Did you love Mike Phipps?"

That did it! I turned toward him and yelled, "Caris, don't you think that's kind of a presumptuous question?"

"I'm sorry . . . wanna go to a show?"

"*No!*" I yelled, losing my cool altogether. "*I don't wanna go to a show. And yes, I loved Phipps!*"

"Do you still love him?"

I gave up. "I don't know. I just wonder what he's doing, but I don't really want to know. Makes a lot of sense, huh?"

"He's a great football player."

As Caris drove me home, he kept gawking at me. "I'm so lucky. I mean, I never thought I would ever see ya again. This was my lucky day."

"Yeah, well, I'm really tired. Thanks for the Coke. See ya."

I had washed my hair and was drying it in the sun by the willow tree when I heard the phone ring inside. Momma had it hooked up again "in case of an emergency."

"Caris Hensley is on the phone," Momma called out to me.

"He is?" I stopped drying my hair.

"Yeah. Is that the little Hensley boy whose daddy runs the fillin' station down yonder?"

"Yes, Momma, that's the one."

"Well, why are ya talkin' to him for?"

"I don't know, Momma. He's a nice person . . . harmless."

"Well, you better go talk ta him, he's a-waitin'."

"Hi."

"Hi, Judy, what's going on?"

"What's going on is that I'm drying my hair. You sound so far away."

" 'Cause I'm callin' you from Lovington. That's where I live now."

"Oh, I didn't know you moved from here."

"Yeah, my daddy and mom have a fillin' station over here. Listen, I'm gonna be comin' over this weekend. Ya wanna go to a show or somethin'?"

"What show?"

"I don't know . . . maybe the drive-in."

"Oh, ya mean the passion pit?"

"The passion pit?"

"Yeah, it's a joke, Caris."

"Well, we could go to the Lampen. I'll see what's playing."

I hesitated. Well, why not? "Okay, Friday night, about seven o'clock."

"I'll be there." Click, buzz.

On Friday night at seven sharp, the doorbell rang. I came to the door dressed in Levis, a windbreaker, and my white Western boots, and carrying my .22 rifle. I opened the door and there was Caris in a starched shirt and a tie. His newly waxed car gleamed as it sat waiting. Caris seemed a little unprepared for meeting a gun at the door.

"Why are you holdin' that?" His voice was edged with panic.

"Caris, have you ever shot a jackrabbit?"

"I've never shot a thing in my life."

"Well, every young man should experience it once. C'mon, I'll show you how."

Caris, who had been dressed to the nines, thinking about how much fun he was going to have with me at the movies, found himself instead driving his choice '55 metallic blue Chevy two-door down a long stretch of desolate road. Instead of holding his hand and demurely sipping my Coke, I was hanging out the window with my .22, feeling some of the energy of my high school days flood back into my mind.

"Now, Caris, you keep an eye out for those turquoise eyes." It felt strange to be with a guy who didn't know the first thing about hunting.

Caris leaned forward and loosened his tie. Suddenly, *bam!* I shot a jack. I must have scared Caris because the car jerked in response.

"Got him. Caris, turn around and go back about two hundred feet. I know where that sucker is."

I got out of the car and picked up the rabbit. Caris didn't budge from the safety of his cockpit.

"You want to see where I shot that jack?" I held up the rabbit. Caris didn't even want to look.

"Yeah, I see . . . good shoot." I think he was trying to keep from throwing up. "Listen, there are lots of them in that mesquite and cactus over there. C'mon. Rev up the car and head off across that way through the desert."

I hadn't thought about what the brush and cactus would do to his paint job, and I think he was afraid to say no. He turned his car into the field, kicking up a storm of dust around it. I hung out of the car and shot, loaded, and shot again.

"God, girl. I heard about you and this stuff, but I thought it was just stories."

"Well, it was true."

"Did you shoot better than Phipps?"

"Sometimes."

"So when I'd see Phipps's car out here on the country roads, you two wasn't . . . in it?"

I turned and looked at him for a moment, the wind blowing my hair over my face. "No, Caris, we were out shootin' jackrabbits . . . both of us."

"Well, I'll be damned."

I slid back down into the seat. It wasn't fun anymore. Nothing was. I asked him to take me home.

After a long, silent drive home, Caris walked me to the front door. I turned and looked at the dirt all over his car.

"Hey, look, I'm real sorry about your car, Caris. How's about I make it up to you by teaching you to shoot? Would you like that?"

"Surely would."

"Well, I tell you what. You pick me up at about three-thirty tomorrow and drive me over to Hobbs. I'll show you there." He looked a little puzzled.

"Why not here?" he said, wiping dust from his eye.

" 'Cause I don't wanna see anybody here. I feel out of place. It's just not where I want to be, that's all."

I went through the same teaching process with Caris that I had gone through with Phipps, only this time I was the teacher and Caris was having a wonderful time learning. As I hiked the gun up to his cheek and showed him how to line up the sight, I confessed to him.

"I had to pretend with Mike that I didn't know how to shoot. I thought it would turn him off. You know, I needed to impress him with my femininity. But not with you. All I have to do to impress you is just be myself."

He aimed and fired, and hit the bottle. "Good, Caris. Pretty soon you'll be able to get a bird flyin' or a lizard runnin'."

"God, woman, you are good." We laughed.

Over the next couple of weeks we went to movies, on picnics, and out shooting together. I enjoyed his company and his friendship. But that was all. We never made out— or even kissed. I appreciated that, too. I think I would have gotten turned off if that had started.

One night we were at the drive-in, and Caris brought back some hot dogs and Cokes to the car. He settled in. The film hadn't started yet.

"Judy, can I ask you something?"

I had been slumped down in the seat on the passenger side. "Sure."

"I've loved you for so long. I mean, I used to come to the football games just to see you. I used to watch you walk home from school with Phipps and think he was the luckiest guy in the world. And now I'm sittin' in this drive-in with you and I can't believe it!"

"Why do you say that?"

"Because I didn't finish school. I didn't play football. I wasn't popular. I wasn't in with the group. So I'm so surprised you're willing to be here . . . with me."

I looked at him and suddenly felt very sorry for him. In so many ways, I was feeling the same things about myself. "I'm really flattered, Caris, but I think you're wrong. Everyone liked you. Really. We just didn't see much of you, that's all."

"Yeah, but you always belonged to what was happening."

"Want to know something? I never really felt I belonged. I always felt lonely. Sounds crazy, but I did. As much as I loved Phipps, and even though we were close, I could never open up to him. I guess I was afraid he might criticize me. I grew up being criticized. For the most part, I really didn't open up to my friends either. I think when a person feels that they can't talk—I mean really talk—they kind of walk around like a time bomb. I had a lot of friends but I still felt totally alone. Maybe if I had been more open, like I'm being with you, maybe things would have been different. Oh well, you can't change the past."

"Can I ask you something?" he said nervously.

"Sure."

"What are you gonna do with your life?"

"Well, I used to think I wanted to grow up, get married, have babies."

"Why did you go to college, then?"

"Because what I really want is to be a lawyer."

"How could you do both?"

"Why not? I would have made an excellent lawyer. I would make an excellent wife and mother."

"Well, would you like to get married . . . to me?"

I was definitely caught off guard with that one. I couldn't believe he would ask me such a stupid question. "Wait a minute!"

"Hey, I don't have anything, but I'd work my ass off for you. I'd put you through school myself. I'd give you everything you ever wanted. So, would you marry me?"

I just stared at him in disbelief. "Caris, I'm not ready to get married. I mean, I'm flattered, but I don't love you. Someday I want to marry someone I love."

"But you just said that you would make an excellent wife and mother."

"Yes, I did. I also said I would make an excellent lawyer, too. Didn't you hear me? I don't love you. I like you, but . . ."

"What else are you gonna do?" he persisted. "You don't want to be in Artesia anymore. So come and live with me in Lovington. You'd be real proud of me. I'd work hard. I'd take care of you and help you go to school. I know you don't love me now, but in time you would learn to love me. It's worth the wait."

I actually found myself considering his proposal. "But what about you? Your education?"

"It don't take a lot to pump gas."

"But it takes an education to run a business."

"Well, my daddy didn't go to school, and he runs his business."

"But don't you want to be something . . . professionally?"

"I want to marry you. And I want to have a brick home and my own gas station. And I want to be happy."

I could not believe that I was having this conversation. The movie had started, but we hadn't even placed the speaker on the window.

"Listen, I know you don't love me . . . but you would learn to, I know it."

"How do you know that?"

"Because, I just know you would. Just give me a chance."

"Caris, have you ever thought that love is just a state of mind? I mean you've talked yourself into this, and now you're trying to convince me, logically, that I will feel the same."

"A what?"

"You know, love is a good topic to write songs about. A good topic to see movies about, like *Splendor in the Grass*. But how do we know it exists? I mean, how do you really know you love me?"

"I just know. Every girl I ever went out with I pretended it was you."

"But don't you see that was something you were making up in your mind? I mean, I was just a fantasy. It's like with movie stars. We convince ourselves we're infatuated with a person, especially if they're forbidden. The more they are forbidden, the more we love 'em. Or we think we do. That's why it's a state of mind."

"Well, Judy, if love is a state of mind to you, then you don't believe in love anyway. So that makes me the best choice around."

I looked at him quietly, showing no emotion. I said that I would marry him . . . that night! Strange, huh? I think we all do a lot of things out of desperation . . . maddening things, on the spur of the moment. We convince ourselves that anything would be better than what we have at the present. My spontaneity was my means of running away again, pulling the rug out from under myself again and doing it in a hurry before I could change my mind.

We left that very night and went to Juarez, Mexico and were married. Then we drove all the way back to Artesia so I could tell my mother the following morning. She was peeling potatoes casually and listened to my news as though she were hearing a weather report. "Why Caris Hensley?"

I couldn't answer her. My face became hot with a deep-ening blush. I was ashamed.

Mother finished peeling the potatoes and put down her knife. She wiped her hands on her apron.

Mother thought I had married beneath me, but all she said was, "C'mon, let's root out your hope chest. You've got some things you'll be a-needin'."

When we announced to Caris's family in Lovington what we had done, they were tickled pink. "Ya got tha prettiest girl in New Mexico," his father said. I was having some difficulty getting excited. I lied a lot.

Gushing with joy, his parents invited us to spend our first full night as a married couple at their house. Caris quickly declined and, in a matter of hours, we found a little white cottage nearby, edged with tall thick lilac bushes. It was quite charming. I immediately threw myself into domesticity, but while making the bed, Caris tried to kiss me. I couldn't get into it. Then he tried to unbutton my blouse. I rebuttoned it.

"But it's our honeymoon." Shit, now what was my ex-cuse going to be? Let's be just friends? It was our wedding night, the first time we would be together intimately. I went to the bathroom, taking my nightgown with me. Caris had turned on a transistor radio that was now playing "Moon River," my all-time favorite. I started brushing my teeth more thoroughly than was really necessary. Trying not to think of what was waiting for me, I put on my powder blue gown and dried my mouth. Suddenly I heard Elvis singing "Sus-picious Minds," a song that Mike and I used to like a lot. I looked at myself in the bathroom mirror, but all I saw was Mike's face . . . the way he made love to me the first time and how tender and patient and loving he was. I was starting to feel sick, trapped.

"Hey, honey, are you all right?"

"Sure, Caris, just getting my teeth nice and clean. Be out in a minute." I couldn't allow myself to think of Mike anymore, but I couldn't open the bathroom door.

"If you don't come out right now, I'm gonna break the door down. I know somethin's wrong."

"No, I'm fine."

I finally opened the door. Caris was standing there in his shorts. He stared at me.

"How beautiful you look . . . c'mon here." He led me to the bed, and we lay down together. He began to kiss me, and I tried to respond. He kept licking his lips and I had the distinct feeling that I appeared to be a soufflé covered in mounds of delicious mayonnaise and ketchup, his idea of bon appetit fare. He pulled down a strap of my gown, I put it back up.

"Hey, we're married now. I love you. I want you. I've always wanted you. Now you're mine." Feeling sick, I submitted.

The following morning we were still asleep when Caris's mother came barging into the bedroom and pulled the covers off of us, just like that.

"Caris Hensley, you got to get up and go to work. Your daddy's waitin' for you."

I sat up in bed, dumbfounded, scrambling for some covers. His mother turned around and walked out, and Caris, like a little boy, scrambled out of bed to the bathroom. I was still in a state of shock, marveling at the brazenness of that woman.

That afternoon, I cooked my first supper for my husband—barbecued chicken, mashed potatoes, and sweet peas with slivered almonds. I had picked a lovely spray of lilacs and put them in a fruit jar in the center of the table. Caris's parents came over and were surveying what I had cooked. I asked them to join us but they refused.

"Well, well, Judy. Caris has himself a fancy cook," said Mrs. Hensley as she tasted the chicken.

"No, it's nothing," I answered, turning to Mrs. Hensley. To my amazement, she was licking barbecue sauce from the chicken and making slurping and smacking noises. I faked a smile and continued. "I'm actually a really good cook. My mother taught me, and I did some of my own improvements."

"Ya know, Judy, Caris used to come home and cry and cry because he loved you so much. We didn't know what ta do with him," Mr. Hensley said. "And now look here. He's gone and married the prettiest girl and the best cook in Artesia."

A feeling of guilt came over me, and for a moment I wanted to run away. I chewed my bottom lip and felt more guilty for even thinking of such a selfish act. After all, I had made Caris and his parents very happy. The Good Book says that it's better to give than to receive. Well, I was giving and I sure hoped that I would start feeling better.

"Well . . ." I began, not sure what I would say, when Caris walked in, said hi to everybody, kissed me on the cheek, and sat down to the dinner he expected to be ready for him.

"Yummmm. This looks fit for some king, Judy. Ya got some mayonnaise?"

"We have mayonnaise, yes." What a peculiar question.

"Well, then, let's have it," he said with a slight hint of demand.

I went to the refrigerator. . . .

"And some ketchup too, please, hon."

"Ketchup?" I didn't think that I had made hot dogs.

Mr. and Mrs. Hensley watched as I placed the jars of mayonnaise and ketchup on the table. They smiled at each other. Food wasn't food without these sauces. Caris scooped out a huge spoonful of mayonnaise and plopped it on the barbecued chicken even before he tasted it. My lilacs also received a generous helping from the splatter. Then he poured about a cup of ketchup over everything. I stared at what he was doing in utter disbelief! Mr. and Mrs. Hensley made "Yummmming" sounds, and Mr. Hensley patted his dear son on the back in approval as Caris dug in.

"This is really good, Jude."

"How can you tell?" I gently snapped.

"How can ya miss? You're the best little wife around."

I went to the sink and started cleaning up. I had lost my appetite.

Later that evening when we were alone, Caris sat on the bed, waiting for me to come out of the bathroom. He had taken off his dirty overalls, greasy boots, socks, and underwear and had strewn them everywhere.

"C'mon, Judy, open up that door. I don't believe there should be no closed doors between husband and wife. We're one person now. There shouldn't be no privacy between us."

I sighed deeply, resenting having to go to bed with him. When I finally opened the bathroom door, I saw his dirty clothes all over. And those boots, why couldn't they have been left on the back doorstep? He had tracked grease all over the floors.

"Caris, why don't you pick up after yourself?"

"Because that's your job. Working hard all day is mine." He walked into the bathroom, and I began picking up his dirty clothes. I happened to glance into the bathroom and saw Caris squatting on the seat, like someone would on a rock or something.

"What's wrong, Caris?" I was shocked. I thought he might be sick. I'd never seen anyone who went to the bathroom like that. Then again, I had never made it a point to study the excretory patterns of *any* species. He acted surprised at my question.

"Ain't nothin' wrong."

"Well, what are you doing?"

"I'm taking a dump."

My mouth fell open. "But why are you doing it like that?"

"I always did it like this."

I turned away in disbelief, whispering to myself, "Oh, my God."

Later that evening, Mr. Weird Dump wanted to make love. Well, I just couldn't get into it. I mean, after all, I couldn't stop thinking about his Neanderthal behavior in the bathroom.

"Please, Caris. I don't feel like it. For heaven's sake, you never give me a chance to feel like it." I tried to roll over.

"Hey, it's not your duty not to want to. I work hard all day, and when I come home at night I expect to be able to love my woman." He leaned up on his elbow, turned me over, and looked down at me. "Do you know how much I love you? I still can't hardly believe this is true." He kissed me on the neck. "So please, let me love you . . . you're my woman now."

I tried to be sensitive. "Okay, but just know, please, that I don't feel like it right now."

"That don't matter to me. I love you anyway, my beautiful wife."

I sighed, submitted, and tried to think of other things.

A month later I was cooking bacon and eggs, but I was having a rough time with the smells. I almost swooned with nausea.

Caris came walking into the kitchen, expecting to have his breakfast on time. "What's wrong? How come the food isn't ready?"

"I'm sorry," I said, wiping my forehead. "I don't know, I just feel real sick. I'll finish off your breakfast." I tried to put the eggs on his plate, but I felt like I was going to throw up, so I ran into the bathroom. Just in time, too. Caris came in and said he would send his mother over. I was lying on the floor trying to keep from moving.

Mrs. Hensley came over later that morning and asked me how long this had been going on. She was the first to figure out the truth. I was pregnant.

"I'm taking you in to see my doctor," she insisted.

Later that same day, I found myself sitting on an examining table with my clothes on. A nurse was taking my medical history. When she finished, she casually requested, "Just take your clothes off and put on that white robe with the opening in the back." The nurse then started for the door.

"What do you mean, take my clothes off? Why do I have to do that?" I did not like the sound of this.

The nurse stopped, then realized that there might be a problem. She was very sweet. "Well, Mrs. Hensley, so the doctor can give you a vaginal examination."

"What's that?"

"You've never been examined by a gynecologist before?"

"No."

"Well, I see. It's a very simple procedure. You just lie on your back. You will be covered with a sheet. You put your feet in these stirrups, so Dr. Quigley can determine if you're pregnant."

"I don't want to do this," I pleaded.

"All right, dear, just wait here a moment."

I tried to calm myself. The door opened and Dr. Quigley walked in. "Now, Mrs. Hensley how are you feeling?" he asked.

"I don't feel so good. But I don't want to have this examination."

"You've never had a gynecological examination before?"

"No, I told the nurse I hadn't. And I still don't want one." I felt hot tears welling up in my eyes.

Dr. Quigley said patiently, "Believe me, I see women every day."

"But I don't see you every day."

"I just need to see if your uterus is swollen. And from that we can determine if you're pregnant and if so, how far along you are."

"But, I don't want this. I can't feel comfortable while I'm lying on this table and you're looking between my legs."

Dr. Quigley began to realize just how traumatic this was for me. "Wait one moment." He left the room and went to consult with Mrs. Hensley.

Moments later, Mrs. Hensley gently opened the door and came in to see me, a smile on her face. "Honey, would you feel better if I stayed in here and held your hand? I've been through so many of these. It's too bad they don't make women doctors, but they don't."

"But, Mrs. Hensley, I don't want to go through with this. I mean, if I'm pregnant, I'm pregnant. That's just the way it is."

"But, honey, it would be better for my little grandbaby if we could see how it's doing. Think of my grandbaby in there. Don't you want the best for it? Come on now, let me help you off with your clothes and I'll hold your hand. It'll all be over in a jiffy."

I reluctantly obeyed.

"Well, Judy, I'd say you're about one and a half months pregnant and everything looks fine," Dr. Quigley announced after his examination.

"Praise tha Lord! I'm really gonna have a grandbaby.

Judy, did you hear that?" Mrs. Hensley was jubilant. I was still so overwhelmed by my "show all" experience that all I felt was ashamed.

In the following eight months of my pregnancy, I had morning, noon, and nighttime sickness. I had only two maternity outfits that I tried to wash daily in Tide. It was also my shampoo. I had very little money. Caris only gave me twenty-five dollars a week for groceries and demanded a T-bone steak twice a week for himself and three square meals a day. He claimed he deserved it because he worked so hard. I never had a T-bone. Those were his. I also never had any spending money. Once, when my sister Wanda came to visit me, I had a craving for a hot-fudge sundae. I asked Caris for fifty cents to buy one, but he refused, claiming it was a waste of money. My sister got very upset and told him off. Terrified of my feisty sister, he slinked out the back door and Wanda treated me to the sundae. My days were spent throwing up, cleaning my little house, doing Caris's laundry, and cooking his meals. Caris would come home, throw his clothes everywhere, expect supper on the table, pour mayonnaise and ketchup all over everything, while I continued to throw up in the bathroom.

My labor came and off to the hospital I went.

"This baby is not positioned correctly. When did the water break?" Dr. Quigley asked.

"What do you mean?" I asked, totally perplexed. I must explain here that as little as I knew about the facts of life, I knew even less about my pregnancy. All that I had been told was "nature will take its course." Obviously, there was a lot that I didn't know about "nature."

"Well, before you came in here, did you experience any water gushing out of you?" Dr. Quigley rephrased his question.

"No, Doctor, I didn't have anything like that," I replied, feeling guilty that this hadn't happened to me.

Dr. Quigley left the room to consult with Momma and Mrs. Hensley, who had rushed to the hospital. When he returned, he told me, "Judy, I think it's time we gave you a saddle-block injection. It won't hurt. I need to go in and turn the baby."

"Whatever you say, Dr. Quigley. I just want the pain to stop."

Dr. Quigley gave me the saddle block.

"Can I go to sleep?" I was exhausted.

"You can do whatever you want, Judy."

I dreamily woke to see Dr. Quigley holding a baby over me. "Judy, I want to introduce you to a beautiful baby boy who just pissed all over me. He just couldn't wait. All this was taking too long."

I tried to focus my eyes. "Is he all right?" I asked drowsily.

"Well, I was afraid he might have a head like a football because of the forceps, but look, not a mark on him." I looked up at him. The baby was calm and beautiful.

"Can I hold him?"

Dr. Quigley handed me my baby. When I looked down upon his little face, I felt alive for the first time in months. Since my marriage, I had found myself waking up every morning wishing I could go back to sleep and never wake up. Even during my pregnancy, I was too depressed to feel any strong emotion toward the small life that was thriving inside of me. But the moment that I held that small bundle of life, I once again felt that there was a purpose to my being. In a few seconds, my world had changed. I cuddled the baby and, without any shyness, opened my gown and began to nurse.

The piped in music began to play. I recognized the song, "Brandy Leave Me Alone." I looked down at my baby boy. You know what? I'm going to call you Brandy. "Do you like that name?" He just continued to nurse, moving his tiny fingers. Caris and Mr. and Mrs. Hensley had assumed that I would name him after Caris and Mr. Hensley. No way!

When I came home from the hospital, my whole life was chaotic. Everyone started coming over. Mr. and Mrs. Hensley would dote for hours over Brandy, claiming different parts of him that they had contributed. Momma would just brag about how all her grandchildren were beautiful. It ran in the family. Meanwhile, I was totally left out of the picture, and so was Brandy. His little features weren't ever his own!

Caris was becoming increasingly possessive of me. I didn't

look like a typical mother, and that made him jealous. His friends would come by the gas station and tell him, "You got the prettiest old lady in town," and he would come fuming home different hours of the day to check up on me. I wasn't allowed to go anywhere alone except to play Bingo on Friday nights.

Because I was always at home, I expressed my creativity through my immediate surroundings and began growing flowers as a hobby. Momma gave me a beautiful hybrid pink rose bush and told me to plant it in the front yard, since it would get the morning sun and the shade in late afternoon. I would spend hours tending to my lawn and flowers while Brandy played gleefully in his playpen.

One morning I got up early and fixed breakfast for Caris. I wanted to get all that out of the way because I had a large bud on the rose bush and I knew it would start to bloom that morning. Out I went in my pink robe, my face scrubbed and my long hair hanging loose down my back. I was so happy; my rose was opening up to the early-morning sun.

"Git in the house. You ain't dressed ta go outside," Caris yelled from the screen door.

"Look at my rose. It's about to bloom," I called back, trying to ignore his overbearing tone.

"I said, git in the house. Look at you with your robe on. Whatta ya trying ta do, get a pickup by some dick?" Oh, I hated him when he got like that.

I went back into the house feeling ashamed and dirty and disappointed. Caris watched me with an indignant glare. As he left, he chastised and cursed me some more while I cowered, feeling as if I deserved it. Then I got dressed and went back out to my rose. "You know what I'm going to do with you, little rose? I'm going to enter you in a flower show. You are so beautiful, I know you'll win—and besides, I want the whole world to see you."

That afternoon over lunch, Caris said he had a surprise for me.

"What is it?" I was touched that he would do such a thing.

"Momma has a real good hairdresser. How would you like her to style your hair?"

"Oh, that's very sweet, but I don't really care to. I like my hair the way it is."

"But my momma says you should really have your hair more styled. She already made the appointment for you."

I felt a little annoyed. They hadn't even asked if I wanted to get my hair fixed.

"Tomorrow morning. I'll take you down myself."

"But I can't. I'm taking my rose to the flower show tomorrow. I know it's going to win. It's—"

"So, it's a pretty rose, eh? You would disappoint my momma, who's gone to all that trouble just to do something nice for you?" He started clenching his jaws.

"What will they do to my hair?"

"Oh, probably just trim it or something. I'd like to see it shorter."

"Shorter? I thought you always loved my hair long!"

"Yeah, but that was a long time ago. I'd like ta see it like my momma's hair. She said you're a married woman and a mother now, an' you shouldn't be havin' to worry about your hair. It takes so much of your time."

Look like his mother? Well, I wasn't fifty years old, and I didn't want to look fifty years old. My hair was beautiful, and it didn't take that much time. And why should he care? I didn't have that much to do in my spare time but grow roses.

"Caris, don't you want to come to the flower show and maybe see my rose win?"

"I don't give a damn about your rose. I do give a damn about your hair!"

He threw down his fork. "I said you're coming to the hair stylist. Not another damn word about it!"

I didn't say anything. I didn't want Brandy to start crying.

Later that afternoon I had supper on the table, but Caris was late, so I went out to water my rose. I heard him come home. He peeled off his dirty clothes and boots and left them on the living room carpet, then looked outside and saw me watering my rose. "Hey, I'm home!"

I rushed in and could smell the booze right away. He sat down and began to go through his ritual of eating while Brandy played up against his knee.

"Caris, how come you've been drinking?" I stood by the stove.

He pushed Brandy down onto the floor, dropped his fork in his mayonnaise, and turned to glare at me. "Me and a bunch of other married guys work damn hard. Damn hard. So we stopped off and had a coupla beers. What the hell is wrong with that?"

"I was just wondering. . . ." I bent over to pick up Brandy.

"What the hell do you do here all day?" I was taken aback by his rudeness.

"I clean the house, do the laundry, make sure all your clothes are ironed and hanging in the closet, make your supper, and take care of Brandy."

"Shit, that's easy. I work hard all day long. I need to get out and be with the guys. You can plop your ass on the couch anytime ya want to and watch television. Shit, that ain't work." There was more than anger in his voice. There was hatred. I didn't understand what was going on.

"Caris, I don't watch television."

"Then what the hell did we buy the fuckin' thing for?"

Brandy began to cry at the tone of his father's voice. Caris got up and took Brandy from me and put him back on the floor, but I picked him right back up and carried him into the bedroom to his crib. I played with the bird mobile over his head and soothed him before returning to the kitchen.

"I have made up my mind," I said. "I don't want to go to the beauty parlor tomorrow."

"All you want to do is take that damn rose to some damn show."

"It's not a *damn* rose. And it's not a *damn* show. Don't you like that there's a beautiful rose out there growing?"

"I don't care about that fuckin' rose." He jumped up from the table and out the door, ripped the rose bush out of the ground, and returned to throw his "kill" on the table. I just stood there looking down at the rose and at all the dirt that had fallen off its roots onto the table and floor. Caris wheeled around and headed for the bathroom. I was numb. I couldn't even cry. I felt like that rose.

I ended up letting Caris take me to the beauty salon. I

would do anything to try to keep peace in the family, so I put myself into the hairdresser's hands. She assured me that I would love my hair when she finished and not to worry.

Two hours later, when I was handed a mirror to look at the back of my hair, I declined. My hair had been cut and styled into a matronly bubble. What's more, it had been dyed black. I looked ten years older and just like Mrs. Hensley! I wanted to cry, hit someone . . . anything. Instead, I solemnly thanked the hairdresser and got up to leave. Caris was waiting for me in the car.

"That's more like it. Now you look beautiful." I got in the car and sat down silently. I was trying to control my fury.

"Caris, I want you to know that I understand why you had this done to me. You want me to look old and just like your mother because you are a jealous man and can't stand it if someone looks at me, not even box boys at the grocery store. Now, no one will look at me, and that makes you happy, doesn't it? I let this awful thing happen to me just to keep us from fighting; it's so upsetting to Brandy. But I swear, I'll never forgive you for this, never!" I turned away and leaned my head on the window. I hated my life.

It took a few months for my hair to grow out, and I looked like a zebra, blond roots and black ends. Brandy was walking now, and he filled my days with joy. Caris was coming home later and later. I had a feeling that he was fooling around on me, but I also felt guilty for having such suspicions, so I tried to ignore them. One day, Brandy was running a fever and I called Caris at work to ask if I could take him to the doctor. He said to go ahead, but there was a lack of concern in his voice.

After a long wait in the doctor's waiting room, it turned out Brandy had the flu. The doctor gave me a prescription to fill.

Blowing snow from a sudden storm made driving home from the pharmacy extremely difficult. Finally I pulled up and noticed a car sitting in the driveway, thickly dusted with snow. I had never seen it before and thought it might be one of Caris's friends. I bundled Brandy up and walked up to the door, the snow whirling around me. As I opened the

front door, a strong gust of wind came screaming from behind me and blew the door out of my hands, crashing it
against the wall. Snow and ice flew into the living room. The
two people seated on the couch jumped up in alarm while
the wind blew stinging bits of ice on their faces. To my
amazement, it was Caris with a woman I did not recognize.
She jumped up, grabbed her coat, made some excuse, and
hastily disappeared out into the storm. I was still standing
in the doorway as she whizzed by.

Calmly, I turned and closed the door, then faced Caris.
He told me it was the Avon lady, and he was ordering some
makeup for me. I just stared at him. The snow was dripping
from his hair and face, but he made no effort to wipe it off.

I put Brandy in his crib, called my mother to come after
me, and then began packing Brandy's things into a brown
paper bag. I didn't say a thing to Caris, and he didn't to me.
He was so terrified of my mother and brothers that he just
got up and left.

Momma, driving down our street, spotted Caris sitting
in his car with a woman. She slowed down, thinking I was
in the car, but the woman had black hair. So she drove by
quickly. When she knocked on the door, I was so happy to
see her that I clung to her for several minutes.

"Girl, if I was you, I would beat tha hell outta him. I'd
just up an smash his sorry face in. Wouldn't make him no
sorrier than he already is. He's just a sorry man, Judy."

The storm howled and the little house creaked and
groaned from the onslaughts of winds that hit it. A shiver
ran through my body, one of relief, not cold. "It doesn't
matter, Momma. I'm leaving him anyway. I'm really tired of
my life."

Two weeks passed and every day I thanked God I was
back home. A January sun shone brilliantly through the windows, bathing the houseplants with warm light. Smells of
fresh-brewed coffee, a baking peach cobbler, and furniture
wax filled my mother's house. Momma was teaching me how
to cut a pattern to make me some clothes. Brandy was playing
under the table with a ball that Momma had bought him.

"Momma, how did you do it all? I mean, how did you

raise all of us with such sorry men around?" I leaned back and sighed.

"Well, ya see, I had ta be the man an the woman. I saw one of my children die, an I seen the rest try ta live. I've been a farmhand, a waitress, a seamstress, an a nurse. I done everythang—even what a man should have been a-doin'. Men has too many rabbits' feet in their souls ta stay married."

I glanced over at a handmade plaque on the wall. "I shall pass through this world but once. Any good thereof that I can do, any kindness that I can show to any human being, let me do it now. Let me not defer or neglect for I shall not pass this way again."

I sighed, remembering the time I had told her about a dream that I had about being someone else. Momma had said that dream was about another life I had lived. She had explained it in simple terms. Like the grass that died in winter and came anew in the spring. I turned back to Momma and asked, "Do you believe we live only once?"

Momma looked at me curiously. "Why do ya ask that?"

"I don't know. It's just that sometimes I get the feeling I've been here before. And I have these dreams about being other people in other times . . . strange dreams. And all of those doll clothes that I used to make for my dolls. You know, the gowns? Sometimes when I made them, I knew exactly how they should look. I used to pretend that they were made by someone named Worth. Funny, though, you used to tell me that 'yeah, they're worth a lot all right' and I tried to tell you that Worth was the name of the designer who made them." I paused, musing over how elaborate those gowns were. "But what's really strange, Momma, I dreamed so many nights that I actually wore them."

We both laughed, and then I remembered the other dreams. "Sometimes I dream I'm a little girl, drowning or something. I always wake up before I finish the dream."

Momma got up and went to an old container that held pictures. She flipped through them, searching for something, then stopped and picked up a picture. She looked at it for a moment without any change in her expression. Then she handed it to me. "I don't think you've ever seen this picture."

"Who is this?" I said, then I caught my breath.

"It's a picture of Bootsie. My first li'l girl that died."

She then pulled another one from the stack and handed it to me. I stared in disbelief. It was a picture of me when I was a baby. Both pictures looked like the same baby. "God, Momma, she looks just like me."

"She surely does," she answered evenly.

I looked up at my mother. "What are you saying, Momma?"

"I don't know. I just always thought it was real curious," she said as she continued to watch me carefully.

"How?"

"Well, sometimes when you was small, I used ta think you was Bootsie."

"That I was Bootsie?"

"That's right."

I looked at my mother, trying to comprehend what she was really saying. Then the phone rang. Mama answered it and looked over at me.

"It's Caris," she said in a flat tone.

"What does he want?" I felt my spirits drop.

"Well, he wants ta talk ta you." She held the phone out to me.

I slowly walked over to the phone. "Hello, Caris. . . . Yes, I'm fine. . . . Brandy is fine. . . . An oil company? Sounds real nice, Caris. . . . I don't know. I'll think about it. I said I'll think about it. Good-bye, Caris." I hung up the phone.

"Well, what's that all 'bout?"

"Caris got a job with an oil company in Hobbs. He says he's really sorry and wants me to come back to him . . . for Brandy's sake."

"Lord have mercy," she replied, shaking her head.

"I'm tired, Momma. I think I'm going to lie down. I don't feel so good. Can you watch Brandy?" Momma said she would, so I went to my old room and lay down on my familiar bed. I began to dream: a little girl, maybe two years old . . . playing with marbles . . . she looks like me, but she isn't . . . a man starts hitting the little girl, cursing, calling her bad names . . . he hurts her arm . . . then throws her out a door . . . she picks up a bag of marbles . . . a dog comes running up, starts licking her face . . . I see her crying, but I can't hear her. She walks to a riverbank . . . the marbles start falling in slow motion out of the bag . . . slowly the water splashes up . . . I see her lean over the water . . . (*No! Stop!*) . . . I'm trying to yell, but she doesn't hear me . . . (*Please stop! Somebody help!*) . . . she slowly falls into the water . . . the water splashes up and a bright light reflects off it . . . (*No!*) . . . the water sweeps above . . . further and further down . . . light pours through the water . . . brighter, brighter . . . (*Help, help, help*) . . .

"HELP!" I was sitting up in bed. I was dripping with perspiration and filled with terror. Momma came rushing into the room.

"What is it?"

"Momma, how did Bootsie die? You never told me. How did she die?"

Mother wouldn't answer at first. She stared instead at a robin outside my window. I sat there wide-eyed, until finally she spoke. "They found her floatin' down a irrigation ditch."

"An irrigation ditch! My God, how did she get there?"

"Nobody knows. The last person ta see her was yer father, Charlie." She continued to watch the robin at the window.

"I know what happened," I said softly. Then, slowly, I told her. I paused when I'd finished, then said, "But Momma, it was as if I was that little girl, but also like I was watching her at the same time."

Momma was real quiet for a long time. "Well, that's why I showed you the pictures."

I felt so strange. "So, do . . . do you think that I'm Bootsie?"

Momma shrugged her shoulders. "I don't know."

I leaned back on the bed. A thought was forming in my head, but I couldn't put it into words. "Maybe my life is *supposed* to be like it is."

"All lives are supposed ta be like they are. I never doubted that fer a minute. Only the Lord knows why. Just knowin' that has kept me goin' all these years."

I stood up and looked out the window. The robin had

ceased his merry song and flown away. A train whistle moaned in the distance. "Momma, I think I'm pregnant again. I wonder who this baby is. Who he's been before . . . and why me? Why am I his mother?"

I stood there wondering about my unusual question.

"Well, he's supposed to be there, an only the good Lord knows why. Maybe you should go back ta Caris."

I continued to gaze out the window in wonderment . . . and in resignation.

CHAPTER THIRTEEN

THE DEATH OF THE ROSE AND LILY

Caris had a very good job with Shell Oil Company. His income allowed us to purchase a very nice brick house only a block away from an elementary school, and we bought some furniture that helped to give the little place more character. My activity outside the home continued to be restricted—Caris was still a very possessive man—so I decided to establish a child-care center in our house for working mothers. Brandy needed someone to play with, and I needed some company. What money I made, after paying back Caris for the food expenses, I kept. It was the first time in our marriage that I actually had any money of my own, and I kept it hidden.

I was about seven months along with my second child by now, and at times I would find myself very fatigued. Even so, I took care of about twelve children and still managed to keep the house clean and get supper on the table precisely at five—whether Caris came home or not.

Caris had the car he had always wanted—a brand-new Chevy Malibu—the house he had always wanted, and the wife he had always wanted. My desires or opinions did not matter. I had resolved to try and make the best of the marriage for the sake of my children. There were times when I wanted to run away from this nightmare or just plain tell him off, but every time I would think of what his mother always said to me—"Girl, you can put up with anything so long as your children have their own daddy"—or I would reflect on my momma's life and all she had to put up with just to make a living, and I would bite my lip so as not to make waves. Sometimes I felt like a pressure cooker, and I wondered if one day I would blow my lid right off.

"How many kids you baby-sitting today?" Caris asked one morning as he left for work.

"About twelve. I thought we might have a coloring session today. I hope that little Tammy comes. She's a dream to take care of."

"Is that the little blond girl whose momma died?" he asked, leaving me at the door and heading for his Malibu.

"Yes, she's my favorite."

"Well, maybe we'll have our own little girl," Caris said as he backed the car down the driveway.

"I'd like that," I yelled. "You gonna be late for dinner again tonight?"

"Hope not. I'll try to call," he lied. He seldom called to say he was going to be late. He drove away.

That evening, after the last of "my children" had left, I prepared a tasty dinner, but when Caris had not come home by six-thirty I put it in the oven to stay warm, and got Brandy ready for bed. I read him a bedtime story about "The Little Red Hen," and before I finished he had drifted off into peaceful dreams. I sat there looking down at my beautiful child, at his Norwegian blond hair trimmed in a "John-John" cut, at his almond-shaped brown eyes and little rosebud mouth, and thought what a wonderful blessing he had been to my life. I gave a prayer of thanksgiving to God for my little son. I started feeling very tired and decided to take a short nap while the house was so quiet. I put on my maternity gown, pulled back the covers of my bed, and lay my weary body down. Within a moment I was lost in a strange but wonderful dream.

I was at this very elegant gathering in a house that seemed familiar to me. Crystal candelabra sparkled, reflecting the flames of their candles. Smells of rose water, lavender, candle wax, exotic oils, champagne, and caviar permeated the air around me. There were many beautiful women wearing feathered plumes high upon their heads, and jewels twinkled from their earlobes. Full bosoms and white shoulders were framed with the silks, satins, and velvets of their gowns, their waists cinched into slenderness and their skirts falling to the floor with graceful ease. I saw bustles worn high on the rear for sensual effect and tiny ivory hands. Men wore dark evening coats, waistcoats of silk, and starched collars, their hair oiled and neatly trimmed. I was in a room filled with so much beauty, animate and inanimate, that one sensed an intolerance of ugliness in any form. If ugliness did exist, it was well hidden by lavish gowns and jewels of immense value.

I seemed to know who my host was: Lord Houghton. His house was on Arlington Street, London. He was the most celebrated host of his time in all of London, and I felt very pleased that I'd been invited. I knew I had been his guest before to lunch, to dinner, and to receptions. He had a son, Lord Crewe, a very famous diplomat, whom I admired. Lord Houghton was a literary man who had published books of excellent poetry. He was quick to perceive the merits of others and would often give a budding genius a lift along the road to fame. No American of merit could pass through London without being welcomed to his lavish Arlington house. All of this was apparent in my dream.

After a twelve-course dinner there was the usual reception. Lord Houghton gracefully led me up to a very tall, lean man with a pale intellectual face, yellow hair so long it lay in curls about his shoulders, a very close-cropped beard, and dreamy blue eyes. I don't remember what he wore, only that it was very unconventional. He was introduced as Joaquin Miller, the poet of the Sierras, a man of nature and perhaps the most picturesque personality of the literary world. After a few moments, he disappeared from the group and only toward the end of the evening did he return. To my astonishment he read me a verse from a torn piece of paper:

To the Jersey Lily:

If all God's world a garden were,
   And women were but flowers,
If men were bees that busied there
   Throughout endless summer hours,
O! I would hum God's garden through
   For honey till I came to you.

When he finished, he added with a very dramatic gesture: "Let this verse stand; it's the only one I ever wrote to a living woman."

I was smiling with composed appreciation, while the applause was muffled by gloved hands. . . . It was fading—the scene . . . the smells . . . the time . . . fading out of my memory . . . I was coming out of the dream back to the waking state. Suddenly a light flashed on. I rolled, trying to see where it was coming from. Then a voice startled my eyes open to the bright light of the bedroom ceiling fixture.

"How come you're sleepin'? Didn't ya hear me come home? C'mon and git my dinner ready, I'm hungry." I sat on the side of the bed for a moment, resisting waking up to this harsh, unromantic moment. I felt so different in my dream. I wanted to go back to it.

"Hey, git up . . . git me my supper. I ain't got all night," Caris yelled as he pulled off his dirty clothes and left them where they dropped. He disappeared into the bathroom and closed the door.

As I pulled the meal out of the oven and tried to make it look fresh, I kept thinking about my dream, afraid I was going to forget it. I decided I would write it down as soon as possible so I wouldn't forget any of it. I remembered that Momma had once said she always recorded her most important dreams. She said it gave her a chance to study them and find their meaning.

Caris came in, grabbed a beer out of the refrigerator, and sat down, complaining I was taking too long with his meal. He asked after Brandy, the other kids, how much money I had made (I lied), and requested that I start ironing his Levis with a better crease. I decided to share my dream with him, but he said he didn't want to hear about no dream . . . there was nothing to them. So I got up, found some paper, and began to record as much of the dream as I could.

I was still writing when Caris finished eating. He belched, and farted several times very loudly. I looked up at him and thought about how crude he was compared to the gentlemen of refinement in my dream. Then he stood by the bedroom door and ordered me to bed. He said it wasn't right for a hard-working man like himself to have to go to bed while I stayed up burning electricity. With great resentment, I put my notes away and went to bed.

Two months later, I was still thinking off and on about my dream. I had recorded as much of it as I could remember because I wanted to go to the library and research some of the people's names. But who would take care of all these children? The only days I had off were Saturday and Sunday, and Caris was home then, jealously watching over me. I put the idea to rest and figured eventually I would find a way to discover the meaning of my most vivid dream.

One day, while I was telling the children a Bible story about how much God loved them, and how if they had faith they could do anything with their lives when they grew up, I began to have a slight pain. I called Dr. Quigley. Because Brandy's birth had been so difficult, he didn't want to take any chances. He wanted to admit me to the hospital right away.

I had a neighbor lady come take over the children and I drove myself to the hospital in our second car.

Dr. Quigley examined me.

"You have a few more hours to go. How do you feel?"

"Like I'm having a baby. It won't be like the last time, will it?" I asked a little anxiously.

"No, Judy. Your pregnancy has been easier and the baby is in the correct position. No forceps this time. I'll be back in a little while. I've got some other women delivering now."

He left just as Caris entered the room, drinking Coke out of a bottle. "Hello, Caris. It will be a while."

Caris walked into the room, trying to be pleasant. "How do you feel?"

"Like I'm having a—" Just then a hard pain came. I screamed and began uncontrollably to bear down. "Caris . . . I think I'm having the baby . . . now."

Caris spit out the Coke in his mouth. "Oh, my God!"

"Quick, run and get Dr. Quigley. Hurry!" I moaned.

Caris rushed out of the room in a state of complete confusion. He ran down the corridors, bumping into people, until he came to a nurse who stopped him.

"Can I help you, sir?" she asked.

"My wife is having her baby. *Now!*" He pointed to my room.

"Now calm down, she won't be delivering for a few more hours. She's not ready yet," she said smoothly.

"But she is in real bad pain and says the baby is coming," he said.

"All right, you just calm down, I'll get the doctor."

All this time the pain had continued. Then, in one hard push, I was relieved of my burden. I lay there for a moment, spent. Dr. Quigley came rushing into my room. I looked up at him. "I had the baby in the bed, Dr. Quigley." I leaned over and pulled up the covers. My baby started crying. Dr. Quigley picked up the crying baby. He was still attached by the cord.

"You lied to me," I said with exhausted laughter. "You said it would be a few more hours."

"Well, it is a full moon, you know. Babies have a way of doing this sort of thing during a full moon," he said as he examined the baby.

Caris, always possessive, was watching Dr. Quigley, trying to see if the good doctor was inspecting *me*!

"What is it?" I asked the doctor.

"It's a boy, Judy. You got another beautiful baby boy."

"Is he all right?" I asked.

"He looks all right to me. I don't know how I'm gonna charge you for this, though. You did it all by yourself."

Caris obviously couldn't take it so he left the room.

Later that same day, after I had been sewn up and the baby bathed, a nurse placed the little bundle in my arms. Smells of baby powder and oil sweetly filled my senses as I gazed into that tender little face. The nurse excused herself and left us alone, and I gently checked him over. Yep, everything was there. Then I noticed the slightly slanted forehead, a cyst on the left eyelid, blue and peeling fingers, and his red skin. I became alarmed and rang for the nurse. Dr. Quigley came in and after close examination said that the forehead would fill in, the peeling would stop in a day or two, and the cyst would disappear. As for the red and blue complexion, Dr. Quigley pointed out that, after all, the little guy had come through an ordeal. He patted me on the shoulder and left. I kissed that sweet banged-up face and said, "I love you and think you are beautiful. I thank God in heaven for you."

When Mr. and Mrs. Hensley came in the room with Caris, I smiled and turned the baby upward so they could have a look. Mrs. Hensley looked at the baby with a scrutinizing expression. "Well, Caris, I guess maybe it is yours! Look at that nose."

Caris shoved both hands into his pockets and said sheepishly, "I told ya, Momma. See, you had nothin' to worry about."

I looked at both of them, shocked. They acted as if nothing had been said. Why wouldn't this baby be Caris's? Who else's could it be? The stork's? I was hurt by their cruelty and asked them to leave, though all I said was that I wasn't feeling well.

The next day I had a wonderful surprise. Momma walked in the room with Loy, who had driven all the way to Hobbs from college. It felt so good to have him and Momma there. I told Loy that I wanted to name my little boy after him. Momma puffed up with pride. Loy, however, said that he never really liked his name, so he thought that the baby should be named "Christopher." He said then we can call him "Chris" or "Chrissy" for short. Loy had such a wonderful time playing with "Christopher." He even went back to the Hensleys' and got Brandy and brought him to the hospital to see his new little brother. The Hensleys were strangely absent when my family was around, and I was glad about that. When Loy and Momma left a week later, once again I felt at the mercy of my suspicious in-laws and hostile husband.

December 4, 1970, we celebrated Christopher's first birthday. It was a cold day with a brisk wind, but the pale sun shone gloriously. I always decorated the house festively for the holiday season, and I always started early in December. Already the tree was up and decorated, the house filled with the smell of fresh fir garlands and pine cones. My little house could have made the Christmas cover of *Better Homes and Gardens*. Caris came home late that night—as usual. He was putting in a lot of overtime "for Christmas gifts," he would say.

Early one morning I woke up and looked at the clock. It was four in the morning. I turned over to see Caris dressed and standing by the chest of drawers.

"Caris, where are you going so early?"

"Working. Go back to sleep. I'll see you later."

"Is everything all right?"

"Yeah, just working too hard for Christmas."

I rolled over and went back to sleep. When I woke up that morning, Caris was gone. I went to check on the boys and prepared breakfast for them. Afterwards, I started to clean up the house while the boys played in Christopher's playpen. Picking up a pair of Caris's trousers from the night before, I noticed a stain on the front by the fly. I examined it closely. It was red. Then I smelled it. It was lipstick . . . by his fly! Then something fell out of his pocket onto the floor. A motel room key! "Oh, my God," I moaned. "And he's stupid, too." In a rage, I flung the trousers across the room. I went to the telephone and dialed his office.

"Mr. Hensley isn't in," the secretary said. "It's Christmas Eve, Mrs. Hensley. I thought he'd be home."

I hung up. I sat down and tried to control my fury. I wasn't jealous, just angry that while I had made a commitment to stay married to that bastard "for the children's sake," while I had been living like some tormented prisoner, he had been out kicking up his heels having an affair with some stupid broad! I was determined to do something about my life once and for all. "Just don't be rash, girl," I told myself. "Think it through . . . plan it out."

There were carols playing on the stereo while I finished decorating some Christmas cookies for the boys.

"Where's Daddy, Momma? Why isn't he here to eat some Christmas cookies, too?" Brandy asked as he munched away. Chris was fingering the frosting that was Santa's face on the cookie.

"He'll be home later. Do you want some more milk?"

A cold rain began to fall and made the evening rather gloomy. Caris still had not appeared. I put the children to bed, reading them "The Night Before Christmas." Then I went back into the living room and stared at the Christmas tree and at the carefully wrapped gifts. I recalled my own first Christmas, how special it had been for me. I had been only six years old. Imagine not knowing about Christmas until you are six years old! I mused on the frugality of my one gift that year as I looked at the abundance of gleaming packages for my children. There were more carefully hidden in the closet. They were from "Santa."

I got up and went to work putting goodies in their stockings, then went to the closet and pulled out the tricycle and rocking horse I had assembled by myself the night before. I placed them under the tree. Santa had finished.

Checking everything over, I decided to pray.

"Heavenly Father, I want to make a bargain with You. I want You to make me a smart and successful woman. I don't want to be a secretary, or a cashier at Safeway. I want to be somebody *important*. I want to set an example for my little boys that a woman, their mother, can be somebody important. I'm going to have to be both a mother and a father to my children, and I don't want to depend on anyone else but You, Father. I don't know how You're going to do this, but whatever it takes, Father, I want You to help me realize this desire. And if You do, I will tell everybody I know that it was You who made it happen." I went to bed knowing my prayer would be answered.

On Christmas Day, Brandy and Chris were having such

a jolly time opening their presents that we didn't hear a car pull up. Caris walked in the door. He had been drinking. He walked over to the tree. Brandy and Chris were trying to get his attention by showing him everything Santa had brought them.

"Merry Christmas, Caris," I said, trying to be civil.

He glared at me. "Big fuckin' deal. How much Goddamn money did you spend on all this?"

"Don't talk like that in front of the children, Caris. It's Christmas, don't spoil it for them," I said, and then I took the boys and some of their toys into their room. I didn't want them to get upset seeing him in such a sorry state.

When I returned calmly to the living room, he was still standing by the tree, waiting for me. "Caris, I think you should get your things together and get out of our lives. I know you've been screwing around on me. I found the motel key in your pocket. I've tried to be a good wife to you, but all you've given me in return is misery. It's finished, Caris. I won't live like this anymore, not for you or anyone else. I think we would all be better off without you."

"Just listen to you," he slurred. "I've been working my ass off for you and those kids. Now you're telling me that you'd be better off without me? You better get your fuckin' head examined."

"Don't give me that crap about you working your ass off for us. Hell, you've been screwing around, Caris, that's what you've been doing. You and I both know that. Don't you be so stupid to think I can't make it without you. I can and I intend to do just that! So you just get out of this house and go work your ass off in motel room three seventy-two." I stood there, defying him to try anything.

With that, Caris picked up Brandy's new tricycle and threw it against the Christmas tree. The ornaments shattered as the tree fell over. I started to scream, "Get out of our lives! I don't care anymore about whether my children have their real father, because you are the poorest excuse for one that I know, Caris Hensley. You don't deserve me or those little boys. *Get out!*"

He started laughing drunkenly. "No! This is *my* house.

I worked for every red cent to buy it, and it's mine. Not yours, baby! You're the ones who's leaving. And you'll be back 'cause you ain't got no other Goddamn place to go!" Then he staggered to the door and left.

I ran to the bedroom where the boys were both crying. I tried to comfort them, telling them we were going where everyone was happy. Then I pulled out the two suitcases I had purchased with green stamps and started to pack. I put in only as much as I needed to take, and the boys started helping with their things. I swiftly packed the car, taking all of the boys' clothes and some of their toys. I had to leave the new tricycle and rocking horse that Santa had brought them. They didn't understand why we had to leave them and started to cry, so I promised them that Santa would bring them even better ones. It seemed to work. When I was finished, I went to my secret hiding place and got out my money. I had saved nearly five hundred dollars. That would take us a long way. I was thankful I had it.

It was cold and raining outside. I started the engine, checked the gas gauge, and turned on the windshield wipers. The radio was playing "Joy to the World." Tears of long-repressed frustration came welling up in my eyes. I didn't know where we were going—I would have to trust God's wisdom for that—but we were free at last, and the joy that I felt made going on blind faith much easier. I pulled the car out of the driveway and drove away, not looking back, only forward to a new life.

I never returned to that house or to Hobbs, New Mexico. I got my divorce within three months of leaving Caris and I was awarded custody of the boys. Caris only made a handful of child-support payments. He and his parents argued that they just couldn't afford it.

I would only see Caris once more, when he came to see the boys at my job in Waco, Texas. He brought along his new wife. Brandy saw him once after that, when at seventeen he wanted to uncover the mystery of his father. He soon discovered why I had left and, his curiosity satisfied, he returned home, never to go back. Christopher does not remember Caris and has had no desire to seek him out. Caris, according to rumor, has been married four times and still, to this day, lives close to his parents.

What good came from this tragic marriage? Many things. First and foremost my two boys, who have always kept me going, pushing for a better life. Also, I learned once again how I pull the rug out from under myself when I compromise my dreams. To deny your personal happiness for the sake of someone else—in my case I did it for the boys—diminishes your chance for self-realization and fulfillment. You can't live for someone else and expect to be happy. This is what my marriage of compromise had taught me.

CHAPTER FOURTEEN

THE BIRTH OF A MOGUL

My journey to freedom took us as far as Roswell, New Mexico, the place of my birth. I found a nice house for us, got settled in, and then began looking for a job. That was difficult since the unemployment rate in Roswell was at an all-time high; you couldn't get a job even with a college degree.

I ended up answering an ad in the local paper that was recruiting salespeople for cable television. The only thing I had ever sold door-to-door was Girl Scout cookies, but I decided to leave that out of my "prior sales experience." The job paid no salary, only a percentage of each sale made, but I was desperate so I took it. The sales manager handed me some subscription forms and told me which area of town to work. That was about it for training. I didn't even know what cable television was all about, which probably explains why I got so many doors slammed in my face. That first day I didn't sell one order, so I didn't make any money. Zero!

Sensing that my ignorance was getting me nowhere, I decided to spend the next day in the cable office learning everything I could. Now, better equipped with product knowledge, I purchased a three-ring binder and created a cable installation on the front. I even cut part of the coaxial cable down to reveal each of its components. I filled the inside of my book with pictures showing the difference between normal antenna reception and cable, and I showed how many more channels were available on cable. I worked hard on my spiel, then prayed hard that I would do it right . . . and make some money.

This next day I made six sales. I was jazzed! Every day that followed I would pray to make just one more sale over the previous day. It worked. Soon I was outselling every other salesperson, including the sales manager. One day, I took off from selling and went into the field with the cable installers. I learned how to climb a telephone pole and do the initial hookup from the box, and then how to do the drop into the customer's house. When I returned later that afternoon, I had a call from the marketing executive in Los Angeles. He had decided to promote me to marketing manager of my office, replacing the old manager. I was elated!

In a short time, I turned that dead-end cable system in Roswell into a profitable one. The sales soared through the efforts of the marketing people I hired and trained. My financial situation was now secure; in fact, I was making more money than Caris had made with Shell Oil. I was independent at last!

One weekend I drove to Artesia to visit Momma and Daddy Bill. Momma was so happy to see Brandy and Chris. But she was very worried. Daddy Bill had gone back into the hospital to have his remaining leg amputated. Gangrene had set in and his toes were black and dead. The doctors were afraid he wouldn't live through the surgery.

I walked into his hospital room and found a withered old man beneath an oxygen tent. He barely recognized me. I told him who I was and he reached out for my hand. I responded and held his cold hand tightly.

"Judy . . . I need to ask you something." He was having a difficult time breathing.

"Anything . . . please ask." I felt such pity looking at him.

"I want to ask you to forgive me. I've treated you pretty poorly in your life . . . and I was wrong . . . very wrong. I'm going to die, I know it. I want to go with a clear heart . . . and with peace. Please, forgive me." He was staring up at me from gray, saddened eyes.

"Of course I forgive you, Daddy Bill. I already have. God has helped me to understand things better, Daddy Bill. You see, I love God, and God loves you. So I can't love God and not love you, too. And I have a lot to thank you for. No, you didn't make my life easy, but because of that I've become a much stronger person. I'm very thankful to you for that. Very thankful. Please, know that and feel at peace with it. I do." He started to cry and it almost broke my heart.

"Judy . . . I'm so scared to die. Please, teach me how to pray . . . how to talk to God."

I was profoundly touched by his request. He had never talked to God before, but in this hour he became humble enough to finally reach to that great source, God, who had been waiting all of Bill's life for that holy touch. I prayed silently for a moment, asking for the right words. They sweetly came.

"Beloved Father, unto this hour I beseech You to look upon me and into my soul for the fear that lies there. Beloved Father, I ask that You remove my fear and bring me peace and the release of the darkened memories of my life. Father, forgive me of my ignorance, that I may be exalted into Thy love and grace this hour, for my life is finished, and unto Your hands I commend my spirit. In the name of the Christ, amen." Daddy Bill repeated every word. He squeezed my hand and told me that he loved me. I knew that the prayer had been heard, and I gave thanks to God for Bill's life and for my own. Bill fell into a peaceful sleep and I quietly left.

I decided to buy him a television for his bedroom at home. I suppose I thought he would get better. I arranged for the television, along with a new refrigerator, to be delivered, and then I went home to tell Momma of my purchase. She met me at the door. The hospital had just called to tell her Daddy Bill had passed away in his sleep.

I stayed on a few more days to help with the funeral arrangements. Most of my family came and gave support to Momma. It was a sad time to have a family reunion, but we were all comforted to be together there. I felt at peace about Daddy Bill. Sort of like reading the last chapter of a book that explains the mystery and brings a final understanding. Daddy Bill was safe with God and, I trust, happy at last.

Two months had passed when I received another call from the head office in Los Angeles. I had been promoted to marketing director for Southern California. I accepted the position and moved the boys and myself to an attractive home in Manhattan Beach, where I enrolled Brandy in kindergarten and Chris in a day-care center nearby. I hired a Negro nanny from Roswell and had her move in with us. Everything was splendid! As director of my new region, I taught my own techniques to the people under me, and the sales really took off.

One day I got a call from Ben Mattson, who was my boss. He wanted to see me. I drove my blue Lincoln Continental into L.A. and up to the curb in front of my company's home office. The parking attendant greeted me in his usual way.

"Good morning, Mrs. Hensley. How are you today?" He smiled as he opened the door for me.

"I'm terrific, Frankie, thanks. Is Mr. Mattson in yet?"

"Yes, ma'am. He arrived just about thirty minutes ago."

I thanked him and made my way through the lobby of the building, my briefcase in tow. Up on the tenth floor I moved through the elegant offices, greeting the girls in the secretarial pool on my way to my small but tasteful office. My secretary buzzed me to let me know that Ben was there to see me. I greeted him at the door with my usual hug.

"Well, beautiful, how's it going this lovely Wednesday morning?" he asked, studying me over his glasses.

"Couldn't be better—except for having to live in California. It's a dreadful place, with all the smog, the traffic. But the boys are doing well, and their nanny, Sarah Lee, is a wonderful housekeeper and cook. A little on the superstitious side, though. She keeps saying there's a spook living with us," I said laughing. "By the way, did you like my last report?"

"Did I like it? You've had more sales than any of your predecessors. I'm still rather amazed that you know so much about rigging a cable complex," he said, leaning back in his chair.

"What's so amazing about that? Just because I'm a woman doesn't mean I have a light lunch upstairs for brains and a soft rump. My momma taught me that a little knowledge and hard work went a long way. She said what we needed were dirtier fingernails and cleaner souls. It's sort of the way God intended it."

"You're a funny young woman, Judy. The way you dress, the way you look, some of the people here feel they should call you Mrs. Hensley. But they feel you're too friendly and warm for such a formal name. On the other hand, Judy doesn't fit either."

"Do you think I need a name that would look good in lights? You know, like they do for the stars?" I teased him. "When I was in New Mexico, some of my workers gave me the nickname Zebra because I wore a lot of black and white."

"Hmmm. Should I call you Zebra, then?"

"You must admit, it is different. Original."

"This may *seem* like a zoo I'm running here, but I like to think it's more chic than that," he said, looking around. "Zebra Hensley, how's that?"

"Please, don't you think that's a little severe?"

"Right . . . let's see, how about Judy Zebra?" He was determined.

"Sounds like a stripper who works in a zebra-striped bikini. Really!"

"You're right again, that would never do. Hmmm, how about abbreviating it?" The lights went on! "We'll cut Judy Zebra down to first initials. How does J.Z. sound?" He wrote the letters on a piece of paper.

I stared at them and whispered "JZ" to myself a couple of times. "I like that. JZ. Hmmm, it's sort of friendly. Hey, I love it. From now on, just call me 'JZ'—and forget about the periods."

"All right, JZ it is. You are a powerful lady; you deserve

a powerful name." He straightened up in his chair. "JZ, I would like you to join my little dinner party at Maison de Gerard. I want to discuss a new marketing proposal, and I feel you should be a part of that discussion."

"I would be happy to join you."

"Be there by eight o'clock." Ben got up and left.

There were six of us at the dinner party. The French cuisine was excellent, and I was enjoying myself very much. It had been a long time since I had had a night on the town. My evenings were always spent with my children, and like most successful people I was single-minded in my pursuit of goals. With that kind of commitment, there was no room for a social life, and certainly not for a suitor. But this was different; it was business.

My thoughts were interrupted by a very good-looking blond, blue-eyed man, dressed in a dark suit and tie. Apparently, he had just arrived for dinner and, seeing Ben, had come over to talk. He kept looking at me in an obvious but subtle way. Ben, taking the hint, introduced us. His name was Lynn de Shane.

"JZ, it is a pleasure to meet you at last," he said smoothly. "I've heard of your remarkable abilities in CATV marketing. But if I may be so bold, you look much too young to have so much experience. I'm very surprised."

"Well, in my short tenure, I've worn out plenty of shoes, broken a lot of fingernails, and burned a lot of midnight oil," I answered, looking up at him. Ben leaned back in his chair and took a sip of his drink.

His polished manner impressed me. Ben, sensing my interest, wasted no time in insisting Lynn join us. In a matter of moments, waiters prepared a place for him. I found it rather odd that he should be dining alone. At least I didn't see anyone else who appeared to be with him. He seated himself gracefully and ordered a drink, but declined dinner. Everyone at the table knew him, so the relaxed atmosphere did not change.

The handsome Lynn received his drink—warmed brandy —and gently rotated the glass. "Do you live here in Los Angeles?" he asked. The candlelight danced softly in his eyes.

"No, I have a little house in Manhattan Beach where my base office is. I'm a small-town girl who prefers small-town living," I answered.

The waiters removed the dirty dishes and placed delicate finger bowls with lemon slices swimming in warm water in front of everyone. I looked down in wonderment. I wasn't sure what they were for. Back home, this could be a con-sommé. Thinking that was what it was, I started to pick it up to sip it, when I noticed that everyone was dipping their fingers in the stuff and wiping their hands. Quickly, I fol-lowed the ritual, and tried to cover my blunder by saying, "Oh, I just love the smell of warmed lemon. It's so healing to the senses." Lynn had been watching me, and my "cover" brought a smile to his lips. I just proceeded to wipe my hands and lips as though I had used finger bowls all my life. "Yes," I told him, "I really like the homey feelings in smaller towns. I'm very old-fashioned, and to me, L.A. is just too racy."

I pushed my chair slightly away from the table and crossed my legs, revealing a beautiful set of knees. I wasn't doing it for effect, merely for comfort, but I'm certain that Lynn, who was still watching me, thought I was flirting. He may have been thrown a bit, though, since my attitude continued to be pure business.

"I'm dedicated to building this company into a very com-petitive business. I would like, someday, to see it become the hottest item on Wall Street. I'm going to grow right along with it, and that makes me very optimistic about my chil-dren's future and my own." That was the truth.

The waiters returned to clear off the finger bowls and pour champagne into crystal glasses. Ben stood up and raised his glass in a toast. "I would like to propose a toast to the imagination of JZ 'Zebra' Hensley, who has shown us that we big-city operators are not as smart as we think we are when it comes to understanding the public's need. She can repair a coaxial drop with her hands and charm the pants off the customers with her smile. To JZ . . . thank you for providing new blood to our company."

Everyone toasted and sipped their sparkling champagne in my honor. I was deeply moved by the gesture. I swallowed my champagne . . . and coughed. It was the first champagne

I had ever tasted and the first time I had drunk alcohol since my dreadful drunk on prom night. I made a face and decided I didn't like this stuff either.

"Excuse me," I said, sounding hoarse. "I think I have something caught in my throat," I lied again to save face. I took another sip in an effort to appear normal, but it was just as bad as the first one. Mr. Handsome was taking it all in.

A waiter appeared bearing a flaming baked Alaska on a huge silver tray. Everyone applauded, and the waiter moved to present the baked Alaska to me as the guest of honor. Everyone was watching, Ben in particular. He was very proud of his little surprise for me. I did not know what this was or what I was supposed to do next. "Why, thank you. It looks . . . just wonderful."

I expected that the waiter would now do something with it, like put out the fire and serve the thing. Little did I know that I was supposed to hoist my arms up over the tray, pick up the huge silver spoon and the spatula, and elegantly serve myself. They never taught me this in home economics!

The waiter waited.

Ben started talking in an attempt to cover my lack of etiquette, hoping somehow I would realize just what I was supposed to do. I finally did.

"Well, well, what *is* this?" I said. I didn't want to get too close, afraid I would singe my eyelashes.

The waiter replied, *"Pardonnez-moi?"*

"What?" I answered. You could tell that French had also been left out of my education.

Lynn leaned over to my ear and whispered, "It's ice cream with meringue, baked in an oven with booze and then ignited." I turned to him, astonished. "It's very good!"

"Really? Ice cream? Well, they couldn't have baked it too long."

"It's all a matter of timing," Lynn whispered again.

I picked up the spoon and spatula and tried to scoop some up. The flaming ice cream was as hard as a rock. I scooped a bit harder into the frozen thing and finally broke a hunk off of the tray—right smack into my lap! I was startled, then embarrassed. "Oh my, that sucker is slippery."

The waiter was mortified, to put it mildly. He was quickly joined by other waiters who were in a tizzy to clean up the dripping mess from the tray, as well as off my dress. No one at the table knew just what to say . . . not even Ben.

"I suppose maybe I'm just a little too old-fashioned," I said. "I can shoot jackrabbits and never miss, but it seems when it comes to, uh, *pardinnezo-moist*, I don't have much of an aim. I'm terribly sorry."

Lynn watched me with dancing eyes. I don't think that he had ever met anyone quite as . . . shall we say original?

Two days later I was walking one of the streets in Manhattan Beach with a woman from the main office. She had taken a definite liking to me and sometimes would drive down just to have lunch and gab about the affair she was having with the company's chairman of the board. Her hang-up was that "Chairman Baby" was married . . . for good! Anyway, she had come to visit and said she wanted to do something outlandish with me.

"So, Twila"—sounds like Ben had christened her with a new name too—"where are you taking me?" I asked.

"It's just a *super* idea, JZ. I'm taking you to see a fortune-teller. I made the appointment. She knows nothing about me. I want to find out what Dumpling-Puss really thinks about me. . . . Great, huh?"

Yeah, right. Why else would you want to do a hare-brained thing like this? I wondered as we walked into the home office of Gypsy, Inc. The lights in the anteroom were low, dimly revealing antique furniture. There was a huge picture of Christ hanging on the wall, surrounded by Indian avatars dressed in saffron robes and towels around their heads. Hmmm, I didn't recall ever seeing any pictures of the Disciples looking like these dudes. An old but graceful Indian woman stepped through the beaded crystal curtain and walked right up to me! Thinking the old lady had made a mistake, Twila stepped forward and said that it was *she* who had made the appointment. The old woman just smiled at her, then looked back to me.

"I have been waiting for you," she said. I thought: Great fortune-teller. She is really with it.

"Uh . . . I think you have us mixed up. I am the one who made this appointment!" Twila repeated.

But the old woman ignored her. "I have been waiting for this one." She gently took my hand and began to lead me through the curtains. I turned and looked at Twila with an expression of "What can I say?" We entered a private room that smelled of incense and was lit by candles. There were more pictures of men in strange garb adorning the walls—one with a mop of hair that looked like the result of a bad perm or of electrocution. A small table with two chairs stood in the center of the room.

"Please, sit down." She nearly whispered it. "Relax, I must tell you things."

Very strange. "But I really don't want to know anything. My friend needs to—" I tried to explain.

"But I must tell you. Make a fist, please, and hold it above your head." I obeyed reluctantly. The old woman didn't even look at my fist; she was gazing at the middle of my forehead. "Now, put your fist in my hand, then slowly open your hand." I complied. The woman looked as if she were in a trance, just staring at my head. "I will first tell you something about your past."

"Fair enough!" I answered smugly. She continued.

"You are an uncertain woman. You married a man you did not love. You had two children from this marriage . . . two boys. You left the man. You are not from here. You are from where the coyotes howl."

Hmmm, this was getting interesting. "Uh, can you tell me what kind of work I do?" That would be the test.

"You are in television . . . communications . . . you market this . . . you are very good!"

Bingo! I swallowed hard.

"Now, I must tell you about your future!" she went on, and I sort of shrugged. "Very soon you will leave this place. You will go where it is hot . . . very hot. You will have fire on your back."

I stiffened. "You mean I will be in a wreck or something?"

"No, only your back will burn. You will be in the place

of heat for three weeks. Then you will have two offers of work. One will be where the sky is dark with business. The other will be a place with great mountains, tall pines, and lakes that shine like mirrors unto the heavens. If you go to the mountains and pines, you will meet The One. Do you understand?"

"I don't understand any of what you are saying." That was the truth!

"You will. . . . If you meet The One, you will have great influence . . . great destiny. I have waited for you. Now, I have told you. It is done." Her face became normal and she stood up.

I was, to say the least, confused, but I was intent on trying to understand all that she said. "Well, thank you. . . . Uh, what do I owe you?"

"Nothing, my dear. Nothing. You owe only to yourself."

I felt as though this last statement of hers rang true. I thanked her again, and she escorted me to the anteroom where Twila was pacing the floor. The old woman paused, looked at Twila, and said, "You give your virtue that is a jewel to a man who only puts it in his pocket." Then she turned around and disappeared through the crystal beaded curtains. Twila's eyes were wide with the realization of what the old woman had told her.

We left the shop and started walking back toward my office.

"I don't know what that was all about," I said. "She says I'm going to have an offer to go to tall trees and mountains or something like that. If I go there, I'll meet The One. Makes a lot of sense, huh?"

"The One? Who's that? Some guy?" she asked.

"You got me. In the meantime, I'm going to have fire on my back. Are you still with me on that one? Oh, well, listen, Twila, I've got to get back to work," I said, checking my watch.

When I arrived at the office, I checked in with my secretary, got my messages, and went into my office. A few moments later my secretary opened the door.

"JZ, there's a guy out here with a jungle for you." She

turned and nodded for the delivery boy to come in. He entered carrying two large white baskets filled with three dozen roses each. He placed them wherever he could and then presented me with the card.

"It looks like a gangster's funeral in here," he said.

I laughed and curiously opened the card. It read, "Coming your way. Love, Lynn de Shane." The delivery boy exited and immediately Lynn appeared. My secretary gave me a coy smile and left, closing the door behind her.

"Was that fast enough?" He smiled, stretching out his arms.

"Like you said, it's all a matter of timing."

Lynn was wearing California white beach trousers, white tennis shoes, and an open-necked shirt revealing a Saint-Tropez tan. His sun-bleached blond hair was tousled a bit, making him look very much like Robert Redford.

"I was in the neighborhood and thought I'd drop by. May I sit down?"

"By all means, make yourself comfortable. What a nice surprise. I wonder how that outfit would look with booze and ice cream on it?" I asked smugly.

He looked down at his pants and smiled. "Not as well as your dress did. I really came down here to hear more about, uh, jackrabbits."

I studied him for a moment, eye to eye. "I'm afraid I don't have the time to explain them to you. I'm busy."

"Oh, come on. Take a break. Let's go for a walk to the beach. It's a beautiful day outside . . . the smog level is way down, and you can actually make out the color of the sky. Anyway, you'll feel better about work when you get back," he said, sweeping his hair away from his eyes.

I thought about it for a moment and decided to go. I got up and put on my beach hat, then buzzed my secretary. "Tell whoever calls that I've gone up the river with a sack of cats."

"A sack of what?" She thought she had heard me wrong.

"Never mind. I'll be back in an hour."

We walked out of the building and down the sidewalk toward the beach.

"Let's get some ice cream that won't slip away," he suggested.

I started laughing. "Okay."

We stopped by the Dairy Queen, got two cones, and walked down to the beach, getting some good licks in on the way. We sat down cross-legged in the sand.

"So, tell me about yourself," he asked. "I really would like to know more about you."

I eyed him suspiciously. Even though I felt he was being a little intrusive, I liked that he was interested in me. "Just what would you like to know, Mr. de Shane?"

He stopped licking and the chocolate started melting down the side of the cone. God, was he beautiful! But men like that are usually treacherous, hung up on themselves. I was not fooled by his suave demeanor.

"All the personal data on JZ. I know you can shoot, ride, fish, trap, pick cotton, and wire up an entire building. You can probably cook, sew, clean, and even throw a mean baseball." He was now licking ice cream off his hand.

"Right on all of the above."

"So tell me, what happened to your husband?"

"How do you know I don't still have one?"

"Ben told me."

"Oh."

"So, what happened between you?"

I hesitated. I didn't want to get too personal with him. "Nothing much."

"Look, if I seem to be prying, it's because I'm genuinely interested in you. You may think you're just another small-town girl, but I can't understand what man would ever let you get away."

"He wasn't a man. He was a child."

"I see. Let's go at it another way. Did you love the child?"

I paused for several moments, pondering that word: "love." Eventually, I replied, "Love, to me, is a state of mind."

"A state of mind?" he said, sounding surprised. I wondered why everyone always acted so dumb when I said that. Good God, doesn't anyone else ever reason this out for themselves?

"Yes, you know, where you think you are but you're

not. I've had a couple of states of mind. In every case, I'm sure I convinced myself it was love, but it was really a state of mind."

"Fair enough." He turned and looked toward the waves.

"So?" I asked, waiting for a reply.

"So?" he asked, still watching the waves.

I felt a little let down that he didn't offer the usual rebuttal. But then I looked at him. He was no down-home, humdrum guy.

"Now that we know more about me," I said, "tell me about you. Fair enough?"

He finished eating the last of the cone and wiped his hands on his napkin. He leaned on one hand in the sand and stretched out his legs. "Fair enough. I was born here in California, which makes me a rare breed. Everyone else is imported. I married my childhood sweetheart and have a son. Things did not work out and we got a divorce. It tore me apart because of my son. He is the light of my life. I see him as often as I can . . . and I also throw a mean baseball."

I listened carefully to what he said and found that there was a gentle and caring man behind that California face. "Are you really only a friend to Ben, or are you associated in some way with the company?"

"Well, Ben and I go back quite a ways. But actually I'm an agent. My office happens to be a floor down from Ben's."

"An agent? What kind of an agent?"

"I'm an actors' agent."

My face lit up. "An actors' agent?"

"Yes."

"You mean, like stars? Movie stars?"

"Yes, some of them are . . . and some are even actors and actresses."

"Do you know Richard Chamberlain? You know, Dr. Kildare?"

"Yes, I know him. But I don't represent him."

"Oh, do you know Ann-Margret? Is she really as beautiful as she looks in the movies?"

Lynn started smiling. "Yes, she's beautiful. But none of the stars are what they seem to be. I mean, if you saw Ann-Margret walking down this beach, you wouldn't stop and look. Almost every woman on this beach is just as beautiful."

I looked around at all the girls. They certainly were all beautiful.

"Most of what you see is illusion. I know, I help create that illusion. It's big business out here."

"Really?"

Lynn was charmed by my naiveté. "Really."

"So who's your favorite movie star? Not just of the ones you represent, but out of all of them, who's your favorite?"

He thought about it for a moment, then said, "Donald Duck."

"Donald Duck?" Oh my stars!

"Yes."

"Well, I always liked Bambi. I felt so sorry for Bambi. I just cried and cried. I really did," I said in all seriousness. I laughed and quickly covered my mouth.

"Why do you always cover your mouth when you laugh?"

I was put off by his close scrutiny. "I don't always cover my mouth."

"Yes, you do."

"I guess because I never thought I had a pretty smile. My teeth are crooked. They remind me of the tires on a John Deere tractor."

"I think you not only have a beautiful mouth, but you have a beautiful character. You don't look or act like anyone else. You are an original in a world of duplicates. You have a light around you."

"A light?"

"Yes, you stand out. You're different."

With that, I began to feel that he was getting too personal. I stiffened. He must have sensed what I was feeling.

"So, are your boys in school?"

"Yes." Click, buzzzz.

"When do I get to meet them?"

Good grief! I needed to get out of this. Enough digging! "I don't know . . . I really must get back to work now."

With that, we got up and walked back to my office. Along the way, he made small talk. I responded with large silences. The Big Chill! He left.

The next day I walked into my office to find the same

delivery boy there with a spray of carnations in the shape of a heart. He squeezed them in between the roses. "I think you must have died and nobody told you."

He handed me the card. It read, "You can't keep a good thing away. Love, Lynn." I looked up, and guess what I saw. You got it. The good thing that doesn't stay away.

"I just couldn't help myself, Mizz Annie Oakley."

"They're beautiful, Lynn. But really . . ."

"Really what? Would you do me the honor of having dinner with me? I promise nothing will be on fire, ma'am." He asked this in a perfect imitation of John Wayne. I couldn't help but laugh.

"But I don't really—"

"Not really: Reilly. It's an old Irish family name. I didn't know you knew them? How about tomorrow night?" Now he was an Irishman rolling his r's.

"Why?" Stupid question, huh?

"Because by tomorrow night you'll be hungry. Please, JZ . . ."

"All right," I relented. "I'll dine with you. After all, who could refuse John Wayne?"

I wore my beautiful white silk dress and let my hair down to flow below my shoulders. Lynn was dressed in a white dinner jacket, looking as California as possible. We were well into our dinner and feeling comfortable with one another.

"I talked to Ben about you. He says you really are an old-fashioned girl."

"Of course I am. Why didn't you believe me?"

He took a sip of his wine. "Because most people I know say they are one thing or another just for effect. Usually they are none of those things."

"Well, what you see is what I am," I said as I looked down and adjusted my dinner napkin in my lap.

"Except you got your district manager fired."

I was truly stunned at this off-the-wall statement. "I never got anybody fired. I was just better at what I did than he was." Really!

"See how honest you are?" He was being coy. "I hear

you helped write the training manual on cable marketing."

"Yes, I did. I wrote it from the firsthand understanding of what people truly wanted."

"Do you want to stay in this business?"

"Of course I do. Why wouldn't I?"

"Have you seen any of those spaghetti Westerns?"

"You mean those movies with Clint Eastwood and Charles Bronson?" He nodded. "Yes, they're actually quite authentic. They certainly know how to ride a horse and handle a gun."

"So can you."

This was becoming a strange conversation. I wondered if the wine was making him a little dizzy. "So?"

"So, you can ride and shoot and you are beautiful. There's a movie starting in Rome in two months. I think you would be great in it." I thought he had just lost his marbles.

"You can't be serious?"

"Yes, I'm quite serious. I want to arrange a screen test for you . . . if you want it."

I put down my fork and looked him straight in the eye. "Look, Lynn, I'm no actress."

"Neither were any of them when they started."

Oh my God, the man is serious, I thought. "No, I don't want to be a phony. I'm not an actress, never have been, and I don't care to start. And besides, I'm not beautiful, and furthermore I'm not leaving my boys for anything, ever!"

"You wouldn't have to become a phony. You *are* beautiful. And you could take your boys with you."

I suddenly became intensely frightened. I'm not sure why; maybe it was that I was being confronted with something I didn't want to face. All my life I had been subject to feelings of inferiority. It had become my identity, and I just couldn't accept any other.

"No, Lynn, I don't want to talk about it anymore, please."

He stared at me in disbelief. "Most women would jump at this opportunity. You can't imagine how many of them fill my waiting room every day, hoping to be discovered. What is going on with you? Why?"

"Nothing is going on. It's like you said, there are lots of women dying for the chance, probably much more qualified for the job than I am. Why don't you pick one of them?

I don't need to be a movie star. Can't you understand that?"

How familiar my reaction sounded. Shades of being se-lected Annual Queen in high school! It was as though I were repeating the words verbatim.

I was becoming visibly upset by the conversation, which provoked a protective feeling in Lynn. He sat back and stud-ied me. It seemed that I was determined to prove my un-worthiness and would go to the mat doing it. I amazed him.

"I've never met anyone like you before." His voice was soft.

"I'm sure that's probably very true," I said, adjusting my napkin.

"Dear lady, you provoke some very deep feelings in me. I'm not sure, at this point, what they are, but they're there."

I looked up at him. "Well, I don't mean to."

"I'm just going to come right out and say it. I very much would like to make love to you . . . very much." He leaned forward and took my hand.

Oh, my stars! The movie bit was difficult enough to handle. Now this! "I mistook you for a gentleman, Lynn." I pulled my hand away and hid it under the napkin in my lap. That napkin was so useful.

"I am very much a gentleman."

"I don't think gentlemen ask questions like that." I felt my face start to redden.

"It wasn't a question. It was a statement of how I feel."

"But I don't love you."

"But you said love was a state of mind."

Nonplussed, I retorted, "Yes, well, it's a state of mind I'm not in." The red on my cheeks deepened two more shades.

"It's a state of mind I could easily be in," he responded. The chase was on.

"How can you say that?"

"It's easy. I just say what I feel."

"Look, I'm a woman who's in business in a man's world. I know a lot of people think that women get ahead in business by sleeping with their bosses. I've heard of the casting couch even in New Mexico. Maybe that's part of your world, but it's not mine. Get it?"

"I don't understand you right now. Would you help me to?" Boy, was he crafty. He sure knew how to handle that one. I was beginning to feel intimidated by this man. I had never been with a man who had his looks, his personality, his power and experience. He scared me. My eyes began to well up and I could hardly hold back the tears.

He leaned forward again. "I'm sorry. Please tell me what you really feel."

I took out a handkerchief and delicately dabbed under my eyes to prevent the mascara from running. "Look, let me be real straight with you. I don't know what I want. I don't want to get involved with you, even though you are nice. I just can't."

"Do you already have someone in your life?"

"No, I don't. My only real friend has been God."

Lynn was astonished. "God?"

"Yes, God. I talk to Him all the time. He's answered my prayers and helped to make me what I am."

"Oh. But when was the last time you ate ice cream in the sand with God?"

"Well, never, but He is always there when I need help." I was wondering if anyone in California ever prayed to anything but fame. Whenever I said anything about God, people treated me as though I were completely out to lunch. There were moments like these that made me feel that I didn't fit in anywhere. An outcast of Poker Flats.

"Yes, but why do you always need help? Why don't you make *yourself* responsible for the help?"

I had never thought of it that way. "Lynn, I've had a hard life. I guess I've just gotten used to expecting His help. I have made my life out of nothing. I *did* do it. But I did it with God's help."

He dropped his eyes to the table and said softly, "Yes, I guess you did."

I continued to dab under my eyes, feeling a strange mixture of courage and self-pity.

"So, what will you do with your life besides be a successful businesswoman?"

I straightened up in my chair. "I don't know. I seem to

be looking for something—or maybe even someone—but I don't know what it is. I really don't think it's a man . . . but it's something, I can feel it, around me, inside of me."

"Don't you think it's *you* you're looking for?"

"I don't know what you mean by that?" It was a strange statement.

"It's what we're all looking for. You just have to go through a lot before you get it . . . before you know who you are."

"Maybe."

"So, you don't want to be Ann-Margret?" He smiled.

"Oh, Lynn, she's so beautiful."

"Just as you are beautiful, sweet lady."

"You know, I have a really hard time with that compliment. I always have. God, I don't know what I would do without Estee Lauder, Clairol, and mix-and-match ready-to-wear."

"You'd look like you . . . which is even more beautiful." Lynn smiled at me and then asked the waiter for the check.

"Can we go for a drive by the ocean?"

"No, Lynn, please take me home. I miss my little boys."

"Can I call you tomorrow so we can talk more about what you are looking for? It's obviously not an agent."

I laughed. "Let me think about it, okay?"

"Fair enough," he sighed. "It's such a shame the world will be robbed of seeing you ride across an Italian sunset with that hair blowing in the wind."

The next day I was in my office on the phone to Ben.

"Yes, Ben, but I don't want to be queen of spaghetti Westerns. . . . All right, so you think I'm crazy. You're not the first one to tell me that. . . . What? Where? . . . Waco, Texas! What, to set up the system? Three weeks? Then on to the next franchise. I'll have to take my boys, Ben. . . . Okay. . . . Yes, and Sarah Lee too. Apartment? Does it have a pool? . . . Okay, I'll leave in three days."

A rare picture of me in a dress. Judith Darlene Hampton, born March 16, 1946.

Here I am in a cotton field in East Texas with my brother Donnie. While my mother picked cotton with the other farm hands, Donnie made sure I stayed out of trouble.

(*Above*) Momma, Donnie, Aunt Pearl, and me in East Texas shortly before we moved to New Mexico.

(*Above right*) My dog Puddles and me in Artesia, New Mexico. I'm wearing the dress my father bought me, the only gift I ever received from him.

Daddy Bill shortly after his marriage to Momma.

The "fancy" new house in Artesia that we moved into after Momma married Daddy Bill.

My third-grade picture. Can you tell who cut my bangs?

Lloyd Gene (Loy), my baby brother, sporting a black eye.

Posing, at age eight, with my older brothers and sister: (*left to right*) Donnie, Gayle, Wanda and Charles.

Dressed in my first real formal. By eighth grade, the little tomboy had blossomed into a bona fide glamorous teenager.

At age sixteen, I was the youngest girl ever to be elected President of Theta Rho (*top row, seventh from the right*).

I. O. O. F.

THETA RHO GIRLS
ASSEMBLY
AND
GRAND JUNIOR LODGE

Eighth Annual Session

INSTALLATION PROGRAM
1962 - 63

Las Cruces, New Mexico
Saturday, June 23, 1962

Riding Slim, my beautiful chestnut friend. My happiest moments as a teen-ager were spent with Slim.

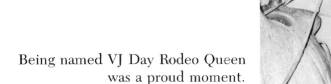

Being named VJ Day Rodeo Queen was a proud moment.

Mike Phipps was a football star, one of the cutest boys in our high school and my first great love.

Mike made me question if love was really just a state of mind . . . or something more.

By age fourteen, Loy was a handsome guy and far more knowledgeable about the facts of life than I.

Here I am as the Spirit of Light in a dance that I created during my senior year. How strange and prophetic.

From my high school yearbook: Who's Who 1964, most beautiful.

When I was chosen Annual Queen of my senior class, Momma bought me a magnificent pink satin dress. Unfortunately, I felt neither happy nor beautiful that night.

My two sons, the greatest joys of my life. Here they are before we left New Mexico. Brandy (*left*) is two and Chris is less than a year.

Here we are, Christmas 1980, in the Great White Structure.

An early Ramtha dialogue. As Ramtha's teachings began to spread, our dialogues would draw several hundred people each weekend.

With Jeremy, Jeff (*far right*) and the members of Earth, Wind and Fire.

My brother Loy, now head coach
of Portalas, New Mexico, High
School.

Momma, who is as feisty and
loving today as she was when
I was a kid.

With my close friend Thomas
Sharkey of the Shirley Mac-
Laine "Simo" fame.

A magnificent site for a sunrise dialogue.

By 1982, I had developed a style of dress—loose-fitting pants and an Indian tunic—that allowed freedom of movement for Ramtha.

An early morning march in Yucca Valley.

Also at a Yucca Valley dialogue.
Ministering to the body as well as the spirit.

This is the ad in an Arabian horse magazine that changed my life by introducing me to the love of my life.

After declaring our love, Jeff and I sought refuge in the home of my dearest friend Anne-Marie Bennstrom.

Soulmates: Jeff and JZ Knight.

The Ram, who opened my eyes and my heart to that grand adventure called "life." PHOTO CREDIT: Thomas Sharkey.

CHAPTER FIFTEEN

THE GHOST AND
SARAH LEE

During the next three days, I busied myself making all the arrangements for leaving Manhattan Beach. Sarah Lee took care of the packing and readied the household things that were to be picked up by the moving company. On the second day, as I was reviewing my office procedures with the new cable manager, I received an urgent call from Sarah Lee. She was in a state of sheer panic. After I got her to calm down, she told me about a remarkable incident that had just occurred.

She had gotten the boys dressed and was in the kitchen preparing their breakfast. As she was frying some eggs, the back door, at the other end of the kitchen, opened up wide and a wind flowed through the kitchen. She said she strongly felt the presence of something in the kitchen. Brandy came running out of his bedroom and stopped short. He looked up at something that was beside Sarah Lee, and he started laughing, obviously very happy to see what was there. "Hi,

Ghost. Are you going to move with us?" Then he turned around and told "Ghost" to follow him to see Christopher.

As Brandy entered the dining room, the shag carpet revealed not only Brandy's little footprints, but another, larger set behind him that followed him all the way to Chris's bedroom. As the footprints disappeared into the bedroom, a wind followed as well, leaving poor, frightened Sarah Lee in a state of shock. She accidentally knocked the frying pan with eggs onto the floor, just missing her feet. That frightened her out of her wits. She thought "Ghost" had done it. As she stood there with her false teeth chattering away, the wind came back through the kitchen and passed Sarah Lee, taking her breath away. She was frozen to the bone with fright.

As the back door gently closed, the boys came frolicking into the kitchen to announce to wide-eyed Sarah Lee that, "Ghost says he's moving to Waco with us. I'm glad. I would cry if Ghost couldn't move. He's our friend." Brandy and Chris began to jump up and down with glee, which must have brought poor dear Sarah Lee back from the dead, for she ran and locked the door, grabbed the boys and the phone, and locked all of them in Brandy's bedroom. When she called me, her teeth were chattering so badly I had trouble making out what she was saying. She pleaded with me to come home right away. I did just that.

When I got home, I heard muffled crying coming from Brandy's room. I tried to open the door but it was locked. At first Sarah Lee wouldn't believe it was me, but finally she opened the door. Brandy and Chris came running and put their arms around my legs and squeezed them. I tried to get Sarah Lee to come out to show her that there were no "spooks" in the house, but she flatly refused. So I went to do the investigation, with Brandy and Chris acting as assistant sleuths.

As we walked into the living room, the large footprints were apparent in the carpet. They tracked from the kitchen to Chris's bedroom and back again. I was alarmed by them and by whatever had made them, but I felt it was imperative not to let the boys know what I was feeling. I proceeded to the kitchen to find the pan lying upside down, butter and eggs splattered all over the floor. Brandy came up to me and tugged on my pants.

"Mommy, Ghost came in the kitchen and scared Nanny Sarah. *She* had the accident on the floor, not me and Ghost. We didn't do nothing. Are we in trouble?" It seemed strange that all Brandy was worried about was getting into trouble. It was odd that this Ghost character had terrified poor Sarah Lee, but not Brandy or Chris.

I sat Brandy and Chris at the kitchen table, then I checked on Sarah Lee. She was moaning and praying and uttering things about goblins and spooks, but she did not want to leave the sanctuary of the bedroom. I returned to the table and sat down with the boys. Chris had climbed onto the table and was "driving" a small car around. I replaced him in his seat, folded my hands, and tried to put into words the questions that I needed the boys to answer.

Before I could ask my first question, Brandy asked me, "Mommy, are we in trouble? Are you mad at us?"

"No, no, son, I'm just a little confused. I wasn't here this morning and I don't really know what happened. But I would like to ask you and Chris to help me understand, okay?" They must have felt relieved that they were not going to be punished, for they nodded with happy contentment.

"Okay now, boys . . . uh, who is Ghost?"

Brandy volunteered first. "He's our friend. He's real tall, like Superman, and he comes to visit us. And he's real bright, like Tinker Bell. He's real nice, Mommy. One time I had a bad dream, and I woke up real scared, and he came in my room and made all the dark go away . . . everything. It all glowed and I wasn't scared anymore. Then he smiled and put his hand on my face, and I went back to sleep and dreamed happy dreams. Are you mad at Ghost, Mommy?"

I might have thought this was just an "imaginary friend" that the boys had made up, but how could something imaginary leave footprints? I answered Brandy's question while pondering this mystery. "No, I'm not mad at Ghost. Uh, Brandy and Chris, are you afraid of Ghost?"

"No, he's our friend—huh, Brandy?" said Chris as he nodded his head at Brandy.

"Well, why were you both crying when I came into your rooms? You looked like you were afraid."

"Because Nanny Sarah scared us. She said it was the devil. Mommy, what's the devil?" Brandy asked.

"The devil doesn't exist, but to a lot of people he's like the bad guys that Superman always fights. Anything that scares some people or anything that happens that's different—like Ghost, for example—some people say is the devil. But God wouldn't create something like that. He loves you and everyone else, and when you love someone, you don't try to hurt them or scare them, do you? Well, neither would God. Even though Ghost is a good guy, because Nanny Sarah can't see him like you can, he is different and that scared her. So, she thinks he is a bad guy. Do you understand what I'm saying?" They listened carefully.

"But if Ghost was a bad guy, he would already have hurt us and he hasn't. He says that he loves us and that he is supposed to protect us. He says that God told him to, but Nanny Sarah doesn't believe me. She just hates him," Brandy said, looking rather sad.

"No, I don't think she *really* hates him. She just isn't friends with him like you are, and so she was frightened."

I cleaned up the mess in the kitchen and started to fix everyone some late breakfast. I kept thinking about Ghost and all that the boys had told me. I found it rather ironic that it wasn't Ghost who had frightened them but Sarah Lee by her hysteria and religious superstition. It's amazing, I thought. It isn't what we can't see that frightens us, it's what we see—it's people! All bound up in ignorance and superstition, so fanatical about their beliefs, crazed by the very culture we live in—no wonder we've had so many wars and so much human suffering. I wish people would stop saying, "The devil made me do it." Shit, people do what they do *because they want to,* not because some boogeyman made them. And the worst of the lot are those who accuse others of being possessed by such idiocy—shit, those hypocrites are the most evil of all of them! How screwed up people are!!

I was struck by what Brandy had said about Ghost. My little boy reasoned that if Ghost were bad, he would have had plenty of chances to hurt us. But obviously he hadn't, and according to Brandy and Chris he had comforted them. I had often prayed for God to protect us, especially here in California, and when I prayed for that protection I did feel a presence. I was comforted by all of this, and I believed my children, even without the evidence of the footprints. Whatever or whoever Ghost was, I gave thanks to God for being blessed with this esteemed guardian.

When the boys were seated and eating their breakfast, I took a tray in to Nanny Sarah. The fright hadn't dampened her appetite; she wolfed down the food. As she ate, I told her of my conversation with the boys and my own thoughts about God and Ghost. When I came to the bit about giving thanks to God for his presence, she jumped up screaming, dumping the tray of food onto the floor. She ran around the room shaking her arms and screaming that the devil had gotten me, too. Then she ran and got her suitcase and started packing up her things. I just sat there aghast!

Sarah Lee finally stopped long enough to tell me that she couldn't live with "no spooks and no devils" and "folks and young 'uns that were friendly with 'em." Nothing I said could change her mind. As my momma would say, "Lord have mercy!" So I called the bus station and arranged for her to go back to New Mexico. She refused to fly—something about the devil flying, too. She wouldn't let me drive her to the bus station, so I called her a "safe" cab. I escorted her to the cab. She was crying all the way. As the cab roared off, I noticed that it had a bumper sticker that said, "Make Love Not War." I'm certain she never saw it.

On our last day in California I managed, with the help of my secretary, to get everything packed and on the moving van. Ben had called to tell me that he would drive me and the boys to the airport. Everything was ready. The boys looked charming in their red-white-and-blue blazers and their little matching neckties. They were very excited about flying in the big plane. When a knock came at the door I assumed it was Ben, but when I answered it, there stood a chauffeur announcing, "Your car, madam." I looked out, and there, waiting, was a shiny black limousine. I questioned him about Ben, but all he said was that Ben couldn't make it and had sent the car instead. He picked up our baggage and we followed him to the car. The boys were "Wowing" while he opened the door for us. To my surprise, there sat Lynn.

"You rang, madam?" he said in a very British accent. I started laughing. He helped the boys inside and introduced himself, then opened a carton of milk and started pouring us all a round. "Ah, this is much better than bubbly, wouldn't you say?"

As we started for the airport, Lynn turned on the TV for the boys, who were "Wowing" even more. I told Lynn the story of Ghost, and he laughed most of the way through. We finally arrived at the airport, and the chauffeur checked the baggage for me and even checked us in for our flight. Lynn carried Christopher in his arms, while I held Brandy's hand all the way to the gate.

"Lynn, it was such a wonderful surprise to see you again. And the car and all of this—it's just so very thoughtful. I have never ridden in a limousine before and the boys, well, I think you can tell by their reactions, it was quite a treat for them as well. Thank you so much."

His eyes were slightly moist and his voice broke to a soft whisper. "You deserve it and much, much more." He paused. "Remember at dinner, when I said I had strong feelings for you? Well, I still do. I'm happy for your new move, but I feel like I had the rarest thing in the world in my hands. I wanted to hold it tight so it wouldn't disappear, but I was afraid I might crush it if I closed my hands. When that plane takes you and your little boys away, it will create a vacuum inside of me . . . something, I guess, has to be there. JZ, I love you for your beauty inside and out, and I would never want to see you lose it just to fit in with someone else's expectations. Trust me when I tell you that if there truly is a God up there, He is going to come into focus for a lot of people just like me because they have been touched by you . . . and that must make the Old Man pretty happy." A small tear formed at the corner of his eye and dropped off when he lowered his head.

I couldn't say anything but how much I appreciated him and how much I enjoyed the few times we were together. The announcement came for our boarding, and I straightened out the boys' jackets. Lynn lifted each boy up and gave him a kiss, then told them to take care of me. I looked at him, and he leaned forward and kissed me long and tenderly. When he opened his eyes, he said, "I love you, JZ. . . . Please let me know where you are from time to time. I'm already missing you so much."

I looked into those beautiful eyes and knew he meant what he had said. "Lynn, I promise I will let you know where I am. Now, go and see your son and throw him a mean baseball."

Waco, Texas, was quite unlike Manhattan Beach. No more backed-up traffic on freeways; in its place was the relaxed pace of come-and-go traffic—with the exception of an occasional drag race at a stoplight. The people looked more "normal," and there were even dogs that whizzed normally on fire hydrants. All in all, this place felt more like Artesia, though I must admit I found the heat and humidity rather appalling.

I had a beautiful apartment with access to a large swimming pool. Within a block there was a day-care center and kindergarten. But my visit to the local cable TV office was a different story. The office itself was rather quaint, and most of the staff didn't possess the savvy to run an efficient system. I was scheduled to meet with the "marketing crew" at ten-thirty that morning. I noticed some people milling around in the back room, and when I asked why they were there, the secretary told me that they were the marketing team.

"This is the marketing crew?" I was aghast. The crew of seven included three men dressed as if they were going to clean sewers. One didn't have a tooth in his head, and when he closed his mouth, his chin hooked up with his nose. There were four women. One was pregnant and wore a thin cotton dress with a safety pin in place of a button to hold the bosom in place. She had large hairy legs and thongs exposing dirty toenails. Another was an ancient senior citizen who, though very pleasant, was almost deaf and looked as though she needed to sit down, not hit the streets selling cable TV. The other two were fine—except one wore a black leather jacket and the other had a passel of kids with her that apparently waited in the car while she worked. There were also two teenagers, one a flower child and the other just a kid in need of work.

The woman with all the kids answered me. "Yes, ma'am. We git in our cars with our dogs and kids and we go door-ta-door. The boss, Mr. Emmet, don't talk ta us much. An' we don't really knowd whut ta do."

"Well, ma'am, I'm the installer, and ever' time I tells Mr. Emmet whut's wrong with thangs, he don't give me no mind. The people here is real good folks, but they don't know much cuz they ain't been taught much."

"That's right, ma'am," the toothless man said. "Ol' Bill here knows. He been a-helpin' us some, but we don't know it all. We got some hungry bellies ta feed, but we's not makin' enough ta do the job."

"Well, I want to thank all of you for coming and enlightening me a little. I see the difficulty here. I've already spoken to Mr. Emmet, and he's not really very happy doing this work anyway. But be that as it may, we are going to make this system something everyone in this room can be proud of. It's my job to see that is accomplished. I'm going to be training each one of you in every aspect of your job, and I'm also going to help improve your appearance, something you all need. The more professional you look to your customers, the more likely they are to buy from you. Now, is that clear to everyone?"

"Ya mean you even goin' ta teach us ta talk right?" asked Bill.

"That's right. And I think that afterwards, you'll be much happier because you'll be making a lot more money." Everyone applauded.

"Bill, I know you're the installer and part-time technician here, but I want to promote you to office manager. Your sincerity alone is all you need to do the job for now. The rest, I'll teach you. I want you to hire five more people, and

I want to have our first training session in two days, starting at seven in the morning." Bill blushed deeply but was very grateful for the promotion.

"The rest of you, I'm going to raise your commission by five percent and you show me what you can do." I got another round of applause.

Two days later, I took them into the field for a training session. I was dressed in my jeans and had my hair pulled back under a hard hat. It was very hot.

"Now, I want you all to learn how to wire up the system in preparation for a drop. That means you'll have to learn to climb these poles. I'll demonstrate." I put on my pulley belt, attached my spurs to my boots, put on my gloves, and scaled the pole to the top and then back down again. I must have astonished everyone because when I came back down and faced them, their mouths were hanging wide open.

"Uh, Mrs. Hensley, I can't climb no poles," said Mrs. Chapman.

"If you're going to work in this company, you will. Now, come on and get your rigging on and get up that pole. Look at the pole as a challenge. When you *believe* you can do something—anything—then you always can do it. Your attitude is everything and everything is your attitude."

One by one, the women did their turns up the pole; their pride in their achievement was evident in all the bragging they did afterwards. The only two who did not climb the pole were the pregnant woman and the dear old senior citizen. Next came the men.

As the training went on, I taught them how to go through crawl spaces of various houses to locate suitable outlets. We dissected a four-way amplifier. I held daily seminars on proper dress and the development of individual sales presentations. And through it all I stressed the importance of a positive attitude in achieving success.

Bill advanced in his knowledge and expertise, including the management of his crew, and was now well on his way to a new career as a cable manager. I felt great pride for everyone in the crew. They had a much better understanding of what they were selling, and more important, their personal attitudes about themselves had changed. They didn't even look like the same crew I had first met. I had done my job well.

I had been working hard for three weeks and decided to stay home with my boys. We had a jolly time swimming and playing in the water. In the afternoon, I put the boys down for a nap in the apartment and I returned to the pool and dozed off on my stomach.

I was awakened by a burning sensation on my back and realized that I had a severe sunburn. I went inside and looked at my back in the bathroom mirror. It was a deep and angry red. Brandy and Chris came in and began oohing and ahing over my back. I sat down and gave them some Noxema to pat on me gently.

"Does it hurt, Mommy?" Christopher said with an expression of pity on his little face.

"Hurt? It's like my back is on fire." I listened to my own words, and suddenly the words of the fortune-teller came ringing in my head. "I can't believe it. . . . It's true, my back is on fire!"

"Mommy, you shouldn't have fallen asleep in the sun," Brandy said.

"You're absolutely right. But maybe it was inevitable. Oh, my goodness, I don't understand this. Never mind. Listen, you two, take a lesson from Mommy and don't stay in the sun too long. See what happens?"

They both nodded in awe.

The following afternoon I lay down on my stomach to take a nap. I never sleep without pajamas or a nightgown, but I couldn't put anything on my back, not even a sheet. I was in a deep sleep when the phone started ringing. Slowly, I woke up and fumbled the phone off the hook.

It was Ben.

"Well, you blew out the computer down here," he said happily. "We've never had two hundred cable sales in one day! Doll, you've turned that loser completely around. Congratulations!"

"Yeah, pretty good, eh? Ben, I was so tired yesterday, I fell asleep in the sun and—"

"Listen, doll, you deserved to take a break."

"Oh really? You wouldn't think so if you could see my hard-working back. It's cooked." I tried to sit up and get a little more comfortable, but moving was painful.

"Your back is sunburned? Hey, JZ, I'm sorry. Can I do anything?" he asked sincerely.

"Oh, sure, Ben you can do a lot from a thousand miles away. . . . So, what's up?"

"I've got a proposal for you," Ben continued. "It includes two choices."

"Two choices for what, my back?" I said, trying to laugh.

"Well, I've seen what you did in that fire hole down there, and I've got two more franchises and they're big and tough. I think you can handle either one, but I need to find out which one you want."

"Please, no wisecracks about fire. Ben, how long have I been here?"

He paused. "Three weeks, doll. Ready to leave?"

"And you have two franchises . . . and you want me to pick one?"

"That's right."

Oh, my God. That fortune-teller had been right on. I was beginning to feel a bit uneasy about someone knowing so much about my future. "What are they, Ben?"

"One is Bethlehem, Pennsylvania. Have you ever been to Bethlehem?"

"Only in the Bible, Ben." I crawled off the bed and made my way to the window.

"Yeah, funny, I admire that dry humor of yours. Anyway, the other one is in the Puget Sound area, around Seattle and Tacoma, Washington."

"Outside of Seattle-Tacoma? Where?" I started chewing at a fingernail.

"A place called Bremerton. It's beautiful up there. Lots of trees and mountains and lakes."

"Of course!" I rolled my eyes. I couldn't believe what he was saying. I pulled the receiver away and stared at it a moment, as if to see if it was real or if I was dreaming this whole conversation.

"If you want my advice, I'd choose Seattle-Tacoma."

"Why that choice, Ben?"

"Because you're a nature person, and there certainly is a lot of nature up there. And Bethlehem has real bad air pollution. Worse than L.A."

"You mean, 'The sky is dark with business'?" I repeated the fortune-teller's words.

"You know, steel factories, industrial parks, and all of that. What I'm saying is, wouldn't you prefer moving to the Pacific Northwest? It will take a long time for you to develop the area, so that'll make for a more stable environment for the boys. You see, doll, I do think of those things."

I was thinking about the uncanniness of the prophecy. There was no room for skepticism; the prophecy was too exact. "Ben, I must tell you that I am beginning to feel my life is being guided somehow."

"Well, I don't mean to be pushy. But you weren't crazy about L.A., were you?" Ben the unenlightened! He didn't understand what I meant at all.

I was still preoccupied. "No, I wasn't." Just then a breeze came flowing through the room, billowing the curtains into my face. It carried a gentle scent of jasmine and ferns.

"So, what do you say?" Ben persisted. "I'd like you to go right away. I'll have the apartment closed up and make all of your arrangements for you."

"Ben, I have fire on my back."

"What the hell are you talking about? Has the heat fried your brains?" he huffed.

"I don't know. I guess that's what I'm going to find out."

"So, do we have a deal?"

"I guess we do, Ben, I guess we do."

"That's my girl. You'll still get twelve percent of everything sold."

"Fifteen," I countered.

"Shit. Okay, fifteen. Uh, two other items. First, Lynn's been asking about you. Have you talked to him lately?"

"Once or twice. What is the other item?"

"Twila told me to tell you something about some old

woman dying . . . and something about how she never found out anything? I hope you can figure that one out."

He must have been talking about the fortune-teller. How strange that she should die now! Or maybe it wasn't so strange; she was pretty old. But still . . . "Uh, Ben, please tell Twila that I think I'm going to meet The One."

"The One? Who's that?"

"I wish I knew."

"Okay, I'll tell her. You sound weird, JZ. We better get you the hell out of that place."

"I'm sure it's just a state of mind, Ben, that's all."

"So you really don't want to be a movie star?" he said teasingly.

"No. I think I'm destined to do something that makes a difference."

"Yeah, well you're already doing that, doll. Talk to you soon."

"And Ben, thanks for the new job." I hung up the phone and just stood there in front of the window, allowing the breeze to cool my body. It felt so good. All of the burning seemed to cease. It was a healing breeze.

As the breeze bathed my back, I said a little prayer. "Dear God, is all of this Your will? Was the fortune-teller guided by You? If so, then I accept the changes in my life and only pray that I will know the right thing to do. Father, grant me the wisdom I need to make all the right moves and all the right decisions. I give great thanks to You for my life and the lives of my children. Keep us safe in Your arms. Oh, I almost forgot, thank you for Ghost. Amen."

It was a long flight from Waco to Seattle-Tacoma International Airport, but the boys amused themselves and enjoyed the in-flight movie. As the flight pattern took us over the Pacific Northwest, I gazed out the window at the most beautiful mountains I had ever seen. The captain announced their names as we flew over them: Mount Saint Helens, Mount Hood, Mount Adams, and the grandest of them all, Mount Rainier. Each mountain rose up out of an emerald green forest of noble and Douglas firs, and was crowned with a glistening white cap. Amid them were many lakes that reflected the sun . . . like mirrors! Suddenly, the fortune-teller's voice came into my head and spoke softly. "The other will be a place with great mountains, tall pines, and lakes that shine like mirrors unto the heavens. If you go to the mountains and pines, you will meet The One. Do you understand?"

"No," I whispered, "I don't understand."

CHAPTER SIXTEEN

THE PROMISED LAND

Washington State was utterly breathtaking. I was in awe of the fact that Christmas trees were everywhere, and of the gentle rain at night that provided the most restful sleep I could ever recall having. Everything was so clean—the roads, the streets, the forests. When I took the boys camping I was amazed to find that the nearby stream was so clear you could actually see the fish in the water. Back in New Mexico the streams were so muddy and murky that when you put your line in the water, you had to have a bobber on the line just so you would know when you had a bite.

One day as I was admiring the beauty that surrounded me, I remembered how much I had enjoyed playing in Momma's greenhouse. I would pretend all the plants were a forest and sprayed the plastic ceiling with the water hose, watching the water fall on the forest like rain. Now, I didn't have to pretend anymore. It was all alive and around me right there.

I thought about how children have favorite play habits, some of which come true later in life, and wondered if as children we somehow choose our destinies. After all, what I play-pretended had come true. There was only one ingredient missing: the rancher I had dreamed of marrying and all his wonderful horses. Oh well, I thought, who knows? Maybe that would come true as well. One thing was certain, this area felt like my home, and I did not ever want to leave it.

I found a beautiful house for us in the Lakewood district of Tacoma, which I leased; I still didn't know for certain where I wanted to plant permanent roots. I chose Tacoma because it was the midway point between several cable TV franchises I was negotiating. Though it was a long drive to Bremerton and to Seattle, I needed to have a home base so the boys could enroll in school on a more stable basis. It was 1972; Brandy was six and needed to be in school, while Chris, now four, was ready for a day-care center. I found a charming, warm older lady to care for the boys when they returned home from school.

By June of 1973 I had completed the marketing of the Brimstone and Seattle cable systems. Then Ben's company collapsed in L.A. There had been an internal dispute followed by a large lawsuit. I was now out of a job. But my reputation in the CATV industry was impeccable. Though I had many offers from marketing firms, I declined them and decided to form my own company. I gave it a masculine name—Mann Communications and Marketing. I negotiated a contract with the *Tacoma News Tribune* to represent their subsidiary, Cable TV Puget Sound. It was a large system that had room for expansion and development. It would provide me with the stability that I needed for quite some time.

I hired a superb team of marketing people and trained them thoroughly. They were all self-motivated, open-minded, creative people with positive attitudes—essential factors for a successful marketing campaign.

One late-winter afternoon, some of my salespeople began returning from the field, pouring themselves some coffee to warm up. I was busy going over their orders, when the phone rang.

"Hello? Yes, Terry. Wait a second. . . ." She was having problems finding anyone home and was asking for a new area. I just closed my eyes, and in a moment I knew where to send her. "Okay, go two blocks over to Vine Maple. You'll have better luck there. And Terry, don't forget to bless the house before you knock on the door." When I hung up, Frank Smith walked in the door. He was one of my most successful salesmen. I liked his attitude from the moment I'd met him.

"Hey, boss, you doing your hocus-pocus number again?" He plopped down in a chair by my desk. The others were milling around, talking about various things. I smiled at him.

"You've turned this whole company around," he continued. "Everybody is impressed, even though they don't understand how it works. How do you know how to tell a salesman where to go?" he asked, sipping some coffee.

"I just have a feeling about it, sort of a hunch, and that's how I know," I said, shrugging my shoulders.

"Like a psychic feeling?" he asked.

I looked at Frank earnestly, eager to understand what he meant by that word. "Psychic? What do you mean?"

Frank gave me an indulgent smile. "You know, it's like a sixth sense. I think you must be psychic, boss," he said in a sturdy voice.

I hesitated. "I don't know . . ." For a moment I felt guilty for even considering that I was psychic. It wasn't me that knew, but God. To think otherwise would be to deprive myself and others of the beauty and mystery that is God.

"Well, whatever you do is beyond scientific marketing techniques . . . really beyond!" he said.

My gaze turned from Frank to the dull light flowing through the windows. It was a bleak brown autumn afternoon, subdued and cheerless. I answered Frank in a listless monotone. "I can't agree I have any sixth sense, Frank. It's God. I pray and trust in God. He's helped me to be what I am."

Frank leaned back a bit in his chair and studied me for a while. I braced myself for the usual rebuttal.

"Boss, you are damn good, and uncommon. But I feel

I should warn you that your trustfulness could be destructive to you. All that 'innate nobility of mankind' you talk about —hell, the general run of mankind is wicked. Forgive me for saying this, boss, but there is a certain stupidity in innocence. All that loving candor makes you naive and defenseless against those who would use you for their own gains. And I suspect that when that happens, you simply think that it's God's will." Frank paused to let what he had said sink in. Then he became wryly amused. "You silly angel, maybe God will reward you someday, but I doubt it. I still think you're psychic."

Frank was an agnostic, and it shocked me. "Frank, if people really understood how much God loves them and how accessible He is to them, if they really understood that, then they could love and trust one another. Unfortunately, most don't understand, so they become wary, wicked, and greedy, even cruel. That saddens me. Doesn't it you?"

Frank pondered, then shook his head. "I think humanity's corruption is caused by unselfish people like you, boss. Your kindness and generosity tempt people to exploit and ridicule you. I think they do it because deep inside they know exactly what they are, and that makes them feel guilty and they need to blame and hate you for it." Suddenly Frank changed the subject. "Hey, boss, I have an aunt who really wants to meet you. I've told her a lot about you. Can you spare an hour tomorrow afternoon and let me take you to her house?"

What Frank had said was making me feel depressed— almost as if I were responsible for the world's unhappiness. I shrugged my shoulders in an effort to rid myself of the gloomy thoughts, then looked up at Frank, grinned, and nodded. Just getting out of there for an hour might do me some good. I had been working as much as sixteen hours a day, and I was beginning to feel the fatigue of it. "Sure, why not."

"Boss, you won't regret it. She's some kind of a psychic. She says she can see things in people . . . something about reading their energy. But"—he shook a long finger at me and laughed—"she says it's a gift from God."

My ears perked up. It sounded like it might be an interesting meeting.

When we got out of Frank's car the following afternoon in front of a two-story house in a middle-class neighborhood, the winter sun was shining and I felt the need for a good stretch. As I stood there feeling blessed by the sun, dogs and cats from all over the neighborhood surrounded the car. The dogs wagged their tails and cats purred and rubbed up against my legs. Frank watched in astonishment.

"What the hell is going on here?" he asked.

"This has been happening a lot lately if I stand still long enough. It's kind of odd, but it's also very nice." I looked at him smugly and added, "I think it has a lot to do with love and trust and being innocent, Frank dear."

I followed Frank into the house. It was decorated with plants and flowers of every description, even herbs hanging upside down from the ceiling to dry. The air was permeated with the musk of clutter. Frank's Aunt Beau came down the stairs in a robe. She had been asleep.

"Aunt Beau, I want to introduce you to my boss, JZ Hensley."

When she reached the bottom of the stairs she said, "Oh, my dear, I've heard so many wonderful things about you. It's such a pleasure to meet you. You must forgive my robe, I do a late-night radio show on health, and I'm afraid I overslept."

She embraced me, then suddenly stepped back. Her hands trembled as she adjusted her bathrobe and smoothed down her drab hair. She glanced at Frank, who seemed to be waiting for some divine confirmation. When she looked back at me, I had the distinct feeling she was studying me with some apprehension. Then, rather unexpectedly, her flabby and colorless face began to burn and her eyes reddened. She began to cry, but she was also smiling as she cried. Frank became alarmed and led her to a chair. He gently pushed her down into it. I stood rigid, confused by her sudden burst of emotion.

"I'm sorry . . . did I offend you?" I asked in a voice that was barely audible.

"Oh my, now I understand. My dear child, you have the most awesome power walking with you."

I was stunned. "A power walking with me? What do you mean? I don't understand."

"I've never seen anything like it . . . it's powerful . . . it's all around you. It's a blazing light, a powerful energy. I've seen energies, but never one like this."

I looked back at Frank. Could she be loony? "Don't we all have some sort of light around us?" I hesitated. "Maybe even a guardian angel—it says that somewhere in the Bible."

She started shaking her head in a determined manner. "No, not like this. This is a timeless energy. It's just more than I can put into words."

Then I remembered Ghost. Maybe he was paying Aunt Beau a visit too. "Maybe it's a . . . ghost?"

"No, it's like a powerful god."

"What does that mean? You mean like God the Father?"

"No, it is *of* God," she answered, sounding as if she were out of breath.

I was still thinking of Ghost. "Could you mean like a person who has died but comes back to haunt us? Or even maybe help us?"

"No, it is as if this power were life itself."

I became engulfed with fear and frustration. I wanted to yell at her, "For God's sake what the hell is it? Get on with it." But instead I started chewing my bottom lip. Frank gave Aunt Beau his handkerchief and she began to wipe her forehead.

I blurted out, "Is this thing an evil force?" A chill ran up my spine. I was almost afraid of her response.

Her oyster-colored eyes were fixed on me, scrutinizing my face. "Oh, no, no, no. It's the opposite. It's holy, child, holy." Then she put her arms up to shield her eyes from something unseen. "I'm sorry, I can't talk about it any further," she muttered. "Please do forgive me for not being more clear to you. I know that, because of your innocence, you don't understand this."

"But you act as if this brings you some anguish, as if what you see is too terrible to look upon," I said.

"Oh, no, dear JZ, this wonderful and holy light that walks with you will change many things in the world."

"But what is this *thing* that you say walks with me?" My voice was quivering now.

"I don't want to confuse you, and I don't want to sound blasphemous, but have you studied Jesus Christ and His teachings?"

"Yes."

"Well, dear child," she said gently, "it's a force on the same scale . . . a great teacher who will help engage the world in peace with his teachings."

"His teachings? This . . . power, uh, light is a man? How will he do that if no one can see him?" I asked in confusion.

"Definitely yes. An immensely powerful, masculine energy," she answered with more confidence. "How he will accomplish it, I cannot say. It is a mystery."

"Please, Aunt Beau, tell me what he looks like," I pleaded.

She raised an eyebrow on her anxious face. "I can't see his face. I can only feel the force and see the magnificent light. It fills this room."

Frank, who had wisely remained silent, regarded me inquisitively. I don't think he was able to cope with Aunt Beau or any more of this business. I was feeling the same way. It had been too much.

"Thank you, Aunt Beau," I said with as much kindness as I could. "I really must be going now."

"Yes, dear . . . I understand. Please take care of your own energy. You seem extremely run-down. This power with you can be profoundly draining unless you are completely rested and peaceful in your own life."

I barely heard what she said as I walked out the door with Frank. On the way back to the office, neither one of us had a word to say. What can you say after an experience like that?

Over the next two weeks I found I was getting weaker and weaker. My stamina was so depleted that I was sleeping through my alarm clock in the morning. I wasn't sure what was going on with me, so I made a doctor's appointment for a week later. But two days after I had made the appointment, as I was sitting at my desk talking to Frank and arranging some yellow roses that another salesman had sent me, I became dizzy and collapsed onto the floor.

I woke up in a hospital bed. A doctor entered my room. He was about forty-five years old and looked just like a matinee idol.

"Hello there," he said with a smile. "I'm Dr. Kiley. Do you feel like sleeping more, or would you like some answers about how you got here?"

"Talk," I said, as I tried to adjust myself on the pillow.

Dr. Kiley sat in a chair next to my bed. "Well, you certainly have exhausted yourself."

"Yes, I suppose I have." I looked up to see that there was an IV running into my right hand.

"It's glucose; it will help give your body some energy. Before I launch into the medical details, tell me something about yourself. I already know where you work, how good you are at what you do, how everyone loves you and calls you 'boss,' and how hard you drive yourself." He was smiling.

"I see." Someone had certainly filled him in.

He asked, "You live alone?"

"No, I live with my two boys." My tongue felt very thick.

"You're not originally from the Pacific Northwest, are you?"

"No, sir, I'm from New Mexico, but I love it up here and I plan to stay here. This is my home."

"You aren't married, then?" As he asked these questions he was making notes on my chart.

"No."

"Can your housekeeper take care of you?" He didn't look up from his notes.

"Not exactly. Why do you ask?"

He flipped over a page, read it over, then looked back up at me. "I've already done some blood tests on you, and one of the first findings indicates that you have mononucleosis. I'll have more results from the lab in a few days."

"Mononucleosis? That's the kissing disease, isn't it?" I was alarmed.

"Well . . ."

"I couldn't possibly have that." There was no way. I had not been kissing anyone for quite a while.

Dr. Kiley laughed. "I see. Well, you have abnormally low blood pressure, you don't have a normal heart rhythm, and more than anything else, you need rest. Lots of rest. I want to put you through a series of tests tomorrow, and one of them will be a glucose-tolerance test. So I need my patient rested."

I didn't reply.

"What can we do to make you feel more comfortable?" He stood up.

"I want to see my boys. Can I call someone to bring them up to see me?"

"Mr. Smith has been very helpful. Would you feel confident about him arranging that?"

"Dr. Kiley, did Frank bring me here?"

"Yes. He was very concerned about you when he brought you in yesterday."

"Yesterday! Oh my God! Did he tell my sons and housekeeper where I was?"

"Yes, I'm sure everything has been taken care of. If it will make you feel better, I'll have the nurse call Mr. Smith and verify that. But for now, you need to rest. We'll take care of everything else."

"Dr. Kiley, how long does it take to get over mononucleosis?"

"I think it would be wiser to wait for the blood analysis and test results before we draw any conclusions."

"Just one more thing. Could this be the reason I've been feeling so tired and lethargic all the time?"

"It could explain part of your exhaustion. Rest now, I'll check on you again after dinner." He smiled and left the room. I closed my eyes and fell asleep again.

A few hours later I was awakened by the familiar sounds of Brandy and Chris. I looked over to see Frank enter the room with the boys. They ran over to my bed and I scooped them up and happily started kissing their little faces off.

"Oh, I've missed you precious little guys. I'm so-o-o happy to see you both." The boys started pulling out draw-ings they had made for me at school, and a get-well card they had made with the housekeeper's help. Frank sat in the chair with a lapful of bottles, perfume, creams, makeup, and hair spray loaded into a box. A small overnight case sat beside him.

"Frank, what have you brought me?"

"The boys showed me your dresser, so I just brought everything that was on it. I don't know a lot about women's cosmetics, so I hope it's what you use. I also packed two nightgowns the housekeeper gave me, and some of your paper work."

"Oh, Frank, aren't you a sweetheart."

"What does the doctor say?"

"I won't know for a few more days, but he think it's mononucleosis."

"You have mono?" He was alarmed. "Well, boss, that's going to put you out of commission for a while." He stepped back and looked at me intensely.

"For God's sake, Frank, I don't have leprosy, and you don't have to worry. I'm not going to jump out of bed and kiss you."

Frank's stiffness softened and he flushed with embarrassment.

Brandy got down off the bed and got me a glass of water from the bathroom, while Chris patted my head as if it hurt. Brandy told me to drink the water, that it would make me feel better. I followed his advice. Then they both began telling me about school and all that was going on back home.

A nurse came in to say that visiting hours were over, and the boys groaned at the idea of leaving me. I groaned, too. I was sad to see those little guys go; I had to stop myself from crying. Frank said he would take care of the office for me until we could figure out something else. Then they all walked out of the door, saying good-bye.

Why was this happening to me? I couldn't afford to be sick. What would happen to my company? How could I run a marketing system from a sickbed? Then I began to worry about my illness. Just then, Dr. Kiley walked in and sat on my bed.

"Your boys are very nice children. I watched them in the waiting room," he said, smiling. "Excellent manners. You've done a very good job with their upbringing, Mrs. Hensley."

I was touched by his kind remarks.

"Thank you, Doctor, I'm very proud of them. They are the light of my life. Please call me JZ; I'm much more comfortable with my first name than with my last."

His eyes twinkled and a smile came over his face. He was a truly handsome man. "All right, JZ, if you're more comfortable with that. Can I get you anything?"

"No, but Dr. Kiley, please tell me what's on your mind. I'm very sick, aren't I?"

"Yes, you are. But hopefully tomorrow's tests can tell us more, and then we can go about getting you well again."

"What other tests are you going to do?"

"Aside from a glucose-tolerance test, I want to do a bone marrow test."

"Bone marrow?"

"JZ, we've gotten some preliminary results that are . . . very unusual. Your white blood count is extremely low, and we need to find out why."

"Do you think I have cancer or something like that?" I was getting scared.

"We won't know that until we have further results. But please, don't be alarmed. I must tell you, some of the tests are very painful, but we will make you as comfortable as possible."

Sensing that I felt frightened, he took my hand and held it very gently. "Please, don't be frightened. The tests are all standard procedure. And you won't be alone; I'll be there with you."

The following day I underwent the grueling glucose-tolerance test, which took eight hours. I almost threw up several times from the syrup I had to drink, and my arms began to look like pin cushions from all the punctures. Later, I submitted to a painful spinal tap, and a bone marrow tap from my hip. It was a dreadful day.

The next morning I dressed myself in a daffodil yellow

nightgown. I had just finished my makeup and was styling my hair when Dr. Kiley entered the room and sat on my bed.

"Well, JZ, you certainly look well. Yellow is a nice color on you." He smiled.

"Thank you." Weirdly, I felt embarrassed about being in bed with my gown on in front of a strange man.

"How do you feel?"

I didn't answer. I lay there wringing my hands in my lap, thinking about my dear children, and feeling an ominous premonition. Without looking up, I muttered, "Worried. Worried about my children, Doctor. I must live. I must, for my children."

Dr. Kiley was very grave. He scratched his chin and smoothed his mustache. "The degenerative mononucleosis is very serious in itself. Your bone marrow, where your blood cells are made, is infected by a virus that seems to be attacking the white blood cells. I'm baffled by it. It's too early yet to reach a definite prognosis, I'm afraid. You will need an extended period of time, and of chemotherapy treatment, before I can say anything more conclusive."

I turned my face away and lay there, numbed by what he was saying.

"JZ, tell me about your religious beliefs."

I turned slowly around and stared into his eyes. I understood without further comment. He nodded, reached down, and touched my hand. His own was warm and gentle. At once I trusted him. I slowly began to tell him what I believed while tears filled my eyes.

"Christ taught and demonstrated God's love for all humanity. I love Him very much and I have endeavored to not judge others but to love them as I love myself. I *do* love God with all my body, soul, and mind.

"I understand that when an acorn falls from the tree, it will live again as another tree. Christ said we would all be born again. In my soul, I know that I will live again. My mother believes I have lived before. I do too. I'm not afraid to die, Dr. Kiley. . . ." My voice broke and large hot tears rolled uncontrolled down my cheeks. I sniffed and tried to wipe them away, but they just kept coming. I took a deep breath and continued. "The only regret I have is leaving my children. I love them so much. They are all that I have, and without them my life would have been over a long time ago." I paused and blew my nose. Dr. Kiley looked down at me, his great blue eyes sparkling with moisture. I continued. "Maybe you think I'm a little crazy, but I know what I am saying is the truth. I know you must have seen a lot of people die . . . and I'm sure it makes you feel very helpless. But Dr. Kiley, they didn't really die; they just went on to another time and another place. Every time a new baby is delivered into the world, you may be bringing back to this life someone that you saw die. I think that when a person faces death, there is a part of him that knows innately that he's coming close to God. That is my belief." I looked down and began to play with the yellow satin bow on my gown. I never thought I would be telling a doctor my beliefs because *I* might be getting ready to die.

Dr. Kiley got up from my bed and walked over to the window. I wasn't certain how he felt about my words. "I've seen a lot of my patients die," he said, "and after a while I built up an immunity to death. It's my way of coping with it. Every doctor does the best he can to save his patient, but sometimes it's just not enough, and we must learn to live with that. When I hear the heartbeat of a newborn child, I know it's alive; when the heartbeat stops, and can't be revived, I know it's dead, gone. Whatever it is that makes the heart beat and then ceases it again, I can only surmise." He walked back to the foot of my bed and put his hands on the metal bars. "I learned something from you . . . touch, feel, and hope. You have profound convictions, but please don't give up on living just because you have them." He turned and left my room.

I looked out my window into the night sky. "Father, whatever this thing is that's got me, I will not yield to it. I don't believe You've meant for me to die . . . not yet. I have two little boys to raise up, and I refuse to let anyone else do that for me. Do you hear me?"

The next day Frank brought Brandy and Chris to visit

me again. My room looked like a playground: Frank was on the floor with Chris, playing with battery-driven cars, and Brandy was playing with his Erector set. I enjoyed watching them play, but I was starting to feel rather tired. Frank glanced up and saw how weary I looked. "So, when do they begin the treatments?"

"It started this morning. And then more tests," I answered in a dull voice.

"Boss, are you in any pain?"

"Frank, I'd rather not talk about it," I snapped. Then I felt guilty. Poor dear, he was just concerned. "Look, I'm sorry. It's just that I feel very sick and weak. Try to understand."

"Aunt Beau says not to worry. She says it all has a good reason for being."

"Excuse me, Frank, but your Aunt Beau ain't me. I'm trying to understand this. I mean, for a woman who's lived as good as good can be, it doesn't make any sense. How can a loving God make you sick?" I was becoming indignant. "I've been lying here trying to figure it all out. What have I done to make this happen?"

"Well, maybe you haven't cared enough about yourself. Maybe you should stop working yourself to death for your kids and start living a little more . . . for you! Hell, you can't even take a compliment. If someone thinks you're beautiful—which you are—you snap their head off."

"You're right, Frank, that's always been a hard one for me, but honestly, I'm mad, mad, mad, mad . . ." I slumped back down in the bed. "Hey, you guys, Mommy needs to go to sleep. I love you so much, but I'm getting real tired. And Frank, thanks for coming. I appreciate everything you're doing for me and the boys. Really I do." After they left I cried a little, feeling bad that I'd sent them away.

A little later one of my other salesmen came by to see me and brought me a bouquet of roses. I was visiting with him when suddenly the door opened. It was Dr. Kiley.

"Oh, excuse me," he apologized, thinking that my salesman must be more than just a salesman.

"Dr. Kiley, this is Gary Marshal."

"Nice to meet you. Would you excuse us, please? Vis-

iting hours are over, and I'd like to speak to my patient."
The doc was being a little curt.

"Sure. What should I do with these flowers?" Gary asked.

"We'll get someone to put them in water. Thank you,"
Dr. Kiley answered.

"Good-bye, JZ. I'll be seeing you." Gary left.

Dr. Kiley came over to my bed, a grim look on his face.
"How do you feel?"

"How do *you* feel? You don't seem too happy. Did you
get some more ugly test results?" I asked.

"Raise up. I want to listen to your heart." He put his
stethoscope on my chest and my back. He was very close to
my face, and when he finished he looked at me and asked,
"I thought you told me you didn't have a relationship?"

"I don't. Why did you ask me that?" I thought about it
for a moment. "Oh, you think that I *should* have a relationship
with someone who can take care of me when I get out of
here."

His face was still close to mine. Those blue eyes of his
shone with intensity, and a faint scent of spice wafted from
him. "I think you should reconsider having your mother
come."

He smoothed back my disheveled hair with slightly quivering hands. "All of the color has gone from your lips and
cheeks."

"I feel fine."

"Well, I'm glad to hear that." There was a long silence
between us as he continued to check my pulse. Then he
pulled the covers back up over my chest and walked toward
the door.

"Dr. Kiley, I'm not going to die . . . I want you to know
that."

He wheeled around and faced me. He was very angry.
"If you don't take care of yourself, you *are* going to die!" He
left abruptly. I thought doctors didn't lose their cool, especially after what he told me about not becoming emotionally
involved with their patients.

As the first light of morning gained strength, I slowly
opened my eyes and observed the movements of the thick

fog outside. For a moment it seemed like a gray phantom whose pale fingers quietly stroked the window. I rolled over and took out my mirror and was aghast at what I saw. My face was puffy and gray, my eyes lost in dark shadow. My disordered hair was dull and lifeless. Death seemed to be moving in. Quickly, I grabbed for my makeup and began to apply instant health to my poor features. I dressed in my blue nightgown and applied a heavy layer of blue eye shadow. There was a gentle knock, and Dr. Kiley walked in with a bouquet of violets.

"Oh, they go with my gown, thank you. You're probably going broke buying all your patients violets," I teased.

"I want to apologize for my unethical outburst. Sometimes I feel the need to be stern with you, in order for you to realize what you're up against."

"I understand." I put my violets on the table and just watched him for a moment.

"How's the nausea?"

"Like having morning sickness every hour of the day. It's horrible."

He sat on the bed. "I know. I've prescribed a powder that might help. It tastes a little chalky, but it might be effective. You're doing very well, considering all you've gone through." He looked out the window.

"You know, Dr. Kiley, I've prayed all my life to God. I was thinking last night about how I have made God my father because I never really had a father." Dr. Kiley gave me a somber look. I continued, "Since I was a little girl, I have talked to God. Do you think that's crazy?"

"Did God talk back?" He gave me a beautiful smile.

"Yes."

"How?" he asked.

"With a kind of a feeling. Did you ever feel a kind of rush come over you, kind of like you felt lifted a little?" I was watching his face for a reaction to my questions.

He replied slowly, "Yes, I've had that feeling a time or two."

"When you were at total peace and nothing worried you? Almost as if you were a part of everything there was? Like you weren't separated from anything?"

"Perhaps."

"When you knew everything was going to be all right . . . because it already was all right?"

"JZ, I know one thing—that you are a very courageous woman."

I looked at him in surprise. "Me? Oh, you are mistaken, Doctor! I have always been afraid. That's why I've always asked for God's help and—"

"Fear and bravery are not mutually exclusive. Those who have reason to fear can be greatly brave."

I shook my head slowly, and tears began to gather in my eyes. "I always had to be brave for my children's sake, but this . . . now . . . When I pray, I feel like I'm not separated from God, alive and vital. But when I'm sick, I falter." I tried to keep from sobbing, but when I remembered the sweet serenity that I'd had in childhood, when I possessed a child's utter faith, in spite of the hardships of my life, the tears ran from my eyes silently.

Dr. Kiley leaned over and gently stroked my hair. "What I am about to tell you may sound odd to you, considering my profession, but I want to say it nonetheless. I've always considered the godless not alive; they are the ones who are truly dead. But then, they never really lived, either."

My tears were dropping heedlessly on my breast, spotting my blue silk gown. He continued to speak, almost in a whisper. "You are alive. You have feelings and depth. A life of feelings that you can share with another human being."

I looked back at the window. "No, I've never had deep feelings for someone else. I've never been in love. Only what I feel for my sons and God."

"JZ, why are you afraid to trust and love another person?"

"Because people are fickle. One minute they think they're in love and the next moment they're not. They play mind games. Or maybe just lust games. Either way it's only a state of mind. How can anyone put trust in that?"

"Could it be," he said cautiously, "that you don't feel you're worth loving, and perhaps that's why you don't trust that love is a real thing?"

"You think you've got it all figured out, don't you?" I

retorted with a vehemence that soon dried my tears and set my face to burning.

"I just—"

"Is this part of your psychological approach to seriously ill patients?" I interrupted, smiling a tight little smile.

He calmly answered me, "It takes more than medicine to get well, JZ. Love and happiness are the most effective medicines."

"But I can laugh and be happy as much as the next person—even if it is a little harder now." I was very uncomfortable with this conversation. He was trying to tell me something about myself that I did not want to hear.

"You know, I've recently come to understand something about myself." I looked at him suspiciously. "No matter how many people I heal, or how 'successful' I am, I honestly feel it's not enough unless I *share* it with someone. It sounds like a cliché, I know. But it's true—for me, anyway. I think it must be true for most people."

"Well—" I was prepared to tell him that I didn't need anyone, but he interrupted me.

"Haven't you ever thought about loving someone completely? Perhaps getting married again, but this time for all the right reasons?"

My eyes began to well up with tears again, and I quickly turned my head on the pillow. Dr. Kiley watched a tear slide slowly down my cheek. I reached out and touched the violets beside me. Dr. Kiley leaned toward me. He looked into my eyes with a gentle smile. I looked back at him, trying to figure out why he was saying all of this to me.

"Have you had many patients that you felt this sorry for?" I whispered.

"Sorry?"

"Are you trying to save me? Am I a challenge to you?"

"My dear, beautiful lady, you don't have the foggiest notion about *human* feelings, do you? Is your world nothing but a nice tidy package of answers supplied by God?"

I blinked at him. "I guess I just don't think like you do." He started to walk away, but I grabbed his arm and pulled until he was very close. "Dr. Kiley . . . I know that you're trying to help me . . . in many ways. I do love you for that.

And I know I have to trust you; you have my life in your hands. But where I grew up was no bed of roses. People hurt people in order to survive. The truth is, there weren't any knights in armor on white horses, just harsh realities. I had feelings for someone once, but I couldn't let go of my own fears to let it go anywhere. Maybe you're right. Maybe I feel I'm not worthy of being loved. But up until now, I was the only one I could count on, never anyone else."

He was listening very intently. Suddenly it struck me what a handsome man he was. I wanted to put my arms around him, hold him. I leaned up and gently kissed him on the cheek. As I pulled away from him, I felt my heart pounding in my chest. "I'm sorry, it's just that you have been so kind and thoughtful."

"No, I needed that from you." He gently wiped my forehead and leaned forward and kissed me on the forehead. "I want you to live and to know what happiness can be with someone who deserves you." He got up and slowly walked out the door.

I was grateful to him and touched by his sensitivity, but I had heard stories about patients getting crushes on their doctors, and I did not want to fall into that foolish trap.

After a week of treatments and lying in bed, my complexion had become sallow and I had lost a lot of weight. The nausea was a permanent routine and my nerves were getting frayed. One day a nurse came into my room. She had tended to me before and I liked her a lot.

"Come on, sweetheart, time for a shower," she said.

"Nurse Emily, I don't feel like moving."

"I know, but you don't want me bending over you giving you those sponge baths all the time, now do you?"

I smiled up at her. "Why are you a nurse, Emily?"

"I like watching beautiful young things get well. Come on. Dr. Kiley will be here in a while." She gently removed my sheets. "He's such a nice man. He certainly does care a lot about you. Wonder why he never married?"

"He cares for all his patients, Emily. And I think he looks after his mother."

She helped me to the shower. My body trembled with

weakness and my head swam. "There we go, now take it easy. Good girl. Yes, I think he's married to helping people."

I took off my hospital robe and stepped into the shower. "God, it's hard to keep my balance with the nausea."

"I know, honey. But when you're clean, somehow everything seems easier."

The warm water felt so good on my body. Emily continued to talk as she straightened up my room. Suddenly she heard a blood-curdling scream from the shower. It was me and I was screaming, "*Nooooo!* "*Nooooo!*"

"What is it? What's wrong?" Emily cried.

She ran to the shower and opened the door. I was standing there frozen, my hair full of shampoo, staring down at the floor. There, clogging the drain, was a thick wad of my hair. More strands were clinging wetly to my chest and legs, and I held another handful in my right hand. I was screaming in panic.

"I know. I know. JZ, listen honey, it will grow back." She reached for me in the shower but I was frozen, unable to move. I was going into shock. Nurse Emily ran from the shower and called for help. I stood there while suds, water, and hair poured down my body.

Three more nurses came into the bathroom. "JZ, come out of there, honey," Emily said, as she shut off the water. "Come on, now."

I couldn't move. Another nurse grabbed a hand mirror from my table and rushed back into the shower. "JZ, look, it's not as bad as you think. Look at yourself, you'll see."

I looked into the mirror and reacted with horror. I ripped the mirror from the nurse's hand and smashed it against the wall.

"Get out of here! All of you. *Get out!*" I was screaming like a mad woman.

"Please, honey, listen, it will grow back. Please believe me," Emily pleaded.

I pushed her against the wall. "Don't look at me! Stop looking at me!"

Nurse Emily grabbed my robe and draped it over my shoulders. I lurched away from her, stumbling back into my room. She quickly grabbed a towel and covered my head.

"Get out! Get out!" I kept screaming.

Dr. Kiley came rushing into my room. "JZ, please don't do this to yourself."

"I hate you. I hate what you've done to me!"

"It will grow back, I promise," he said as he tried to take hold of me.

"Don't touch me! Get out of here and leave me alone!" I was like a terrified animal trapped in a corner.

"Give her the shot, nurse!" he ordered.

I whirled around. "Don't you touch me!"

Dr. Kiley and the other nurses grabbed me. They forced me onto the bed. I was screaming at them violently. Nurse Emily administered the shot.

"Noooo!" I screamed.

"Don't do this to yourself," Dr. Kiley pleaded with me.

"Me? Me do it to me? *You* did it to me. I can't stand this anymore!"

"You *will* be all right. You are beautiful, remember that," he said.

"How can you talk to me like that? You've taken away my dignity!" I was crying now.

"No, JZ. It's only temporary." His calm voice was edged in panic.

"Temporary! Maybe being alive is temporary!" I kicked my wheelchair toward Dr. Kiley. "Don't you understand, you big medical expert? Don't you understand a person can die of humiliation!"

My words blasted him in the face. Then the shot began to hit me. As I crumpled onto the bed, sobbing, the last thing I saw was Dr. Kiley quietly leaving the room while poor Nurse Emily looked on, paralyzed.

The next morning I was lying in bed with a scarf wrapped and tied around my head. I was numb from the events of the day before and I felt like my soul was searching for answers . . . but none came.

As time wore on I became a recluse in my own dark world of depression. Sometimes I would spend hours staring out my window, or just lying in bed, not responding to nurses, Dr. Kiley, or even to my little boys. I could not eat

and ended up being fed intravenously. Even with the scarf
that I kept permanently over my head, when I went to the
bathroom I would not look into the mirror. One day I just
hung a towel over the mirror. I could feel no joy, no hope
for my existence. I wondered how many people had suffered
this way and simply died of a broken spirit rather than of
any disease.

One morning a woman opened the door and entered
my room. She was attractive and exuded cheery energy. She
was carrying four round boxes with her. I didn't acknowledge her presence as she sat down next to my bed.

"Hello, Mrs. Hensley, my name is Betty Jo Taft. Dr. Kiley
called me in to prepare you a lovely wig. I've brought along
some pieces of exquisite quality."

I didn't say anything.

"I hear you have beautiful hair," she continued.

I turned and frowned at her with impatience and faint
disgust.

"Some of these pieces are really quite lovely. Here, let
me just show you what I have." Betty leaned down, opened
a box, and took out a medium-long blond wig. She shook it
until the hair bounced freely. "I don't know about you, but
I love to work with hair. Here, I have a picture of you." She
took a picture out of her bag and handed it to me. It was
one that had been taken with my head installer at Puget
Sound Cable TV. I stared at how beautifully my hair flowed
down my back. "Your length of hair is my favorite to work
with. Most of the time people have much shorter hair. As
you can see, I tried to duplicate your length and color. I'm
very proud of this piece."

I continued to glare at her with anger. How presumptuous she was with her stupid remarks.

She held the wig up to the light, and I watched the sun's
rays dance and flicker through it. Every bright wave and curl
glistened. It really was beautiful.

"I've never lost my own hair," Betty continued, "but
I've worked with many people who have. Here, just feel this,
isn't it wonderful?"

I looked at her and then at the wig. Slowly I reached

out and touched it. It was fine and soft and fell through my fingers, just the way my own used to.

"See, I tried to capture from your picture how your hair looked. We can style it together if you wish. Come on, let's try it on."

Betty reached toward my head, but I quickly put my hands up to hold the scarf on.

"I want you to know," she said gently, "that I've seen many people with no hair, Mrs. Hensley. It isn't shocking or disgusting to me in the least. It makes me feel so good to be able to do something like this for others. Please trust me."

I listened to what she said and finally brought my hands down from the scarf. "Did you ever read the Bible when you were a little girl?" I asked her. She was taken aback by my off-the-wall question.

"A little . . . I did go to Bible school once."

"There's a verse in the Bible that says a woman's hair is her crown and glory." As I spoke I started to cry. "I've been unglorified. Look at me, no eyebrows, no eyelashes . . ."

Betty became very sympathetic. "Oh, it will grow back. Just give nature time. Everything takes time. Please, let me try to help you. You might even enjoy it."

Feeling a little scared, I pulled the scarf off my head. Betty looked at me carefully. There were still a few clumps of hair left. "Well, it's not as bad as I thought." She took a mirror from one of her boxes and handed it to me. I pushed it away. Betty then began to feel my hair. "Oh, this is good hair you have." She leaned in a little closer. "You're very lucky. Now, can you sit up for me? I'll brush your own hair back so I can place the wig over your head to get a good fit."

I straightened up and, without saying a word, allowed her to brush my hair. When she finished, she placed the blond wig on my head. I felt the hair fall to my shoulders. I started touching it. It felt wonderful.

"Now, if you want the bangs trimmed, that's what we'll do." I blew the hair out of my eyes as she handed me the mirror. "Now look at it. It's gorgeous!"

I couldn't believe it. I looked almost like me. I started

smiling. "Oh, dear God! It does look like my own hair. It's beautiful."

Betty was smiling at her own achievement. "How does it feel? If it's too snug, you'll get a headache. Let's leave it on for a while and see how it feels."

I reached for a brush to style it. Betty held it at the crown so that I wouldn't pull it off. I began to back-comb the sides and pull them out and away from my face. Then I began to work with the front. "Have you got some hair spray?" I asked.

Betty seemed pleased, and a little surprised, that I was so quickly styling it for myself. "Oh, you are going to have so much fun with this."

I whipped up my own style and then picked up the mirror again. "What do we do with my bald face?" I said as I touched my sparse eyebrows and lashes.

"You don't think I came here unprepared, do you? I'm a woman, remember?" she chuckled. Betty pulled out some professionally woven eyebrows and dabbed them on with some glue.

"I thought about being a movie star once," I said. "I guess they do this every day, don't they?"

Betty laughed. "Now for those peepers." She handed me false eyelashes with the glue already applied. "See how naturally they're blended? Not like the five-and-ten numbers."

I applied the first one and looked up at her. It was very crooked.

"Did you particularly want to look like Bette Davis?" I laughed. "Here, straighten it out," she said, holding up the mirror.

I straightened it and applied the other one, then looked up and blinked mischievously. Betty handed me the eyeliner. "Now, just follow the natural line of your eye and cover the edge of the lashes." I followed her instructions. "You see? Hospital cosmetology at its best."

When I looked back in the mirror I couldn't believe how pretty I looked—almost like my old self. I didn't look like some circus queen as I'd expected, more like a Barbie doll. Tears started to well up in my eyes.

"No, no crying with these lashes. They'll fall off. Or else pull your mouth down like this so the tears will spill out of the sides of your eyes. And don't blink." She demonstrated.

I made the face. "Like this?" A big tear spilled out of my eye. "I guess we're all held together by glue, hair spray and Max Factor, aren't we?"

"I always say, it helps to pick up where God left off. Sometimes I think *He* should take a course in cosmetology!"

We were both lost in laughter when Dr. Kiley walked in the door. "Oops!" He closed the door, knocked, and then came in again. He stood there with his face lit up with approval. "When did Marilyn Monroe check in here?"

Betty and I laughed.

"Well, you certainly look beautiful this morning, Mrs. Hensley," he said. I batted my eyelashes rapidly.

Betty gathered up her mirror and boxes. "Well, I'll be going now. Here's my card. If you need me for anything, just give me a call."

"Thank you, Betty. You made my day."

"Thank you. You've made my week. You look beautiful, Mrs. Hensley." Betty shook hands with Dr. Kiley and left.

Dr. Kiley stood there a moment gazing at me. "Do you want to be alone for a while with your mirror?"

"I don't have one," I said, looking around.

Dr. Kiley pulled out a gift-wrapped present from behind his back. "You do now. I'll see you later."

CHAPTER SEVENTEEN

IF YOU BELIEVED . . .

A week later I was sitting in my room reading *The Lord of the Rings*—a present from Frank—when the hobbits' adventures were interrupted by a knock on the door. I called out, "Come in," and Dr. Kiley entered in a beautiful suit. I had never seen him in anything but his medical coat before. He looked like he had just walked out of some men's magazine. Quite handsome, he was. "Hi, James. My, you look wonderful!"

"Oh, the suit? Well, even doctors can show a little class from time to time," he said, smiling at me. "I wanted my favorite patient to see me at my best when I discharged her." He came and sat on the bed.

"Am I well?"

"No, not yet. I'm still puzzled about this disease, but I've done all I can for the time being. You'll be an outpatient until we see further results from the chemo."

I was so happy about going home, I sat up in wide-eyed

anticipation. "You mean I can smell my petunias, play with my boys, take them fishing, and feel the rain fall?"

James smiled very lovingly at my simple desires. "Well, yes, you can do all of that, but I don't want you to overexert yourself, JZ."

"Oh, James, I'm so happy." As I looked at him I realized how much I appreciated him. "I know some of this has been rough on you . . . but thank you, James, thank you so much."

"I called your mother in New Mexico," he said flatly.

"You *what?*"

"I felt you should have someone with you that you can trust. Someone who can help you with the boys and take care of you."

"James, you shouldn't have done that." I was shocked that he had made this decision on his own.

"You never told her about your sickness." He sounded perplexed.

"Of course I didn't, James. I didn't want her to know. I didn't want anyone to know." I was outraged.

"JZ, she'll help care for you. She wants to help you. She already sensed something was seriously wrong. As a matter of fact, she told *me* what was wrong. I just confirmed it."

"Look, my mother doesn't need to take care of yet another sick person in her life. She's had enough of that."

"Well, JZ, she doesn't feel that way at all. She rushed here as soon as she heard."

"You mean she's at my house now?" I was ticked that he had done this. How dare he? "So, once again you feel you know more than I do about what's best for me!"

He flared, "Why don't you accept that there are people who love you and want to care for you? Is it that you think you're not good enough to love? Or do you feel you're so Godlike you don't need human emotion? Don't you see how self-centered that is? Don't you ever think about anyone but yourself? I think you're afraid of love. You run away from the possibility of real passion. It's as if you were afraid that happiness with another human being would rob you of your identity."

I was stunned by his words. I had never in my life been spoken to so directly. The point was, he was right.

"Listen, James, if I'm not afraid to die, why would I be afraid to feel passion or to love?"

His face darkened. "Because you'd rather be a martyr! That's much easier for you to handle. Sure, you can spit in the eye of death, but you can't look love in the eye without cringing or running away. If you'd take a look at loving a person the way you love your God, you'd soon see you'd be looking at yourself, and *that* you are not ready to do. Someone somewhere convinced you that you were nothing. Why can't you listen to someone else, someone who's telling you the truth?"

As I pondered his words, weighing their truthfulness, I slowly began to realize for the first time that James was trying to tell me he loved me. Alarmed, I smoothed my hair and bit my bottom lip, but I never took my eyes from his.

His expression softened, and after a moment he said, "You'll be leaving tomorrow, and I want you to think about letting someone else into your life besides work and God. It's possible you might feel real happiness for the first time. When you love only God, you're loving your own perceptions. That's easy, God doesn't argue with you."

I think James wanted to tell me directly how he felt, but he was unsure of what I was feeling. He got up to leave, his face revealing all the frustration he was holding back.

"So, we'll make arrangements for your outpatient appointments. Please don't overdo." He paused. "Oh, and another thing. I won't be here tomorrow when you check out. But I'll see you in two weeks, all right?"

I nodded silently.

James hesitated, obviously reluctant to leave the room. I knew there was more he wanted to say and I wanted him to express it. I raised myself up to tell him not to leave, when James suddenly came back and embraced me. He leaned down and kissed me, then put both his hands around my face. "I've tried very hard not to become involved with you, JZ, but I haven't done a very good job of following my own prescription. I want to take care of you. I need to, JZ. Please, let me . . . let me be that someone. I'm very much in love with you."

I looked up into his face and knew that he was sincere, but what good would I be to him as an invalid? Or maybe I wouldn't get well. What could I possibly offer him besides worries, just as my stepfather had done to my mother? I couldn't bear to put that on another person.

James moved closer and bent his head toward me. He whispered, "JZ, my beloved, will you marry me and let me take care of you? I'll build you a wonderful house with beautiful gardens." I remained so still that he thought I had not heard him. "JZ, I am filled with emptiness," he said, grasping my hand.

"James, there are deep and precious feelings I have for you. You mean more to me than you realize. I know you don't want to accept what I'm saying, but in time the person, the happiness, that you are looking for will come to you. You don't need me and the suffering I would bring you. Please understand. I'll take care of myself, James, the best that I can, but I need to be in control from here on out."

His face dropped, and for a moment he opened his mouth as if to reason with me. But his body slumped and he gently let go of my hand. "Yes, I know."

He walked out of the room and closed the door. I continued to stare at the door until I finally broke down and wept.

I awoke the next morning to mellow sunlight streaming through my window. Above the noise and clatter in the hallway, I heard the songs of birds outside. How wonderful their music was. As I turned to get out of bed, I noticed a roll of paper tied neatly with a blue ribbon sitting on my nightstand. I looked at it curiously, wondering how it got there. I pulled the bow and the ribbon fell loose to reveal a handwritten note: "Life belongs to God; for the activity of the mind is life, and He is that activity. Pure self-activity of reason is God's most blessed and everlasting life. We say that God is living, eternal and perfect; and that continuous and everlasting life is God's for God is eternal life. Aristotle." Tears of joy came to my eyes; the writing could have been none other than James's.

Frank drove me home from the hospital. When we pulled

into the driveway, the living room curtains dropped back into place as if someone had been staring out the window, waiting. As I got out of the car, the door flew open and out poured Brandy, Chris, Momma, and the housekeeper. The sun was shining, the flowers in my yard were in bloom, and my family was together again. It was grand to be alive.

The boys hugged and kissed me while I held my wig in place. No one at home knew I had lost my hair, and I wanted to keep it that way.

Frank carried my suitcases into the house and politely left us to get on with our lives. I sat down on the porch feeling tired, but I didn't want to go in. I just wanted to be outside to smell the air and the flowers and life. Momma was sensitive to my feelings, so she made us some iced tea and sat down with me. The boys had their pet frog, Harvey, on the driveway, bragging about his skills as a hopper. He didn't budge.

"Oh, Momma, I wish Dr. Kiley hadn't called you. You've had enough worry in your life. I don't want to add to the long list."

"Well, young lady, I know'd ya was sick. I had dreams an big feelings 'bout it. I come up here either ta bury ya or see to it that ya git well. That's all." She took a swig of her tea and patted her foot.

"Thanks for coming. I am glad to see you, but I'll be all right. I just don't want to talk about it."

"You're lookin' good. . . . Ya know, I saw ol' Janet the other day. Why, did ya know she married a friend of Loy Gene's? That gal's a character. . . . Well anyway, she told me ta tell ya ta write to her. I think ya better eat somethin' an then ya better rest awhile." She was eye-balling me.

"I need to call the insurance company and see about my bills, Momma."

"Well, don't ya worry your head about that now."

A few weeks later I was digging around in my flower beds, occasionally raising my face to the sun to feel its warmth. I was so glad to be a little part of nature's beauty and life. While I was taking a deep breath of a flower, a car drove up. It was Frank, and he had an attractive young woman with him.

"Hi, Frank. Come on over and look at my roses. Did God ever make anything more beautiful?"

"He sure did. He made Joanie here. JZ, this is my fiancée, Joan Parker. I met her two weeks ago and finally found the woman for me. We're getting married."

I rose and wiped off my hands and looked at Joan. "Well, I'll be. Joan, it is a pleasure to meet you. This man is the salt of the earth. He is a friend . . . a true friend." I embraced her.

"Thank you. Frank has told me so much about you. You mean a lot to him, he admires your courage." I didn't react to what she said.

"I know you'll be happy. Oh, Frank, how wonderful for you." I gathered up my gardening tools. "Let's go in and have some tea."

The sun was setting and its golden light filled the living room with a warm glow.

"Well, how are you feeling? What does James say?" asked Frank.

"I don't know. I'm not feeling very well, Frank. I guess I've been doing too much for the past few weeks. James is still having problems with this virus, or whatever it is. He says the medication hasn't been as effective as it should have been." I sighed.

"Uh, listen, that's why Joanie and I dropped by. We're going to a big revival meeting on the other side of Seattle. There's a real good evangelist preacher there, and he's healed quite a few people."

"A revival meeting? In a tent?" I was stunned. "Why, Frank, it sounds like you've found God after all."

"That's right," Frank answered. High color filled his bony features.

"Frank, I was raised with that hellfire-and-brimstone stuff. It's crap! It's not about God."

"Well, it all depends on how you look at it," he answered smoothly.

Joanie sat quietly. She had closed her eyes and was praying. I had seen this before.

"Frank, I'm not walking down any aisle so somebody can save me from the devil."

"Well, we've been praying for you. I wish you'd try it." He was pleading.

"Frank, I have tried it . . . for most of my childhood. I saw what that stuff did to people. It scared them. It humiliated them. As a matter of fact, I renounced evangelism while standing in a church while my sister-in-law knelt sobbing on her knees. And you know what? I never went back!"

I looked over at Joan. She was still praying silently with her eyes closed.

"JZ, would you try it just one more time?"

"No."

Frank got up and came over to me. He touched my arm. "JZ, would you do it for me? Never mind the church. Just do it for me so I won't feel I haven't tried to help you."

I looked up at him and then at Joan, who was . . . you guessed it. I realized that, due to Joan, Frank was now deeply involved with a new faith.

"This would mean a lot to you?" I asked.

"Yes, it would," he answered.

"I really don't want to, but . . . okay," I sighed. "For you."

Even though I was exhausted, I changed my clothes and went with them. On the way, I saw Mount Rainier in the distance, glowing like a giant magenta pyramid in the setting sun. It was breathtaking.

We finally arrived at a huge tent with hundreds of cars parked outside. We went in. People were singing hymns and swaying, caught up in the ecstasy of religious fervor. Frank and Joan were holding hands, swaying and singing, too. I was very uncomfortable. I rolled my eyes and then closed them. I was in pain and I was very tired.

"Brothers and sisters, let us come together now. All of you who are in need of special healing, come on down here. Come on down here," the preacher yelled.

Many people began to file down the middle aisle to the altar.

"Jesus is waiting. Jesus is waiting. Come on down and renounce Satan . . . renounce your sins. Come on down and ask forgiveness for your souls that you may be healed."

Frank took my hand. "Come on . . . let's do it."

"Oh, Frank, I've seen this all before. I know the game."

"What have you got to lose?"

I chuckled sarcastically.

"For me?" he whispered.

Slowly I got up from my seat. I could hardly stand. I had a real bad pain in my lower back. Frank gently helped me to the aisle. It was all so reminiscent of what I had gone through as a child . . . and here I was again, only this time it was me going to the altar.

Frank helped me to walk down the aisle, many other ill and desperate people surrounding us. He led me to the altar and left me there. Right next to me was a woman about seventy-five years old, very thin and frail.

The preacher was now laying hands on the heads of the unfortunate who stood in line waiting to be saved.

"Oh, Jesus. Oh, Jesus, save this man from his temptations. Save him from the wrath of Satan. Deliver him up into God's pure love."

The man continued to pray silently awhile, and the woman next to him cried out, "Jesus, oh, Jesus, hear my prayer. I renounce Satan. I will be lifted into Your loving arms . . . glory, glory, oh, Jesus."

She continued to wail as the preacher laid his hands on her head.

When the preacher finally got to the old woman next to me, she asked, "Brother?"

"Yes, sister. Yes, sister. What is it, sister? Open your sins to Jesus. Open up your sins."

"Oh, brother preacher, my husband needs work. Pray to the Lord Jesus to have mercy on our souls. We have sinned. We have sinned. Forgive us so that he may find work," she cried.

The preacher silently prayed for the old woman as he closed his eyes and touched her head. The old woman began to sob and sway.

"Yea, sister. The Lord Jesus will help our sister here . . . renounce Satan who heeds you. Renounce Satan . . . pray for our sister."

The congregation prayed for her, and the preacher then moved in front of me.

"Yea, sister. What is it, sister?" he asked.

I looked him in the eye and with defiance said, "Before you begin with me, I want to tell you something. I love God more than you can conceive and more than you can preach. I denounced Satan a long time ago because he doesn't exist. He never did. When you understand the love of God, there is no room for evil or sin. Now I am dying. When you lay your hands on me, you pray for one who loves God. Don't even mention the name of Satan. He has no place here. He never has."

The preacher was stunned by my intensity. I'm sure he felt I was both courageous and blasphemous. With trepidation, he placed his hands on my head. With my head bowed, I told him, "Remember, don't mention anyone's name but God's."

I had intimidated him.

"Oh, God, our Father, look upon this child and lift her life so that she may be healed. Oh, God! Oh, God!"

Before he could go any further, there was a sudden flash of blue light from the top of the tent. The flash became an electrical streak, almost like lightning and just as bright. The blue lightning streak went vertically down, straight through my body. It was so powerful that it knocked the preacher and the elderly woman to the ground. The whole congregation witnessed the light and they all gasped. Then there was a moment of complete silence.

I didn't fall. I just looked above me questioningly. Then I closed my eyes. God had heard me!

The people in the tent began to murmur in hushed tones. Then the tones built until there was screaming and moaning. Some of them rushed to lift the old woman from the floor. The preacher stood up, shaking.

"Who are you?" His eyes were dilated and there was a shocked expression on his face.

I looked back at him. "One of God's own."

Frank and Joan rushed down the aisle to me. The throng were slowly making their way to the altar to see me, some trying to touch me. Frank grabbed my hand.

"Let's get out of here," he demanded.

"Frank, the pain is gone. I feel different," I said, reveling in the warmth and lightness of well-being.

"Let's get out of here before we get mobbed." He took my hand and hurried me out of the tent and to the car.

Joan kept looking at me curiously. "I've never seen anything like that," she said in an excited voice.

"There was this streak of light," Frank said. "From where we were sitting, I could see the whole thing. Did you feel anything?"

"Yes, I felt electricity, like a surge of electrical energy," I said in a mellow tone.

"But . . . it was like lightning, it went through you," he answered.

I turned and looked at him. "Do you think that's what it was, Frank?"

"I don't know . . . but that's what it looked like to me."

I got in the car and looked out the window up at the stars. They were very vivid. I felt a peacefulness and detachment that kept me from talking about what had happened. It was like the release at the moment of birth after enduring the hard labor of delivery. Once you see the baby, you don't think about the pain, but only of the bliss of the child.

"Frank, Joan, have you ever seen the stars look like this? Look at them; they're like crystals close enough to touch."

Frank casually looked up at them, then back to me. "JZ, are you all right?"

"Frank, I want to thank you for this. You felt the rightness of something that I was unable to see."

"Jesus saved you," Joan said adamantly. "Jesus saved you."

I turned and looked at her for a moment. "No, Joan. Jesus didn't save me. I saved myself. I saved myself by trusting in God." She gasped.

"But why did this happen . . . like this, now, here?" Frank asked.

"Because I was ready for it to happen," I said evenly.

"But I've seen you suffer. You've always been ready for the cure."

"No, Frank, I might have been ready for God, but I wasn't ready for me. God needs help, too. We are the only way God can express Himself for us."

Frank and Joan looked at me, trying to understand what I had said. I guess when you've always believed that God is separate from that which He really is, you can never understand the miracle you are.

We drove slowly back to my home. I watched the passing landscape under a moonlit night. Somewhere inside of me I felt a connection to this quiet splendor. I also understood the mystery of God's grand plan. It was beyond words, but I knew.

The next day I walked into James's office.

"JZ, you look great! Your color is back. What happened? You want to tell me why you look so healthy?" He was staring at me with disbelief.

"James, how long will it take to have my blood analyzed?"

"It usually takes a few days. Why?"

"Could you ask them if they could give my tests priority?" I asked.

"I could, yes. . . . Why do you want it now?"

"I'll tell you after you see the analysis. Please see if you can do it for me."

James seemed puzzled by my behavior. "All right. It will be a few hours, though. I'll have the nurse draw the blood. Can you come back at the end of the day? I should know something by then."

I smiled and thanked him.

Walking down the street, I felt so happy that I twirled around in the sunlight. Somebody honked their horn at me. I just waved.

At the end of the day I went back to James's office. After a brief wait the nurse sent me into James's examining room. He stood up as I walked in and then motioned for me to sit down.

I sat down. "You want to tell me what happened now?"

"No, tell me what my blood test says first, James."

He was still looking closely at me, almost marveling at me. "Remember once I asked you where you were really from, and you said Alpha Centauri?"

I started laughing. "Yes."

"Well, the tests have come back . . . absolutely normal. They don't even *resemble* your last test. It's almost as if they belonged to two different people."

I started to beam while he continued. "There is not a trace of pathology. I'm baffled. But there is something else. The lab found a cell that we don't understand."

"What do you mean?"

"They said they've never seen it before, in you or anyone else. JZ, you should be honest with me. Something very dramatic has happened to your blood, which means that something has happened to your whole body."

"James, let me make it simple. Frank came by yesterday with his new fiancée. I think she's a born-again Christian."

"That should be something you would understand."

"Yeah, well, they took me to a hellfire-and-brimstone revival meeting."

"You must be joking. I thought you rejected that kind of thing."

I went on to retell the event while he listened intently, sometimes smiling.

". . . and I felt so peaceful. So calm. James, I had no more pain at all. In fact, I felt incredible and I still do. That's what happened."

James cleared his throat and began pacing nervously. "Now let me understand this. You actually felt an electrical shock run through your body?"

"Yes, James, it was incredible."

"And your pain disappeared—immediately?"

"Well, I didn't realize it was gone at first because I was so stunned. But then I focused on my body and, yes, the pain and the exhaustion were gone. It was like I had had a transfusion of energy!"

James was taking me seriously. After all, the proof was sitting in front of him and the tests lay on his desk.

"And you told the preacher not to speak of Satan?"

"That's right, I did. I don't believe in evil, James. It's devastating to believe in the power of evil. I mean, those preachers try to scare you into loving God by punching you in the rear end with a pitchfork. Really, it was important for me to tell that preacher that I didn't believe in Satan. That I only believed in God. And that I loved God!"

"Yes, I know." James nodded.

"Listen, James, by renouncing Satan's existence, I was renouncing his religion and he knew it. But God isn't about religion. It's about God. They are two different things. God is everything. There is no evil in God. I wanted that preacher to know that, because I know that he thought I got sick because I was a sinner. He preaches more about the devil and evil than he does about the love of God. And I didn't want him to . . . not with me."

James walked to his doorway and looked out. I just sat there quietly.

"JZ, what do you think caused this to happen?"

"I don't really know. But I know I have a purpose in my life now. I don't know what it is, James. I just know I have a different sense about myself."

James shook his head and returned to his desk to look again at the test reports.

"James, do you believe in miracles?"

"I guess I've just seen one."

"And as my doctor, would you say that I am healed?"

"I hardly know what to say, JZ."

"James, remember you told me that if I loved myself more, my body would reflect that?"

He nodded his head.

"Well, you were absolutely right. I was loving God as if He were someone on the outside of me. I don't feel that anymore. Now, I feel that God is somewhere within me . . . within us all. And if that's true, then it's essential that I love who I am. James, you were right. I did get sick because I didn't think enough of myself. I felt I was nothing. I have for a long time. I was taught that by my religious training and by all the things that I went through as a child. My illness was the final result of all that. James, I know this goes against all conventional medical knowledge, but I really feel illness is a state of mind."

I hesitated, searching for the clearest way to express what I was feeling. "This may sound bold, but maybe I created that lightning bolt. If I can create disease, then I can heal it. I think what we call a miracle is another way of saying we can do anything if we know we are worth it. So, James you might consider yourself a medical doctor, and I'm certain you can't explain this from a medical point of view, but you helped me to see something that I never even saw in the Bible. You might have been antagonized by the love I have for God, but *you* helped me see a little of that same God in me. And that's what made me well."

My own words made me remember something else. I quickly opened my handbag and pulled out a little scroll. I rolled it open and read aloud. "Life belongs to God; for the activity of the mind is life, and He is that activity. Pure self-activity of reason is God's most blessed and everlasting life. We say that God is living, eternal and perfect; and that continuous and everlasting life is God's for God is eternal life. Aristotle." I rolled up the note and smiled at him.

James's face flushed with embarrassment. He walked across the room again, attempting to stay in control of himself.

"Assuming you *are* cured—and I'd like you to come back in a few weeks to confirm that 'medically'—what will you do now? Return to your business?"

"I'm going to take some time to think a lot of things over. I need to take care of my medical and hospital bills, but I've made up my mind that I don't want to continue in the cable business. I want to do something different."

James smiled in appreciation.

"James, I once told you I loved you for taking such good care of me, and that there was a lot that I never told you. But maybe after some time goes by I will."

He perked up. "Like what?"

"Well, it has to do with my capacity to see what is unseen."

He looked up aghast and threw up his hands. "Go away, you star child. Go away before I lose the 'state of mind' that lets me be a practical, functioning scientist."

James laughed, and as he escorted me out of his office I turned to kiss him and hug him. It was good-bye.

CHAPTER EIGHTEEN

AN ABNORMAL BUSINESS CALLED LIFE

For the next four years, my life was rather uneventful. I had a new appreciation of life and found myself savoring the small miracles of my precious existence. I dedicated a lot of time to my boys and became more involved in their lives. Though I was still dedicated to my work, I was more inclined to let it take a backseat to my family. As a result, the companies I developed were not successful, but I didn't feel like a failure because they weren't. Success was simply no longer important. Living and being happy was.

In January of 1977, Brandy was ten years old and Chris was eight. Though the three of us were very close, I began to feel the boys needed a masculine influence in their lives. So one night I prayed, asking God to send someone who could love and take care of us, someone who could provide the boys with the father-friend influence they would need as they approached their teenage years. I knew that if the right person existed, God would send him to us. And of course, if he was the right person, I would be happy as well. After being sole provider for so many years, I wanted to be a housewife and a homemaker, so whoever it was would have to be happy with my wishes and not need me to work and help provide for the family. I trusted that my prayer would be answered.

One evening after work, Martha, a dear woman I had met at a local restaurant, dropped by.

"JZ, I thought about you all day. I get tired just thinking about you," she said, laughing. "You work harder than anyone I know, girl. So I had a great idea. Let's have a girls' night out with a few of the girls at work. We'll go to the Roadway Lounge. You know, that one down on I-5. It's a great place, girl."

She eyed me mischievously. I curled my upper lip and tilted my head to one side. "Okay, but only for a little while. I don't like booze joints."

She shook her finger at me and said, "There is more to life than work, girl. Oh, hell, it'll be good for you."

The four of us—Martha, Kitty, Sue, and I—arrived at the Roadway. As we walked in I was assailed by loud ugly music and the offensive smells of liquor, cigarette smoke, perfume, and cheese. I stood there adjusting my eyes and trying to imagine having a good time. The lounge was filled with businessmen, doctors, lawyers, secretaries, and some free agents on the prowl. As we made our way to a clean table, I was approached by two men who wanted to "boogie." I tried not to snarl as I politely said no.

The waitress came with everyone's drinks and our cheese fondue. I was busy with my fondue and milk while warding off the wolves with my free hand. "You know, girls, this is what I call 'hein'-and-shein' joint."

Martha stared over her drink and batted her false eyelashes at me. "A what?"

"You know, he and she? Oh, for heaven's sake, Martha, a meat market." I shouted over the blaring of "Proud Mary."

To Martha's delight a man walked up and asked her to dance. Immediately her voice took on the cooing of a South-

ern belle. I distinctly remember her saying to him, "Charmed,
I'm shore." Then two more came over and asked the other
two girls to dance.

"What a game," I said to myself. Suddenly a man grabbed
hold of my arm as I dipped into the fondue.

"Gorgeous, they're playing our song."

I yanked my arm away and gave him one of those "bug
off, creep-o" looks. "Thanks, but it isn't our song. I'm eating."

I continued to eat, alone, observing the call of the wild
during mating season. Then a man came and planted his
feet firmly beside my table and stared down at me. I looked
up and was going to say beat it when, "Howdy, ma'am,"
he said in a good imitation of John Wayne. "I surely would
be beholdin' to ya iffen you would do me tha honor of this
dance."

I blinked my eyes a few times and answered, "Thanks
but no thanks, John, dear. Some other time."

He didn't budge. "Well, ma'am, I jest can't take no for
no answer."

"You shore do have a fine line fer tha ladies, but it ain't
a-workin' with me. So why don't ya make like a grasshopper
and hop on to another table."

I turned away to ignore him. He just stood there watching me eat. Finally I turned around and glared at him. "Can't
you take a hint, buster? Buzz off!"

"Naw, I'm just gonna be a-standin' here till you is ready."

My shoulders slumped. I wiped my mouth with the
napkin and sighed. "Just this one. Promise?"

"Yes, ma'am." He pulled the chair out for me and escorted me to the dance floor. Martha spied me and began to
applaud. Jeremy started boogying, and I followed.

After a while he shouted, "So, what do you do?"

I ignored him.

"I'm a tooth fairy, ma'am." He beamed.

"You're a fairy?" I said, raising my eyebrows.

"No, ma'am. I'm a tooth fairy."

I laughed. "Right."

"I'm a dentist."

That was a relief. I continued to ignore him.

"Well, ma'am, most ladies are impressed by me being a doctor and all."

"Well, I suppose you done gone and picked one who ain't, now. By the way, why do you talk like that?"

He changed his impersonation to Cary Grant. "Judy, Judy, Judy, my dear. I speak in many voices, depending on what is appropriate. You see, in my business I'm usually required to do all the talking because the people have their mouths open."

I couldn't help myself, I started laughing. His face beamed. "Ah. Now, my dear, this is a bit personal, but may I have the honor of knowing your name?"

"JZ Hensley. And what would yours be?"

"My name is Jeremy. Jeremy Wilder. And after a hard day of drilling, filling, and billing I am, in the main, an honest man."

The music finally stopped. He took hold of my arm and asked for another dance.

"I would like to sit down. Thank you for the dance, Doctor."

He led me back to the table. Martha and Kitty were sipping their drinks while they whispered and giggled. I sat down and, to my surprise, the tooth fairy pulled up a chair and forced it between Martha and me.

Martha stared at him with righteous indignation. He ignored the glare and turned to me. "Now, where do you work and how can I get in touch with you, ma'am?"

"JZ, who's your gentleman caller?" Martha twanged.

"Oh, this is John Cary Grant Wayne," I said smugly.

"Oh, really. Charming," she purred.

Jeremy didn't even look at her. "Ma'am, I'd like ta spend some time with you, but I need ta know where ta find you."

Even though he was charming and funny, I did not want to tell him where I worked or where I lived. I was glad I had an unlisted phone number.

"Sir, I think you have drunk entirely too much," Martha snapped. I laughed to myself.

He didn't even acknowledge her. He simply replied, "I

may have indulged excessively in the bubbly; however, it has not impaired my vision," looking at me adoringly.

Martha straightened her chair and huffed, "Sir, this place is for dancing, not for pickups. You are out of line."

He calmly turned around and said smoothly, "Well then, ma'am, why don't you dance?"

"Please, let us be civil, for heaven's sake," I said.

"My apologies, ma'am. But I didn't just fall off the turnip wagon, and I know a good woman when I see one. Can we speak . . . alone?"

He got up to help me with my chair before I could even answer. Martha lost her Southern charm and jumped up. "JZ, you don't have to tolerate this, let's go."

"She isn't going anywhere until I find out a few more details. As for you"—he smiled sarcastically at Martha—"I suggest you sit your pretty little rump down and have a drink on me."

Martha froze. She was livid with anger.

"Excuse me, but I will leave anytime I get ready to," I replied smartly to Jeremy.

"Just one question, ma'am. Are you married, engaged, or otherwise affiliated?"

"No. I love God."

He scratched his head. "Woman, you sure know how to make it hard on a fella."

"Let's get out of here before he gets more obnoxious," Martha insisted.

I stood up, smiled, and said, "I'm sorry, but I do have to go. Good luck with your drilling, filling, and billing, Doctor."

Martha, Kitty, and I made our way out of the lounge. Sue was sitting at another table with some pickup. She waved good-bye. As we left the building for the car, Martha turned around and, to her horror, saw Jeremy hot on our heels. "Good God. This sucker is sticking like glue," she groaned.

"Did you ever have the feeling someone was following you?" Jeremy asked.

I wheeled around and snapped, "Did you ever feel unwanted?"

"Ma'am, I want to know why you love God so much. I love God, too. So with so much in common, I thought we could have a talk about our mutual friend."

"Oh, please! I have to go. Go talk to him yourself," I snapped.

Then he took hold of my arm gently. I stared down at his hand holding my arm. "Look, you may very well be the tooth fairy, but I'm the princess who can turn you into a frog."

His face became gentle and sincere. "Please, tell me where I can find you."

"Boy are you pushy! I mean, you don't let up."

"I'm sorry, but God does help those who help themselves," he reasoned.

He pulled his hand away and put both of them in his pockets, rocking slightly on his heels. I looked up at him. My goodness he was tall. His face was pleading like a puppy's. I sighed and told him to meet me the next afternoon at the restaurant where Martha worked.

Successful at last, he bowed deeply, like a knight in King Arthur's court. "Good night, fair lady. Tomorrow is another day."

I chuckled, but Martha, who was already in the car, stuck her head out the window and said in a Clark Gable voice, "And frankly, Scarlett, I don't give a damn."

We drove away leaving Jeremy gazing at the stars.

The following afternoon I left work early and met Martha at the restaurant. She served me a cup of tea and merrily regaled me with gossip. I wasn't listening, just nodding and really thinking about whether I should go through with meeting Jeremy. I hadn't decided yet if I should when Martha cried, "Don't look now, honey, but King Arthur is here."

"Oh, panther piss! Uh, tell him I left, uh, I got sick. Something!"

Panicked, I jumped up to run to the ladies' room when I heard, "I never forget a face, ma'am."

I stopped in my tracks and put on a sweet smile. "Oh, my goodness, if it isn't the tooth fairy. Right here in broad daylight."

He smiled and walked toward me. "Could I interest you in a cup of coffee?"

"Milk."

"I beg your pardon?"

"Milk, I love milk." I smiled and gestured to a table. "Let's sit here and have a lovely visit."

We sat down. As he took his coat off I studied him intently. The thought had crossed my mind earlier that day that I might not recognize him, what with all the smoke and dim lights the night before. I was surprised to see what a handsome man he was—well over six feet tall, lean, and well built. He had shiny black hair, ice blue eyes rimmed with thick dark lashes, and a fair complexion. He sported a thick mustache that he often smoothed with his fingers. His hands were slender and soft, with clean nails, and his clothes fit him very well. The man exuded class. Could this really be the same person I had met last night?

"Tell me, don't you drill, fill, and bill during normal hours?"

"Oh, I had a couple of cancellations." His coffee arrived and he took a sip.

"You sure don't waste time, do you?"

"Ma'am, I told you I didn't fall off the ol' turnip wagon yesterday. I know a good thing when I see it."

"Yeah, well, I've heard that before."

"I bet you have." He smiled and his eyes sparkled like blue fire. "Tell me what you meant about loving God. Are you a religious person?"

I stared into my milk and took a deep breath. I sort of dreaded getting into the conversation. "Not religious like you think. It's just that I see things. Things like ghosts. I have one living with me. I also believe in reincarnation because I was my own sister in another life. I experienced a UFO, and I talk to God because he answers back."

Jeremy had a coughing attack. "Really?"

"Really. Don't you think I'm odd?" I was hoping he would.

"I don't think 'odd' is the right word. Maybe 'fortunate' is a better word. It's wonderful, because I believe in all those things, too. But in my profession, you can't talk about them."

My eyebrows narrowed as I scrutinized him. "Oh, of course."

"I definitely think there's more to those UFOs than the government lets on," he said very seriously.

"You do?"

"What do you think of those new sightings over Brazil?"

"Brazil?"

"Yes, Brazil," he said.

"Oh, were there sightings of UFOs over Brazil?" I felt my face grow pale.

"It's in all the papers."

"Oh, yes, that. Brazil. Actually . . ."

"They're friendly, of course," he said in a tone of authority.

"The ones over Brazil?"

"You know, South America?" He narrowed his eyes suspiciously.

"The saucers over Brazil are . . . well, you know, that's quite common." I was embarrassed that I wasn't up enough on current events to know about the Brazilian UFO incident. I remembered what my science teacher had said about the Air Force dismissing them as weather balloons.

"So, you believe in reincarnation too. Interesting." He pursed his lips and nodded in approval. "Very interesting. You know, when I'm in the woods hunting, I have this feeling that I've lived as a mountain man. Sure, I can't prove it, but I feel different when I'm in the woods. I think different, like—well, as if I were someone else."

"Do you hunt?" I was mesmerized.

"Yep, ma'am, purty good at it too."

"That's wonderful. So do I—or rather, I used to."

He was delighted. "You mean to tell me I've done gone an' met up with a beautiful, intelligent woman who loves God, has lived before, has her own personal ghost, and can shoot a gun?"

I laughed. "Kind of looks that way, doesn't it?"

"Tell me, wonder woman, how do you think reincarnation fits into the scheme of heaven and hell?"

So the afternoon wore on while we had in-depth discussions about everything you ever wanted to know but felt too stupid to ask. Our relationship developed very quickly. We had so many things in common that the weeks that followed were packed with adventures. Jeremy took the boys and me on mountain hikes in the Cascade and Olympic mountain ranges. We went fishing and scouted out deer trails. We picked wild huckleberries and I made a pie of them. Jeremy opened a new world for Brandy and Chris. He liked the kinds of things that most little boys like to do—and overgrown tomboys, too.

Jeremy was a breath of fresh air in my life. He had become my best friend, my lover, and a prayer answered. When he asked me to marry him, I didn't think twice because I loved him, I trusted him, and above all, he loved me and my boys. On August 27, 1977, I became Mrs. Jeremy Wilder. Brandy did the honors of giving the bride away, while Chris was the best man.

I became a happy housewife and mother. My husband delighted in my good cooking and homemaking, while I adored doing them for him. Weekends would come and we all would head for the mountains or lakes. Occasionally, Jeremy would take me out to dinner with friends and business associates, and it was at one such dinner that his friend George Kensy made that memorable comment about pyramid power. That conversation eventually led to Ramtha's debut in my life and to our hasty move to the great white structure.

So there I sat in my new living room, having vividly relived my life, and though I had learned a great deal more about who I was, I still didn't have the answer to the sixty-four-thousand-dollar question: Why me? And who—or what—was Ramtha? I was sitting there pondering this, when directly behind me Ramtha materialized.

"Indeed, beloved woman. I am here."

I whirled around in my chair. "Oh, you scared me!" I said, holding my chest.

"Fear is a no thing, entity. Fear be that which is termed

a perception that is removed by love." He smiled and walked around in front of me.

"I *do* know when I'm afraid and when I'm not," I protested. "It's very real to me!"

"Why believe you fear me, beloved entity?" Ramtha continued to smile.

"Come on, you're not everyday . . . not normal, Ramtha. It's a little crazy to be sitting here talking to a . . . ghost . . . spirit . . . whatever, who says he's thirty-five thousand years old."

"Beloved woman, I was a Lemurian who was part of the pilgrimage that went into that which is termed Atlantis."

"What were you? What did you do for a living?" Dumb question, huh?

"I was that which is termed a warrior."

"Oh, I see. Did you kill people?" I asked sarcastically.

"Indeed, I was a barbarian. Know you a barbarian?"

"Are you still one . . . a barbarian, I mean?"

He laughed. "I came to love indeed that which you have loved for so long, entity."

"What was that?"

"That which you term God."

"You were a barbarian who loved God? My God?"

"Indeed. I knew not what God be when I was a barbarian."

"Well, why were you one?"

"For mine was a destitute people who were termed slaves and soulless. I was the conqueror who freed my people from tyranny. Indeed, I became the greatest of all warriors. For great was my ignorance and hatred, and feared I nothing."

"And how did you change?"

"Beloved woman, may I sit upon the cushions?" I offered him a chair. He walked over to it as though made up of liquid illumination, leaving glittering light behind. When he sat upon the chair, it almost looked as if he and that chair became the same thing. His purple robes flowed onto the carpet, seeming to possess a life of their own. How majestic and utterly beautiful he was, sitting there. He looked like some fabulous king on a throne . . . in *my* living room.

I was so dazzled by him that I wanted to touch that magical robe of his. "May I touch you?"

"Indeed, but you will feel nothing, for that which I be, be that which is materialized thought, entity."

"Materialized thought?"

"Indeed, beloved woman, for that which I be, I be through the lowering of my own thought frequencies, that you may see that which I am. I am vibrating at a slower rate in your time. For I exist where there is no time, indeed no limitations of measurement. I be that which be pure light synthesis of thought, indeed!"

I was really trying to understand this. "You mean, your light is even brighter than I can see?"

"Indeed, for my light be brighter than a thousand suns. I shall tell you a great truth, beloved entity. The highest vibratory frequency of light be that of thought which is love."

"Love?"

"Indeed! That is correct. Your Great Master, Yeshua Ben Joseph, achieved that state of pure love, pure thought."

"Uh, who was he?"

"You know him in your history as the man Jesus."

"What did you say Jesus accomplished?"

"The Great Master vibrated at the highest rate of light, which be termed pure love. Therefore, his ascension was made possible."

"This all sounds so scientific." I shook my head.

"Indeed! But that which you term science in your understanding disregards these great dimensions. For they be limited unto that which is linear. One day, in your time, your sciences will embrace the great truth."

"What great truth?"

"That all be God in understanding which everything is. For that which is the unseen governs the science of the seen."

"Well, I understand God," I said rather smugly.

His smile broadened. "Beloved woman, soon you will understand even more of the God you have, indeed, loved for so long."

I stared at him for a moment, still not understanding all that he had said to me. I was still struggling to understand "light synthesis," and my limited mind was literally being stretched to comprehend his presence in my living room.

"Ramtha, I've been trying to figure out what I did to bring about this unbelievable experience. Why are you here in my life?"

"Indeed, to bring forth unto you that which is termed greater understanding."

"Are you my guardian angel?"

"Beloved woman, I have been with you throughout this lifetime, indeed throughout all of your lifetimes!"

"Did you ever live again? Here on earth, I mean."

"I did not need to choose to be of that which is termed flesh again. For, entity, in one lifetime I became God."

"You are a god?"

"Indeed! Beloved entity, so be you God also. The only difference between that which be you and that which be I, is that I know that I am and you, beloved woman, do not!"

"Honestly, Ramtha, don't you think it's a little presumptuous of you to say you are a god?"

"Honestly? Indeed, I am *honestly*! Entity, it would be that which is termed presumptuous of me to say I was *not* God." He smiled and continued, "We all are a part of God. We are each that divine perfection."

"We are perfect?" I asked, surprised. I had grown up, like most other people, hearing the phrase "No one's perfect."

"Beloved woman, the dire diseasement upon your plane is that which is termed spiritual ignorance. Humanoids do not understand that each individual be that which is God. Entities are arrogant in setting themselves apart from the divinity that all is. They, indeed, stand outside of the Great Knowingness and desire to be separate from the All. No thing exists outside of the life force, indeed, not even man. God be that which is termed your birthright."

I was still contemplating the possibility of God being all of us as I gazed upon Ramtha's beautiful cinnamon-colored hands. "Ramtha, isn't God up there?" I pointed my finger toward the ceiling. "He's our Father that protects us."

"God is within you, beloved entity. God be the life force

of the All. It is liken unto what Master Jesus said, 'I and the Father are one.' Indeed, so it is with you."

"So, you're telling me that I am God? You really believe that?"

"No, I don't believe anything, I know it. There is a vast difference, indeed, between *believe* and *know*."

"So Jeremy is God . . . Brandy and Chris are God?"

"Indeed!"

"So, everybody is God?"

"Indeed! Beloved woman, when mankind realizes that truth, that which you know as war will cease."

I didn't respond for a few moments. This was a hard pill to swallow. If the God that I had been praying to up there in heaven, smiling down on me and everyone else, really *was* me and everyone else, how could I profess to love God and yet not like so many people? If I truly loved God, I would have to love everyone. Ramtha was reading my thoughts.

"Beloved woman, indeed, to love all people is, indeed, to love God. For God, the life force, the source, be all people. That be what is termed the love of Christ, unconditional love. Indeed, it be an arduous thing, for all people express differently and, indeed, what be different in one threatens the difference in another, thus there be war. Beloved woman, though all be different, there lies the commonness between them all, and that be that they be of God. The master first learns to accept the God that he is. For, indeed, when love he completely that which he is, he loves completely God. That love be termed 'unconditional love.' Then the master sees and loves in others that commonness called God. It is the love of self and God that allows the master to love everyone regardless of their differences."

"I see. Ramtha, you said you have been with me and that you protected me. Well, if that is so, why didn't you help me when I was so sick?"

"Beloved entity, you created the experience in order to learn from it, indeed! It was for you to learn and realize your own power unto yourself. Is that not what occurred?"

"Yes . . . I suppose so."

"Beloved woman, you have been progressing in a most unlimited manner. You are now ready for greater understanding of your Father's business."

"Wait a minute, Ramtha. I am a very simple person. I don't profess to have great intelligence. I just love God. Period!"

Ramtha smiled in a delightful manner, his black eyes flashing copper lights. "Indeed."

I felt a little apprehensive about his merry little attitude. "I don't understand why all of this is happening to me!"

"Beloved woman, there be a great purpose and reason for this, which I will demonstrate at another time in your time."

"But I want to know now. Don't you think I should? Honestly, I just want to continue to love God, Ramtha. I don't want to be involved in a 'great purpose.' "

"You will, entity, you will."

I thought he was acting real bossy, and since he knew what I thought, I didn't have to say it! He smiled. I frowned! I turned away from him and looked instead around the house. Then I remembered that we had this house because of him.

"Oh, it's great!" I said, signaling with my hands that I meant the house. "Thank you. You really hit the nail right on the head about the old house, didn't you?"

"Hit the nail on the head? What be that meaning to you, Master?"

"Uh, it's just an expression to say that you were right. That's all."

"Indeed! I am always right. If the hammer is, indeed, struck with the truth, then the nail becomes your servant!"

"Uh-huh . . . yeah, right. Did the realtor, Roy Burnsides, know about you, too?"

"Master Burnsides is a most delightful entity who enjoys a challenge. Indeed, I knew he would be a grand runner."

"Runner? Uh, did he think I was nuts?" I asked.

"Know you the term *bizarre*? A most appropriate word. Am I not bizarre also, entity?"

Ramtha then threw back his head and let out a roar of laughter that made my chair vibrate. As I watched him laugh,

I started laughing too—at myself and at the insanity of this whole experience. Then Ramtha got up and began to inspect the "great white structure." His huge materialized form floated into the kitchen. He didn't even duck under the doorway; he just walked through it. He turned on the faucets and put his long graceful fingers under the water. The water fell around his fingers. Ramtha started to chuckle at the instant waterfall in the kitchen. Then he moseyed on over to the stove, turned the knobs, and the blue flames magically appeared. He had the most delighted look on his face.

"Indeed, beloved woman, this is most wondrous! Call you this instant fire a miracle?"

I was taken aback at his interest in my kitchen. It was as if he had never seen one before. I suppose he hadn't. But his innocence was so beautiful. I really had never thought of my stove as a miracle before. "Well, Ramtha, it's what I call a gas bill. You pay for the miracle."

He leaned down and opened the oven door. "What be this small room for, entity?"

"Well, that's for baking and cooking. It has fire miracles in it too."

"Ah, a modern hearth; most convenient, entity! Most appropriate, indeed, when there is rainfall! Beloved woman, in my day this would indeed have been a miracle. Anything, beloved, that is inaccessible and longed for becomes a miracle. Yet, if one desires such, it becomes manifest through creative mind. Then it becomes that which is ordinary."

"Hmm, I guess so. Ramtha, you didn't live inside a house in your day?"

"Indeed! I was continually on what you term a march."

"Oh. And how many warriors were there in your army?"

"Multitudes." He continued to inspect my miracle kitchen.

"What did you do with an army that was so big?"

"Indeed, I plundered and killed. It is, indeed, beloved woman, as I have told you. I was that which was a barbarian until I became enlightened."

He turned and glided into the foyer, making it look like some grand cathedral with his light dancing off the ceiling and reflecting in the polished wood floor. As I watched this beautiful entity, I couldn't help wondering why, if he lived thirty-five thousand years ago, he didn't look like a run-of-the-mill caveman.

"Uh, Ramtha, you said that you lived some thirty-five thousand years ago, right?" He smiled and nodded. "Well, our researchers, called anthropologists, say that people in your time were ignorant cave dwellers that wore skins and bones and stuff. That would have been around the Ice Age, I think. But you don't look like those old bones, and well, you don't look like an ape. Uh, I mean, I'm glad you don't, but if you did, look like an ape-man that is, your story would add up. I mean, you should look like a Neanderthal or a Cro-Magnon type person."

"Cro-Magnon?"

"Yeah, skins, bones, stringy hair, and B.O. . . ." What other description could I offer?

He contemplated this for a moment, then his face lit up even more. "Ah, indeed, I understand that which you ask. That which is termed man has been developing and, indeed, evolving since ten million years in your time and counting. That which was of my lineage will be found in that which is termed Africa; they shall say that his bones are seventy thousand years old. Those that were of that period became advanced through the aeons and would later be called the Atlantians. Those of my lineage would migrate and through their adaptation into Lemuria I thus came. My people were not that which you term ape-men for they did not possess the genetics of stouten entities with muscular necks, indeed, large boned and deformed brows. Such entities you term Neanderthal were much earlier and were the experimental phase of mankind. Indeed, they did not resemble what you term Cro-Magnon. Nor were the two species linked genetically. There existed two superior species, both being that which you term Cro-Magnon, that began to evolve much differently. Indeed, one was called the Atlantian, bearing red skin, and the other the Lemurian, bearing brown skin. Indeed, both evolved from the great ones in that which is Africa—indeed, Eden as you term it. Those who remained, flourished to later become the fair Ionians. That which you

termed Neanderthals intermingled through breeding to create yet a different genetic species.

"Beloved woman, your scientists will discover many
wonderful things of your past—indeed, they will discover
that that which I was, that is termed Cro-Magnon, were the
wise peoples with a powerful seat of reasoning, due to our
frontal lobes. Indeed, that I of my day had the ability of
thought, indeed, of adaptation and of invention. As for that
which you term skins and bones, I and my people dressed
in cloth of reeds, robes of wool, and that which is termed
fur. We were adorned in tunics and undergarments and,
indeed, wore soft sandals. Our jewel adornments were of
ivory beads and the stone of blue fire. Indeed, we did not
dwell in caves liken unto the animals, but of hovels made
upon the grounds. We often rode what you call horses. My
people believed in the Unknown God and always prepared
for an afterlife. We believed that once you died, indeed, that
you would live again. There was no thing to tell us different,
entity. Now, beloved woman, still think you that that which
think you I am, Cro-Magnon, be ignorant and, indeed, smelling bad?"

I blushed at my own ignorance. Who would have thought
that a Cro-Magnon would believe in reincarnation, smell good,
and know all this? I wondered what the anthropologists would
think. Hmmm, I thought, I guess they'll just have to keep
digging. Ramtha smiled and said, "They will, indeed, and
they shall find many wonderful truths."

Ramtha waved the discussion away with his hand and
glided up the staircase. I went trailing after the illuminated
Cro-Magnon.

"You are pleased with the whiteness of your surroundings, beloved woman?"

"It's really nice, Ramtha."

Ramtha turned to face me, looking down as I looked up.
"Indeed, beloved woman, you are most appreciative. The
whiteness of your hovel is liken unto the soul of your attitude." He then turned and went into our bedroom. "You
will learn great truths in your dreams upon these cushions,
entity." He sat on the king-size bed, his robes of light flowing

and dancing around the white carpet on the floor. As he sat there, I noticed how he made a deep impression on the bed underneath him.

"Ramtha, I see evidence of you sitting on my bed, but you say that you are a spirit."

"I desire, indeed, to feel the dimension of the body. It is an exquisite sensation."

"Then why don't you just materialize and become one of us modern Homo sapiens?"

"I do not choose the experience again, for know I all. I am a grand teacher for the dimension of the spirit, indeed, for I have grand things to teach you modern Homo sapiens, as you have termed it."

"How can we help? I mean, what are we supposed to do?"

Ramtha sat up very straight and put his wonderful hands on his knees and leaned toward me. "In time . . . indeed, beloved entity. Be you happy with your marriage union?" A broad smile came over his face.

"Yes. Did we do the right thing?"

"Indeed, it is the fulfillment of an aspect of destiny unfulfilled."

"What does that mean?"

"I shall tell you this, beloved woman: you were one of my daughters in the army of my time. Your beloved husbandman was one of my centurians. Indeed, at the age of thirteen years, as you term it, I promised my daughter to him. But, indeed, you refused. Your heart was my strategy of armaments—indeed, beloved woman, you wished to be a warrior. Indeed, in this lifetime you are fulfilling that which was unfulfilled."

I was amazed, to say the least.

"I bless this union. You will learn much from one another." He stood up and said, "So be it." A wind blew through my window and Ramtha, the beautiful Cro-Magnon who was God, disappeared.

That evening when my husband came home, I told him about my visitation from Ramtha, about the stove, the lights from his robe, perfumed Cro-Magnons, reincarnation, and

God. As Jeremy finished warming a little hot toddy and sat down, Ramtha appeared again. I knew Jeremy couldn't see him, but from the way he started looking around, he definitely felt him.

Ramtha addressed Jeremy. I became the interpreter, involuntarily. "My beloved physician, I am Ramtha, the Enlightened One. I come unto you this hour from that which is another dimension."

"Ramtha, welcome. You mean you lived at some other time?"

"Indeed, I lived. I was the Ram, the Great Conqueror. I was the first Great God of the people of Indus."

"You mean India? Were you born in India?"

My mouth was moving with Ramtha's words, but my eyes were trying to tell Jeremy that we had already discussed this stuff.

"No, Master. I am a Lemurian who lived in Atlatia."

"In Atlatia? Oh, you mean Atlantis. You were from Atlantis? Ramtha, why do you call me 'Master'?" Jeremy asked.

"Indeed, you are all masters, unaware of your own greatness."

Although I was mouthing Ramtha's words, I started to become a little frightened by it.

"Jeremy, I'm frightened. It says in the Bible that the Antichrist will appear as an angel of God and deceive the world. God, maybe this is the Antichrist!"

No sooner had I made that ludicrous statement, than I began to hear the faraway sound of a musical horn. Then I began to hear the chanting of multitudinous voices. "Ram . . . Ram . . . Ram . . ." Then my kitchen disappeared, the walls of the house falling away into a mist. My ceiling had become a clear blue sky and I seemed to be on a mountain. There were three people standing in a vapor in front of me. Two were like warriors; the one that was the tallest must have been Ramtha. He was dressed in battle gear, with a helmet that shadowed his eyes. He wore a breastplate of leather and some silver things on it. In the center of the breastplate was a carving of the head of a ram. Again I heard a horn blow. It seemed to be coming from the mountains and echoing all around me. Then the chanting began again, "Ram . . . Ram . . . Ram . . ."

Ramtha's left hand held a sword at the hilt, the point resting on the ground. He wore a huge ring with a bright blue stone. There was another warrior to his right. And in front was a woman poised serenely on pillows with a gentle smile on her face. Her thick black hair was done up in plaits that coiled around her head. She wore a white garment, and in the center of the girdle around her waist was the same blue stone. None of the three said anything. It was as if they were suspended in time. The horn began to blow again, hauntingly, far away. The vision faded and the robed Ramtha came back into view. The time warp had disappeared and we were back in the present.

"My beloved woman, I am the Great Warrior. I am not that which you term Antichrist. There never was such a thing. It only exists for the fear it brings those who harbor it within their souls."

I was still confused, but Jeremy had no trouble accepting what was happening.

"I *knew* you were a warrior. I could sense it, because I've always thought that I was. But Ramtha, why can't I actually see you as JZ does?"

"Indeed, beloved physician, she sees many unseen realities. This is that which you term her destiny. She will be a light unto the world, beloved one, and that which is termed you shall dance with me in the sun."

Jeremy was overjoyed with Ramtha's message, but I was having difficulty even accepting that these things were coming out of my mouth.

Ramtha then turned and looked at me. "My beloved woman, be at peace. All is in harmony, it is as it should be. So be it!" Ramtha faded away.

I just shook my head as though I were coming out of a trance. Jeremy embraced me. "Oh, Zebra, this is wonderful. We actually have made contact with an entity beyond this dimension."

"Jeremy, what's going on? I could feel myself mouthing his words, but they were *his* words, not *mine!* Anybody else would think I was having a conversation with myself. Loony Tunes time!"

"My Zebra, I know Ramtha was here."

I looked at him curiously. "Why aren't you having any difficulty with this?"

"Because I accept it. And I know it's all right."

I sighed. "We should both be committed!"

"My Zebra, you've had this entity with you most of your life. You said he was your guardian angel. Why are you having trouble with him now?"

"God, Jeremy, he seems so real. He talks . . . I talk. He talks to you . . . I'm talking to you. Lord!"

"Well then, if he's real, why do you think you're crazy?"

My mouth dropped open. I could not believe he asked me such an asinine question. Jesus, had *he* gone mad? I got up and walked out of the room.

A week or so later on Saturday morning, Jeremy had just gotten out of the shower and wrapped a towel around his waist. He was going to the closet to get dressed. I was standing in front of the vanity mirror putting on my makeup. Just as I had outlined my top lip with a lipstick pencil, Ramtha appeared in the mirror behind me. He startled me and I dropped the pencil, leaving the job half done. I just stood there blinking my eyelashes at him in the mirror. I smiled and asked sarcastically, "Can I help you, Ramtha?"

At that moment Jeremy dashed back out of the closet with this towel still wrapped around his waist. I smiled at him and said, "He's right over there."

"Beloved physician, wear you loincloths?"

Jeremy blushed and tried to explain a shower to him. I interrupted. "Uh Jeremy, remember that Cro-Mags knew nothing of showers." Jeremy shot me a "come-off-it" look.

I looked at Ramtha and motioned with my head. "The shower's in there. Be my guest!"

"Zebra!" Jeremy admonished, shocked by my sarcasm. Ramtha laughed!

"Beloved physician, indeed, shall we feel the warmth of the hearth below? I desire to speak to you of that which is termed gold."

"Money?" Jeremy asked.

"Indeed! Prepare yourself into your proper dress."

Jeremy got dressed quickly, then ran downstairs and built a nice fire. Ramtha sat on the sofa, which he called "beauteous cushions." The boys came in and sat too!

"Indeed, you will find it necessary to amass gold for the payment of this abode, is that not correct, beloved physician?"

"You mean money?" Jeremy asked.

"Indeed. In your counting, what earn you for your services as a tooth physician?"

"How much do I make? Enough to get by on."

"Desire you to make more?"

"Sure, Ramtha, that's why God made stockbrokers and investment analysts . . . to make more money." Jeremy chuckled.

"Indeed. He did and you can. I desire you to bless each individual who sits in your chair, for indeed, you will heal them greater."

"All right, but what I need are more patients, Ramtha."

"Indeed, that be a great truth. Alas, Master, the masses must become aware of you, correct?"

"You mean advertising?" He sort of choked on that one.

"Indeed! Callers in the marketplace."

"But Ramtha, that would be against the ADA's ethics committee."

"It is termed wrong to hail forth your services in the marketplace?"

"You mean like taking out an ad in the paper or the phone book?"

"Indeed, they are callers, are they not?"

"No one has done it, exactly."

"Master, I charge you to be the first. Indeed, there will be those who will try to enslave you, only because you would pose a threat to their own services. But, beloved Master, because of this boldness, others will come forward and also hail their services in the places of such advertisement."

"I trust you know what you are doing," Jeremy said.

"Indeed, beloved physician, I always know what I am doing, for that which I am doing is how I am known."

Jeremy sat there considering what Ramtha had said.

"Jeremy, I don't like this," I interrupted. "You know, you could be blackballed by all your friends and the ethics committee."

"Beloved woman, there is always the black before the dawning of light."

I just glared at Ramtha. How could he know any of this stuff about ethics and blackballing?

"Ramtha, why are you suggesting ways for me to become more successful?" asked Jeremy. "It doesn't seem to be in keeping with what a spiritual entity would do."

"Master, why think you that abundance be not spiritual? Everything be God. To be fruitful in that which is one's work is to manifest the joy of abundance on your plane."

"I always thought that really spiritual people were poor. They didn't need wealth."

"Master, that be a creative truth created by those to induce poverty upon others in the name of spirituality, to take their wealth away from them! Those entities that created that truth are the richest of all. They be that which is termed religions. If say you to them that, for them to be spiritual, they must then tear down their cathedrals, melt down all their gold, and give up their treasures back to those they took in from, think you they would follow their own truth?"

Jeremy laughed. "Can't say they would."

"That which is termed abundance is also God. A spiritual entity enjoys the happiness and possibilities of all that he creatively manifests. He does not intimidate others out of it, nor does he rob them, but rather he evenly creates it for himself. That be God."

Ramtha looked at Brandy and Chris sitting on the floor. "Beloved Masters, in your days to come, when speak you of me, there will be much controversy indeed. There will come, indeed, an hour that you shall deny that which I am. But say I unto you, I will become a grand teacher upon this plane. Remember this, I will still love that which you are and I shall be with you as I always have been. Know that you are greatly loved. So be it!"

Ramtha disappeared in a blaze of light. I shook my head and became focused again.

"Now he's running your business," I said in a huff.

"Zebra, let's give it a shot. I trust him."

"He's too manipulative, Jeremy!"

"Well, I think the old boy is just showing me how to be more creative in getting some new patients. Who would I really be hurting?"

I just stared at him for a moment, then got up and angrily left the room.

"What's wrong with Mom?" Brandy asked.

"There's just a lot of new stuff to adjust to, Brandy. Who else do you know has a guardian angel hanging around?"

"Maybe she's scared it won't work," Chris said as he got up off the floor.

Over the next few weeks, Jeremy took Ramtha's advice and started running some ads in the newspaper and later in the phone book. His waiting room filled up with new patients every day. Of course, Jeremy was blackballed by the ethics committee, but even though he felt isolated from other dentists, he stood his ground and became an overnight success.

I, on the other hand, had difficulty dealing with the ill feelings that resulted in his ostracism. I felt so sorry for my wonderful husband. But Ramtha had been right; other dentists began to follow suit. My husband had walked away from the pack and had become a trailblazer.

Some weeks later, as Jeremy and I were fawning over our new dining room set, he observed, "Well, my Zebra, we made over three times more this month than the month before. The old boy was right."

"Yes, but it's not as if it came without a price. I don't know what to think. Ramtha comes in here, gives you tips on P.R., and then we don't hear from him. I mean, what kind of spiritual teacher is that?" I huffed.

"I don't know, Zebra . . . but he was right!"

CHAPTER NINETEEN

THE ONE

Lt was now September of 1977 and that meant grouse and early deer season had opened. Jeremy and I spent many days hunting in the forests of the Olympic Mountains. We both enjoyed being outdoors and were both excellent hunters, but what I particularly loved was walking the pitch-dark forest of early morning to my stand. I would sit very still and watch the light spread throughout the forest around me. I saw the squirrels wake up and begin their morning escapades, gathering acorns for breakfast. Woodpeckers would begin drilling nearby trees for termite larvae as blue jays screeched and tried to rob the nests of other birds. Often a doe appeared in a clearing with her fawns, and I would watch them for hours. They had gotten so used to my being there that once, when I was late getting to my stand, instead of running away they casually watched me walk into the clearing and take my seat. I became so much a part of my surroundings that once a hawk landed on the end of my shotgun, thinking it was a branch. I loved the serenity of the forest and the harmony of the animals that lived there. Oftentimes, I did not want to return home at the end of the day.

Though Ramtha had been absent for a time from our household, I would catch myself thinking about him with reservation. Even though he had told me a little about why he had chosen to appear to me, I was still bothered by him. I wondered if others had had similar experiences and, if so, what they had done about it.

I had remained very closemouthed about Ramtha. After all, most of my friends would think I had gone off the deep end. Even I had thought so at first. Looking back, I think one of the reasons I wanted to stay out in the forest was to avoid thinking about Ramtha and all the questions that still bothered me about him.

One day in September while Jeremy was at his office, I decided maybe I should call around to some churches to see if someone could help me understand this a little better. Why the churches? Because I remembered that when I was younger, a few of the members of my church testified about being visited by angels, or even by Jesus Himself. So I went to the Yellow Pages and started with the first church. I gave them a ring.

"Hello? Yes, someone told me you could help me with a problem I'm having in my home. . . . Yes, I've been saved . . . and baptized. . . . No, no, you don't understand; my husband is *very* faithful and . . . No, he's not a sinner. . . . Uh, could I just interrupt you for a moment? Thank you. Well, I have this spirit that appears off and on in my home, and he says that he is a God and . . . What? Well, I wouldn't say that he is evil to me. I never really believed in such a thing. . . . Yes, I have been saved. I just didn't know who else to call. . . . What do you mean you don't want to have anything to do with me? Hello? Hello?"

When the phone went dead, I just went to the next number and dialed.

"Hello? I'm Mrs. Wilder and I would like to speak to

someone who can help me with a spirit in my home. . . . But I don't know who else to contact. . . . Call back next week? But I need to have some kind of explanation now. Aren't you in the business of helping people? . . . I see! Thank you!"

I made five more phone calls and in each case found no one willing to help me. I was becoming more angry and frustrated with each call. By the sixth call, I was livid.

"Listen, what's going on with you pious people? You church people are supposed to help people in times of trouble, aren't you? Now I understand why I never really believed in you. You're nothing but a bunch of hypocrites! I'm dealing here with a spirit from the spiritual world, and I might need an exorcism or something, and nobody will help me! Why can't I come down to your church; isn't it open for business? Why would I want to fly to Chicago? Are you nuts? To be exorcised? You want me to tell you what I really think of your religion?" Click, buzz. What the . . . ? I slammed down the receiver. Then I tried another church, this time to be told by one of the secretaries in secretive tones that I should wear garlic around my neck and the rest of the family do the same. Then I should put garlic in all my windows and above the doors and I should burn white candles in every room. If all this fails, I should move! Good God, I could just see Jeremy doing a root canal on some patient while his garlic dangled in her face. Or the boys explaining it as a new defense measure in football!

Just as I was about to write off the churches and people in general, I happened to see the name "Spiritualist Church." I dialed the number.

"Spiritualist Church?" Just as I began, Ramtha appeared in the kitchen and told me to ask for a Michael. "Uh, do you have a Michael there?" My forehead felt hot.

"I'm Michael," a soft voice replied.

"Yes, well, I'd like to talk to you about a problem I'm having."

"I'm a psychic. Perhaps I could help you," he said.

"A what?"

"I'm a psychic."

"Are you a fortune-teller?"

"No, I'm a psychic."

I'm really making progress here. "Really? Then can you tell me why I'm calling?"

"You have a problem. You have dark brown hair and are rather heavy. You are married. The problem is your marriage. I feel great distress coming from you."

"I think I've dialed the wrong number."

"No, you haven't, but I have described you perfectly," he said, unruffled.

"Oh yeah? I'm blond and I'm not overweight . . . but I am married," I huffed. "My problem is that I have a spirit in my home and I— Come right down? Where are you? 1802 Federal Way? I'll be there in two hours and I'll bring my husband."

I called Jeremy and described my conversation with the hit-and-miss psychic. Even though he was off base, the fact that he didn't sound shocked when I spoke of spirits convinced me we should pay him a visit. Then I dressed in an all-yellow skirt and sweater outfit, with matching heels and handbag—I was, after all, going to church—and waited for Jeremy to pick me up.

We finally found a small white house that was set off the main highway. We drove up and parked alongside some other cars there. I checked my hair and then we walked up and knocked. No one answered, so we crept into what appeared to have once been a living room. There were about forty folding chairs that faced a pulpit. The walls were adorned with two huge pictures of Jesus. We walked through a kitchen and then to the back door. In the backyard was a long table with fourteen men and women sitting around it. The women wore double-knit pantsuits and the men were dressed casually with open-necked shirts and slacks. They had been gabbing away until they saw us standing on the back porch. Jeremy and I looked at each other and then walked over to their table. No one said a thing!

Finally I said, "My name is Mrs. Wilder, and this is my husband, Dr. Jeremy Wilder. He's a dentist."

No one said anything. I stood there remembering all

those earlier phone calls to churches and I got very mad. They were giving us the cold shoulder. So I just grabbed one of their chairs, pulled it up to the table, and sat down.

"I called and talked to a man named Michael about a problem we are having in our house. He said to come right over. Well, we are here, and I'm not leaving this table until someone here helps us!" I was impertinent and defiant.

An older woman with gray hair stood up. "I am Pastor Lorraine Graham. Michael told me a little of what you said. Now, what can I do for you?"

She gestured for Jeremy to take a chair next to me, while she sat on the edge of the table. Everyone else quietly got up and left us alone.

"Well, it's a long story. . . ." I told her everything we had experienced with Ramtha, and even with Ghost prior to our marriage. During different parts of the story Jeremy became a little restless, but Pastor Graham listened intently. She was not alarmed.

When I had finished, she smiled knowingly and said, "First of all, please call me Lorraine. Second, I don't think you're crazy at all."

"You don't?" I looked up at her in amazement.

She shook her head. "As a matter of fact, the Spiritualist Frontier Movement prophesied some years ago that a spiritual entity called The One would manifest on this plane as a profound and great teacher."

I began to wring my hands when I heard her say, "The One." My mind shot back to the fortune-teller in Manhattan Beach. "I don't think this is the same teacher."

"Perhaps not. Would you and Dr. Wilder like to come upstairs where we can talk more comfortably?"

Jeremy and I were surprised at Lorraine's easy acceptance. We all walked back into the house and up a narrow staircase to a niche of a bedroom. There was a small bed covered with a patchwork quilt, and a round table with four chairs. There were books and memorabilia everywhere.

"This is where I sleep when I come here to give lectures. Please have a seat," she said.

Jeremy and I sat down at the small round table, trying

to make ourselves comfortable. Lorraine was quite relaxed. She pulled a book from beside the bed and put it on the table. It was titled *Roots of Consciousness*. She flipped through the pages.

"What do you know about mediumship?" she asked casually.

"Mediumship? What are you talking about? I'm afraid I don't understand."

Lorraine eyed me with those bright blue eyes of hers and realized that she was talking to a novice.

"I see. Well, certain individuals have the vibratory energy and frequency in their physical makeup that gives them the ability to connect with spiritual teachers on the other side." She was watching my expression and seemed to know that I lost her on "the other side." "When I talk about the other side, I'm referring to those who have died but still live after their death. These spiritual teachers speak through certain individuals who are gifted with a high frequency. Edgar Cayce, for example, was one of those individuals."

"Who?"

She looked at me incredulously. "You don't know who Edgar Cayce was?"

I looked at Jeremy and he was a blank. "I never heard of him," I told her.

"Edgar Cayce was one of the great mediums of this century. He provided spiritual information from the other side, medical diagnoses, predictions of human events, and so on."

"Was the stuff correct?" I was very interested in what she was saying.

"In the main, yes. You see, spiritual entities from the other side aren't limited to our three dimensions, or even to our time, so their understanding is more comprehensive."

She paused to see if we were understanding, and, sensing that we were to some degree, she continued. "Now, I want you to visualize a scene for me. It will help you to understand more clearly. Visualize a canoe floating down a river. You are in the canoe. You can see only what is immediately behind and immediately ahead of you. Now suppose for a moment that you were a hundred feet above that canoe. Your vision downriver, meaning the past, and upriver, meaning the future, is much more extensive. Individuals— or 'souls' as I call them—living in the spiritual dimension have that same vista. They see physical life in the form of energy, or light. This vision is called inner vision, which means they can sense your vibrational frequency. If the frequency of your energy is high enough, then you can become an instrument through which a contact can be made from the other side. A medium is a telephone. If you wish to call long-distance to the other side, you use the telephone. You, Mrs. Wilder, are a medium."

I laughed nervously. "Please, call me JZ. So you are saying that I am a medium through which this spiritual thing called Ramtha speaks?"

"Yes. Because of your electromagnetic frequency. When you raise your own vibration, you can then see the spirit. But I think he must lower his own frequency in order to meet yours. That is what makes him visible."

"Hmmm, I seem to recall him saying something about that. I just didn't understand. It's all Greek to me."

"Oh, my dear JZ, it's really quite scientific. Our limited sciences just haven't recognized it yet. They have yet to develop the instruments or techniques to pronounce it real. Of course, to those who can't see spirit it's a hoax, but to those who do it's real. The Spiritualist Frontier Movement has devoted itself to the study of psychic phenomena. Perhaps one day the public won't be so skeptical and will benefit from the wonders it could offer the human race. But for now they call such things 'occult.' "

"What does 'occult' mean, Lorraine?" I asked.

"It's a word that means 'hidden.' That's all. It's funny, but this word could even apply to the standard religions, since in essence they, too, worship a spirit. Well, JZ, you are experiencing a hidden reality. You aren't crazy, just gifted."

To this day, I don't really know what happened to me after that, so the following account is based on what Lorraine and Jeremy described to me.

My body suddenly sat up very straight and my arms

went far above my head, stretching as if to reach the ceiling. My face began to change completely. Though my features were the same, I took on someone else's expressions. A powerful energy filled the room. I pushed back my chair and opened my legs under my full skirt. I planted my legs apart and positioned my feet firmly. My once slender neck doubled in size, becoming muscled and masculine, and my body grew astonishingly large. I leaned forward and smiled in a way that was clearly not my smile, and then looked intently at Jeremy and Lorraine. Both were transfixed by this transfiguration. The energy that was coming from my eyes was penetrating and intense. Lorraine seemed paralyzed. Jeremy swallowed hard and then spoke.

"Ramtha, it's you, isn't it?"

"Indeed, my beloved physician. Be you well?"

"Well, partner, I'm doing just fine."

"Indeed, you are learning new knowledge?"

Lorraine came out of her paralytic state and began to beam with joy.

"Indeed, beloved teacher, be you well?" Ramtha asked Lorraine.

"Oh, my. I don't have any words."

"Indeed, beloved woman, you need not say any one thing. Be at peace. You have, indeed, been unto my daughteren and my beloved physician a most wondrous runner. This I say unto you: for that which is termed melanoma that is within your arms and that which is in your bosom is, indeed, subsiding and, unto an hour, you shall have your bosom removed, for that is your decision. I will help you, indeed, for little shall be your pain. You are a courageous warrior. Know that you are greatly loved."

Lorraine's eyes began to fill with tears and she began to heave with emotion.

"I will speak through my beloved daughteren. I am Ramtha, the Enlightened One. That which I be, I be; that which I am, I am. My daughteren will become a great light unto this world . . . a light that shall blaze through the dogmas of your plane. Indeed."

Tears were spilling from Lorraine's eyes and dropping

off her face. Jeremy got up and got some tissue for her. Ramtha then leaned forward and took Lorraine's hands and kissed their palms and their backs.

"I desire you to be a runner of understanding for my beloved daughteren and beloved physician—indeed?"

"Yes, yes, Holy One, I will."

Ramtha then turned to Jeremy. "My beloved physician, I desire you to support your beloved woman in all these most confusing times—indeed?"

"You got it, partner. I'll do my best." Jeremy smiled.

"Beauteous entity, you have learned a grand lesson with gold. It was, indeed, all for purposeful good—indeed?"

"I guess so."

"Indeed, it is enough. For the body is weary. I will come again when you least expect me. Know that you are loved. So be it!"

Ramtha left my body and I crumpled slightly. I felt like I had only had a little dizzy spell, so I continued my conversation with Lorraine.

"So, the word *occult* means 'hidden.' I didn't realize that. I always thought it had to do with supposed evil activities and stuff. Well, I still don't understand a lot of this. . . ." Suddenly I realized that Lorraine had been crying. "Lorraine, what's wrong? Did I say something wrong?" I looked at Jeremy, trying to find out what I had said, but he was looking at me strangely.

"Jeremy, why are you looking like that? What's happened?" I was alarmed at their strange manner.

"Zebra, the Ram was here," Jeremy said.

I looked around, but I didn't see him in the room. "I don't see him."

Lorraine blew her nose hard and began to wipe away her tears.

"Will someone here at this table tell me what's going on?"

"Well, the Ram just came *through* you, Zebra," said Jeremy.

"Came through me? I'm sorry, but I don't see him anywhere, and I didn't talk to him, either."

"Zebra, you know how you would use your voice to speak to me for him?"

"Yes."

"Well, this time you just disappeared somewhere else, but your body changed too . . . I guess to look something like Ramtha's. He spoke to us, Lorraine and me, and it was through your body, Zebra. It was wonderful."

Now I was really alarmed. I hadn't gone anywhere. "What do you mean, I went someplace else? I didn't go *anywhere!*"

Lorraine tried to comfort me. "Now, JZ, it's all right, dear, you're safe. It was what I was trying to explain to you before. You are a medium, an extraordinary one at that. I've seen many mediums in my day, but never one to compare with you . . . or Ramtha. Your husband's right, JZ, he is powerful. More powerful than anything I have ever seen. And his eyes! My God, those eyes of his were penetrating, ancient, all-encompassing. I am rambling on, but you must believe me. Ramtha is like nothing that I have ever witnessed. Most spirits do not manifest themselves in broad daylight, and they don't open their eyes. And the touch . . . my dear child, it is known that you cannot touch a medium in a trance; it distorts the ectoplasm of the spirit and could easily kill the medium. But Ramtha *touched* me. I just know that this spirit is something much greater than any I have ever known."

"But I didn't go anywhere," I protested. "Are you guys going crazy? I'm sorry, I just don't believe you!"

"Zebra, it's true. I knew it was Ramtha before he even opened his mouth. The feeling was the same one I have when he's at our house. He talked as he usually does, only this time he was in your body, not just in your voice. And, Zebra, I finally got to see and talk to him face-to-face. It was wonderful."

I jumped up from my chair, nearly knocking it over, and began to pace the floor. "Then what you are saying is that I'm possessed? Is that what you're saying, I'm possessed by Ramtha?" Images of exorcists filled my head.

Lorraine got up and took me by the shoulders. "Please listen to me, JZ. Ramtha asked me to help you understand what's happening to you. I want to do just that. I can't right at this moment; there are people coming in downstairs that I must see. But I want you to know something: there is nothing to be afraid of, believe me. This is a monumental adjustment you are having to make, but with understanding and knowledge it will become more reasonable and clear."

I began to cry in utter desperation. "All I know is that once I had a ghost who was my family's guardian, and that I have always loved and trusted God. That was simple to me. I'm a simple person with simple needs. All I want to do is raise my children, be a good wife, grow roses in my garden, and bake cherry pies for my husband. I don't want to be a telephone to spirits. If I have to go any further with this crap, I'll lose my mind."

"Listen to me, JZ, you were chosen. Chosen to be the instrument of this magnificent and powerful teacher. And may I tell you something else? I have known many mediums; I have studied this phenomenon throughout the years. I have talked to a whole host of different spirits through the mediums. I'm well acquainted with this process. But like I told you, the entity who calls himself Ramtha, the Enlightened One, possesses compassion and love unlike any I've ever seen. You, my dear child, are very blessed. You just need to understand it better."

I looked into her eyes and softly replied, "Lorraine, I don't want to understand it. I just want to be the way I am. I'm simple, not special."

"I'm certain that is precisely why you were chosen, my dear." She hugged me.

Jeremy got up and came over to me. "Zebra, let's not talk about it anymore for now. All right?"

Lorraine turned to Jeremy. "Dr. Wilder, I would recommend that you not discuss this with *anyone* until I can meet again with you both. I'd like the two of you to come to my home in Portland as soon as you can. Stay a day or so with me. I have all my great books there and we can go through them together. If you don't take advantage of this knowledge, it is possible, with the state of mind JZ is in, she may become dangerously confused. I'm here to help you. That is why you were guided to me."

"Oh, Jeremy, I don't . . ." I moaned.

"All right, we'll talk about it, Lorraine. Can I have your phone number and address?" Jeremy asked.

Lorraine jotted down the information. "JZ, I have been waiting for this day most of my life. I was beginning to think it would never happen," she said as she handed Jeremy the paper.

I was so agitated I wasn't sure what I was saying. "Thank you. I'm not sure *what* I'm thanking you for. Maybe you're just as crazy as I apparently am."

Lorraine smiled and gave me and Jeremy a hug, then we all quietly descended the stairs. On the way home Jeremy and I didn't exchange a word.

Later that same night I was sitting on the edge of my bed, just staring at the wall. I was angry, confused, and depressed.

"Ramtha? Can you hear me?"

No response.

"Ramtha, if you are around, I want you to know you are fired as my guardian angel! Furthermore, I'm quitting the phone business! I don't want to see your lit-up face in my life again. Do you hear me? No popping in, lighting up, or blowing your horn! Do you hear me?"

I looked around. Nothing. I got up and sighed, then left the room, slamming my hand on the wall as I left. I headed down the stairs and into the family room, where Jeremy was sitting reading *The Lord of the Rings* in his chair by the fire. I plopped down on the couch.

"Jeremy? I just told Ramtha to get out of our lives. I fired him."

He looked up from his book. "Was he here?"

"How would I know? I just said it to thin air."

Jeremy closed his book. "Well, Zebra, I can understand why you did that."

I watched the light of the fire flicker on his shiny black hair and twinkle in his eyes. Jeremy was such a strong yet gentle man. I felt like a bomb just ticking away; he was my link to reality. "Jeremy, I just want us to get back down to earth and be happy. You know, sensible and normal," I pleaded.

He nodded with understanding. "My Zebra, I think a lot of things need to be answered. It's like hunting. If you don't scout out the trails, and find out where the big buck is in the summer, you sure won't find him when the season opens. You end up frustrated because you didn't do your homework. Don't be too hasty before we find out where this trail is leading."

"I don't care about where it's leading. I just want to lead a normal life. I want to go to Safeway like a regular housewife, buy regular food and pay regular money for it. I want to love you and make love with you without feeling that someone is watching everything we do. I don't understand this psychic crap and I sure as hell don't want to be a puppet."

"Okay, I just think we should go a little further and find out more about Ramtha," Jeremy replied.

"Come on, Jeremy, you don't like this, either," I argued.

"Zebra, I don't have a problem with Ramtha, you are the one that does. I think Ramtha is a good teacher who is trying to help us."

"What do you think it would feel like, Jeremy, to have *yourself* used like I was today?"

"Can't rightly say how I would feel."

"Well, I felt like a witch . . . a distorted witch," I snapped. "And I don't want my state of mind to become any more distorted than it already is."

"I know, Zebra, that's why I think we should go to Portland and stay with Lorraine. She can help you understand this better. I'm sure of it!"

"No, I don't want to go to Portland. I'll just be getting in deeper." I crossed my arms defiantly.

"Zebra, I got news for you, you're already up to your pretty little neck. Look, just keep an open mind for a little while longer."

"You know something, Jeremy, you are doing a lousy job of protecting my well-being in all of this." Snap, snap, snap.

"Protecting you from what? Has anything hurt you?"
He got snappy back.

"Yes, that . . . that guardian-angel Cro-Mag thing. The
one that says 'indeed' forty thousand times in one sentence."

"Zebra, how can you say that? How many times have
you told me he's protected you and the boys? Why are you
backtracking on all of that now? Wasn't it the truth?"

I glared at him. "Look, I'm not qualified to be an instrument, or whatever you call it—not for him or the whole
friggin' world. Light to the world! Please!"

"Zebra, don't you think your problem is *you*, not Ramtha?"

"How can you say that?" I was fuming.

"You always say you're so simple. A simple person not
worth anything, right? Why don't you accept the truth that
you *are* somebody? In business you were a genius, no problem, but when it comes to you personally? Everything stops
there. Did it ever occur to you that perhaps the reason Ramtha, and all those little miracles, happened was to prove to
you that you are somebody? I know a lot of somebodies who
would kill just to have one of your simple-person miracles.
You're amazing, really amazing. I don't know anyone else
who would slam the door in the face of a heavenly being
just to prove they weren't worthy."

His words rang in the air. I had heard them before. Was
this really a matter of psychic phenomena, or of confronting
my own self-worth? I sat there rubbing my toe against the
coffee table. I looked up at Jeremy, who was still glaring at
me.

"All I want is to be happy, nothing more."

"Zebra, I don't think you could ever be happy without
confronting yourself. That kind of happiness only comes to
people who know themselves and find contentment within
themselves." Jeremy struck the chord of truth, and I listened.
"Come on, let's go to Portland and see Lorraine. Give it a
try. I've wanted to learn more about this all my life. Now I
have that opportunity."

I looked at him and my heart melted. He had done so
much for me; how could I possibly say no?

"Okay, you win, but if we go down there and one weird thing happens, I'm leaving, Jeremy."

He was relieved. "Weirder than what's already happened?"

I got up and stretched. "Okay, I'll get someone to sit with the boys. And I guess Mr. Wonderful will probably be here whether I like it or not."

Jeremy looked up. "Well, ma'am, I do intend to hang around iffen it's all the same to ya!" Jeremy, aka John Wayne.

I punched him and laughed. "Not you, dummy, the other Mr. Wonderful who blitzes in and lights everything up." He pulled me down into his lap and together we watched the fire dance and crackle in the fireplace.

CHAPTER TWENTY

A MOST GENTLE PERSUASION

Our drive to Portland was pleasant and soothing in many ways. I kept my eyes on the passing landscape. I don't think I could ever tire of watching nature in its grand beauty.

At one point in our journey we crossed over a bridge that spanned a large body of water. The water was like a huge mirror that reflected the sky, clouds, and trees. I contemplated the vision and then remembered what that old fortune-teller had told me.

"Jeremy, a long time ago, when I was in California, I went with a friend to a fortune-teller. She told me I would come to live in this area, and she also told me I would meet 'The One.' It's kind of odd how all of what she said really did happen."

"The One?" Jeremy asked.

"Yeah, I thought it was a man or something. But I have this very strong feeling that it really means Ramtha."

"Oh, so she didn't mean me." He smiled.

"Well, I suppose you, too." I looked over and smiled at him. "Or maybe I'm all wrong and The One is really me. I wonder if that's it."

"When you come right down to it, Zebra, what would the difference be?"

"You mean you think I'm making this all up?" I was shocked.

"He wouldn't be around without you, but that's not what I meant. I mean that through Ramtha, you'll meet yourself. If the Ram's purpose is for us to know ourselves, then *you're* The One you'll meet."

I became irritated at his presumption. "So what you're really saying is that I'm having trouble knowing who I am, and that's why all of this is going on."

"Well, isn't that everybody's problem, not just yours?"

I stared at him in disbelief for a moment, then sighed and returned to watching the passing scenery. We finally reached Lorraine's little house, and she met us at the door.

"Come in. Come in. Bless you both for coming. I'm so happy you made the decision to come. Now, you'll just have to excuse the clutter. I don't even notice it anymore," she said happily.

"That's all right, Lorraine." I looked around to find that "clutter" was putting it mildly. There were books stacked in every conceivable space—under tables and chairs, piled in high columns in the corners and packed solid in small bookcases. It looked like an unorganized library with a few plants thrown in for color. There were two small couches and a rocking chair that were covered in crocheted doilies. Jeremy put our overnight case in the guest bedroom and returned to the living room.

"Sit down. I have some tea ready." Lorraine went into her tiny kitchen and returned with tea served in fruit jars. I was a little surprised by this odd tea service. Jeremy didn't even notice.

"Did you have a pleasant drive down?" she asked.

"It's God's country to me," Jeremy said with sincerity. "Even if you are on a freeway, it's still a beautiful drive. I tell you, whenever the pressure at the office begins to get to me, I just take to the woods. A day or so out in the forest gets me vitalized again.''

"Well, nature is a most profound teacher.''

I was feeling a bit uncomfortable with this chitchat. Lorraine noticed my discomfort.

"I want you to know up front," I said, "that I'm only here because my husband begged me to come. He feels very strongly that I have something to learn about myself and all this . . . stuff." I waved at the ten thousand books in the room.

"I agree with him, you do need to learn a few things. I think I can help you." She smiled as she took off her glasses and wiped them on the hem of her blouse.

I just nodded sarcastically.

She put her glasses back on and continued. "Since I came back from our meeting, I've been doing a lot of reading. I reread some books I had forgotten I owned. And I was right in something I remembered. Arthur Ford was one of the Spiritual Frontier Movement's great mediums. Fletcher, his spirit teacher, prophesied that a great teacher would come during the latter years of this century and would manifest himself through the body of a woman. He said he would be an epic entity. JZ, I believe more strongly than ever that that teacher is your Ramtha, the Enlightened One." She peered at me through the upper part of her glasses.

"I see," I answered. "And could you be so kind as to tell me why he would be greater than, well, any other teacher?"

"Because, JZ, we on the earth plane have been suffering under the concept of good and evil. The churches teach us that the devil will get you if you don't go to church and live according to their doctrines. They have set themselves up as the only arbiter between man and God."

"Yes, I know," I said.

"Well, the spiritualist movement, even though its understanding is advanced, has fallen into the same trap. They speak of evil spirits, and the dark force, and so on. I always felt isolated from the church and the spiritualist movement because something in me just refused to believe in that kind of polarity between good and evil. I really don't believe there is any such thing as evil, but on the other hand, I don't know how to explain why there is so much suffering in the world, so much despair. When I met your Ramtha the other day, I felt very strongly that he is a profound teacher and can somehow make it clear. JZ, people are crying out for an explanation of their existence, and they're not getting it from the churches or anywhere else, as far as I can see. So many of them seem to love God out of fear. That can't be a true motivation, can it?"

"I never thought so," I answered. "To me, the love of God is as natural as breathing . . . and I was never afraid to breathe."

"Now, to address so much of this confusion, I feel that people who are searching for answers need enlightenment, not programming. And I feel that the mysticism which surrounds spiritual dogma is just as limited."

Lorraine lifted her fruit jar and took a long drink of tea before she continued. "What we all need to understand is that we are unlimited and that God is within us, just as the Christ Jesus said He was. He is just not out there somewhere beyond the sun but in here. [She pointed to her heart.] I believe Ramtha can help us understand and work with that principle. If we continue to separate ourselves from God, I frankly don't see how we are going to survive. I know that we and the Father are One. Can you imagine such a state of awareness in everyone? Oh, what peace and joy that would bring to the world." She was caught up in the rapture of her words. Then her eyes came to rest on Jeremy and me. "I'm very sorry. I feel like I'm lecturing you. To be honest, I'm inspired by you." A soft and beautiful smile lit up her face.

"By me?" I was taken aback.

"Why, yes. You are the key to all of this. You are an instrument of our learning, my dear child. You could help so many people. Don't you understand how you could help people who are confused by the duality of good and evil?"

"Yeah. An instrument. Like a Ouija board," I said.

"Yes, *I* have a Ouija board. It's right over there." She got up to retrieve the ominous thing from under a stack of newspapers. I crossed my legs and began to tap my foot against the table. Here I thought I had been talking to some-one who was relatively intelligent. Good grief! "Thanks, Lor-raine, but no thanks."

"Oh, my dear, the Ouija board is only an instrument to me. It all depends on what you use it for, *how* you use it. I must tell you, JZ, if it weren't for my Ouija board, I would have lost all hope with my melanoma." She sat back down with the board in her hand.

"What do you mean, you would have lost all hope?" I asked.

"Well, my doctors told me I would never regain the use of my arm after they removed the marrow. And they also told me I was going to die. My guides on the other side, speaking through the board, told me that if I believed I would, then I would. Well, I'm just not ready to die yet, so I chose to believe my spiritual guides. And here I am. You have access to great truths without a board."

Jeremy raised one eyebrow. He had taken an immediate interest. "Lorraine, can I see your Ouija board?"

I was horrified. "Oh, no, Jeremy, I think we have had enough of that!"

He ignored me. Lorraine cleared off the coffee table and laid the board out. I was infuriated.

"Let's just see what happens here." Lorraine put her hand on the board and was silent for a moment. Jeremy pulled a pad and pencil from his pocket. The pawn on the board began to move swiftly, almost too swiftly for Jeremy to register. Jeremy was writing very fast while I looked around the room at the books, feigning detachment. I desperately wanted to get up and get out of that room.

Suddenly the movement stopped. Lorraine looked up at Jeremy. "What was the message?" she asked.

Jeremy was deciphering his own shorthand and began to read the message. "We salute you, wise one. You will bring great joy and answers. We hail your enlightenment. You are in the palm of the hand of God."

Then the pawn began to spell again. "Outside."

Lorraine jumped up. "Outside. I feel we should go out-side . . . right now."

We all got up and went outside, but frankly I was exasperated. Night had fallen, and the stars were unusually bright in the clear sky. We walked over to the car and leaned on it. Lorraine told us to look up. I began to shiver from the cool night air. Just about the time I was thinking this was a waste of time, from out of the northern sky came a huge ball of light. It moved very fast and was only a few hundred feet in the air. I was astonished. I had seen comets and falling stars before, and this was neither. Just as I was regaining my wits, another whizzed by over my head, only this time it divided and became eight smaller balls of light. There was absolutely no sound accompanying this display.

Jeremy was very excited. "My God, I've never seen anything like this. What are they?" I just stood there in awe of what I was seeing.

"I would say they are saluting you, JZ," Lorraine said softly.

I shook my head. "Oh, no . . . no."

The eight balls of light disappeared over the treetops. We stood transfixed by the heavenly light show. Finally, I moved away from them and sat down on the front porch. I was overcome by the experience, yet desperately trying to deny that it had happened. Jeremy opened the car door and turned on the radio. A disc jockey's voice was talking excitedly.

"Yes, I hear what you're saying, sir. Well, there are high-level aircraft. No sound? Hmm, that's interesting. Perhaps we'll have some information later on in the program. Yes, all right. Thanks for calling in, and stay tuned. Well folks, our switchboard is lighting up with reports of unidentified flying objects. I don't know what they are, but stay tuned and we'll keep you updated."

Jeremy turned off the radio. He walked over to me. "Well, Zebra, is that what you would classify as weird?"

I waved my hand helplessly at the sky. "I saw something like that once when I was a kid. Only, I didn't remember it until a few years later. It was as though it had been wiped from my mind. Oh, Jeremy, what should I do? What does this all mean?"

"Do you have a choice?" he said.

"Don't we all have a choice?" I retorted defiantly.

We slowly got up and walked back to Lorraine, who was sort of meditating by the car.

"Listen, Lorraine, please answer me one question. Do I have anything to say about this at all? I mean, am I chosen even if I don't want to be?"

"JZ, your freedom is more important than anything else in the world. If you want nothing more to do with Ramtha, he will leave you alone. That's cosmic law, my dear," she answered.

"And what happens to all those people you say need his teachings?"

"They'll just have to wait. There is no such thing as time anyway. Perhaps, in a later lifetime, an instrument such as yourself will come along, or there may be one even now. But one thing is for certain; it will happen, because it needs to."

I thought for a moment. "What exactly do you want to do with me here?"

She turned around to face me. "I want you to read some of my books. I want to give them to you to take home. And I want to talk some more with you, to help you understand the things you'll read about. When I accomplish all of that, my part is finished."

"Then, what?" I asked.

"I don't profess to understand the full spectrum of your mission," she answered.

"Mission? Listen, Lorraine, I'm no missionary."

"All right. Perhaps that was the wrong word. You asked what you would do after you come to understand. I'm not sure, maybe you will channel. I'm still getting used to the word *channel* since all that has ever been before are trance mediums."

"Channel?" I asked

"Yes, you are a channel for Ramtha. As I understand it, a channel leaves her body, as in death, and allows the entity to express his own personality. A medium serves only as a bridge between dimensions but does not entirely leave her body. It is a rare phenomenon for one to allow herself to be used like that. It's really up to you to make that decision."

"I feel I have no safe place," I sighed.

"My dear child, the only safe place is within yourself. That is what you must contemplate." She took my hand and gently squeezed it.

I looked back up at the sky again. I felt dwarfed by its foreverness. "There are so many secrets up there, quietly snuggled between twinkling stars. Sometimes I wish the sky could just talk to us."

"And as above, so below," whispered Lorraine. I turned and looked at this wonderfully wise little woman who had endured so much in her life. A pang of pity ran through me as I recognized how small and helpless she was in her desire to help the world. I was touched by her sincerity.

"I guess we had better get started on my homework," I chuckled. "I have a feeling I'm going to be reading quite a lot." The three of us walked back into the house.

Over the next two days, Lorraine taught us all she could of her spiritual knowledge. Oftentimes arguments would break out over different concepts. We pored over Lorraine's books from early morning until late at night. Lorraine showed me pictures of Indian avatars, books by Madame Blavatsky, the readings of Edgar Cayce, and the books of Arthur Ford. One startling connection that tied this spiritual world with the Christian faith was that Jesus was acknowledged as the Christ by both. Moreover, the spiritual movement believed Jesus' teaching that the Father is within, and they endeavored to practice that great teaching. They also practiced the teaching of Jesus that said whoever is without sin, let him cast the first stone. The different teachers and writers were never critical of one another, or even of those who ridiculed them. That I found to be rare and refreshing.

By twilight of the second day we were piling books into the backseat of our car. Lorraine waved good-bye to us, tears streaming down her face. She felt she had accomplished what she had been born to do.

The next morning, after I had gotten Jeremy off to work and the boys off to school, I was sitting alone feeling the soft fresh breeze as it came through my kitchen window. My thoughts were on Ramtha and who he really was. I took a sip of my tea and heard the whooshing sound of Ramtha's marvelous robes. I got up, opened the sliding glass door, and looked around, but he wasn't there. So I went into the dining room. Nothing. I returned to the kitchen to find Ramtha standing next to the oven that he had found so intriguing. He was beaming a dazzling smile, his purple robes flowing around him.

"Hi, and where have you been?" I asked, smiling.

"Indeed, beloved daughter." He walked over and took my hands and kissed them.

"Ramtha, why do you keep calling me that?"

"That be who you are."

"Was I really your daughter?" I queried.

"Indeed, of the flesh, no. For never I made a union with a woman. I was immersed in hatred, ignorance, and the ravages of that which is termed war. You were given unto my house by a woman of that which is termed destitution."

"When you were here before, Ramtha, I saw a vision of three strange-looking people. I think one of them was you. But then there was this woman with thick black braids. Who was she?"

He led me into the living room and motioned for me to be seated, then seated his kingly self on the sofa. "That, beloved woman, be you. Such was, indeed, the reason for the wondrous vision."

"Did you make that vision happen?"

"Indeed. You had identified me as the Antichrist. It has despaired me that you see me in such an understanding."

"Who was the other man, the one beside you?"

"The entity's name be Gustavan Monocoluas; that be your beloved physician. Indeed, we have been together before, long ago in your time as you know it."

"Oh, so Jeremy and I were around you then?" As I sat there looking at this beautiful being, I wondered how come some of him hadn't rubbed off on us if we were once together.

"Indeed."

"Well, how come neither of us remembers any of that, Ramtha?"

"Entity, it be that which be a long time in counting since

this union be together. One day in your time is liken unto that which is a lifetime in other times. Remember you when be you ten years of age, on the thirteenth day of the month of Julius, or July, at noon, what you were doing? You cannot. 'Tis be the same with lifetimes. You be that many people since then, beloved woman. I am here because you desire me to be here."

I frowned. I certainly didn't remember desiring him to be there. "Oh, no. I didn't desire you to be here at all. I was just sitting here thinking about springtime and flowers and stuff."

"Entity, I hear your thoughts."

I thought for a moment. Ramtha was smiling patiently. "Does God judge us?"

"God, that which is the Is, is without judgment. God be that which is ongoing Isness. Eternal everness. God is the Isness that allows that which is creativeness. It be you who judges you, entity. It is you who judge people. It be you who must live on your own path. Everyone's path be that which is different."

"So what you are saying is that I and each person decides if something is right or wrong?"

"Indeed! There shall come a time when you will understand that all life is only an adventure which endows you with wisdom, and it is the wisdom that will make you as I am."

"And what are you, Ramtha? I mean, really?"

Ramtha laughed. "I am God, as you are. Indeed, I am the manifestation of the Father, as you are."

"So, I've always been right in believing there was no such thing as the devil?"

"Indeed."

"So the others who believe in the devil are wrong!"

"No, entity, they are right in knowing that. That be their desire. God allows all desire, thus there be no wrong or right, or that which is good or evil . . . only there be experience."

"But what kind of world would we have if nobody believed anything was wrong?" I retorted.

"Indeed, entity, what kind of world do you have now?"

Hmm, I had stepped right into that one. "Yes, it's not very nice. But Ramtha, with all the crime and violence around, how can you say that's not wrong?"

"Beauteous entity, there are no victims in life that is everlasting. Entities draw nigh unto them experiences to learn from. Know you that wisdom comes from experiences?"

"Ramtha, if someone murders someone else, you mean the victim wanted to die?"

"That which you term victim doesn't die, entity. No one ever dies, that be a great truth. All experiences learned bring forth wisdom to enrich the soul of life which be God."

"Was that what Lorraine meant when she told me about karma?"

"Karma be the experience of the human drama, entity. Karma be not punitive. There be no such truth as punishment. Man is, indeed, hungry for experience." He paused, obviously checking to see if I was still with him.

"But Ramtha, you said that you killed lots of people. Why didn't you get killed?"

"Beloved woman, I spend many years, in your time as you know it, contemplating what, indeed, I was doing, even in the name of human freedom, as it were. I was, indeed, a driven entity, a barbarian who despised the tyranny with which man ruled his brothers. I despised this greatly, and fought as it were, expecting to die. Beloved woman, I did not have the fear of dying that many of my people did, for, indeed, I wanted to die, honorably. I never knew fear, only knew I hate.

"I led my armies in the front of the charge, with none on either side of me. Indeed, I was the spectacle of hate to be hewed down by the most noble of foes. Yet none did me the honor. I, as it were, had chosen the worthiest of opponents to bring forth my demise, but, beloved woman, because of my absence of fear, there was only the presence of conquering. Thus, indeed, I became a great conqueror, indeed, what is termed a great entity. Know you what be a hero?"

I had been caught up in the images of the story Ramtha had been telling me. Deep within me, I was feeling some ancient emotion that I could not articulate. It was all so very familiar to me. I slowly shook my head no to his question.

He smiled and continued. "A hero be one who salvages life and, indeed, puts an ending to all the wrongs of life. I realized not, beloved woman, that in righting the wrongs, indeed, I was only creating a wrong. I desired to do away with all the odious forms of tyranny, and indeed I did, only to become the very thing that I despised. A tyrant! Beloved woman, I was driven to make myself and the color of my skin more respectable. Indeed, unto all the sieges and battles that were put forth, the lands that my army crossed, indeed, all the peoples I freed, one by one, my army grew . . . unto the legend of the Ram and his army."

Ramtha paused and sighed. The great light around him appeared to dim a bit. The dancing black eyes seemed to flicker with remembered sorrow, from some remote past. For a moment, I too felt this subtle sadness as my eyes began to well up with tears. What a pity that emotions could not linger with the fossil remains of the people of Ramtha's time. For they were, after all, human beings, feeling individuals, just like this great warrior sitting in front of me. No wonder we consider our ancestors not very intelligent. We forget that they had emotions, too. Ramtha lifted his left hand and waved it eloquently in an effort to continue on.

"Beloved woman, I indeed was an imbecile, a barbarian, a buffoon, an ignorant entity of savage acclaim. I marched for ten years and warred upon many until, one fine morn, I was betrayed in a trap and run through by a sword. I fell upon a snowy white marble flooring that seemingly was perfect, yet I watched as the scarlet river of my blood found a crack in it. Woman, I lay there on the cold floor, watching my own blood issue forth from my being, when there came a voice to that which is I. The voice spoke to me to stand up. Again it spoke, 'Stand up!' Indeed, I pulled up my head and put forth my palms, then I began to pull under me the knees of my being. I raised my countenance, beloved woman, so that my head, indeed, was erect and even. I pulled up my left foot and stabilized it. Beloved woman, I gathered all of my strength. I put my hand upon my knee, my fist into my wound . . . and I stood up. Blood was issuing from my mouth, flowing through my fingers, and running down my legs. My assailants, who were, indeed, now certain that I was immortal, fled from me. My soldiers laid siege to their city and, indeed, burned it to the ground."

I sat there teary eyed. My mind kept thinking about where that voice had come from. Ramtha read my thoughts.

"Ah, the voice. Lady, I would never forget that voice that made me stand up, for it kept me from dying. Indeed, in the years to come, I would seek to find the very face and the wonderment of that voice."

I wiped a tear away with my fingers and then reached into my pocket for a tissue to blow my nose. I tried to blow very femininely, but I let out a honk that was most embarrassing. Ramtha, startled at the noise, let out a wonderful laugh. I laughed too.

"Well, who was the voice? Did you ever find out?" I asked.

"The Unknown God. Yet even that, beloved woman, is not suitable to such a practical mind as yours." He laughed again. "Indeed, I was given to the court of women in my march that I be cared for. Lady, I had to endure the stinking poultices of vulture grease that was put upon my chest. The vileness of its stench kept me awake. Indeed I, the Ram, was bossed by the women and undressed before their eyes. I could not even urinate or spill dung from my anus in private, but rather in front of them, for be that I was helpless in their care. Indeed, it was a most humiliating experience! For of the period of my convalescence, the greatness of my pride and hate had given way to that of survival.

"I ordered that my stay be in solitude, and found I a large rock that overlooked the encampment. There, on that rock, I sat and contemplated for nigh seven years in your counting. I was served only by a beloved old woman who loved me greatly. There came a day while recovering from my ghastly wound that I watched my old woman pass from this plane. Indeed, she was at the river, and I saw her collapse. I made my way down to where she lay. She was clutching heartily the crudely woven linen she had made for her son, who had, indeed, perished long ago. I saw the old woman pass in the light of the noonday sun, the life ebbing from her body in strokes of weeping. I watched the old woman shrivel in the light, her mouth opened to an aghast expression, and, indeed, her eyes became glazed, unaffected by the light of the sun. I stood there. Nothing moved save the breeze through her silver hair. Beloved woman, I thought about the old woman, her cursing, her kindness, and her love for that which is I. I wondered at her great intelligence. I turned my head and looked back at the sun, which never perished. I knew that it was the very same sun that had shone through a crack in the roof of her hovel when she was first delivered as a babe. Indeed, now it was the last thing she saw when she died. I stared at the sun. It was oblivious to the fact that my old woman, who had cared for me, had died. I ordered that she be not burnt, but rather buried under a great tree by the river."

"Oh, dear . . . was she your mother, Ramtha?"

"No, not what you would term a mother, but like a mother in manner and tenderness. She was my old woman," Ramtha said tenderly. His light was still a little dim.

"I see. . . . I'm very sorry, please accept my sympathy. I know that's a tough thing, Ramtha." It occurred to me that I was giving sympathy to a warrior angel that apparently had gone to heaven already. But how else would you tell a departed spirit that you're sorry his old woman has died and gone to heaven? Cute. "So, uh, why were you so concerned about the sun?"

"I wasn't concerned, beloved woman, I cursed it. I watched it sit like a mantle on the mountains, like some great fiery jewel, scarlet eyed. I looked upon the purpled mountains and the valley, already shrouded in mist, and saw rods of the sun's light gild all things and, indeed, make them illusionarily beautiful. I looked upon clouds, that once be the pallor of blue, transfigured vividly alive in hues of scarlet, fire rose, and the brilliance of pink. I sat there on my rock and watched the great light as it retired behind the mountains that now loomed like piercing teeth on the distant horizon. I watched until the last rod of its beauty had descended behind the last mount. Beloved woman, in the twilight I heard a night bird cry above me; I looked into the heavens to see the pale majesty of the moon waxing against a darkening sky. I looked upon the great silence of forever, the timelessness of the midnight sky, and realized that it wept for no man or no woman. Then came, indeed, a gentle breeze that rustled quietly through my beard and hair. As I wept, it dried straight away my tears and I was sickened within my being."

Ramtha turned his beardless face and looked out the windows to the sky. He was impassioned, that was obvious, and his emotion had softened me. God must have worked some grand miracle for Ramtha to be there with me, and I was finding that I was giving up my resistance to Ramtha. I shrugged my shoulders.

Ramtha looked back at me and a look of suppressed amusement came dancing into his eyes. "My lady, I am a miracle of God, just as you are."

"I'm sure that's true," I said carefully. "I'm sorry, sorry for my ignorance, Ramtha. I mean, just look at you . . . here in my living room. I know that you are real. I can see you, hear you, I'm bowled over by your beauty, you astound me with your ability to read my thoughts. But I still can't believe that you are happening at all." I jumped up in frustration and walked over to the window. I stood there, scarcely moving, feeling a surge of self-hatred for not accepting this beautiful being God had sent me. Had I not always asked God for help, and did He not answer my prayers? How many times had I longed to see an angel? Oh, and the times I had staunchly sworn that if God or Jesus ever appeared to me, I would never deny Him like the disciples did. What a joke! I was feeling like the biggest hypocrite in the world.

"My beloved lady, you are too arduous on your being. Why, indeed, don't you treat yourself more gently? You are, indeed, a woman of sincere love, not one bought by gold and reputation toward fame. The common dregs of the populace care nothing of their hypocrisy. It is their way of life. You, great lady, have a soulful thirst for God, the living God."

"What do you mean by all that?" I asked.

"Simply that, unlike most of your brothers, if you were to die soon, you would seek God more eagerly, even if it were to seem bad to you. Then, you would spend every moment worrying if you have been pleasing in the eyes of God. You do not live for frivolity, but for truth." I was stunned. "Why think you it is necessary to maltreat yourself to love God? The flesh is not evil. The material world, as it is known, was created by God, and so be that of human bodies that are hallowed by the incarnation. Indeed, lady, why do you banish yourself and punish yourself?"

I sighed and looked around the room. Everything was in its place, neat and clean. I worked vigorously to keep my home in order. The truth was I had dedicated my life to preserving order and traditions that have kept me from embracing the concept of God. That was what was sticking in my craw. "The truth is, Ramtha, I can't accept you. If I do, all this supposed happiness around me, this middle-American life-style, will be threatened by your existence. I know this sounds crazy, but you see, your very existence, in this room, in my life, diminishes the importance of all my possessions. Things that are supposed to be important, stuff that people work for all their lives to have, and somewhere in the midst of their achievements they place God on a convenient table and dust him regularly with nimble prayers. I mean, don't you see, that *God* has to fit in with the decor? He's gotta blend, complement the surroundings but not dominate it. That's scary. You make me see the unimportance of everything around me, and worse yet, you tell me that I 'thirst for God.' C'mon, take a look around you. I feel guilty because I don't know if I could give all of this up, even if I knew that one day I could look and be like you. Jesus, what am I saying?" What *was* I saying? "Look, I just think that we need simplicity, stillness, quiet, but Ramtha I do invent unnecessary needs for trivial things, and they begin to accumulate, demanding attention from me. They distract me from the Truth. That is why monks go to monasteries. Silence provides the ears for Truth. Monks trade this cluttered world for heaven, but the rest of us live for the cluttered world and organize God on the coffee table." I understood, at that moment, what I was saying; there was no mistaking the longing that came from within me when I spoke of monasticism. I was being hard on myself because I was living a confused duality, a hypocrisy that I bitterly disliked.

"Ramtha," I whispered, "I'm sorry for my exasperation. I'm just very confused. I do love what I have and am very thankful that I've been blessed, but I feel remorse that I'm not living the way God would want me to live. I sat here listening to your story and felt moved to tears by it. You did do something right. God let you come here and help me. How did you know what to do? Who told you?"

"Indeed," Ramtha said in a mellow voice. There was another minute of silence, and then he said, "All I wanted was to know. Liken unto your monks, as you term them, I had the silence to ponder the Unknown God. That, indeed, was the only thing I truly wanted, to understand that which seemed so awesome, indeed, so mysterious and so very far away from my understanding. What was man? What *was* he? Why be not man greater than the sun? Why couldn't the old woman live like the sun? Why was man the most vulnerable of all creation? If man be so important, as my people told me, why then wasn't he important enough that when he perished, the sun stood still in quiet array to mourn his passing? Indeed, why did the moon turn purple? Or the wildfowl cease to fly? Lady, man was very unimportant, it seemed unto me, for all life continued in spite of his peril.

"I did not have any one entity as a teacher to teach me of the Unknown God, for I did not trust any man. For I had seen and lost much through the wickedness of man and his altered thinking. No, lady, there was no man living that I would have as my teacher, for, indeed, any living man had altered thinking. I wanted not a god created through man's understanding, for if man created the god, the god was, indeed, fallible."

"You can say that again," I replied. A curious look came over Ramtha's face. He paused for a moment and then, to my astonishment, began to repeat, "I did not have any one entity as a teacher—"

"Oh, for heaven's sake, I didn't really mean you should say that again. I meant I agreed with you. It's an expression of agreement, Ramtha. Sorry." I flushed with embarrassment.

"Ahh, indeed," he said. "The gods of man are propped up with argument and proof. That which is, soon becomes toppled down with proof and argument. Man feels that he must continually prove his God by disproving its opposition. Know you, lady, that to approve of its opposite is to, indeed, disprove it?"

"Uh-huh." I nodded my head, but truly I was lost on that one.

Ramtha laughed. "God has no opposites. Indeed, how shall you prove or disprove *Him?*"

I sat there searching my mind for some answer or consoling word, but nothing came.

"The only teacher that I had was life's elements, indeed, the truest teacher of all. I learned from the days, from the nights; I learned from the tender, insignificant life that flourished even in the face of destruction and, indeed, war.

"I contemplated the sun in its advent of glory upon the far horizon. I watched its journey through the heavens, ending up in the western sphere and passing into its deep sleep. Indeed, I learned that the great jewel, the sun, subtly controlled life; for all who were, indeed, brave and gallant and warring with one another ceased their warring when the sun set in the west. I watched the enchantress moon in her pale light as she danced across the heaven of forever, illuminating the dank and darkness in mysterious and wondrous ways. I watched the fires from our encampment and how they lit up the evening sky with the hues of russet orange. I listened to the wildfowl landing on the water, birds rustling in their nearby night nest, and the laughter of children busy at their merriment. I observed the falling of starry lights, the frost on the reeds, and the ponds slivered with ice, creating the illusion of another world. I watched the miracle of olive leaves turning from emerald to silver as the wind blew through them.

"I watched women standing in the river as they gathered

water in their urns, their clothing tied up in knots to reveal their alabaster knees. I listened to the clatter of the women's gossip and the teasing in their laughter. I smelled the fragrant loaves of fresh bread, baked during the cool of the night; of honey cakes, of dung, of unwashed flesh, of perfumes, of sewage, of spices, of smoke from distant fires and the garlic and wine on the breath of my men. Everywhere, lady, these were the sounds, color, and smells of life, and it stunned me.

"It was not, indeed, until I observed and pondered life and its ongoingness that I discovered who be the Unknown God. I reasoned that the Unknown God was not the gods created through the altered thinking of man. For, indeed, I realized that the gods in men's minds are only the person-alities of the things that they fear and respect the most; that the true God is the ongoing essence that permits man to create and play out his illusions however he chooses, and that will still be there when man returns yet again, hallowed in his incarnation, in another spring, another life. Indeed, I realized that it is in the power and the ongoingness of the life force that the Unknown God truly is."

"But who is the Unknown God?" I asked, still feeling confused.

"I . . . and the birds in their night nest, the river reeds, the morning dawn and the evening sky. It was the sun and the moon, children and their laughter, alabaster knees, olive leaves, the smell of garlic and leather and dung and perfume. Ah, lady, in my silence, this understanding took a long time as you know time to be, to grasp its simplicity, though it had been right in front of me all the time. The Unknown God wasn't beyond the sun and the moon. It was all around me. With this new birthing of reasoning, I began to embrace life; indeed, to hold it in endearment to me and alas, find the reason to live, to be, to feel, to think, to imagine, to know, indeed, to become, those most Holy Understandings."

I was sitting there staring at Ramtha's robes, feeling as if I were dreaming it all. Why me? I wondered. Why is this happening to me?

Ramtha smiled as though his whole being were lit up

with loving understanding, and then he answered my thought. "You are a beloved woman who does thirst for God. To one who has a God-seeking heart, all roads will lead to God, indeed, as yours has. Lady, your destiny will be a work not to sow truth, but rather to prepare men for its awakening. That which is the seed of truth is within all men and all things. Know that you are worthy of the love of God and of His confidence."

I sat there, awestruck and dumbfounded, not daring to ask what he meant. Ramtha reached out to clasp my hands and then kissed them gently like a loving parent. He fixed his large bright eyes on me, bowed, and vanished.

A moment later, after watching Ramtha leave and trying to follow his light as it had disappeared, I came out of my daze.

It had been a long session with Ramtha, and it left me feeling melancholy. I began to cry. All I wanted was to go somewhere private. I ran upstairs, locked my bedroom door, and buried my head in the pillows. Emotion and fatigue overtook me and I fell into a dreamless sleep.

I was awakened by someone knocking on the door. The room was dark. I jumped up, turned on the light and unlocked the door. It was my husband. I was caught off guard, for I never had slept so late in the afternoon. I stopped short in the doorway, my heart pounding; I could feel my face going hot. It was a reaction left over from my marriage with Caris, when sleeping and not having his dinner ready and on the table would have been considered a major crime. But as soon as Jeremy saw me, he smiled with delight and hugged me.

After dinner, Jeremy and the boys were sitting with me by the fire. I was feeling a little nervous about telling Jeremy what Ramtha had said.

"Zebra, what all did Ramtha tell you . . . anything new?" He took a sip of his hot toddy.

"He was telling me about fear and, well, uh, how it didn't really exist unless we let it exist. . . . I know it was profound stuff, but I don't know if I can live that way. I mean, I can't help but be afraid of some things." I wiped my forehead and rested my chin in my hand. Suddenly a light appeared by the fireplace. It was, of course, Ramtha.

Jeremy looked around and said, "He's here, isn't he?"

"Yep."

I started feeling like I was in a daze again. I began repeating what Ramtha said.

"Beloved entities, I have been observing you. Be you happy?" Ramtha said as he warmed his hands over the fire.

"Why did I fail my math test?" Chris asked, looking around.

"Ah, the test. Master Christopher, you did not *know* you would succeed. You were not living in the moment of the numbers for you were distracted by your game with the ball."

"You mean the baseball game?" Chris asked.

"Indeed. Live any moment in your time fully and you will succeed in its moments."

"Why do you like to warm your hands by the fire if you're a spirit?" Brandy inquired.

"The fire has vibrational frequency, Master Brandon. I enjoy that feeling from my understanding. Don't you?"

"Yeah, but what do you think about when you feel the fire?"

"I don't think, beloved Master Brandon, I am. I am the wood that becomes flame that in turn becomes ashes. You see, it is as life . . . I feel the life. Nothing dies, Master, it merely changes form."

"Ramtha, I missed you when you were gone," Jeremy said with heartfelt emotion.

"Indeed."

"No, I mean I feel empty without you."

"What means empty to you, beloved physician?"

"I don't know . . . sort of like I wanted to talk to my comrade. I was lonely because you weren't here. Man does get lonely, Ramtha."

The Ram smiled. "Beloved physician, you are the friend to yourself. You are the entity you were lonely for. I simply reflect what you are and what you are not."

"Yeah, but I never really had anybody to talk to about

these things. Now I have you. Partner, that means a lot to me."

"Indeed. You have your woods and, indeed, your beloved woman."

"True, that's true. I never feel lonely when I'm in the woods. And I've got my Zebra. But ol' buddy, it just ain't the same."

"Beloved physician, the hinds, or deer, as you term them, are coming into their season in two weeks of your time. Observe their activities and you will understand the absence of loneliness. The deer are drawn to the moment of communing in propagation, yet soon they return to the simple Isness of being. Be aware for there is a great lesson for you with the deer."

Jeremy mused for a moment on what the Ram had said. "I wish wildlife lived closer to this house. I mean, wouldn't it be great if I could just look out that sliding glass door and see a huge wild pheasant?"

"Indeed. I contemplated the wildfowl for many of my days. They are wondrous creatures for they know the heavens as well as the earth. Ah, they ride on the wind which becomes their chariot. It was remarkable, indeed, to me that a chariot was invisible. In the wind, I understood the reality of the unseen."

Jeremy was smiling and nodding in appreciation of what Ramtha had said. He gazed at the place where the Ram stood by the fire. "You know, you make such exquisite pictures with the English language. Where did you learn that?"

"I speak in the language of the one who hears. My beautiful images would not be heard had you not the capacity to imagine them, Master."

"So, what is imagination, Ramtha?"

"Imagination be the language of the soul contemplating its unlimitedness."

"Is it real?"

"Anything your heart or mind or soul thinks or feels is real to the one experiencing it, is it not?"

"Yes, but we usually stop ourselves and say it's our imagination. It's not logical."

"Master, logic is the crutches for one who is crippled in wisdom by his own lack of imagination. To stop your imagination is to cripple your unlimitedness."

"Ram, it sure is good to have you around."

"Indeed, enjoy your glorious evening as your flames play upon the unstaked realms of your imagination. Know that you are loved and that I am with you always."

Ramtha disappeared in his familiar blaze of light. Chris started clapping gleefully, and then he and Brandy ran upstairs. Their clatter jarred me back from my seeming daze. "Where is he? Where did he go? He was just here." I turned to look in the kitchen.

"Zebra, the Ram just left." Jeremy chuckled. "I think maybe he's preparing you to be a channel. He was speaking through your voice, but it wasn't *your* voice. It was almost like you were in a trance or something. Remember what Lorraine explained to you about this?"

I shifted uneasily in the chair and stared in disbelief at Jeremy. I still couldn't believe this was happening to me.

"Do you remember any of the conversation?" There was not the least bit of concern in his voice.

"Conversation? No, I only remember seeing him. After that, it was as though I were somewhere else." My brain began to race to find the "somewhere else."

Jeremy put his hand on my knee in a comforting gesture. "Zebra, try to remember what Lorraine said about channeling being sort of like a time warp."

Right. Loony Tunes times. The next saga of *Star Trek*. Spock goes to warp factor five in search of the missing channel—me. "That's what it feels like . . . warp factor five." I laughed nervously. "Well, I guess it's like blanking out. I don't know where I went. It looks like I stayed here, but no time has passed for me."

Jeremy leaned a little closer, his face more solemn. "Hey, does the feeling bother you?"

I looked up at him and rubbed my hand through his hair. "I guess it's something I'll get used to. God knows there's been a lot of getting-used-to these months." We both went upstairs to get ready for bed.

As I was putting my nightgown on, I noticed that my tummy was swollen a bit. Then I noticed that my wedding ring was very snug on my finger. That was odd. George (that was my code name for my monthly period) wasn't due for another week. I lingered another moment on my pudginess and then forgot about it and went to bed.

Two weeks went by with the Ram intermittently appearing, reading my thoughts, and teaching me. "Master, think each thought as if it were written in the sky for the whole of the world to see . . . for indeed, it is." Or, "Beloved lady, listen to your thoughts . . . for when, indeed, you listen to them, you will know who be you. Know you that the voice of God, entity, is the river of thought . . . purely that. The altered ego is the dispenser, the alteredness, the judger of pure thoughts. All of your thoughts that you have termed mundane or illogical are where all of your answers have been." Then he would disappear again, leaving me either exalted or utterly bummed out, depending on what I had been thinking.

Of course, there were those nightly interludes with Jeremy and the Ram. And I would spend most Saturday and Sunday going into my time-warp state. Then to top it all off, I was plumping up like the Pillsbury Dough Boy. I was becoming increasingly depressed. My husband was spending more time with the Ram than with me. We no longer shared intimate conversations. Every other word was, "The Ram did this," or "The Ram said that," or "I want to talk to the Big Boy." My relationship with my husband was going downhill fast.

That was when I started my escape from this unreal reality by buying every book I could find on this sort of phenomenon. I read incessantly, but not one book ever talked about the process of channeling. There was a lot written about trance mediums, but nothing on what was happening to me. Even more depressing was that some of these mediums professed they felt energized after each session with their guides. One even said he danced around with a new-found vitality, while another said that he experienced "immense sexual desires" afterward. Oh, Lord, give me a break! Where did they get this stuff?

One Saturday morning I had cooking detail and was in the process of making a delicious cherry pie. Jeremy was sitting at the other end of the counter having coffee, thinking either about his upcoming conversation with our new "house guest" or about some new area to scout for deer season. As I was putting the finishing architectural designs on my pie, Jeremy let out an *"Oh my God, I don't believe my eyes!"* He startled me so much that my cherry masterpiece became airborne and crash-landed on the floor, cherry debris sticking to my fuzzy slippers, the oven, and the helpless refrigerator.

A rush of emotions swept through me; I was horrified, shocked, dazed, bitter, and pissed off. "Shit!" Jeremy, always suave and cool, got up and stood rigidly still. I rolled off a few more altered-ego thought words to be written in the sky for all the neighbors to see, then took a step forward to see what Jeremy was staring at. I slipped on a dough glob and landed across the counter, knocking his coffee cup to the floor.

Jeremy looked angrily at me and shushed me. Jesus, what a gentleman! He looked back at the sliding glass door. "If anybody had told me this, I wouldn't believe it. Zebra, look. Have you ever seen one that big? My God, right here . . . on my patio . . . in our neighborhood."

I craned my neck to see what the big deal was. Oh, my stars! There, standing on the patio deck and peering in the window at us, was the biggest Chinese ring-necked pheasant I had ever seen.

"Zebra, that's incredible. You know, not too long ago I told the Ram that I would love to see one on my patio . . . and look. There it is. The ol' boy made a miracle for me."

About that time, the boys came downstairs and wanted to know what all of the racket was about. Brandy ran up to Jeremy and was delighted to see the pheasant. All he could say was, "Cool." Chris, on the other hand, walked toward the kitchen. His eyes widened when he noticed the mess on the floor. He then bent down, scooped up some cherries with a finger and aimed it at his mouth. I turned just in time.

"Christopher, don't you dare put that dirty cherry in your mouth," I screamed.

"I was just going to help you clean it up, Mama," he lied.

"Sure you were. Go wash your hands. *Now.*"

Chris returned, and we all watched as the astro-manifested pheasant got bored watching us. Then he spied an apple that one of the boys had taken a bite out of and thrown to the corner of the lawn. He delicately walked over and proceeded to make lunch out of the apple. He was enjoying it immensely. Well, that beautiful pheasant stayed for three days, and on the third day, disappeared. It was truly a beautiful manifestation, for Jeremy in particular. The Ram confirmed his own gift to Jeremy, and the two of them had a jolly laugh about it.

The following Monday morning I got the good doctor off to work, my two ideal children off to school, and after my cup of tea, I started in on the housework. I had to go to the grocery store that day and run a few errands. I did the dishes and then started to mop the kitchen floor. I was in a hurry, so when three Cheerios that had become glued to the floor wouldn't come up with the mop, I threw the mop to the side and tried to pry them loose with the toe of my shoe. They refused to budge, so I muttered a few vile threats at them and then opened the silverware drawer, took out a butter knife, dropped to my knees, and began to chisel the little suckers off with a butter knife. At that moment the Ram appeared in front of me by the sink, but I was too engrossed in my war with the Cheerios. He stooped down, put his hands on the floor, and came eye level with me and the O's. I stopped my prying and looked at him. Of all the . . . He didn't say a word, just put one of those long cinnamon fingers on one stubborn O and it lifted off with the greatest of ease. He did the same with the remaining two. I dropped my head in my hands and muttered, "Thanks, the next time I need a helping—glowing—hand, I'll call ya."

I got up and asked my new housekeeper to step aside so I could dispose of the Cheerios in the garbage disposal. He was amazed that a machine in the sink ate. Then I started to dust and polish the dining room table. He watched me. Finally I looked up at him and said, "Ramtha, if you don't mind, I'm in a hurry. I have a lot to do today. So can we skip whatever I need to know today?"

He watched me, smiling. "Indeed. And you will roast the meat of oxen in your interior brazier, am I not correct?"

I stopped polishing for a moment, rolled my eyes, and sighed. "If you mean, am I going to have a roast beef tonight, yes . . . yes, Ramtha, I am."

"And you have in your mind to create one of your circular fruit sweetmeats?"

I gave up on my polishing, exasperated. "A huckleberry pie, yes. With the wild huckleberries we picked."

"Ah, indeed, they are a most delightful treat, lady. I especially enjoy observing your fruit pictures on the surface."

"What? Oh, when I decorate the pie with dough faces for the kids. Yeah, they are rather delightful." I paused for a moment, reveling in my creativity.

"Indeed. The faces create new huckleberry beings." With that Ramtha laughed uproariously and slapped his knee, then pulled out a chair and sat down.

"Huh? Oh, come on, I'm not in the mood for your weird jokes. I've got work to do." I sprayed some more and buffed some more, trying to ignore him. I hoped he would just buzz off.

"Weird?"

"Yes, weird," I huffed as I pulled back a lock of hair that had fallen into my eyes.

"Ohhh, indeed, I have learned a new idiomatic expression. It means 'unusual' in your language, eh?"

"No, it just means 'weird.' "

"Indeed, I feel your emotional meaning."

"All right. Look, if you're going to hang out with me, why don't you do some work too. Or are you above that? That was a pun, get it? *Above* work?" He didn't get it.

His eyes focused on the table, and in a moment it started shimmering and then it just sparkled. I gawked.

When I turned to go upstairs, Ramtha followed. I hurried up the stairs and turned to look back for the Ram. He was gone. I shrugged and continued up the stairs. There he stood. As I passed him, rather huffily, he graciously bowed with his foot and arm outstretched. Really!

I began in Brandy's room, which was a mess. I started piling his toys in the toy box. Then I picked up one of his stuffed bears; a dried chicken leg was stuck to the fur. The toy box was obviously the place to hide stolen snacks. I ripped off the leg; it broke in half. "Why in the world are kids so messy?" I muttered. "God, this chicken leg must be four months old!"

Ramtha leaned over to inspect the remains and said, "A sense of order is not part of a child's world. Did you not say that your world is organized clutter? Did you not say it made you unhappy? Look upon your children; are they not free and happy?"

"That's different. My kids are slobs. Just look at this room. Of course they are happy, Ramtha, they've got me to keep it organized for them!" I stuffed the chicken leg in my apron pocket and started making the bed. Boy, was I fuming. Boy, was he right.

"Lady, find the good in your children. Expand upon that which is good, that, indeed, they are, and love them in freedom. There are many out there in the world of our brothers that will find faults in them. Do not be the one that will lead the charge against them."

"Oh, good God. I'm not going to lead any charge against them. I love them. I just want them to be responsible, so they can grow up to become responsible men. I mean, I don't think I'm out of line wanting that. That's part of being a good mother."

"Children do not come into your life, Master, to be liken unto you. They come in to fulfill their acts in their life according to what they have obtained in their life prior to you. You are merely the divine and sweet mother that has given unto them the perfect body to exude their brilliance and their beauty from. They do not inherit the characteristics in mind that the motheren or fatheren has, as they are agents independent of one another.

"Entities liken your children, Master Brandon and Master Christopher, came as siblings through that which is termed parents, like you, as a vehicle. They were drawn to one or the other parent because of an association or a familiarity in thought processes. Then there are those entities that are not drawn to either parents; parents are simply a means through which the entity can emerge and have a life of expression.

"Parents, lady, are under the assumption, through that which is termed ignorance, that they somehow own their children, that they are the ultimate creators, and that if the child does not react how the parents think it should react, then, of course, their world is torn to shreds, as it were, and they cannot understand how they could have created something that does not coexist with them happily. I will tell you, lady, your children are sovereign entities. They do not belong to you, but rather their relation to you is one that is called your brothers in God. These children have lived thousands of lives before they came to you; thus they have experienced a great abundance of life, just as you. When you realize that your children are as old and ancient as you, you will realize that they are gods, gods with the things that they must do to fulfill their souls.

"Children are a wonderful blessing. They hold a little life within them that is accepting the world in an innocent way again. And their truth is very much like God in His truth: they smile at everyone and have a trusting for everyone, and their curiosity of life in all of its splendor is quite glorious. Perhaps the only error in that which is termed the foundations of humanity is that everyone grows up."

I listened intently to what the Ram said. It made a lot of sense. I'm not so sure I felt happy about cleaning up their happiness, but it did open my eyes to the mysteries of children.

Ramtha sighed. "Your beautiful children don't concern themselves with the future. They live only in the now . . . the moment, as it were. In God there is no time, only now. Observing a child is a great lesson, lady. You are, indeed, fortunate to have the observation."

"You sound like you learn from everything. Do you?"

"Indeed. Learning is the wonderment of life. Life is a

schoolroom where all lessons are learned." He beamed a beautiful smile. God, you just couldn't help liking this guy.

"Well, don't you learn any lessons where you live?"

"Indeed, I am continually learning that I am God." Take two on the beaming smile.

I rolled my eyes. "When will you graduate?"

"Hmmm, that's up to those whom, indeed, my excellence of truth is learned from." He put his hands on his sides and roared in laughter.

"Cut it out. I have to go to Safeway." With that, I picked up the dirty clothes and headed to the laundry chute, down the hall.

Ramtha, on my heels, asked, "What be a Safeway?"

I opened the chute and threw the clothes down into the abyss. "It's a market where you buy groceries."

"Groceries?"

I turned on my heel and headed toward Chris's room. "Yeah, you know, you probably used to come into a village and go down to the marketplace and trade things for your brazier, didn't you? I mean, after you conquered the place?"

I was rapidly repeating the cleaning ritual in Chris's room, only this time it was a stash of Oreo cookies under the covers at the foot of the bed.

"Ahh, the purchasing of foodstuffs. Indeed. That be a Safeway?"

"Yeah, that be a Safeway."

Quickly I replaced the crumb-covered sheets with fresh ones and continued to tidy up the mess. The Ram watched as he fingered a guitar. He was enjoying the sounds. I thought it was rather off-key, but to each his own. Then I noticed that he was watching the air above the guitar. I bent over, trying to see what he was looking at. I saw nothing.

"Uh . . . what are you looking at?"

"I am watching the sound vibrations of this most unique instrument. They are beauteous indeed. A bit slower than, say, violet or yellow."

"What? Color from sounds?"

"Indeed, all life be a question of vibration. Vibrational

frequency determines that which are levels of thought density. Life forms."

"Well, does the wood in that guitar have a vibrational frequency?"

"Indeed. It be frequency that distinguishes it from a piece of cloth or a lion's whiskers."

"Lion's whiskers . . . you're funny . . . cute."

"The ancients developed what you term alchemy in an effort to alter the frequency of sand into gold."

"Hmm, I did read something about that."

"But, lady, every frequency exists in harmony with every other frequency. Know you that sand be as important as gold? From my perspective, that is the harmony and the music of the spheres."

"Ramtha dear, around here, in the real world, if you tried to pawn sand off for gold, they would lock you up and the only music you would hear would be loony tunes." Curious, I asked, "Is music beautiful for you to hear?"

"Indeed. And it be more beautiful to *see*."

"You can *see* music? My goodness."

"Indeed. And I can *hear* gold."

"Is there anything you can't do?"

Ramtha smiled and put the guitar back where he had picked it up. "I cannot feel my heart break in sorrow or my stomach clutch in fear. I am beyond that experience. I no longer desire it."

"Do you ever cry?"

"I weep for that which is a deep love."

"A deep love of what?"

"A deep love of God. It is a most poignant remembrance of the past. Indeed, my most exquisite memory." He then picked up a comic book—I think it was *Spider-Man*—and started flipping through it. Then he continued, "Lady, there be no passion as deeply experienced as the love of God. None. It is, in fact, the passion that causes your earth to clash and war in battle."

"What are you talking about now?"

"Your world is embroiled in battling the interpretation of God. Each nation, each individual, feels that its interpretation of God is the correct interpretation. Such is the lust of the warlords. This lust for ownership of God's Word throws them into a continual turmoil, indeed, into the ever struggle to snatch it from the hands of those who hold it. And, indeed, all the while, man who is God is trampled underfoot. Such warlords are bloodthirsty and, indeed, crazed, and not for one moment do they look upon the monstrous ugliness of human suffering that they have created. Ignorance is the truth of religious fervor. Because of ignorance, there are wars and bloodshed. Such fervor is rewarded by the putrefying of the dead, the slandering of another's belief, and the conquering of another by putting them in bondage on a narrow path of belief. Their ignorance justifies it all by uttering, 'In the name of God, we are victorious.' Imagine, lady, they kill their neighbors that they may live and worship in peace. Indeed, a most strange spectacle. The world is poor, indeed, in understanding and, indeed, love."

"So what is the alternative?"

"Peace. When man grows up into the God that he truly be, there comes an understanding that is unveiled. That be victory. Peace is established forever and ever within his being. Even in the midst of conflict. Without this understanding of his divinity, man suffers the duality of ignorance, and in that he makes a dual world on which breeds continual strife and war. Man glorified with the awareness of the God that he be makes for a singular world, one that is at peace. Remember, lady, it takes two to create war. When man knows that he be God, in that awareness there is nothing to battle another about. For if you be the king of you, what does it matter who rules your body? Indeed, when the great Forever be yours, what does it matter, indeed, who has dominion over this or that part of the earth, or what they believe or don't believe?"

I tucked the bedspread around the bed. "Ramtha, do you really believe people will ever understand all of that?"

"Beloved woman, all people already know this. They just don't believe it. It is all too simple for their complex small minds."

"Too simple? You gotta be kidding."

"I will not kid you. Man complicates the simple truth in order to sustain his individual dual identity. Man feels he would lose his identity if he recognized that all are equal and all are one." He then eyed a small plastic horse on Chris's windowsill. "This be a magnificent steed. My steed that I had I called him Shamiradin. It means 'Ride with the Wind.' One day, lady, you shall have many such steeds."

"I will? Are you serious? I will have a lot of horses? How wonderful, Ramtha," I gushed.

"Indeed, and a few of them shall win great honors, but many people will hate you for it."

"Why would they hate me for having horses? That doesn't make any sense."

"One day, indeed, you will understand and you will own a great truth from that understanding." He waved his beautiful hand to dismiss further conversation on the subject of horses.

I was overjoyed at the possibility of having many horses as I had dreamed as a child I would, but I was confused about why people would hate me if I did. I let it drop. Then I thought about the wind. I hesitated for a moment as another memory passed through my mind. My big red balloon. Why did I think about that?

"Ah, the mother of your being had trekked a long journey for foodstuffs . . . to Safeway. The magical balloon, as you term it, was a prize, was it not?"

"Well, aren't you something? Ramtha, does anything surprise you? I had never seen a balloon before. Why did the wind blow it away? Or rather, why did you?"

"It created happiness, then it created sadness. The red balloon has remained in your memory so that we could speak of it today in your time. Lady, without that memory you would not recognize that it was I."

"Oh, I see. You did it to make a big impression."

"The impression was more precious to you than the balloon."

"I see. Thanks a lot."

I finished the room and turned to Ramtha. "Okay. All done. I have to go now, see ya." I turned and headed down the stairs, hoping that he would get the hint. But no, he slid down the staircase railing. At the bottom, he proudly announced, "I have observed your children doing this."

"Well, for your information, they aren't suppose to," I huffed. "Uh, what does it feel like? Whizzing down the rail, I mean."

"It is good practice for the balance of what you term gravity. Desire you to ride the rail?"

"No. You're too much." I turned and walked through the living room and picked up my handbag. "Now listen, if I go to Safeway and you try popping in, say at the checkout stand, will other people see you?"

"You are concerned with what you term weirdness?"

"Oh crap, I don't care. It just would be nice to know I'm not the only one who can see your Most Perfect Self. On the other hand, I think it would be better if you stayed home . . . I mean *go* home. I really don't have time to discuss celestial stuff over the meat counter." At that I turned and started out the door.

"You are a very beautiful entity."

I stopped. "You mean you think I'm beautiful? How sweet."

"I see your beauty as I see it in everyone. Know you that you are beautiful?"

I started twisting the strap on my purse. "Well, I've always had problems with that."

"Indeed."

"Why do some people judge others so cruelly?"

"People judge in others what they see in themselves, beloved woman."

"Well, I never thought anybody was better than me," I retorted rather smugly.

"Precisely. You thought you were less."

"Oh, no, I didn't. I may not have thought I was beautiful, but I never thought I was less."

"That be a creative truth. The worth that you possessed was not known to you. But, indeed, that will change."

"Yeah, right." With that I turned and left.

CHAPTER TWENTY-ONE

PORK CHOPS, PINK BLOUSES, AND PENITENCE

Somehow, I had this sort of holy feeling going to the Safeway. I smiled at everyone. I was divinely patient and forgiving when a box boy ran over my toes with a grocery cart. I lied to him when I said it was all right. I started pushing my shopping cart down the aisles, picking up my grocery items. When I came to the canned veggie section, I saw an elderly woman standing by her cart and looking at the top shelf with an expression of frustration on her little face. "Oh dear, I just can't reach that far." I thought she was about to cry.

I stopped to see if I could help her. "Excuse me. Is something wrong? Can I help you?" She smiled and turned her head to expose her ear, saying she couldn't hear me. So I got a little closer to her ear and repeated myself. When I did, I smelled a perfume that I had not smelled since I was a little girl. It was Evening in Paris.

"Oh, you dear child, I can't understand why they put the single servings on the very top shelf. Most people my age just can't reach that far. I was looking for Jolly Green Giant peas."

She was right. All the single-serving cans were on the very top shelf. Of course, I thought. So many of the people who bought the single servings would be elderly. It made me a little sad. I pulled down several cans of peas for the charming lady.

"Maybe you should complain to the manager about this," I said as I let her pick out one of the cans.

"Oh, they'd never listen to me," she said evenly.

"Well, have you ever tried?" I yelled it so she could ·hear.

"No, I haven't . . . but no one listens to old people anymore."

She was right, of course. No one listens to them or even sees them. It's as if they no longer existed in our ultrabeautiful, ultrathin, and ultrayoung world. What a pity. "Try it. It can't hurt," I said, and then went about my business.

The store was so crowded that I would have to reposition my cart several times as I made my way down an aisle, just to let myself or other shoppers get by. Something else I noticed that I hadn't before was that no one ever said "excuse me" or "thank you." They reminded me more of gunslingers headed for a shoot-out at the O.K. Corral. By that time I was becoming irritable. I had to either shove or be shoved, push or be pushed, hog the breakfast cereal section to search for more Cheerios or go home empty-handed. So I strapped on my Colt .45, buckled my spurs, and let my trigger finger twitch. It was survival of the fittest!

I finally arrived at the meat section with blood in my eyes. I was after pork chops and a roast. But most of that section was barricaded by a huge woman whose dirty, bawling child stood in the cart screaming at the top of his lungs. I stopped short and checked the scene over. The little boy —he was about three years old—was wearing a dirty diaper. He was filthy, with a runny nose leaking into his mouth, a dirty shirt, and tears streaming down his face. His mother looked even worse. She was about 250 pounds and had long, stringy, greasy hair which she probably hadn't washed in two weeks, because she couldn't fit a shampoo in between meals, snacks, and more meals. She wore some kind of gray thing over her ample body that split up the seams of the sleeves because her arms were so fat. She also smelled. *She* needed some Evening in Paris—along with a bath. Oh, my stars, was she grotesque, and she was hogging the pork chop section. There probably wouldn't be any left to buy when she finished. Well, the poor thing never turned around, so I didn't see her face. Nor, for that matter, did she see mine, which was contorted into an expression of utter disgust.

I whirled around and started muttering nasty things, tnen headed for the dairy section. God knows, I had to get there before King Kong did. "Some people." As I approached the dairy section, I was startled to see . . . yeah, you guessed it, Ramtha standing in front of the cheese. I almost swallowed my tongue. I should have. I looked around to see if anyone could see him. Well, they just walked right past him and probably thought nothing of the cool air that sometimes accompanies his Most Illuminating Self. They probably thought it was just cold coming from the dairy section.

"Beloved woman," he said, without the usual smile on his face.

"Yes," I whispered, then looked to see if anyone had heard me.

"Indeed, did you not a moment ago in your time say to me that you did not judge people?" He crossed his arms.

I sheepishly answered, "Yes . . . I think so."

"Know you that you have just judged another? The woman and the child? You are in ignorance as to the epic story behind her bereavement." I closed my eyes in shame. He continued. "Return to the woman and her child. Look into their eyes; find the God within them that you may see it within yourself."

I opened my eyes, checking to see whether anyone had observed this shameful exchange. No one had. I slowly pushed my cart back to the meat section where the pork chops were last seen. I stopped my cart in front of hers, with the little boy watching me. I smiled and rubbed my hand over his hair. He stopped crying and started smiling back at me. Just then, the huge woman turned around to put her meat in the basket. She looked up and over at me. I stared at her face. I was astonished. Her peaches-and-cream complexion needed no makeup. It was flawless—no wrinkles, no zits, and no freckles. But even more striking were her deep violet blue eyes rimmed with thick long lashes that touched her rosy cheeks when she looked down. I was stunned.

"Excuse me, but I have always wanted to have lashes like yours. Your eyes are the most beautiful I've ever seen." That was the truth.

She smiled the most beautiful smile back to me. "Why thank you. What a nice thing to say. No one has ever said that to me," her soft voice replied.

I smiled at her and then back at the little boy, who by this time was giggling. I told her to have a nice day and hurriedly pushed my cart away. I looked over my shoulder to see if Ramtha was still by the dairy case, but he had gone. At first I wanted to be praised for what I had done, but I felt so naturally good inside myself that that was reward enough.

I finished my shopping and then got into the checkout line. It was very long. My immediate reaction was to show my impatience by a sour face and tapping my toes. But a conversation caught my ear two lines down. There was my little old lady talking to the manager. He was having to shout for her to hear him. She was showing him her single serving of peas and pointing to the top shelves. He nodded, patted her on the back, and smiled. It must have worked, for she was beaming. Then I began looking—I mean really looking —at all the people around me. I found in their faces the beauty that came from knowing they were all God's children. I loved the Ram for revealing this loving understanding to me. I *loved* him! "I love you, Ramtha. God bless you, forever." A gust of wind came in through the store doors and ruffled my hair. He had heard.

That evening after dinner, I recounted my wonderful story to Jeremy. He sighed and nodded and gently kissed my forehead, but his thoughts weren't on my story but on Brandy. He was angry at Brandy because of his poor grades in school and had sent him to his room without dinner. The tension that was building between Jeremy and the boys was becoming more and more apparent. Brandy, who once had been recommended for the gifted-child program in the second grade, now seemed disinterested in school. Something was wrong. Brandy had been coming home from school with rashes on his body and his hands swollen. I had taken him to his doctor, and a battery of allergy tests were scheduled in a few days.

I sneaked upstairs to see him. He had been crying as he tried to do his homework. I tried to talk to him about what was bothering him, but he just clammed up. I put my arms around him and told him I loved him and that if he ever needed to talk, I'd be there for him. When I got up to leave, he ran and put his arms around my waist and buried his little head in my stomach. I felt a pang of motherly guilt run through me.

I knew that he and Chris were not Jeremy's little boys, but I had hoped that he could love them as his own. Deep inside of me, I didn't feel he could. That hurt. I thought about how Caris's mother would tell me I should put up with anything so long as my children had their real daddy. I thought about my real father and all that my poor mother had put up with so we could have him with us. But wasn't my mom just like me, and when she couldn't take it any longer didn't she leave? Didn't she try to provide Loy and me with a respectable stepfather and a decent home? And what of Daddy Bill? He never did show me any love, and that hurt me. Was that what Brandy was feeling? The absence of fatherly love? Jeremy didn't abuse the boys, but Daddy Bill never really abused Loy or me, either. Both men provided a good home and both were good men, but both had difficulty showing affection. A child can starve to death in the wealthiest of homes from the lack of love.

Why, I asked myself, did I really marry Jeremy? Was it because I was needy and he was an answer to a prayer? Did I really *love* Jeremy? How could I expect him to love my boys if I didn't love him? Of course I didn't love him. Remember, love is just a state of mind. Actually, I did love Jeremy. I utterly respected him as a man. He had been nothing but wonderful and considerate of my needs. But I knew I wasn't *in* love with him—whatever that was. Jesus, I was a hypocrite—worse yet, an unhappy one. And just look at what I'd done here. My boys were not happy; Brandy was sick; Jeremy sought the Ram's company more than mine; and poor little Chris just tried to hide his feelings and stay out of the way. Oh, God, what was I going to do?

I squeezed Brandy a little harder as fat tears poured down my face. Brandy looked up. "Mom, don't cry. I'm sorry I made you cry. Please stop, I'll do better in school, I promise. I love you, Mom. You're my only mother."

I sniffed and wiped away my tears with Brandy's help. I faked a laugh. "Oh, no, no. You didn't make me cry. It just made me so happy that you hugged me. I haven't had a hug like that in a long time . . . really. I can tell you one thing, Bran, I love you to pieces and I want you to be happy. The most important thing in the world to me is for you and Chris to be happy."

"Even more important than Ramtha?"

I was stunned. "Of course even more than Ramtha. More than anything. Why did you ask me that?" I looked steadily into his beautiful almond-shaped brown eyes.

" 'Cause . . . well, 'cause he is from God, and . . . 'cause Jeremy loves him . . . and, well . . . he takes you away a lot. Everybody's always talking about the Ram . . . but no one wants ta listen ta me an' Chris. I wish I was as important as Ramtha."

Tears rolled down his little cheeks and I felt my throat choke up. This wasn't sibling rivalry with the Ram, it was lack of love and attention. He was right . . . a simple truth. I tried to form my words carefully. "Brandy, you must know that you are more important than Ramtha to me. But you are right, a lot of attention has been diverted from you and Chris because of what Ramtha has been trying to teach us. I'm very sorry. Please forgive me. But son, Ramtha didn't come to us to separate us; he came to help each of us to *love* more and be more understanding of others. That is what we are trying to learn from him. Talking to Ramtha is just like going to school and learning from your teachers. Do you see?" He nodded his head. "Ramtha loves you, Brandy, and he loves Chris, too. Why, just the other day I was cleaning up your room and I told him that you guys were slobs—I was just kidding, of course—but instead of agreeing with me, he sort of told me off, in a nice way naturally, but he made me understand and appreciate you and Chris. He's trying to help me be a better mother, someone you can be proud to call your mom. I don't know everything, and I do make mistakes—we all do—but with the Ram's help . . . and yours . . . I can make fewer of them and become a lot happier. With God's help, too."

Brandy had stopped crying and was listening carefully. "Brandy, I know it is definitely weird to hear Ramtha speaking through your mom's mouth, but for some reason, somewhere along the line, I did something right. God loved me enough to allow the weirdness to actually be a miracle. What matters isn't the weirdness of Ramtha using my voice, but the beauty of the words that come out. It's the love, it's definitely God's purpose and truth, and it works. Just look at how the Ram manifested that pheasant for us all to see on our patio. Isn't that terrific? I mean, not any ol' voice can do that. But more important, son, is how you feel about all this. If it's too weird for you to talk about with your friends, then don't. You don't have to. None of my friends know about the Ram. To be honest, I don't want to talk to anyone about him. Face it, they just wouldn't understand. So, that's okay . . . do you understand?"

He nodded. "Yeah, I don't think the Ram's dumb or weird. I think he's cool. I'm just glad ya love me and Chris."

"Wild horses couldn't drag me away from you or make me stop loving you, kid." I laughed but was interrupted when the door opened. It was Jeremy.

"What's going on, Brandy? I want all that homework done before I go to bed. Do you hear me?"

Brandy replied, "Yes, sir," very solemnly.

I gave him a big kiss and then joined Jeremy, who was

waiting for me in the hallway. "He'll be fine. I think he just needed someone to tell him they still love him." I waited for a response, but Jeremy didn't reply.

Later that evening I was sitting in bed, trying to read a book. But the brilliant little lights of yellow, violet, blue, and white that normally danced across the pages were not there. I had gotten used to those little lights. Lights, you're probably asking, what lights?

When I started going to the bookstores, looking for books to explain what was happening to me, I would pick up some insignificant book and another would fall out of the shelves onto the floor, my foot, or my head. Those were the books I was *supposed* to read. I took the hint and starting buying them instead. When I started reading those books, little colored lights would appear. Their activity would become frantic when there was something on a particular page that was important. At first I thought it was my eyes. But after a doctor's examination and an explanation from Ramtha, I learned that these were "runners," or light beings, and (I know this sounds crazy) they were there to show me that I wasn't crazy. Anyway, they seemed to go with me wherever I went and sort of "light the way."

On this particular evening I just couldn't get into my book. The lights seemed to know I wasn't ready to learn so they went out. My thoughts kept returning to my conversation with Brandy and my confusion about my marriage to Jeremy. And, of course, to Ramtha. I was feeling that everything was about to go haywire, which, needless to say, depressed me deeply. I put the book on the nightstand and lay there silently, not wanting to utter a word since Jeremy was in his "library" reading. Instead, I just felt all these thoughts and began to cry. I stared at my wedding band of gold and, in my agitated state, tried to twist it. It didn't budge. My fingers, as well as the rest of my body, was getting fat. That realization, on top of everything else, brought on another bout of crying.

I heard Jeremy stir and flush in his "library." When he came out he proclaimed excitedly, "Zebra . . . look at this."

He handed me an open book. It was Thomas Sugrue's book, *The Story of Edgar Cayce: There Is a River*. Jeremy pointed to a sentence, which I read. "Ten thousand years before the Ram entered India . . ."

"Zebra, don't you understand what that says? It means that for the first time, we have found Ramtha in history. I know it's the same Ram."

I wasn't impressed. "So what's the big deal, Jeremy? I mean, look at the book you are reading. It's about a medium. The world doesn't give much credit to such stuff."

"I wouldn't be saying that if I were you," he chastised me.

I jerked my head around and narrowed my eyes. "Why?"

"Because one of these days, my Zebra, you just might be doing the same thing, and someone just may write about you and the Ram, and there just might be someone out there just like me who will read it and then show it to someone just like you, who may just say the same thing," he said smoothly.

"Don't be cute. I'm not in the mood." With that I turned over and turned out my lamp.

That night I had another exquisite dream. I heard beautiful, haunting melodies being played on a piano, although I never saw the pianist. As the playing continued, someone put three white ostrich plumes on the crown of my head. I kept feeling my coiled knot of hair at the nape of my neck. I looked into a mirror and saw myself wearing the most extraordinary gown. It was ivory brocade and hung beautifully from the shoulders in the style of Empress Josephine. On both shoulders were pale yellow roses that matched the lining of the train. My waist was very small and long and the bodice seemed to be of satin. I turned to walk out of the room, when a woman handed me an enormous bouquet of pale yellow roses, which I took, seeming to understand why I was carrying them. I felt a little sick, or maybe faint, I'm not sure, but I had the sensation of preparing to experience something that would be quite an ordeal for me.

The piano filled the void for a moment, and then I was approaching a petite woman who was sitting. She was dressed simply, in a black dress with a low neck and very short sleeves. Across her ample bodice was a blue ribbon studded with diamond pins and jewels. I looked at the strands of pearls around her neck; they seemed to glow. This little woman wore a small diamond crown that flashed brilliantly with her slightest movement, and a tulle veil with black feathers. She looked straight in front of her, stiff and unmoving, and extended her hand to me in a most graceful manner but without the least flicker of a smile on her face. Her face seemed tired and forlorn.

At that moment everything changed. I still saw the face, but it was the face of a man that I seemed to know. Then everything changed again, like the next scene in a movie. I saw my own hands playing the music on the piano! It was exquisite. I watched as my fingers glided over the ivory keys as if playing the piano were second nature to me. The tones echoed sweetly in my mind . . . and in my dream. At the moment I began to awake, the melody became fainter, almost as if it were fleeing back into my dream where it lived.

I opened my eyes to hear the singing of birds outside my window. I thought about the dream, trying to figure out just what it meant. I couldn't come up with a meaning, but the music, the piano, was so real to me that I decided I would coax Jeremy into letting me get a piano. I just knew that I knew how to play it. I was thrilled with my decision. It was something to look forward to.

The following morning, after finishing my morning housework—without my "helper"—I got ready to leave for the big sale at Nordstrom's. As I started out the door, Ramtha appeared again in the kitchen.

"Hi . . . uh, I don't like to be discourteous, but I really want to get to that sale."

"Indeed, you are in need of *more* clothing?" he beamed.

"Not *more* clothing, Ramtha, just some that will fit. Thanks to you," I retorted.

He bowed and smiled. "You need not thank me, as it were; you simply desire *more*."

"Don't be so smug. You know what I mean. I'm *fat*. And

you *made* me that way. I did not desire to be fat." I was getting very huffy, but as usual, he was undaunted by my attitude.

"Ahh, indeed, think you you are not beautiful because you're fat, as you term it?"

"I know that I'm to look for the God in everyone, and it does make me feel good, but"—I pinched more than an inch on my waistline—"this fat does not make me feel good about me. I can't see any God in this stuff, it's *cellulite*, as I term it, not God as you know it. So there." My face had turned a light shade of crimson.

"Indeed, beloved lady, I understand your plight. I desire you to know that your beloved body is responding to the change in vibratory frequency, indeed, when I speak through you. Your vibration must be raised in the body to meet my lowered one. It is most wondrous. Indeed, this shift in energy creates energy; indeed, life engenders life. Indeed, it is by changing the energy, spending your body, that indeed offers that which is I to become. Your body is rich in energy. Thus for this miracle the body responds by retaining and amassing aqueous substance, for water is the conduit of electrical fields . . . indeed, energy frequencies raised."

I frowned. "Oh, I see. So in other words, if I want to take off, say, ten pounds and fit back into my bathing suit, I have to give you advance notice to buzz off so the fat frequencies have time to melt back down to low skinny frequencies?"

He just smiled.

I flipped my handbag over my back, gave him a long hard look. Once I was satisfied that he got my message, I left. I had forgotten all about asking him about my dream and what he thought of my getting a piano. Oh, well, I had had enough of him for one morning. I would pursue it another day, when I had some time.

As I drove around and around the parking lot of the Tacoma Mall, looking for a parking place, I noticed that "Nordie's" doors had already been opened to the sales-hungry mob. I was one of the mob. I panicked. I parked and ran up the steps as fast as my high heels could go, shoving, mashing, and squeezing myself through the throng to start grabbing the items that were on sale. The place was jammed with frantic, salivating housewives and screaming children. People were yelling, buying, charging, and waiting for credit approval. Salespeople were smiling, biting their lips, wiping the sweat from their foreheads, and selling, selling, selling. Somewhere amid the chaos, faint sounds emerged from a piano, far, far away, playing Beethoven's Fifth. I was bumped, hit, snarled at, and pummeled as I tried to maintain my cool. I blessed, blessed, and blessed some more—until a baby buggy ran over my foot. I jerked around, muffled a few screaming no-no's, and then turned back with a smile as I patted the bawling baby. Jesus. How could God get a kick out of this?

Finally I made my way to a rack of blouses, feeling like I had marched ten long miles of hard road to get there. It was then that I spied the very object of my desire—a pink 100 percent cotton blouse with a button-down collar. I reached to pull the blouse from the rack, but it didn't come off the rack. I pulled harder, and somehow it just jerked right out of my hot little paws. I suspected that Ramtha was meddling, so I grabbed it again and gave a hard jerk, and to my amazement it tried to jerk back. I glanced up and saw a woman on the other side of the rack. Her face—maybe it was the lighting—had a predatory expression. Her eyes, yellow blue and beady, were fastened upon me in a most cunning way. She was giving me the evil eye.

"Excuse me. I want this blouse," I said with stern politeness.

"You can't have this blouse; it's mine." Her smile looked more like the sneer of a wild animal.

I clutched the sleeve savagely, trying to pull it away from the hanger that was hung up with Ms. Ugly. She, of course, was doing the same. Finally I spied a salesgirl. I put my fingers in my mouth and blew a blood-curdling whistle, the kind that I used to call the dogs or the kids. It was so shrill that for a moment everyone stopped and stared at me in horror; babies started screaming louder from their fright. I didn't dare look at Ms. Ugly. I ignored the shocked onlookers. But I did get the attention of the salesgirl.

"Excuse me, but I would like to buy this blouse . . .

now," I said heatedly while I continued my death grip on the blouse.

"Oh, no you don't. I got here first." Ms. Ugly leaned over so the confused salesgirl could grab her handbag from her shoulder. "Here, take my wallet out of my bag, get my credit card out, and ring it up. I'll wait here for you."

"Well, of all the nerve! I'll rip it in two and give you half . . . just like King Solomon did in the Bible with the baby. That should be fair," I hissed at her.

Her eyes widened. "You wouldn't *dare.*" The salesgirl started to sweat.

I snarled and wrinkled my nose. "Just watch me, sister."

"Now, now," the salesgirl intervened. "I don't think that will be at all necessary. I think I might have another one in the back. Let me go and see." She scampered off, leaving the two of us still clutching the blouse. Suddenly I saw something glitter out of the corner of my eye. I turned a little more to see . . . Mr. Beautiful Light Robes himself. I slowly closed my eyes and whispered under my breath. "Oh, shit, not you . . . not again."

"Beloved woman."

I turned back to look at him. I saw again how beautiful he was. He was bathed in that unearthly light that no words could describe. I looked at his magnificent robes—purple light trimmed with dancing lights of gold, white, and rose. Bejeweled with lights, the robe itself looked alive.

"Ramtha, this blouse is one hundred percent cotton, and it's pink. I love pink. And pink in a one hundred percent cotton is hard to find," I pleaded—in vain, I might add.

"Do you like my robes of light, lady?" At that question, he must have turned up the power, for his light robe glistened and glowed brighter than ever before.

"Of course I do; what a silly question. But what has that got to do with anything?" I wished I had just shut up.

"There will come an hour, beloved, when you will be wearing a robe of light."

That did it. I closed my eyes and turned back to face the nice lady holding the other end of . . . uh, nothing really important. Before I opened my mouth she screeched, "Why, you're nuttier than a fruitcake. Standing there talking to thin air . . . *thin air.* If you think I'm gonna feel sorry for your mental condition and give you this blouse, you had just better go back to Washington State Hospital. *Empty-handed. Ya nut.*"

I closed my mouth, blessed her sweet self, and then smiled. "I'm sorry, really I am. I've just been selfish and ugly. To think that I did that for this blouse. I'm sorry, you can have it."

With that, I ran from the store. Since then, I have never, ever gone to another sale.

On the way home, I stopped at a music store in Lakewood to check out some pianos. As I browsed, I came upon the most splendid baby grand. I knew right then that I had to have it. The more I looked at it, the more it screamed— in the key of F—for me to buy it! So when the salesman came over, about to deliver his pitch about its virtues, I interrupted him and asked the price. He replied that he could give it to me for 20 percent off the asking price. Again I asked what the price was, and he said seven thousand dollars. I swallowed hard. There was no way I could approach Jeremy for such an exorbitant amount. He would clench his teeth and then lecture me on the importance of frugality and the sin of frivolity. I chewed my lip and thought I had just better leave before I was seduced into the sin of extravagance. That's when the kind but persistent salesman told me I could rent it for forty-five dollars a month, and if I desired to purchase it at any time, the rental fee would be applied to the purchase price. I smiled deviously and signed the papers, paid two months rent in advance, and purchased some beginner's music books. My soulful piano would be delivered in two days.

That evening I prepared a fabulous roast with New England potatoes and asparagus bathed in butter and slivered almonds. I sat the feast before my appreciative family. After the bananas flambé on vanilla ice cream, I gently told Jeremy of the dream and the "divine inspiration" to rent the piano. I was nearly pleading with him to let me fulfill my great destiny of becoming a spiritual pianist. He smoldered silently, but after a moment or two of teeth gnashing he told me to try it out. If I didn't fulfill this "spiritual destiny," the divine thing had to go back.

The next day, Brandy's doctor concluded after a painful allergy test that Brandy was allergic to everything except bread and water. A special serum was made up, and it was arranged that Brandy would have a shot every Wednesday. These were to last for five years, maybe ten, maybe for the rest of his life. I was devastated. The doctor could give no reason why Brandy had developed such an allergic reaction to *life*.

So, for the next couple of months Brandy went in to get his shots. Not something that he relished doing at all. Then, one afternoon, I was upstairs reading when Brandy burst in the room with a friend of his from school. He was nearly in tears. His hands and fingers were so swollen, he could not bend them. The least bit of movement caused dreadful pain. I tried not to panic, and told him I would call the doctor right away. At that moment, the room filled with a wind. The friend thought it was coming from the window . . . which wasn't open. I turned to look and there stood Ramtha in the corner. I wasn't about to start having a conversation with him while Brandy's friend was in the room, so I just looked up and shrugged my shoulders in an effort to say, "Can you help my son?"

At which the Ram replied, "Ask for your beloved son to come forward, indeed. Then take his hands and ask him to repeat these wondrous words." I just looked at the Ram for a moment, and then back to the boys. They hadn't heard a thing. I nervously asked Brandy to come sit on the bed beside me, and then asked him to give me his hands. I waited for further instruction.

The Ram smiled and then said softly, "Master Brandon, know you that you are loved of God?"

I looked into Brandy's eyes and repeated this, but I left off the "Master." Brandy said yes evenly.

"Master Brandon, know you that God lives within you?" Ramtha continued.

I repeated this, again omitting the "Master." Brandy didn't hesitate.

"Yes, I know God lives within me." His pure innocence and total acceptance made my heart ache. Tears began to fill my eyes.

"Master Brandon, the God who lives within you has made you whole. So be it."

I repeated this last and most powerful sentence, and this time I didn't leave anything out.

"My God who lives within me has made me whole. *So be it.*" Brandy looked at me with a smile on his face. I gently removed my hands. To my utter amazement, Brandy's hands were totally normal! I sat there stunned into immobility.

Brandy screamed with delight, "*I'm healed. I'm healed. Look at my hands.*" He ran around the room, jumping up and down with joy. He jumped on my bed and off again. His friend, who had watched, was as stunned as I was. Brandy stopped and showed him his hands. The kid just shook his head in disbelief and then joined Brandy in his dance of joy.

Tears of appreciation and relief were flowing like a river down my face. I looked down at my hands, turning them over to examine them. Just normal run-of-the-mill hands, but they were the most loving hands in the world to me. I looked up at the Ram, who was observing this scene in silent amusement and delight. The thought I sent him made my trembling lips move quietly, "I love you, Ramtha. I love you so. God bless you for healing my little boy. God bless you, you wonderful being."

He smiled and said, "Beloved woman, 'twas not I, but the Father within Master Brandon that hath made him whole. Beloved lady, that which you and I be are facilitators of truth which Master Brandon has accepted through simple innocence. His acceptance has, indeed, made this miracle. We be but facilitators of love. Your beloved son will experience many dark days in his future before he reaches his own steadfastness in love. But know you, he will, indeed, survive them, for I will always be with him. One day, he shall do a great thing for humanity and will remember this sweet day that hath allowed him the courage to do so. For now, revel in the joy, for indeed, this is a miracle of God's love for Master Brandon."

I was inspired to later tell Brandy that it would be wise to pray and give thanks to God within him for his healing. So he did . . . gladly. When I called and canceled Brandy's Wednesday shots, the doctor was concerned. But when I told him that Brandy had been healed by prayer, he conceded that God's medicine was the best of all medicines.

Even though miracles began to become a regular part of our lives, they were never taken for granted. Still there was a growing uneasiness within me about my "organized and cluttered" emotions. Life continued as usual, and yet a sense of unreality was challenging my organized reality and often left me with an inability to grasp these changing times. A sort of emotional duality.

Then in late November of 1978, as I was making one of my pies, the phone rang. I answered it with some pie dough still on my hands.

"Hello. Yes, this is JZ Wilder. What kind of spiritual center are you? . . . Rama Center? Well, I'm not in the habit of speaking to groups. . . . Uh, excuse me, I didn't hear you. . . . Ramtha? Who told you about me? . . . Oregon? Boy, word sure travels fast. Okay, well, what does all this entail?"

As I was talking, the Ram appeared by my oven. I glanced over at him and shrugged, sort of looking for some advice. Mum was the word with him.

"Well, uh . . . all right. When is it again? Could you give me the address? Yeah, all right. I'll be there with my husband."

I hung up the phone slowly, realizing what I had just committed my poor husband and myself to. A public display! Why on earth did I do that? I turned to Mr. Wonderful for some comfort.

"Beloved woman, do not be afraid. It is the beginning of your great destiny." He glided over to the other end of the counter.

"Uh, excuse me?" I swallowed hard. "What destiny?"

"To become a light to the world. Indeed, to help prepare within man the awakening of his great truth. That be a grand and noble destiny, lady." He beamed a delicious smile.

I dropped my chin into my hand. "Ramtha, I trust you

implicitly. But one little question: Just *how* am I supposed to do this?"

"Indeed, beloved woman, you will bloom completely into that which is termed a channel. Be it known, not that which be a medium—there are rivers of consciousness in difference between them. You will abdicate the entirety of that which be your body . . . liken unto one passing from this plane. Indeed, in the twinkling of an eye you will be changed and, indeed, you will follow a great light until you become that light. Within a moment in your time you shall return unto your body and, indeed, time will have ebbed by. In the moments of your journey to the light, I will, indeed, surround the body, and indeed, that which is I shall become known. No thing shall be lost of my power, indeed, my Love, indeed, my wisdom, indeed, my knowingness, indeed, I. For all that shall be lost shall be my face, indeed, my countenance. For it be not what I look like, but what, indeed, I say and do. For the one who is in dire need of worship and love shall be those to whom I speak. So grand shall this union be, beloved woman, that there shall come a day when the whole of the world shall know about this your work. Of the world, many will rediscover, alas, the Kingdom of Heaven within, indeed, God the Father within, indeed, and all realities perceived and received shall be unlimited in the consciousness of man. Indeed, then tolerance shall prevail that will, indeed, allow peace, the new Age of Understanding, to be unveiled."

A year ago, or even six months ago, I would not have been ready for Ramtha's message. But now, deep within me, there arose that "thirst for God," that desire to experience the thirst completely and quench it. Somehow, I also knew that *this* was "why me." I was, for the moment, at peace with my destiny.

"Ramtha, what is this light that I will go to?" I asked.

"God."

"Will I know that? I mean, will I remember that light when I get back to me? Will I remember *anything* about what happens in my absence?" It was the normal sort of question one would ask in an abnormal situation.

"Indeed God, the light, is an understanding that is wholly

without the stage or moment of time. For time becomes a duality when it moves from the *Is*, or God. Indeed, man's denial of self comes when he is within the axis of time and in time there exists good and evil. Remember, time and its past, indeed, lady, do not exist within the light, yet *all-know-ingness is the light.* Slowly, in your life, the all-knowingness of the light will manifest through the slowly lived demise of your own duality. Indeed, that duality that subjugates you into self-denial. Indeed, each limitation owned, each duality resolved, the great light of understanding and truth will, indeed, begin to shine forth. But indeed, beloved woman, it will take living to accomplish that unveiling."

His eyes danced and my heart soared with an understanding that I did not yet understand. He continued. "Though multitudes shall come to hear and to know, indeed, seemingly you are left out, indeed, missing. But, grand lady, know that you will be in the light of loving understanding that will engender life within you, life that is without words. This be your blessing, indeed, your gift of the Father that *you* have searched for. This be your destiny, that which the entirety of your life has prepared you for. Many challenges of the heart and soul still await you, indeed, and you shall arise to meet them; thus is the life of a master. Be not afraid, you are loved greatly."

Ramtha disappeared. As I reviewed all he had told me, I felt apprehensive and a nervous chill ran through my body. I went out on the patio and looked at the beauty of nature that was all around me. I remembered that the Ram had once told me that he found the Unknown God in nature, in life. With that thought the spell of fear left me. I prayed to God, giving thanks for my life and that of my family . . . and also for Ramtha, God's miracle "runner."

When we arrived at the Rama Center, there were about thirty people milling around, having coffee and chatting. Every last bit of space in the room was filled with chairs and people. I didn't know a soul except for Jeremy. I wished that Brandy and Chris could have come, but Jeremy thought it best they didn't—not this time at least. A woman walked up to me.

"So *you're* JZ Wilder. My goodness, dear, they didn't tell me you were so young . . . and so beautiful . . . and, oh, you are so dressed up." She was rather heavy, wearing a black pantsuit and lots of strange-looking ornaments around her neck.

I blushed and looked down at my high heels and suit skirt. It never occurred to me how I should dress or look for Ramtha. I felt a wee bit uneasy.

Then the woman grabbed another woman, also dressed in black, and introduced her to me. "Yes, Maudy, she's a little different from your reading of her, huh? JZ looks more like a model than a psychic." She narrowed her eyes and smiled. I didn't like the way she smiled at me.

"Psychic? Oh, I'm not a psychic, I'm married, a wife and mother . . ." I stammered.

Just then a "normal"-looking woman came over to me. She was dressed very tastefully in a beautiful rust cashmere sweater with matching skirt and heels. She had auburn hair and striking blue eyes that reminded me of Linda Evans's beautiful eyes.

"Hi, JZ, my name is Mary Redhead. I'm so happy to meet you," she said.

When she told me her name was Redhead I immediately looked at her hair. They matched. This was a very organized lady.

I chatted with her for a few moments and, to my horror, found out that all these people were mediums, psychics, and healers.

"Oh, my God. You're kidding. I've never met a medium before. I've read about them, but everyone here looks like they're in mourning. Everyone but you, Mary."

She laughed and looked at me rather strangely. "You didn't know that these were . . . 'spiritual' people? Oh, how delightful. You want to meet *them*? They all came here to meet *you*. As for the black, well, I guess it makes them more—shall we say, 'mystifying'?"

"Oh, I see . . ." I said as my voice trailed off.

Mary helped get everyone organized and in their chairs. Then she introduced Jeremy and myself. Everyone ap-

plauded courteously, and I sat down in the front and tried
to figure out what I was supposed to say. As I glanced around
the room at the thirty people, my heart started pounding.
Everyone looked friendly enough, but I was scared to death
I would not live up to their expectations.

One woman had placed a reel-to-reel tape recorder in
the middle of the room, the microphone aimed directly at
me. I swallowed hard. It looked so big and black, so cold
and antagonistic. In those first few difficult moments I sat
there, alone, in silence. It was the beginning of the greatest
role that I have ever played, yet I was too frightened to know
of the masterpiece that would follow while I "moved toward
the light."

"Ramtha, please get me out of here," I whispered.

"Indeed, beloved woman, go in peace," came the answer.

In the wisp of a moment I felt like a great hand had
come and jerked me from my body. I faintly remember seeing
the room from the ceiling . . . everything and everyone seemed
frozen. I looked down and saw the top of my own head. My
beautiful hair was casting a light, something like a bright
golden white light seen through a slight mist. Then the misted
light filled the room, dancing and flashing like brilliant stones
fired by lightning. I somehow *felt* and *knew* that I was part,
yet all, of that light. A flash came—I don't know where
from—but I was going somewhere. I was racing or flowing
down a tunnel, but I couldn't see the sides. I just remember
that there appeared to be a *wind* taking me toward a brilliant
light at the other end of the tunnel. I focused on the growing
brilliance of that whiter-than-white, brighter-than-bright illuminating light. I head a voice: "Go toward the light." I
knew that the voice *was* the light. The closer I came, the more
brilliant the light was. Its lightning flashes began to bathe
me in a warm peaceful glow that I cannot possibly explain.
I just know that I had no fear, no regrets, and no limitations.
I was rapturously free. I had no thoughts or fears about my
husband, my children, the house mortgage, the bulldog, my
cellulite, my kitchen, the kids' grades in school, my past, my
present, my future, or the people in the room I had left

behind. No sorrow, no pain . . . just oneness with the great light. Within it, I knew and understood all things completely in a fashion that transcended the logical and petty mind. I *knew* that what I had left behind was a dream of the altered state of God: man. I was not detached from the whole but *was* the whole. I did not want to leave the light. Then a flash came and I felt heavy once more, with eyelids, arms, legs that tingled as if they were asleep, and a head that pounded. I slowly opened my eyes. Things were blurred at first. I barely remember my husband holding my hands and head and saying something to me. Images were moving, and voices that were faint were becoming audible. People were crowded around me, faces in my face, hands on my unfeeling feet, and there was an air of excitement everywhere. I focused my eyes on a woman. It was that sweet woman, Mary Redhead. I started and tried to jump up, but I wasn't ready. I had not completely become me again. My mind began to race with questions about what, if anything, had happened. I remembered asking the Ram for help and remembered the jolt . . . but nothing else. I looked around with what must have been an expression of anxiety on my face, because Mary, my husband, and others started saying, "It's all right, everything's all right. It's a miracle."

I wanted to get to the bathroom. I was helped through the throng of people. Everyone around me was either crying or stunned or happy. People were trying to hug me, touch me, and one even fell to the floor and kissed my high heels. I was shocked. I turned and looked at Jeremy for comfort.

"My dearest Zebra, you have made many people here joyful and thankful. They feel grateful to you and the Ram," he said with reverence. "Including me."

He hugged me close; others hugged us both. I pulled away and looked deep into his eyes.

"Jeremy, did it happen? You know, did . . . did . . . ?" I was almost afraid to ask. To me, it seemed as though I just sat down, closed my eyes, dozed for a moment, and then woke up again. But why was everyone else so changed?

"You mean did the Big Boy come in? Oh, yes, in his normal kingly and beautiful way. Zebra, he talked to everyone, read their minds, answered their questions and, all in all, shocked everyone with his power, wit, and love. Hey, come over here, Zebra, you gotta see this." He started laughing, along with Mary.

We moved through the crowd back into the room. There, in the middle of the room, was a piled up heap of magnetic tape that looked like a giant bird's nest. Just beyond it was the woman with the recorder. She was in a daze, just staring at the mess.

Jeremy and Mary started talking at once, then Mary gave way to Jeremy. "When the Ram came to this woman, he just stared at her for a moment after she asked him some question—I don't remember what it was. Anyhow, he didn't answer at first. Then he looked at the recorder. All of a sudden, the thing just started spinning out of control. It was going so fast that the tape started spinning right off the reel. It went crazy. It was spinning in the air and then landing all over the place. The woman kept trying to reach out and turn it off, but the tape went wild and sort of chased her back to her seat. You should have seen everyone's face. My God, Zebra, they were shocked right out of their skins. I started laughing and I couldn't stop, so I grabbed one of these flyers and put it up in front of my face until I could regain my composure."

"You're kidding! But what's wrong with the woman? Is she all right? She looks sort of . . . sort of not with it," I asked with concern.

"Oh, I'm sure she will be fine," Mary said. "I'm sure she's still trying to make heads and tails out of her question . . . and *this*." She pointed to the black bird's nest all over the floor.

"Miss, are you okay?" I asked. She nodded slightly. "What was her question?" I asked Mary.

Whispering, Mary explained, "When the Ram came to her, she said she was a great psychic and she acknowledged Ramtha as a great and profound teacher, but then she asked him to acknowledge her as one for the benefit of the others. See, sometimes there's a lot of heavy competition among these readers to be king of the mountain. You know what I mean—kind of like car dealers. Well, then the Ram looked at her recorder and, well, like your husband said, it just went crazy. When every inch of tape had gone out of the machine, my goodness, you could have heard a pin drop in this room. Nobody even *breathed*. Then the Ram told her something very profound. He said something like, 'The God within you is very forbearing and, indeed, kind and loving, yet you extinguish his dazzling brilliance that is your own beauty by tarnishing it with the shame of your frivolity and greedy intolerance of your brothers. Thus, you seek to exalt and redeem yourself through the belittlement of those around you, beloved woman. You seek further this praise as a talisman to dangle before your foes. You have dimmed further the light of the living God within you. Indeed, thus I, beloved woman, have wrought such upon a rubbish heap in front of you. Indeed, behold your talisman and contemplate it long, for in doing so, you will once again behold the love of God within your naked being. You are loved, greatly.' So that's what she is doing, I imagine: thinking about what he said to her."

I stared at the "rubbish heap" and then at the woman. My thoughts ran back to the Safeway and Nordie's. I felt a surge of pity for the woman, but whatever she was supposed to learn, maybe this would help. I hoped so. I again asked Mary if she could show me the way to the bathroom. Once there, Mary hugged me with tears in her eyes and told me she was grateful to me for allowing the Ram to manifest himself through me. She said he had changed her life in one afternoon. I blushed and tried to tell her that I didn't really *do* anything. But she refused to listen to that. Truth was, I didn't know how to say thank you. It would be a long time before I learned how to do that.

On the way home, Jeremy told me everything that had gone on in my "absence." It was still so hard to accept the reality of my "warp factor five to hyperconsciousness" and Ramtha. I pondered everything he said.

"Zebra, the ol' boy was more powerful than I have ever seen him before. What I mean is, I *really* saw him in those eyes of yours, and I forgot that it was your body at all. It was a complete transfiguration. You could *see* and *feel* as well as hear him. It was incredible, just incredible, Zebra. You weren't anywhere to be found. Do you remember anything about where you went?"

I studied him for a moment as he drove, trying desperately to remember just what had happened to me. Try as I might, all I remembered feeling was a jerk, and then waking up again thinking nothing had happened. I explained this to Jeremy and I think he was a little let down. As for myself, well, I felt like I was no longer me, at least not the old me. I sensed that nothing in my life would ever be the same again. I was right, of course; I knew that from the light.

CHAPTER TWENTY-TWO

COWBOY

Shortly after our debut at the Rama Center, my life started its unbelievable change from normal to chaotic. The phone started to ring off the hook with people asking for advice about their problems. People who "just happened to be in the neighborhood" started stopping by unannounced at any hour of the day. Often Mary brought people by who wanted to discuss Ramtha and the phenomenon. In the midst of this, I tried feverishly to keep my house in order, serve everyone food, and tend to my family. Thank God for Mary, she ran herself ragged trying to help me.

When people from the Rama Center showed up I would channel Ramtha for them because I thought I *had* to, and then after each session I would be bombarded with questions, most of which I couldn't answer since I didn't know what the Ram had said to them. And afterward, I would get up to prepare them food and beverages. No one offered to pick up a dirty ashtray, their Coke cans, coffee cups, or help to prepare the food. They may have been "spiritual" but they sure were lazy suckers. The only thing they wanted was for Ramtha to help, help, help them . . . nothing else. Quite frankly, I don't know how they expected to be helped when it was obvious they weren't helping themselves. I began to feel guilty and unqualified to do what they expected of me, but when I tried to express my qualms some of the people would remind me that it was my spiritual obligation to help them. Frankly, I was doing all that I could. And I was finding less and less time to spend with Jeremy and the boys.

The boys started leaving the house more and more frequently because they didn't know how to handle this rude intrusion on our lives. School was becoming harder and harder for them to deal with because they lacked a support system at home. It was becoming common for the school to call and report that Chris or Brandy or both had been caught fighting. My dream of a happy home with cherry pies and roses was shattering. I began to look as exhausted as I felt. Dark circles appeared under my eyes. (Some "guest" offered to heal them, but I declined the healer when I noticed he complained a lot about his ulcer.) It finally dawned on me that I was being used. Jeremy tried to make me feel better, but quite frankly, I was too damn tired to listen or even care.

One afternoon I took the telephone off the hook, put some earplugs in my ears, and lay down for an afternoon nap. I was staring at the bedroom wall, trying to get used to the deafening silence, when the Ram appeared brilliantly on the wall. Oh God, even he couldn't give me a moment's peace, I thought. I pretended I didn't see him and just rolled over and pulled the covers over my head.

All of a sudden, a spark of some kind shot through my body. It was like an electrical shock. I bolted upright and stared at him with blood in my eyes.

"Good Lord, Ramtha, what was that for? Can't you see I'm tired and want to be left alone?" I snapped.

"I desire to speak evenly about your destiny," he beamed.

"My destiny, yeah. Well, I've been giving this destiny some thought too. I think we should discuss *your* destiny,

Ramtha. Like, why don't you just walk out there and do it yourself? You would save me a lot of worry and frustration. After all, you don't have to clean up after those spiritually hungry gods of yours. *I* do, and I'm *sick* of it."

"Indeed, it is not the way. Know you, lady, that you are living in a time of that which is the worship of heroes and idols? Your brothers worship images and hear not the truth of the image. None shall see my face, indeed my robes, indeed none shall see my light. They will only hear my truth, indeed, see my manifestations. For in that way, beloved woman, they will understand that the love of themselves and the love of God are one and the same. It is themselves they should see."

"But Ramtha, dear, it would be so much more effective if *you* did it," I tried to reason with him.

"Beloved woman, it is more fitting that they have nothing to remember me by but my truth as it were. Indeed, they will have no picture of me to decorate their walls or their beings. They cannot burn incense in my honor, and there shall be no temple in which they can worship me. Indeed, when they leave my audience, they will be wholly of themselves. They will remember only the truth that their souls grasp and remember. It is *they* they must learn to worship, for only then do they touch the living God."

I listened to what he said and then I understood his purpose.

"What am I to do then about all of these spiritual freeloaders?"

"Indeed, you will know. Entities will approach you and, beloved woman, you are to ask for a tally of gold when, indeed, they come to learn."

I frowned. "Gold? You mean that people should pay to come see this? I mean . . . to see you? You mean I should charge admission?"

"Indeed." He crossed his arms behind his back and just smiled benignly at me.

"You've got to be kidding! Ramtha, I can't do that; you just can't do that."

"Indeed, why not?"

I tried to pull my confused thoughts together. "What you are saying is that people should pay to learn about God. Ramtha, that's as bad as those evangelists I used to go see."

"Beloved woman, how define you gold?"

"It's money. I use it to buy pork chops, clothes, and, uh, pay for the house."

"What is it?"

I sighed. "What do you mean? It's made of paper and metals."

"What be that?"

I ran my fingers through my hair. My God, he could be so difficult with his needling. "Do you want me to say that money is God, too?"

"Indeed. Money be God. Everything be God. What isn't? Money is energy. Energy creates energy . . . it's your economic system. Everything be God."

"Okay, now what about the Bible saying that it's easier for a camel to go through the eye of a needle than for a rich man to get into heaven?" Hmm, maybe I had him for once.

Instead Ramtha leaned back and laughed uproariously. "Beloved woman, a poor man wrote that verse . . . after he gave all his riches to a priest."

I started chuckling, but I still wasn't impressed. "Oh, Ramtha, I just can't do this. It doesn't *feel* right."

"Beloved woman, you will expend great energy in allowing me to use your beloved body. You will not be aware of large amounts of your time. When you are gone, indeed, that time of your life, in living, will be gone forever. It can never be relived. You will be giving up your body so that others can learn. It be even to ask for gold. For if people deeply desire to learn, they will create their gold in order to do so. They create energy to create energy."

"But Ramtha—"

"Woman, know you the groups of entities that have been within your household?"

"Do I know them? I wish I didn't." I frowned.

"Did they not weary you and, indeed, demand of you?"

"Yes. Why did you allow that to happen?"

"In that which be your present value system, if they are

not asked to expend gold, they continue to ask the same question. They, indeed, ask, they do not *do*. They desire to be entertained. I desired for you to see that and understand your worth, lady."

"You mean to tell me that if I had charged these people money every time they came over here, they would have showed up much less?" The lights were beginning to go on.

"Indeed. Rather than being happily unemployed, they would have been moved to be gainfully employed."

"Oh . . . I see. But people say this is a gift from God and from you, Ramtha."

"And you. It be your body, beloved woman . . . your life. You will see. Indeed, you will be giving up your conscious awareness for others."

I slumped. "I can never make a point with you . . . ever."

"Ahh, you are learning, indeed. Did not your beloved physician pay gold in order to learn knowledge of his craft?"

"Yes. It was really hard for him to pay off that loan, Ramtha. He had to do without a lot of things."

"Indeed, and now he be a physician who attends to the needs of his brothers. And indeed, the people pay gold for those services."

"Sure."

"Are not his services a gift from God?"

"Well . . . yes, you could say that."

"Lady, if you don't require gold for *your* services, you should inform the physician that he needn't either. The man who tills the soil is borrowing the soil from God. Yet he makes a profit from it. All services are a gift from God. Be it known, lady, the knowledge of God will provide the grandest profit of all. For this you should be compensated."

"Yeah, right. Okay, what should I charge for my services?" The word "charge" got stuck in my throat.

"One hundred tally of gold in your understanding."

"One hundred pieces of gold? Are you kidding? Gold is at three seventy-five an ounce right now. That's ridiculous. No way, Ramtha."

Ramtha laughed. "One hundred of equal amounts in your understanding."

I thought that over for a bit. "You mean a hundred dollars?"

"Indeed. Dollars. Tell me, lady, be a dollar liken unto a shekel or a rupee?"

I smiled. "Somewhere in between."

"You will charge one hundred of your dollars. It is even."

"Wait a minute . . . how do I explain this to people?"

"Indeed, tell them that God be your employer." He laughed, and with that he disappeared.

The next day I was sipping a cup of tea alone at my kitchen counter, musing over my conversation with Ramtha about money. I stared aimlessly at my kitchen. It was a mess. Every once in a while, my thoughts would be interrupted by the clatter of voices and laughter in the family room. Yep, the freeloaders were jolly well back. At that moment, Jeremy called to me.

"Come on in, Zebra. Listen to this."

I quietly continued to sip my tea and ignore him. Then the phone rang. I answered hesitantly.

"Hello? Hi Mary, what's up? Channel for twelve people? When? Where? Your house? Okay. Just one thing, though. Ramtha has instructed me to charge one hundred dollars per person. Hello? Hello, Mary, are you still there?" I heard a muffled conversation and held on until she got back on the line. "Oh, just six people. Okay, I'll be there."

I hung up the phone proudly. "He works fast," I said to myself. Then I went into the Spiritual Den and made that same announcement. To say the least, this overturned everyone's spiritual applecart. I walked out of the room with a delicious smile on my face and began to clean up the kitchen. I opened the fridge, poured a Coke over some ice, and then got a pack of Planter's peanuts and emptied them into the glass. I drank, chewed, and whistled the old tune, "Oh, we ain't got a barrel of money, maybe we're ragged and funny, but we're travelin' along, singing a song, side by side." I didn't even notice the crowd disperse.

On December 18, 1978, I channeled the first paid Dialogue in my dear friend Mary Redhead's living room. Ramtha was a hit, and from that day forward into 1979, Mary helped to organize these splendid events and Ramtha's fame began to spread. Soon the groups went up to fifty people. Then, a call came from a woman named Pat Mueller in New Jersey. She was a most delightful person. I loved her immediately. She organized a Dialogue in her home in New Jersey. I was so excited that I went to Nordie's to get some chic clothes for Jeremy and me to travel in. On top of all the other changes I had stopped smoking and had put on nearly forty pounds. I didn't like the way I looked, but Jeremy didn't seem to mind, so I tried not to make a big deal out of it. Anyway, the Dialogue consisted of twelve people, and everyone left feeling happy.

It was there in Pat's home that I met her two children: Steven, who was about fourteen, and Karen, sixteen. I loved them immediately. Little did I realize then that one day Steven and Karen would play a major role in Ramtha's work.

Then I was called by a woman named Gini Hashii in New York, this time to bring the Ram to the Big Apple. The *Philadelphia Inquirer* did a cover story on Ramtha and the New York event. The reporter commented on my fur coat, saying that business must be good. That made me mad since the coat had been a gift from my husband, and not from "the business." A wire service picked up the exchange and ran it all over the country. It was my first experience with the press, but it wouldn't be the last. Nor would it be the last of the slanted reporting. When I grumbled about this to Ramtha, he said that one day he would be fashionable, outrageous, and controversial, for the light always brings out the shadows. I didn't think much about his prophecy at the time, but I knew one thing for certain: I would no longer believe everything I read.

Ram's teaching began to spread. Time after time I went back to New York, and I met many people who became dear friends to me. Two of them were Thomas Sharkey and Gini Hashii, one of the best coordinators I ever had.

During all of this, I began to develop a style of dress that would allow freedom of movement for Ramtha. I wore loose-fitting pantsuits with an Indian tunic over them. I wore my hair pulled back in a ponytail, and socks without shoes because my feet were always swollen. I was also developing confidence and getting better at imparting my experiences articulately and with clarity. Ramtha no longer just popped in anymore. *I* decided when I was ready for him. I would go to my light while the Ram became the body in a most masculine way. He was so powerful that once he picked up a two-hundred-pound man in a Dialogue and carried him back to his chair, healing him from his pain.

But there were limits to how long the Ram could stay in my body. Over three hours at a time and I was utterly exhausted and had difficulty getting "back." I would end up in a sort of "twilight zone" for many hours.

In New York, as the groups grew, we moved from Gini's living room to a dance studio, then to a church auditorium. That's how large the groups were becoming. Then back home for more of the same. Off again to Dallas for Dialogues with men and women in cowboy hats and boots. To Atlanta, Chicago, Denver, and San Francisco.

In airports, waiting for flights, I would sit slumped in my chair next to Jeremy, sick of smelling jet fuel. I remembered Ramtha saying I would be expending so much of my energy. He'd also said great hunks of my life would be lost in time forever. And how I missed my little boys! I was always wondering if they were lonesome. I was paying a price much greater than the profit I received in money.

After a New York Dialogue, we boarded our plane for the long flight home. I fidgeted with my dinner, while Jeremy ate his graciously. Then the movie came on. It was *The Electric Horseman.* In the movie, when Robert Redford freed the stallion to run free back to the open wilds, my mind flashed back to the fields of New Mexico. Just me and Slim, my horse, riding in freedom . . . happy. Slowly I began to cry. I was soon crying so hard that I couldn't stop. I knew I was embarrassing Jeremy, so I buried my head in a pillow on the window. Oh God, how I wished for those days to return. I never fully realized just how unhappy I had become until that moment. I will never forget the sorrow that I heaved out of my soul on that flight.

A week later, as I was driving along to Jeremy's office,

I noticed two young girls on horses in front of the Hoagie
Shop. They had stopped to get something to drink. One girl
had a shiny chestnut mare with a white blaze and flaxen
mane and tail. She was a quarterhorse. I turned sharply into
the parking lot, got out of my car, and walked up to the
young girl.

"Hi, what's the name of your mare?" I asked, delighted
at how beautifully the mare had been taken care of.

"Fancy, but her registered name is Modoc's Fancy Me.
She's purebred quarterhorse, you know," the girl answered
very smartly.

"Fancy, what an appropriate name. Would you consider
selling her?"

"Well, I've thought about it. You know, she's won a lot
of championships for me. I've got the ribbons and trophies
at home."

"I believe it. She's really beautiful. Well, want to sell
her?"

Now, you have to understand something about me here.
This little girl was a smart businesswoman. She was extolling
the virtues of her horse in order to justify the price she wanted.
I, on the other hand, well, I've never been a tire kicker in
my life. Nor have I been crafty at dickering. I always just
paid the price asked. In other words, I've never been a horse
trader. If I wanted something, I just got it. Even if I had
champagne tastes on a beer-bottle budget.

"Yeah, I guess I'd sell her," the girl answered. "But I
want seven hundred dollars for her. I paid—"

"You got it. Stay right here while I get my checkbook."
I paid her, hugged my Fancy around the neck with great
passion while she nibbled at my slacks. I started to cry. The
little girl didn't realize how much this meant to me.

It turned out Fancy was boarded just down the road
from Jeremy's office, so I made arrangements for her to continue on there. Next, I went to a Western tack store and
bought everything from a saddle to hoof picks, then ran
home to change into my trusty Levis and headed for the
barn. I groomed and groomed Fancy while she feasted on
the generous helping of carrots I brought her. I've got to tell

you, there is something about the sweet smell of a horse that's sheer freedom and joy. I loved it, and for once I was jazzed. All that was left to do was to tell Jeremy and the boys about my new life.

So, I prepared a sumptuous dinner for Jeremy and the boys. You know, feed 'em and lay it on 'em. . . .

"See, why should we go out? You're the best cook in the country." Jeremy smiled as he took another bite of his beef Wellington.

The boys agreed.

"Oh, Jeremy, you'll never guess what I did today." I took a deep drink of my iced tea.

"I give up."

"I bought a horse today." Then I flashed those pearls of mine in glee.

He stopped chewing and stared blankly at me. "You bought a horse?"

"Cool," screamed Brandy.

"Where is it?" Chris asked as the two boys jumped up from the table and ran to the glass doors, looking for it in the backyard.

"Brandy, Chris," Jeremy said calmly, "get back to this table and settle down right now."

I laughed nervously. "She's a beautiful chestnut mare with a white blaze."

"And what are you going to do with a horse, Zebra?"

"Ride it," I said.

"With all that you've got to do? You're going to ride?"

I lowered my voice and put my hand on his arm. "I need to, Jeremy. My life is too closed in. I don't have anybody to talk to . . . they all want to talk to the Ram. I need to be back outside . . . free, Jeremy, free, so I can ride and talk to my horse. Horses always listen."

"That's just fine. Whatever you say. Just remember, it's a big responsibility. Speaking of which, I need to talk to the Ram."

I stared at him for a moment. "Why don't you ask me . . . talk to me?"

He chuckled. "Well, I'd rather just talk to the ol' boy."

I dropped my eyes to stare at the ice in my glass. "You know, Jeremy, you're one of the people who don't talk to me anymore."

He stared at me in disbelief. "What do you mean? We're always together."

"Yeah, I know, but there are so many things I would like you to share with me. *Me*," I said, pointing to myself. The boys, sensing an argument, asked if they could be excused and left the table. "Instead, you're more interested in the Ram," I went on.

"Zebra, that's the most asinine thing I have ever heard you say. Come one, let's eat. This is just too stupid to talk about any further. But I do need to talk to the Ram about something that happened to me today."

"What? Ask me. Maybe I can help," I pressed on.

"Look. I don't want to go through it twice. He'll give me the right answer."

"Just maybe *I* could give you the right answer, too." I felt my face getting hot.

Jeremy stopped eating again and gave me a look as though I were dingie. "Well, maybe. But I think I'm too tired, anyway."

I looked long at him, then I slowly got up from the table. I went to bed leaving the dirty dishes on the table and Jeremy in stony silence. I didn't give a damn.

Over the next few weeks—in between the Dialogues, of course—I took the boys to the barn with me. I delighted in watching them ride. Then one day I noticed how good Chris looked on top of Fancy and that Fancy seemed to have taken a fancy to Chris. Suddenly I had a stroke of genius. I asked the boys if they would like to have horses of their own. They were jazzed to the max. So I gave Chris my Fancy, then found an ad in the paper for a half-Arabian snow white filly, broke to ride, and decided to go take a look.

Jeremy, the boys, and I made our way to a country farm where we met the owner, his wife, and his filly Lily. Well, she was very pretty, and Brandy decided on the spot that he would love to own her. About the time Jeremy began to negotiate the deal, Brandy started squalling and rubbing his head like mad. After Jeremy caught him, an examination showed that Brandy had received a helping of mites off of dear Lily. The shocked farmer took Brandy in the house and shampooed his hair. I was determined that Brandy should have Lily anyway. We could cure those mites, and besides, the price had dropped substantially due to the mites. So, Lily was delivered and stabled right alongside Fancy. I then found myself a beautiful snow white quarterhorse gelding whose name was Grey. I loved this humorous horse. I swear, he must have been a comic in another lifetime.

A young girl—there were lots of them at the stables—started giving the boys riding lessons. One day, I watched as Brandy saddled up Lily, who for the most part acted like she was suffering from PMS, and took off with Chris and some other young girls. As I watched with satisfaction, thinking that this was the way kids should be raised, to my horror I saw Brandy start sliding with his saddle to one side of ol' Lily. Well, I had heard of sidesaddle, but this was ridiculous. Brandy let out a screech and hit the ground. I jumped up and ran after him. He wasn't hurt, but his pride had been badly bruised. Well, you know, around the girls and all. I started laughing—I just couldn't help it—but he was vowing to give Lil a piece of his mind. As if she really cared.

The young trainer decided to take Chris and Fancy to a horse show. Well, I decked the kid up like Roy Rogers. I even bought him a new saddle pad with his name on the side. Brandy had declined to participate with "PMS." When the big day finally came, I was so excited I was a nervous wreck. I gave Chris and Fancy a big smooch each and then took my place in the bleachers. I proudly announced to one and all that "Chris, *my son,* is riding his *champion* mare, Modoc's Fancy Me, in the next class."

As the gate opened and the organ music started wailing "Your Cheatin' Heart," the kids rode in one by one. I started clapping for each one of them . . . only to find that I was the only one clapping. I looked around and muttered something about everyone being deadheads. Then I spied my own offspring. Jesus, I gave a few shrill whistles . . . hollered . . .

clapped, and then yelled, "That's my boy." All of this to Chris's total embarrassment. Well, he and Fancy just went around so . . . so proper. I just knew the judge was going to pick him the winner. Then, all of a sudden I saw Chris begin to lean in that same "sidesaddle" fashion. Well, Tex Ritter slid, saddle and all, off onto the ground. There was a gasp among the living dead, and I jumped up and ran to my child. Fancy had stopped and was licking his face.

Chris was helped up. He brushed himself off with help from the judge, resaddled Fancy, and continued on bravely. Turns out it was that damn saddle pad. It was too stiff. Chris didn't get a ribbon, but he did get applause . . . from me. I admired Chris for his steadiness and his tenacity. That little boy had a lot of courage and will. I was so proud of him.

One day I was out riding Grey just to be alone. I rode through some woods to a nearby stream. As much as I craved to be out in majestic nature, I was still very troubled. I got down off Grey and let him drink while I lay back, looking up at the sky. "Hey, Greybers, did you know that I love you? Huh? I think you are the most handsome man." He looked down at me. I think he already knew that—rather conceited, he was. Then I started remembering my life as a young woman, and I felt the loneliness of that time come over me. I shivered. I never wanted that to happen to me again . . . yet in a way, it was happening. I shivered some more and noticed that the sun was going down. Reluctantly, I mounted Grey and headed for the barn.

After I had groomed Grey, I gave him a big kiss and said good-bye. I got into the pickup and headed for the tack shop. As I was driving and thinking, suddenly the Ram appeared in the seat beside me.

"Good grief . . . you could get us both killed, scaring me like that. What's going on?" I hit a pothole in the road and we bounced up and down in the seat. I snickered to myself, wondering what Ramtha *really* thought of riding in a pickup.

"Beloved woman, I desire you to know that you need not be alone."

"Yeah, I know, but I'm very lonely, Ramtha. Now I

know you can be surrounded by your family or ten thousand admirers and still feel, and be, alone," I said.

"Prepare yourself to become a woman."

I hit another pothole, and after we stopped bouncing I retorted, "So what do you think *this* is? Dog food?" I pointed at myself. "Just what the . . . ?" Ramtha, the sneaky, just disappeared.

I continued to drive, wondering what he had meant. I was still wondering as I browsed through the tack shop, when I noticed an Arabian horse magazine I hadn't seen before. I picked it up but the magazine dropped from my hands onto the floor, landing open to an ad for a horse farm that had a picture of a cowboy on a beautiful horse. I picked it up and examined the picture more closely. The man's cowboy hat covered part of his face, but he appeared to be young, with curly black hair. Something shot through me . . . like electricity. I felt as though my heart were going to leap out of my chest. I almost had to gasp for breath. That's when the proprietor came over to me.

"Ma'am, could I help you with something?"

"Uh, no. Just this magazine." I shut the magazine almost furtively, paid for it, and left without getting my change.

As I drove home, I felt like I was in a dream, a confusing one. My thoughts kept returning to the mysterious cowboy. It was as if my thoughts and feelings were trying to recapture memories that I had no conscious recollection of.

For dinner I threw some meaningless stuff together, shoved it in front of my family, then made some excuse about not being hungry and quickly went upstairs. Jeremy's blue eyes were sharp upon my back as I made my retreat.

I ran a hot bath and poured lots of milk bath into the water, then vigorously ripped off my boots, peeled off my Levis and blouse, and stepped in. I lay there relaxing as I opened the magazine and thoughtfully eyed the picture. A gust of wind came up and caused the house to creak. Then I heard the sounds of harsh patterings as large drops of rain fell on the roof like stones. I shivered and began to close the magazine, but the cowboy's face looked almost alive. A kind of horror came over me, thinking about that face being closed up in the magazine.

"I don't understand this at all. Who *is* this man?" I said to myself. "He's certainly handsome enough."

I got out and dried off, put on my flannel gown, and sat on the bed, magazine still in hand. Then I opened the book to the advertisement again, grabbed the phone, and started dialing the number of his ranch in California. "After all," I said, looking up at the ceiling, "it's natural to be curious about people!"

"Hello, this is Mrs. Wilder. Uh, may I speak to Jeff Knight, please? . . . Oh, I see. No, I'm just interested in the ad in this Arabian magazine. . . . Yes, the horse. Well, I'm calling from Tacoma, Washington." I left my number. "Thank you, I'll be expecting his call."

As I hung up the phone my shoulders drooped. Then Jeremy came into the room.

"Are you okay? You look like a waxwork of yourself. Zebra, you're acting very mysterious."

I looked at him and felt a pang of guilt. "No . . . I just had a nice milk bath and was . . . just sitting here . . . thinking," I answered quietly. His eyes lost their iciness and became soft and mellow. He came over and sat beside me on the bed.

"What's that magazine?" he asked gently.

I did not answer him for a moment. My smile slowly faded, then I said in a low voice, "Oh, it's just a magazine about Arabian horses. I just love Arabians. They are so beautiful."

Jeremy began to flip through the pages. I made an effort to be lively again. I held out my hand and helped him go through the pages, pointing to different horses. "See, aren't they delightful?"

Then he stopped on a page. Seeing it, I was aghast. I folded my hands in my lap and looked down at them while he stared at the picture with quiet intensity. He raised his eyebrows and said, "I wonder who that poor clod is," pointing to the cowboy.

My face lit up with pleasure. "Isn't it magnificent . . . the horse?"

"They're all beautiful, but these aren't no ordinary horses, Zebra. They probably cost twice as much as the ones we have. Do these guys really dress this way when they ride these horses?'' He chuckled pompously.

I studied him with some anxiety. ''That horse is the most beautiful one in the book. I was just calling about it.''

He turned and stared at me with sudden penetration. His blue eyes now showed a flicker of anger. ''I'll be damned. You what?'' he asked.

I turned and studied his face closely. As I did, I could almost hear his thoughts. He detested what he called my extravagance. The things I loved, he often thought were meaningless, decadent. To me, money was to be spent to make existence joyous and charming. To Jeremy, money was desirable for its own sake and should not be spent except on investments to make more money. He thought I was reckless and frivolous. Jeremy had been very poor as a child, and though his practice had become profitable, memories of his poor days inhibited him and made him fearful. No, I didn't love money, as I, too, had worked very hard to survive, but Jeremy had an intense fear of poverty which he tried to offset by concentrating on his investments and business and bank accounts.

I gently disengaged myself from thoughts. ''Don't worry,'' I sighed. ''There was no one there, and the horse probably isn't for sale anyway.'' The wind shrieked against the house. I shivered.

Jeremy handed me back the magazine and I took another look at the handsome cowboy. He made me tingle—a strange feeling, and I felt quite naughty. I closed the book and let it drop to the floor, then watched Jeremy get undressed. He was very tall and lean, and though his posture was stiff, he had a certain grace. He had a well-shaped face with a some-what solemn mouth shadowed by a well-trimmed mustache. His cold blue eyes, at times bold and merciless, could often be soft and loving. He was a most handsome man. I was married; I loved Jeremy. That was enough. I looked down at the floor at the magazine and thought, ''What does a damned picture matter? It's just a romantic fantasy . . . yes, that's it.'' I despised myself for my adulterous fantasy. Goose bumps appeared on my flesh and I shivered. I avoided any further questioning from Jeremy by rolling over. He turned on the television and I lay there staring out the window into the night gloom.

Tree branches were rubbing across the house as the wind hurled glistening rain over the window. I stared at the tumultuous water sheeting the window. I shivered and buried myself under the covers and let myself drift off into oblivion.

The following Monday morning was a bit chilly, but a mellow sun was shining and I felt very cheery as I cleared away the breakfast dishes. Then the phone rang. Cathy, my recently hired secretary, came into the kitchen to say that a Mr. Jeff Knight was on the phone. I stared at her for a moment in indecision, then said I would take it. I dried my hands and picked up the receiver.

"Hello."

"Mrs. Wilder? This is Jeff Knight. You called when I was out about Cederidge?" His voice was almost shy; quiet and calm. It was beautiful.

"Yes . . . uh, that's a beautiful horse. I was wondering, is he for sale?" My heart was pounding. I pressed my knees together.

"Yeah, he is. But the owner only wants to sell you a quarter of him. He's asking seventy-five thousand," he replied smoothly.

I gasped. "Seventy-five thousand!" My smile had gone away. I may have been a spendthrift, but Jesus, that was absurd! And for a horse! Without realizing it, I muttered this cute little statement: "Well, how much is the cowboy?"

"Pardon me?" he asked. I'm sure he heard exactly what I had said, but couldn't believe I had said it.

"Oh . . . I just said something to my secretary. So, the price is seventy-five thousand?"

"Yes," he answered calmly.

I was so taken aback that I didn't know how to proceed with this conversation. I didn't answer him for a moment. Then, in an effort to be lively, I said, "Oh, just seventy-five thousand. Isn't that a bargain. Well, thank you, Mr. Knight. I'm going to have to meditate on this, I guess." I swallowed hard.

"Meditate?"

"Yes, I meditate. Don't you know what that is?" I asked rather defensively.

"Yes, I do. A woman friend of mine taught me how to meditate. I try to do it every morning, but I'm not very good at it."

I listened intently to the way he spoke. I loved his soft tone, shy but still affirmative. "To still your mind, huh? Well, I sort of teach meditation too." I felt it was too early in our relationship to say that it was Ramtha who taught it—or for that matter that he didn't really teach how to meditate. That was my terminology. Ramtha's was *knowingness*. Anyway, I fudged.

"Really? How do you teach it?" His voice rose in excitement.

I balked. Well, now I've gone and let the cat out of the bag. How do I explain Ramtha? "I have a . . . teacher who teaches me. He's really *good*."

"What's the name of the teacher? Maybe my friend knows him."

"I don't think she would know him, but, uh, his name is Ramtha, the Enlightened One." I stiffened, not knowing what his reaction would be.

"Ramtha, the Enlightened One?" he asked very calmly.

I started chewing away my thumbnail. "Yes, I'd love to explain who Ramtha is . . . but it would take some time. Maybe you would like to come to one of my seminars? I'll be down in California in three weeks . . . Beverly Hills. Would you like to come as my guest?"

"You're coming to California? Thank you, I'd like to come."

"I don't have the address in front of me, but I can send you some information that will tell you all about it." I was nervous but excited.

"Okay, you've got my number and I live right here at the stables. The address is on the ad."

"Great! Well, I'll send it to you and maybe we can meet and talk a little more about Cederidge, okay?"

"I look forward to it. Thanks for calling."

"Yes, me too. Thank you for returning my call. Bye." I

hung up in the throes of absolute elation . . . and I didn't know why.

One afternoon a week later, the phone rang. Cathy had gone to the post office, so I answered. It was a Mr. Halley, the owner of Cederidge, and he proceeded to give me a sales pitch.

"I don't know . . . it's an awful lot of money. I'm just learning about Arabian horses and—" He interrupted me.

"I would be happy to discuss this further with you," he pressed. I stopped and thought about just hanging up on him, in a nice way, of course, but then I had this over-powering feeling that Jeff was on the phone with him. I couldn't resist finding out.

"Uh, Jeff Knight? Are you on the other line?" I crossed my fingers.

"Yes, I'm here," he answered shyly.

"I thought so. I'm happy you are. I wanted to let you know that I sent out that information about my seminars to you. They are called 'Ramtha Dialogues.' So maybe when I see you at the Dialogue, we can discuss the horse further."

"That's fine," he almost whispered.

"Good. Thank you, Mr. Halley, for your call. And, Jeff, I'll be talking with you soon."

The two weeks until the Dialogue in California dragged on. I couldn't wait. My life continued as usual, but the stony doldrums that I had been feeling disappeared. I felt gay, lighthearted, filled with expectant happiness. Jeremy found this very invigorating and sexy. Nothing, absolutely nothing, dimmed my zeal. I even went out and bought a stunning pink outfit to wear at the longed-for meeting.

I went by the tack shop once to buy some more books about Arabian horses—and also to look for more pictures of him. All I found were horses and more horses, but I did read the books to begin enlightening myself.

Finally the moment arrived. As we drove from the air-port to the home where the Dialogue would be held, it oc-curred to me that I might not even recognize him . . . *him!* After all, I had only seen a small portion of his mouth and chin. The rest was shaded by his Western hat in that now-

worn picture. A ripple of panic swept through me. Just then
the car came to a halt, and we were greeted by our host and
surrounded by people who were enthusiastically hugging
and talking to us. I looked around shyly, but *he* wasn't in
the crowd. Then someone said there were more people inside, so I took a deep breath and walked through the door.
My eyes fell upon three cowboys sitting in the front row.
My heart was about to leap out of my chest. I recognized
Jeff immediately. I walked over to them and coolly put out
my hand to the one in the middle.

"You're Jeff Knight, aren't you?" I said. My face, I'm
sure, was lit up like the sun.

He had a full head of shiny thick black hair—a little long
in the back as soft black curls lay upon his shirt collar. He
had soft chocolate brown eyes rimmed in thick pale lashes.
His skin was a deep sun-golden brown, and his nose shone
a bit, giving him a fresh-scrubbed look. He was the most
beautiful man I had ever seen. He smiled and his eyes twinkled a dark fire.

"Yes . . . I knew it was you the moment you came in
the door. Uh, this is Joe and Hal."

I barely glanced at his friends as I shook their hands; I
was caught up in *him* and his charming way of speaking.
"Well, you're about to witness something that I don't have
a lot to do with. But I hope to see you when I come back."

"Where are you going?" Jeff asked, his face registering
alarm.

"It would take a month to answer that question."

"Oh," he answered softly.

"You'll see." With that I smiled deeply into his eyes,
turned, and walked away to change into my Dialogue outfit.
When I returned to do my usual introduction, Jeremy did
his usual thing of opening a book and reading. It was his
way of showing his impatience with me and what he called
my "idle chatter." He always told me that no one came to
listen to me, but to Ramtha. Reading was his way of chas-
tising me. So I began my "story," except that as I talked I
found my eyes kept going to Jeff and I couldn't take them
off him. I botched the story a few times, forgetting what I

was saying. I would blush, continue on, and then look back to my beautiful man. I felt like a giggly teenager again.

When the Dialogue was over, Ramtha took my body back to a bedroom and let me come back in peace. Once I was stabilized, I changed back into "my" clothes and carefully reapplied my makeup and fixed my hair. Then I walked back out to the waiting crowd. Everyone was buzzing and very happy. People came over and began to tell me of their experiences with the Ram, but I was listening in a detached sort of way. I kept trying to find *him*. Then I saw him with his friends. His face was like the golden sun. I walked over to him.

"Hi," I said sheepishly.

"Hi. It was great," he said, smiling. "That's more than meditation. Ramtha said a lot of interesting things to me. I'll have to meditate on them."

I looked down at the floor, trying to regain my composure. "I just couldn't explain Ramtha to you on the phone. I was hoping you'd like it."

"I don't think 'like' is the right word. I thought Ramtha was fantastic. . . . I had this funny feeling that I knew him," he said thoughtfully.

At that moment more people came around, asking more questions. I was put out because I wanted to spend what time I had left with Jeff. When I turned around he had disappeared into the crowd. My heart sank.

When it was time to head for the airport, I gathered up my things and began saying good-bye to everyone. People came up and hugged me with great emotion. Then, as we started out the door, I stopped short and turned around for one last look. There was Jeff at the other end of the room, standing there just watching me. I walked swiftly over to him, looked into his beautiful face, and then did something very impetuous. I put my arms around him. He put his arms around me without hesitation. I felt his heart pounding in his chest. I smelled his wonderful fresh clean smell and I just wanted to stay there with him. But I regained my senses and pulled away. To my astonishment, there were tears in his eyes. I took a deep breath and said, "It meant a lot to me to meet you. Maybe, one day, I can see you again, Jeff."

"It meant a lot to me, too, JZ . . . a lot," he said softly, and I walked swiftly out the door.

Two weeks later Jeff called and asked if I would do a Dialogue at his ranch. He said a lot of friends would be there. I quickly accepted and set about making the arrangements. In the meantime, a call came in from Joan Hackett, the actress. She was going to attend the Dialogue at the ranch. She had been listening to many of the Ramtha audio tapes that had been made available to the public and was emphatic about her love for the Ram and how he had changed her life. We'd had many phone conversations and were becoming fast friends. I was looking forward to meeting her in person.

Upon our arrival at the ranch, Hal and Jeff began to show me around while Mary and Jeremy saw to the arrangements. I was delighted to meet Cederidge and all the other horses, but I noticed a sadness about Jeff. I studied him. He looked so handsome in his Levis, boots, and blue-and-white Western shirt with those vivid black curls lying on the collar. I couldn't help feeling wild, impassioned feelings about him. I didn't know it, but I was falling in love for the first time ever in my life. It wasn't a state of mind, either. My stony limp self was pulsating with the throb of hormones racing through my body and making my head dizzy.

Someone came to the barn and got Hal to take care of some business, leaving me alone with Jeff.

"So, you live right here with your horses?" I asked.

"Yep. Come on, I'll show you where." He led me through rows of horses to a small room near the end. It was a small room, spartan and immaculately clean. The outside light drifted through the dusty golden window and filled the little room with a warm yellow glow. The room smelled richly of oiled pine planks, leather, aftershave, and sweet, fresh-laundered linens. There was a plain single bed covered with a faded blue spread. At the foot of the bed was a banged-up blue metal trunk. There was also a wooden rocker that looked comfortable and an old faded chest of drawers. As I walked forward the planks squeaked under my feet. I looked at the show ribbons that were hung on the wall with obvious pride. Then I came across a single picture, framed in a modest frame, hanging on the plain wall. It was Jeff riding Cederidge in the show ring. The horse was at a gallop and his long mane flowed over Jeff's hands. I could clearly see Jeff's sweet features under his Western hat.

"Oh, Jeff, what a beautiful picture. God, I love it." As I turned to him I thought I detected a blush, so to spare him, I looked again around the room.

"I don't need much," he said. "My life is the horses. I guess you could say I'm as simple as they are."

"I know what you mean. I'm simple like that too. I used to love riding my horse out alone." I looked at him adoringly, and again I noticed he looked sort of sad. "Jeff, is something wrong?"

"I just had a big falling-out with Hal. I think he's just a user. When Ramtha talked to me at that Dialogue, one thing he told me was that I would experience a great conflict here at the stable—something about an ending of relationships— and that I would make a great journey beyond the mountains. He said I would find complete fulfillment there. He said I might be afraid of the change, but that I would go to this place . . . where my destiny really was. I tried to ask him where that was, but he just said things would change very fast and that I would see."

"Are you having problems here, Jeff?"

"Yeah. Hal can be a real bastard, real difficult to work with. But I stay because I love the horses. They're my business and my life."

I looked at him closely. My mind was going crazy. I knew it was all too fast, but I decided to say what was on my mind.

"Listen, Jeff, I've been thinking seriously of doing something with the horses I have. These Dialogues I do take a lot of my energy and time and, well, I need something to do that's fun . . . something I can look forward to. I haven't spoken to my husband yet, but would you consider coming to Washington State? It's great country, and I was thinking you could help teach us about horses and maybe help us buy some more and train them."

Jeff was looking at me with his mouth agape. "Oh! You're married?"

I felt myself go cold as I said, "Yes, I am."

Hal was calling for Jeff outside. I continued, "I also have two boys, and they would love to learn more about riding."

He raised his eyebrows. "You have two children?"

"Yes, you'd love them. They're great kids." Suddenly I became aware of how old I was. Then I studied Jeff. He was younger than I was—and worse yet, I didn't know if he had a girlfriend, or was maybe engaged. Or even married. I glanced down at his finger. No ring.

"I shouldn't be going on and on about you coming to Washington and all. For all I know you might be married, or have a girlfriend here." I batted my eyelashes and peered at him demurely.

"No, I broke up with my girlfriend. She married someone else. It's just me and my horses."

My heart leapt and I felt a warm relief come over me. "Oh, I'm sorry."

Hal walked in. "What's going on with you two? All the people are here. Hey, did you know that Joan Hackett was here?" he said excitedly.

I looked up at him calmly. "Jeff was just showing me around and telling me about the horses. I like the way Jeff feels about horses. I used to feel the same way."

When the Dialogue was over, Joan came over and told me what the Ram had said to her. She couldn't believe that Ramtha knew all those things—things, she said, that no one knew. Ram also said he was going to send her three movie offers, one of which she would win an award for. She said she would call me and tell me more of what Ramtha had said to me. I had to leave to catch my plane.

Everyone except Jeff was hugging and saying their good-byes. He was nowhere to be seen. I felt such disappointment. But just as we all had climbed into the car and begun to drive off, I looked back to see Jeff running after us from the barn. I yelled for the car to stop and ran to meet him.

"I was so afraid I'd missed you," he said. "But you know, it's Mother's Day, and, well, you gave up the day with your boys to be with us, so I wanted to give you something." He pulled a brown paper sack from behind his back and handed it to me. "Please excuse the wrapping job, but I didn't have any paper. Go ahead, open it."

I unwrapped the humble paper, and to my immense joy, Jeff had gifted me with the picture of him on his horse that I'd seen hanging on his wall. It was his only picture. I was so touched, huge tears gathered in my eyes and began to spill onto the glass.

"Oh, Jeff, it's beautiful . . . so beautiful. I just love it. But I can't accept this picture; I mean, it's your treasure."

"It's a treasure, but I want you to have it. It's such a small thing compared to all you have given me." With that he hugged me. I pulled away slightly and kissed his cheek. "Happy Mother's Day, JZ."

"You've made me happier than you could possibly know," I told him. "You're so thoughtful. I'll hang it right by my bed. Thank you, thank you so much." I kissed his cheek again and then ran back to the car before he saw me crying. I got in, wiped my eyes, and watched him standing there as we drove away. I got out my hankie and blew my nose like a longshoreman. Mary tried to inspect the picture, but I had a death grip on my prize and no one could budge it out of my hands.

On the long flight home, I was in a daze about my feelings for Jeff. I kept looking at the picture, recalling everything I could about him. I was so enraptured with the man that I knew there must be something more to our meeting. Somehow, I *knew* I was not leaving him behind, but rather he was waiting for me . . . somewhere in my future.

CHAPTER TWENTY-THREE

NO REGRETS, MY LOVE

The evening after the ranch Dialogue I sat with Jeremy by the fire, trying to figure out how to approach him with the idea of Jeff's coming to work with our horses. I finally just spilled the beans. I told him of Jeff's plight with his partner, and what the Ram had told him. Jeremy listened quietly. Finally, he made a comment about the superb cognac he was sipping and got up to walk to the patio window. He stood there gazing out into the dark. I remained quiet, awaiting his reaction.

Without turning around, he asked, "How do you intend to pay for all of this, my Zebra? Jeff's salary; the expenses; we'll likely need a new location for the horses. Zebra, all that takes money. How do you think you are going to swing it, my dear?"

I felt disappointed at the curtness of his reply. "With the money I'm making. That way it doesn't have to come out of your pocket."

I waited for his rebuttal, but instead he sat back down, picked up a newspaper, and began to read. I watched him for a moment and then felt a pang of guilt. I adored Jeremy. He was reluctantly allowing me to pursue my dreams. I appreciated him so for that. I got up and hugged him around the neck. "Jeremy, I know I must be tiresome at times . . . I am even to myself. But I want you to know how much I do appreciate you. No matter whatever happens, please don't forget that. You have been better to me than anyone has in my life. Just know that, please."

He looked at me with understanding.

It was a beautiful morning in May. A mellow sun flooded my kitchen with a golden light. I stopped cleaning and opened the window wide to look at my petunias, brilliantly alive in their window box. The music of birds danced on a gentle breeze as it carried its sweet cargo—the fragrance of roses, of grass and woods. I felt a limitless peace creep over me and I forgot everything but the joy of being in that moment. I felt like a young girl again, soft and hopeful.

When the phone rang, disturbing my moment, I answered it reluctantly. It was Jeff. My heart soared.

"JZ, does that offer about going beyond the mountains still stand?" he asked in a low and uncertain voice.

My face lit up. "Absolutely. You just topped off my morning."

He laughed softly. "Well, when should I come up there? I can leave anytime."

"Did something happen?"

"Yeah, it was just like the Ram said. Hal and me got into a big fight. I told him I'd had enough of his bullshit and that I was leaving. I'm ready to go over the mountains," he sighed.

"I see. Well, I'm sorry how things worked out for you, but maybe it's for the best. Look, I'll send you the airfare and you can stay here at the house until we find you a place. I have a really nice guest room."

"That's nice of you, thanks a lot. So, Joe and I will plan to be up there next week. Is that all right?"

"Joe?"

"Joe's my partner, remember? You met him at the Dialogue down here. We work very well together."

I hadn't exactly expected Joe to be coming too, but I rationalized that having him around would take some of the pressure off of what I had felt so quickly for Jeff. I was still as naive as I had ever been.

"Okay, if that's what you want. I'll send you the tickets. And Jeff, I hope you will be happy here. I know I'm happy you made the decision to come."

When I picked them up at the airport two weeks later, I had to hire a cab to take all their trunks of tack back to the house. I showed them their room and they began to unpack their things. Jeff had only one suitcase full of clothes, all a little outdated, but he had packed them meticulously and now placed them with great care into the chest of drawers. This was an appreciative man whose world was one of order and tidiness. I smiled with approval.

When we arrived at the farm where our horses were stabled, I noticed Jeff's face register disappointment. Then I showed him our horses with great pride. Joe and Jeff looked at them with undisguised disapproval.

"You're disappointed, aren't you?"

Joe, with a cocky smile and smugness in his voice, answered, "Hey, I'm just used to working with purebred, expensive horses, with training areas and arenas. This just isn't an ideal situation."

While I glared at him, feeling a bit hurt, Jeff said, "Let's see what the lady has in mind. We'll work with what we've got."

He was my hero. "I do want to learn. I was hoping you guys could teach me."

Everyone nodded, so the adventure was on.

Later that evening, as I was preparing dinner, Jeff came down and offered to help. I was surprised at his interest in domesticity, but I loved it. He was a little shy, but he willingly took over the task of peeling the potatoes and did it like a pro. Joe was up in the guest room brooding over the misfortune of taking a job with low-grade horses.

Jeremy, home from work, walked into the kitchen.

"Hi, Jeremy. Well, here's Jeff," I said. "He's been helping me make dinner."

"Welcome. Hope you guys are comfortable here till you
find your own place." He shook hands with Jeff. "I think a
little brandy is in order." He went into the dining room,
poured the brandy, and then returned with two crystal glasses
filled with the golden liquid. He gestured to Jeff and handed
him a glass. "Drink it," Jeremy said as he scrutinized Jeff's
appearance. "Slowly."

Jeff automatically put the glass to his lips and sipped.
The stinging brandy touched his tongue. "Thank you," he
said, and coughed.

Jeremy raised his eyebrows and sipped a little. "Smooth,
eh?"

"No," Jeff said, smiling slightly. "I could never develop
a taste for brandy." He coughed again.

Jeremy went over to one of the counter chairs and, looking at me, said, "Tell me, Jeff, have you ever known what
it is to be poor? Broke? Fools say that poverty isn't really a
crime, but it is. Everywhere you look, the world impresses
that on you very severely. The world treats you much worse
when you are poor than if you were say a murderer or a
madman. I know, I know very well. And the funniest thing
of all is that when you're poor, it's the poor who are more
vicious toward you than the rich; they never quite forgive
you for being one of them . . . not really. When you're poor,
your poor neighbors are afraid that you'll ask them to share
what little they have with you. When they refuse, or have
to refuse, they despise you for making them uneasy . . . do
you understand?" His voice was without emotion, cold and
controlled.

Jeff did not understand but just stared into his glass. He
was speechless.

I was staring at Jeremy, giving him my full and bewildered attention. He seemed to be completely off the wall.

"Money is the only thing that can stand between you
and failure. I used to think that it was the only fortress that
a man had. You can talk about your successes all you want,
but they are really nothing if you are still poor. Without

money, you're wide open to the world and what it can do to you, and what it does do is the most contemptible thing imaginable. It exploits and dehumanizes you as if you were an animal. Well, I had to beat all of that and work hard to rise above the world and its contempt. I worked hard, damned hard, to get where I'm at. But a funny thing happened to me one day; I had everything, but I was still poor. Oh, I had money, but I was poor because my life was empty . . . my face was empty. Then I met this angel." He turned and pointed to me. "She made my life rich . . . richer in ways most of the rich don't understand. I became a happy man the day I met her and, well, in return for that, I've tried to give her everything that I could. Well, almost everything. Some of which are these horses . . . and you and your partner coming up here. It makes her happy. But I don't want her to become poor—if you catch my drift—pursuing this dream of hers. Because every red cent is being paid out of *her* pocket. So I want you to be honest with her and try to keep her in mind, whatever you do with these horses, because, partner, she deserves that. Do you catch my meaning?" Jeremy eyed Jeff with a determined gaze.

I stood there feeling perturbed and embarrassed by Jeremy's speech. I gave Jeff a sly glance out of the corner of my eye.

He looked back evenly at Jeremy and then nodded. "I'm a pretty simple man, Jeremy. I've never really been poor, but I have never really been rich, either. I've been happy even without money. I think that there's more to living than money. It's true I'm not an educated man with a college degree, but I do think and think very deeply. I don't believe that God is interested in me because I have money or don't have money and to me that is just how I feel about everyone. It's how I feel about JZ, and about you. I know your wife is some kind of angel, and I'm grateful to her for giving me the opportunity to move up here. Maybe there are some wicked people in the world who would take advantage of her generosity, but I'm not one of them. All I can say is that I will do my best to make her happy with the horses. If for some reason it doesn't work out, I'll be the first to say so."

Jeremy was silent. He pursed his lips together and continued to sip his brandy.

I stood there for a few moments thinking about Jeremy's distorted view of life. Sure, he had had experiences that had made it hard for him to trust people. But I had also lived in this world poor and alone. My experiences hadn't led me to the conclusion that every man and woman was detestable and spiritually diseased, corrupt, cruel, and merciless. Some of the most blessed people I've known had no money; others a great deal. I felt saddened that Jeremy didn't truly recognize the goodness in others. Jeff was one of those noble people.

Jeff tried to break the silence by saying, "Well, we saw your horses today. I think we can work with them."

"*Her* horses," Jeremy muttered.

I pressed my palms together and looked over at Jeff. He was staring at the uncooked food rather forlornly. "Well, we'll take the boys to the stables tomorrow, Jeremy. Jeff is going to start their riding lessons."

Shrugging his shoulders, Jeremy said, "Fine . . . that's just fine, Zebra. I'll just go along drilling, filling, and billing."

Over the following weeks, Jeff and Joe taught Brandy, Chris, and me how to groom, brush, and wash our horses. Daily riding lessons were fun for everyone—with the exception of Joe. He still suffered the humiliation of working with just plain horses. Everyone would return from the barn, and over dinner we would explain to Jeremy what was going on. Jeff would help me with the dishes while Joe carried out the trash. When he could, Jeff spent time helping me with the housework, doing everything from vacuuming to folding laundry. I had never had a man help me like that before, and I found it very refreshing.

All through the summer of 1980, Jeff and Joe worked feverishly at training the horses. Before much time had passed, other people heard they were training horses and soon Jeff had a full barn of paying customers. This delighted Jeremy. I felt more fulfilled than I ever had. There was no evidence —at least not on the surface—that the relationship between Jeff and me was developing into anything more than platonic. But Jeremy was beginning to resent the lack of privacy in his own home. He had come to like Jeff and Joe, but . . .

On a Tuesday morning, after Jeff and Joe had gone to the stables, taking Brandy and Chris with them, Jeremy broached the subject as we finished breakfast.

"Zebra, I've been doing some thinking and, well, I think it's time the guys found their own house. I mean, it's not natural for two single guys not to be able to have relationships, not to have privacy to have them in. Guys on the loose need their own place, know what I mean?"

I knew he was right. "I think so too," I agreed, "but let's do it after Christmas . . . so at least they won't be alone for the holidays. Okay?"

Jeremy sighed, took another sip of his coffee, and said, "Okay." He got up, kissed me good-bye, and went to work.

Feeling restless, I changed into a linen blouse and some loose-fitting sweatpants, put on my sun hat, and went to work in my little flower garden. I sat down by some large irises my mom had sent me two years before. It was very warm, so I rolled up my sleeves to reveal a light golden tan on my arms. I stared at the light that fell through the cedar trees, and I considered my life with sadness.

The thought of Jeff's moving filled me with pain and loneliness. I had never really loved any man but Jeff in this passionate way. But when he left, it would be as if my life —pleasant, full of flowers, music, laughter, gentle talks, and beauty—had shattered. I felt abandoned. Here I was Jeremy's wife, enduring the secret anguish of guilt and self-torment. There wasn't anyone that I could talk to about my dilemma, my selfish duality. If I had tried, they would only say that it was a woman's fantasy and that it would pass. Jeff was only a passing fancy; Jeremy was my husband, permanent and stable. I would have to hide my emotions and allow them to fester in me silently. It was important for me to repress them, not so much for my sake as for the sake of Brandy and Chris, whose young lives must not be ruined. Oh, how I wished I could just get this all out in the open and let my grief, my adulterous thoughts, be known so that my life wouldn't be poisoned by these feelings.

For years my sole purpose had been to be strong and

self-sufficient for my two boys. The presence of a man did not seem necessary. I was determined to become successful on my own to compensate for my own inner lack of security. However, during the past two years I had allowed my goals to become secondary to my marriage to Jeremy. I had let myself become dependent upon him. Though we shared a bed, passion and sexual desire had never been an important part of the relationship, at least not for me. They did not drive me, and having never experienced them in my life, I never really missed them. Now, at age thirty-four. my passions had been aroused by Jeff Knight. At times when I was with him, my body felt as urgently needy as a young girl's, and Jeff's awareness of this kept me looking and feeling unusually young for my age.

I now realized that I had married out of a need for security. I had become the "angel" of a trustworthy and prudent man who allowed all my dreams to come true. However comfortable my marriage, I knew that there would be no warm nights of excitement, no confidences in the dark, no naughty laughter and kisses, no sense of being completely aroused and fulfilled. I realized that many people around the country regarded me as a guru of sorts because of my involvement and dedication to the grand works of Ramtha, but these grand works could not be the sole aim of my life. I was a human being who longed for a private life of joy, pleasure, and intimacy. Did not the Ram teach that joy is the aim of an awakening God? Was I somehow exempt from this? Did I have to suffer, as I once thought, to seek God and the joy of freedom? I felt that I could not continue my work with Ramtha, who taught of sovereignty and joy and living the truth, if my own life was a travesty of these teachings. I just could not.

A group of bluejays began to squawk in the nearby Japanese cherry trees, and a moist, warm September breeze rustled the flower beds. I watched as a timid rabbit poked its way from the end of the driveway into the garden, breakfasting on flowers and leaves as he went. "Go away," I said listlessly. "I didn't plant my petunias to be your late lunch. Shoo." I lifted the weight of my hair from around my neck and threw it over my shoulders. I pulled out a hankie and dabbed the small beads of sweat from my forehead. As I did, I looked up at my cherry trees and saw the faint browning of their leaves. I was unbearably depressed. Soon everything would begin to take on the deepening topaz of autumn; then would come the dreaded winter that had once made me happy, and with it the departure of my youthful joy . . . my beloved Jeff.

I sat there fingering a brilliant pink petunia, when a bright golden light appeared above the cherry trees and floated down in front of me. It was Ramtha. His transfiguration became solid, but the light, nonetheless, danced merrily around him. He stooped down.

"Where have you been all this time?" I chided him. "I've wanted to talk to you so desperately. Have a minute or so you can spare?" I looked at him pleadingly from under my hat.

He chuckled and began to smell all the flowers around him. I must say, his appreciation of small things was a delight to watch, even for one with a heavy heart. He picked a lavender rose and buried his nose in it; I thought for a moment he was going to vacuum it right up into his nose. Then he let out a pleased sigh and said, "My beloved woman, I am always with you."

I frowned. "Sometimes it doesn't feel like you are." I pouted, dropping my bottom lip rather childishly.

Ramtha just continued to smile at me. Nothing ever seemed to alter his delightful mood of peace. He certainly wasn't the type to console you by getting down and being pitiful with you. At times like that, his attitude could be irritating. I flashed a mock-smile back to him.

"Ramtha, I have a big and hurtful problem and—"

"A problem? There be no such thing, entity, as a problem."

I slowly shut my mouth, then quickly opened it again. "Oh, come on, that's not fair! To me it is a problem . . . and it hurts, Ramtha. Damn, you gotta remember that I'm not where you are. I'm here, in the real world of feelings and emotions." I pointed to the ground and stuck my finger in the soft dirt.

"Indeed, beloved lady, as it should be. That be the reason for life on your plane." He picked some petunias and tossed them over the hedge to the thankful rabbit.

"Okay, but with your insight and wisdom, I thought that maybe you could help me a little. You see, I think that I've fallen in love with this man, Jeff Knight. I think I've loved him since the first time I ever saw his picture. You know, this has never happened to me in my whole life, Ramtha! I can't seem to stop thinking about him, and I get these . . . these feelings, like . . . moving, strong female urges that I can't get rid of. Oh, we haven't *done* anything . . . not even a kiss . . . a real kiss. I don't even think he *knows* about this. I don't even think he thinks I exist. I'm just good ol' JZ, the boss, the channel, the wife, the mother . . . just someone. Then there's Jeremy, the beloved physician, my husband . . . I feel so guilty. I don't want to hurt him, and I know that if I told him I would. I feel like a dishonest, lustful old bat!" I kept my eyes on the hem of my blouse that I had been twisting the life out of.

"Ahh, indeed, my beauteous woman, you are becoming a real woman at last."

"At last? What do you think I've been all this life? An androgynous thing with boobs?" He just smiled. I looked at him in shocked silence. Oh, God, how would *he* know . . . He's a *man!* So I continued, ignoring his comment. "Jeff works so hard at everything he does. He's simple and very honest. Sometimes when I look at him I feel like I'm kind of looking at myself. I feel that if I could hold him, it would be like holding myself. I dream about him every night and I think about him all the time. When he walks into my kitchen while I'm fixing dinner, things fall out of my hands, like the pork chops the other night, skillet and all. Or I forget to turn the stove on and come back after an hour to find my pies are just as I left them . . . undone. It's crazy. I see the compassion that is his naturally. I can talk with him for hours about everything . . . well, almost everything. Then when he gets up to leave, I don't want him to leave. God, what should I do?"

"Indeed, you have a great fire for Master Jeffrey."

"I have feelings now that I never had in my life. Why? Why?"

"There be much you will learn through the simple splendor of Master Jeffrey."

"But what should I do?"

"Do? Beloved woman, just be. Allow yourself to be."

"Be, huh? Tell me, Ramtha, is *he supposed* to be here? I mean, was this destined somehow?"

"You have created it, beloved woman. You be unfolding into that which be you. You are waking up from a dream of limitation. In awakening, that which is lost and, indeed, suppressed must come to the conscious surface to be realized, embraced, and, indeed, owned."

"Did Jeff create this too . . . I mean, being here?"

"Indeed. Once he was oppressed, confused. He knew not his own identity, indeed, he knew not his self-worth, liken unto you. You be awakening through the emotional identity that Master Jeffrey possesses, you be recognizing yourself in him. He prayed and cried out for help. I heard."

My face lit up and my mouth fell open. "Really?"

"I will tell you, beloved woman, had no one heard him, he would have taken his own life, a measure many take from the inner collapse of an unjoyous and unfulfilled life."

"Jeffrey?"

"Indeed."

"Is all of this your doing? Did you make me see that picture, and did you arrange for him to leave his work in California?" Maybe I could lay the blame for my unblessed situation on Ramtha. My old modus operandi lived: make it someone else's fault.

"Indeed, I was part of it."

"What utter manipulation, Ramtha! Wouldn't you say so?" I narrowed my eyes, vehemently challenging him.

"Lady, one does not manipulate against the will of God. I have merely facilitated a cry for help and, indeed, fulfilled only that which is a growing need of recognition within you. You wanted it and, indeed, needed it."

My shoulders slumped and I hung my head. "What should I do? What does God want me to do, Ramtha?"

"Allow yourself to feel. Allow. In this, indeed, what is destiny and, indeed, natural evolution your soul will know. Listen to yourself."

"But Ramtha, I . . ." He had disappeared. Run out on me, I thought.

I got up, dusted the soil off my pants, and walked inside. I climbed up the stairs to Jeff and Joe's room and stood in the doorway. Everything was so neat and orderly . . . just like Jeff. Slowly, I walked into my room and sat on the bed. I reached out and caressed the satin bedspread. Then I had a thought. I walked into my closet and picked out an all-yellow outfit. I got dressed and called Mary, asking her to meet me at a lovely restaurant for a champagne lunch. She was delighted. So off I went to drown my troubles in some Asti Spumante. I rarely drank, but if I did it was Asti. It tasted like liquid bubble gum. Some bubble gum was exactly what I wanted.

Mary was delightful. We chattered away between bites of salad and glass after glass of Asti. Then, when I was completely blitzed, I excused myself and told Mary that I needed to go to the drunk-ladies' room. I lied, of course. What I did was go for the pay phone. I hadn't felt like this since my senior prom drunk, which had also been prompted by a man. Jesus, do men really drive women to drink? Looking around the room, I figured there must have been a lot of hurt going around judging from all the women having their liquid lunches. With difficulty, I focused my eyes on the phone buttons and called Jeff.

Jeff answered the phone in his soft, sexy voice. I swallowed hard and, fixing my gaze on my yellow heels, began. "Jeffrey . . . hi, it's me."

"Hi. You sound funny."

"I sound funny? Funny, but I don't think I'm sounding funny at all. Funny, huh?"

"JZ, you sound like you've been drinking." I sensed laughter in his voice.

"Me? Drinking? Naw . . . I'm fine. That's funny, Jeffie." I wanted to laugh and cry, but not to slur my words.

"JZ, where are you? Are you alone?"

"Where am I?" I looked around and saw a man come out of the john. He gave me one of those "looks," sort of flirty and dirty, but all I wondered was if he had washed his hands after he'd bled his lizard. I looked back down at my shoes and continued, "Uh . . . where was I? Oh, yeah, I don't remember the name of thisss place, but it'sss a place, all right. Yep, and it's got a phone . . . thank God."

"It sure does."

"Uh, listen, Jeffie . . . I wanted ta tell ya somethin'."

"Go ahead. I'm listening."

"Well, ya know . . . I'm a pretty honest person and all . . ."

"Yeah."

"Jeffrey, I just wanted ta say that . . . just say that . . . I love you a lot." My brazen statement just sort of hung in the silence on the other end.

"I love you a lot too. You've really been good to me. A good friend."

"No, no. I mean I really love you. There."

"I really love you too, JZ."

I stood there in my drunken daze trying to figure out if he was dumb or maybe just putting me off on purpose.

"Jeffrey, I want you to know I'm in love with you."

There was another moment of silence on his end of the line.

"JZ, I respect you and I love you in many ways, too, but as a friend, not as a lover."

I hesitated. "Really? You mean you don't have any of those feelings for me? Hey, I know I'm older than you, and I know you could have any girl you wanted, but—"

"I feel friendship."

I was mortified. "Nothing more than that? Is it because I'm old? Is that it?"

"No. You're not old, and you're one of the most beautiful ladies I've ever met. Listen, I think you'd better get sobered up and go home to your husband."

I closed my eyes in utter humiliation. I hung up the phone, staggered back to the table, and told Mary some stupid lie about having to leave. I threw some money on the table and walked out of the restaurant with my head held so high that I couldn't really see where I was going. I hadn't given Mary a moment to protest that I was too drunk to drive.

I stumbled on the stairs once or twice on the way to the parking lot. I looked around furtively to see if anyone had observed me, then made my way to the car. I fumbled for my car keys, found them, but then I couldn't find the keyhole. I looked up at the violet blue evening sky, with its first bright stars, and yelled, *"Shut up!"* I dropped the keys, got down on my hands and knees like some blind mole, found them, and then had trouble getting back up. After much maneuvering, I opened the car door and climbed in, knees first—the praying position. I nobly arranged myself behind the wheel, then went through the same ignition-finding process that I did with the door lock. Finally, having started the car, I took a deep breath and stepped on the gas. The car lurched forward; I didn't even notice. Then I began to drive it in circles around the parking lot. I couldn't find my way out, and I didn't know where to go even if I could. Finally, I saw the exit sign and drove off.

When I got home, Jeremy was having a sandwich and reading an Arabian horse magazine. He turned to see me as I dropped my handbag on the kitchen floor and fell to my knees to look for it.

"Zebra, what have you been doing?"

"I've been out with the pope. What does it look like I've been doing? Drinking . . . like I always do."

He chuckled. "How's come you didn't call me? I'd have come right over."

"Cuz, you were drilling and filling and billing," I said drunkenly, still crawling around searching for my enormous handbag.

"While you were guzzling," he said flatly.

I looked up at him and felt a throbbing pain in my head. He continued. "I've never seen a drunk Zebra before. Do you know which of your stripes are black and which are white?"

I hissed, "I don't care. I have a headache." I pulled my miserable self up.

"Here, let me help you."

I waved him away. "I can do it myself."

Jeremy started laughing. "Well, well, I don't know what got into you, ol' girl." I glared at him. "But whatever it is, it'll be over in the morning and you are not going to feel good about it at all."

As I fumbled to stand up, my right ankle gave way and the heel broke off my right shoe. "Don't remind me, okay?" I fumed, and weaved and hobbled my way up the stairs to bed. I flopped down on the bed and stared at the revolving ceiling. I was getting sick. I rolled over, passed out, and had a dreamless sleep.

When I woke up, Jeremy was asleep beside me and it was still dark. My head was pounding like a sledgehammer and I was terribly thirsty. I slowly rose out of bed, still dressed in my yellow suit, and I shuffled down the stairs to the kitchen. I poured a huge glass of ice water from the fridge, then went to sit in the formal living room. The huge bay window was flowing with light from the full moon. Shadows of the leaves danced on the walls, on the thick white carpet and the polished furniture. I looked over at my piano and laughed to myself about those dreams of my magical fingers playing melodious masterpieces. All I'd ever managed was the two-finger version of "Chopsticks" every time I sat there to play. What a fantasy world I lived in sometimes.

As I sat there on the couch, drinking my water in the moonlit room, I started to cry. What a stupid, ignorant, clumsy, and totally naive person I had been. Stupid, stupid. Then I heard the sound of soft footsteps on the stairs. I quickly wiped away my tears, thinking it was one of the boys, but as I turned I saw Jeff standing in the shadows at the entry to the living room. His hair looked sleek and shimmered in the light of the moon, his face shadowed. He just stood there quietly watching me with those observant eyes.

As he walked into the room, he asked me where I had been. His voice was low and courteous. He sat down and politely listened for my answer.

"In my room . . . passed out, I guess." I sniffed.

"No, I mean before. Today, when you called me."

"Today?" I repeated, raising my eyebrows. "Oh, I don't

remember. I was having lunch with Mary. I drank a lot of Asti. Then I drove around in circles."

I looked up at him sitting on the other couch. The subtle silver light deepened the shadows of his cheekbones and played on the contours of his face. His sensitive mouth glistened with moisture. His expression was sad and gentle. As we sat there in silence, I felt ashamed. I had put him on the spot, and now I felt as though I had hurt him also.

"What·do you think, JZ?"

I was vague in my reply. "What do you mean, what do I think? I made a mistake . . . a shameful one, that's all. Everybody makes mistakes. Even Ramtha's channel."

"Listen, I've known for a long time that you cared a lot for me," he said softly.

"Thanks for acknowledging that you noticed," I snapped.

He hesitated, seeing only anger and repudiation in my face, in the way my eyelids jerked spasmodically, in the way I put my hands to my cheeks. He had never seen me so shaken.

"I've cared a lot about you," he said at last. "I wouldn't have come up here, leaving my business, my clients, and my horses behind, if I didn't care. And I wouldn't have stayed," he said with more courage. "But when I saw your family and your house—I don't know, it was all wrong. I like Jeremy a lot. I respect him. You have a great guy for a husband."

"Great? Why do you call him great?"

"He's a nice man who has a respectable position in the world. He went to college and he's educated. I'm not. I could never compare to him. I don't have anything. Look at this beautiful house. I could never have one like this." He paused, bent over, and clasped his hands together. "I don't want to do anything that would break up this happy home and marriage."

I started to cry openly now. I felt bewildered; he didn't understand. He had no way of understanding that I loved him and that my love was constantly growing, expanding to become the most important thing in the world to me. I felt old and afraid and isolated in my bewilderment.

Jeff came over and sat down beside me. I just sat there

in silence, tears rolling from my eyes, my hands trembling. He put his arm around me and laid my head on his shoulder as he began to tenderly wipe my wet eyes and face.

As I began to speak, I felt and sounded like a weepy little girl. "Jeffrey, I don't know why I love you like this. I have from the first moment I saw your picture. You've made me feel alive for the first time in my whole life. I get these huge butterflies in my stomach whenever I see you. You've done something to me that no one else ever has in my life. You make me happy. I can tell you one thing, Jeff Knight: if you had only a dime in your pocket, I'd give up all this in a minute if you wanted me to. Things don't make a person happy . . . I know that."

He kissed my moist cheek almost reverently. "You should never be that foolish."

"Foolish? Is love foolish? Do you have any idea what I'm talking about?"

"Yes. But I could never be a good enough man for you, or a good enough father to the boys."

"What are your values all about, Jeff? Property and assets? Money? If they are, then you're not as enlightened as I thought you were." I felt fiery inside.

"Maybe I'm not, but I love my horses, and I love you and the kids and Jeremy, too. I don't want to cause any problems. I don't want to ruin a good marriage."

We both lapsed into silence. I had stopped crying. All I could feel was that he was coolly abandoning me.

"I think maybe I should go back to California."

"I can hardly believe this bad dream," I said sadly. "Perhaps you should if that would make you happier."

"Yeah, maybe I should."

Jeff got up slowly. "I'm sorry, JZ. I sure didn't mean for you to get hurt."

"No, it's all right. I'll be fine. Please, just go back to bed."

Jeffrey left. I looked around at the empty room and doubled over in anguish. I sobbed in silence. Then I raised my head and looked up to the ceiling.

"Father in heaven, Ramtha, I want you to do something

for me. I don't want to feel this way. I don't want to love this man anymore. I want you to rip this love out of me, it doesn't belong to me. Please, if you love me, you will make this love and these wretched feelings go away."

I was determined that this should be so. I sat there silently weeping for maybe an hour longer. When I finally got up to leave, I walked past my piano and suddenly had this urge to play. So I quietly lifted the cover and sat down. I laid my fingers on the keys, first just pressing them for sound. Then, as my thoughts became lost in my grief and sorrow, I became disconnected from my own movements. I felt like electricity was flowing through my body and out my fingers. My hands began to move, and the keys began to sound a symphony of music. I felt like some master sitting there while my hands moved wild and free, creating an enchanting and skillful recital. It sounded like Beethoven or maybe Tchaikovsky. . . . I was in a delirium with the miraculous sound. It lasted for maybe half an hour. When I finished, the electricity had left my hands and the tears had dried on my face. I was shocked at what had happened. It was as if my old dream had finally manifested itself that night. Apparently my emotions were stronger than the logic that always told me I couldn't play the piano like the dream. I turned to get up, and there sat Jeremy, Brandy, Chris, Jeff, and Joe, all in their robes, staring at me in disbelief.

I felt a deep flush as Jeremy fumbled to turn on a lamp. I squinted my swollen eyes and muttered, "Forgive me. I'm sorry I woke all of you up. I just forgot about everyone when this incredible thing happened with me and the piano."

Everyone looked at one another, then Jeremy said, "Zebra, it sounded like Beethoven himself was at the keyboard. None of us knew you could play so well. How did you do it? Were you channeling someone . . . maybe Beethoven? My God, Zebra, you played like a master."

I blushed some more and told them about the dream I'd had so long ago that convinced me I'd be able to play. I was thrilled about it, of course, I told them, but, well, I felt kind of sick and all I wanted was to go to bed. Everyone applauded as I left the room.

I washed my face, put on my flannel gown, and went to bed. I prayed again to God, and Ramtha, for this feeling to leave me. As I closed my eyes, I knew that my prayer would be answered and that tomorrow would bring a much-needed sense of peace. I wanted love to go back to being just a state of mind . . . and never come back.

CHAPTER TWENTY-FOUR

HOPE, THE WAKING DREAM

It was a partly cloudy day with sun breaks that filled my kitchen with glowing light. Sudden gusts of wind blew in through the window, delivering moist mountain air. A hummingbird silently drank the nectar of the petunias in my window box while the light reflected the metallic emerald feathers of its head. Everything was cheery, with sounds of the coffeepot perking and bacon sizzling. The sweet tang of fresh orange juice filled the air as I poured it into the juice glasses. I sat at the counter, which was set with white dishes and blue-and-white linen napkins. A glazed white milk pitcher held a fresh bouquet of Alaskan white daisies and delicate lavender petunias. I hummed "Moon River" to myself as I finished preparing the food; I felt genuinely happy and composed, a lightheartedness that topped the morning off splendidly. As each of my family came down the stairs and into the kitchen, I gave him a big hug and chattered merrily about insignificant stuff. As Jeff entered along with Joe, I showed them each the same sunny love that I was feeling for everyone else.

I poured their coffee and some for myself. Everyone took note since I had never drunk coffee in my life.

"Okay, you sweet dubies, dig in. I have a lot of stuff to do upstairs . . . so enjoy."

Jeff stared at me as he began to help himself. Then Chris, who had been observing as I poured myself a cup of coffee, remarked, "Mom, why are you drinking that coffee? You never drink that stuff."

I had taken a sip and thought it might taste better with some cream, then some more, and then more, until finally it was half and half. It tasted pretty good. So I giggled, leaned over the counter to him, and answered. "When I was a little girl, my mom used to drink coffee with the other grown-ups when they sat around talking. One day I climbed up to the crate that held the tin cups and sneaked myself some coffee, too. I took a drink and it burned my tongue. Well, I bawled awhile, and my mom came in to see what I had been up to. She took the cup away from me and scolded me severely. She told me that if I drank coffee while I was little, it would turn my neck black. I was horrified. Then an old colored man I just loved came in and showed me his neck and said that it got that way from not minding his mammy and drinking coffee. Well, from that day forward, I never drank any coffee, even when I was considered a grown-up. Until now . . . I think I'm safe."

"Grandma told you that? Is it true?" He stopped chewing and stared in wide-eyed disbelief.

I laughed, and so did everyone else. "Na . . . but you must admit the trick worked."

"What made you decide to try it now, Mom?" Brandy asked.

"I don't know . . . I guess I felt like trying it. Something new. Anyway, it's not so bad as long as there's a lot of cream in it. Now, I've got to run upstairs."

Later that morning I was sitting in a comfortable chair in the bedroom making some notes. I looked up and Jeff was standing there with a cup of coffee.

"Hi, come on in. Have a seat. Here's a coaster for your coffee cup," I said rather casually.

"Thanks. Thought I would just chat with you for a few moments before I leave," he said as he sat down.

"That's fine. Hey, it looks like a chilly day outside this morning. You guys better dress warmly. Listen, I assume you and Joe will want to be back in California for Christmas?" I chewed a bit on the end of my eraser.

"Yes, our families want us to spend Christmas with them. What about the horses? Who will take care of them while we are gone?" His voice held a trace of regret.

"I was thinking about that this morning. I love these horses of ours. I'm going to go ahead and keep them. I figure I can get myself another trainer, and you know what? I think I can turn this horse breeding into a profitable business."

"If you do that, I think you should consider maybe finding a really good stallion and possibly one or two good mares to breed to him. But it's a big responsibility."

"Anytime you undertake a new business it's a big responsibility. But at least it's one that makes me happy." I paused, thinking about the wisest way to proceed. "I've been thinking about Padron as the stallion I would like to breed to. I have this feeling about that young stallion. I think he's going to be a National Champion, and it would be wise to lock in a definite breeding price before the price goes up. And I was thinking I'd maybe get me a small farm and just see how everything goes. I really feel good about this. Once I start a breeding program with the right mares, I'll have a depreciation write-off, and I can write off the interest on the loan for the farm as well."

Jeff looked startled by this sudden change in me. "Well, look, if you need any advice or help, just call me."

"Oh, I will. By the way, thanks for the talk last night. You were right. We are such good friends, and nothing should get in the way of that. I'll always be very grateful for what you've done for me."

He pressed his lips together as he smiled halfheartedly. "That goes for me, too. You and the Ram have helped me a lot."

"I guess we all learn from one another. It's funny how

things work out sometimes. I knew you were in my life for a reason, and I think it was because you put me on the right track toward knowing myself better. Like the Ram says, everyone mirrors to one another a dimension of themselves."

"Really?" He was rather surprised.

"Yes, really. The horse business is a new adventure for me. In fact, I feel like it's a new me. You are a wonderful man, Jeff, and someday you're going to make some lucky gal the best husband in the world." I smiled and felt delighted about the way our conversation was going.

"Thanks, JZ . . ." I noticed a shadow pass over his face.

"So, listen, let me know when you guys want to leave, okay?"

He nodded his head slowly as he stared into his coffee, which by now had cooled considerably. He opened his mouth as if to say something more, but then closed it again. He slowly got up and said good-bye. I waved and went back to my notes, thinking nothing more of our conversation or of Jeff. Everything was copacetic.

Autumn arrived in Washington with its usual brilliant display of colors, aromas, and sounds. The rains came often, accompanied by chilly winds that washed the brightly hued leaves of yellow, scarlet red, and deep topaz into heaps of color beneath naked trees. The nights were filled with the smells of alder fires, decaying leaves, spice, and the rain-washed air. A large orange harvest moon would appear above the treetops, silhouetting them like black spiral towers, a befitting setting for glowing jack-o'-lanterns to bob and dance. I continued my usual odd life-style of Ramtha, the Dialogues, baking fruit pies, painting Canadian geese, being homeroom mother to both boys' classes at school, planning parties, riding my horses, and helping Jeremy on emergency calls. All in all it was a happy time.

After Thanksgiving, the great search for *the* Christmas tree took place. It had to be at least eighteen feet tall, and a thick noble fir. It was found and erected in the foyer, where it missed touching the ceiling by an inch. The white staircase railing was decked with garlands of holly and bright velvet ribbons. Then we decorated the tree with five thousand small twinkling lights, delighting in its beauty while we drank cups of nutmegged eggnog.

One of my specialties was gift wrapping. Each present was individually designed and each massive silk or satin bow made by hand, some as big as a foot long. The effect when they were all placed under the tree was magical and enchanting.

One night in early December of 1980, everyone with the exception of Jeremy, who was downstairs sipping spiced brandy, was up in my bedroom wrapping gifts. I was in my element, showing Chris and Brandy how to make the renowned fluffy bows. Jeff struggled with his, trying to make eye contact with me. I truly didn't notice. Then he asked for help with his bow, and I enthusiastically complied. The phone rang downstairs and after a moment Jeremy called for the boys to come to the phone; it was one of their friends. Jeff and I were alone.

"Uh, JZ, can we talk?"

"Sure . . . here, put your finger on the ribbon while I tie a knot."

"I'm sorry, but I've been doing some thinking about going home."

"Uh-huh?"

"Well, I don't want to quit my job here."

"Now you can take your finger off . . . uh, why?"

"Well, I'd like to go home for Christmas and stay maybe a week and then just see how I feel."

I stared at him for a moment. Everything had been arranged. What was going on? "What changed your mind?" I asked.

He ran his fingers nervously through his hair. "Since our conversation a couple months ago, I just haven't been able to stop thinking about what we talked about."

I sighed and started fingering some blue ribbon. "It's over with, don't worry, Jeff. I told you, I'm at peace with everything."

"But I'm not. I know I really hurt you a lot. I was cruel to you, JZ."

"No, you were honest, that's all," I muttered.

"No, I wasn't exactly honest with you, either." His voice was clear and quiet.

"You weren't? I don't understand."

"No, I was cruel to you on purpose."

"Well, Jeff, sometimes the truth is cruel. That's why people lie so much."

"But it wasn't the truth. I . . ." His voice choked with emotion. "I've been in love with you from the beginning, too. I didn't know how to deal with it. And worse, I didn't realize that you were married until you came to the ranch. I honestly don't feel good enough for you. And I don't want to break up your family, either. But I also wanted to tell you that I love you . . . always will."

I reached over and gently squeezed his hand. "Jeff."

"I didn't want you to love me. I didn't want that problem . . . never even thought it could happen."

I sat there not knowing what to do. Finally I said, "Jeff, I can't change the attitude you have about yourself . . . not feeling like you're good enough. You have to be who you are. That's all. You are such a priceless man just the way you are. Please try to know that about yourself. You can't make yourself over for someone else.

"You may not believe this, but I went through the same thing over you. I never gave much thought to how old I was or how I looked until I met you. Then I went nuts. I got this female phobia about my age—you know you *are* ten years younger than me. I'm the one that's older, and in our society, it's okay for a man to be older than a woman, sometimes a lot older, but it's not okay the other way around. I started hating myself for how old I was. I became really paranoid about my age, then my weight, then my face. Then when you rejected me, I blamed myself. I was too old, too fat. I wasn't what would make you happy. I guess by now I've been able to transform my feelings for you. Yes, it's true you hurt me, but not as much as I hurt myself, and it took what you said to me to make me realize I can only be who I am and to be happy with that. The Ram teaches us to love ourselves . . . and maybe that's why all of this happened. The thing is, you have to come to a similar understanding about yourself. I'm not going to leave my husband. I'm really at peace with it all."

Jeff stared at me, puzzled. "I just wanted to tell you the truth and how sorry I am that I did what I did."

"Hey, it's okay. Really. Listen, if you want to go home, fine. If you don't, that's fine too. Now, let's wrap your present. Your mother is going to be shocked to see how beautiful it is."

He went back to his wrapping but was unusually quiet.

One afternoon two days later I put some packages under the tree and stood back to admire the effect. Jeremy was still at the office and Jeff had come home early to do some laundry. A bright light appeared at the top of the tree and descended to the floor. It was Ramtha.

"Oh, there you are. Merry Christmas, Ramtha."

He bent over, inspecting the lights and the satin balls that I had made myself. "Beloved woman, and what be these beautiful baubles?"

"Oh, they're Christmas decorations, Ramtha. It's an old custom for us, but I guess it doesn't go back to your day."

"What be its purpose?"

"It's an annual celebration of Jesus' birthday. We'll do this again next year, too. Then, of course, there is Santa Claus."

"Santa Claus?"

"Yes, but he's really a spirit. He represents the spirit of Christmas. We give each other gifts, but we say he delivered them by flying to our rooftops on a sleigh pulled by reindeer that fly. He jumps down our chimneys with a bag full of toys and presents, has some chocolate-chip cookies and a glass of milk, and then goes back up through the chimney to his sleigh and off he flies to the next house and the next. But we really do it . . . he is just the spirit that we imitate. Do you understand?"

"Ahh, I see. Peoples do believe in the unseen, eh?"

"Yeah, it's good business."

"Indeed, it be most beauteous. But now, beloved woman, I desire you to ascend your stairs."

My mouth flew open. "Ascend my stairs? I thought you

and Jesus and Buddha were the only ones that ascended."

"Master Jeffrey is waiting for me. He wishes, indeed, to have a Dialogue."

"Jeff? Upstairs? Oh."

"Indeed, he be waiting."

I glanced upstairs and answered, "Okay."

I slowly walked—not ascended—up the stairs and went to Jeff's room. The room was empty. I turned and went to my room. There, on a chair in the sitting area, sat Jeff.

"Jeff? Oh, hi. I guess you and the Ram want to talk to each other. So I'll just . . . leave." I sat down and in a moment was gone to the light. The following conversation was told to me by Jeff.

"Indeed, beloved Master Jeffrey."

"Indeed, Ramtha, how are you?"

"I am always well," he laughed.

"I wish I could say the same."

"You are desiring to speak with me? I heard your thoughts."

"Yeah, you're right. I need to speak with somebody. I don't know what's going on with me and JZ."

"Indeed, alas, the love of men and women."

"Yes, I love JZ, Ramtha, and I know that if I leave here even for a week I'll never come back." Jeff started to cry softly.

"Why conceive you that idea?"

"I think I've destroyed her feelings for me, that's why."

"There be no such thing as destruction, Master Jeffrey. What can anyone destroy that is of God?"

"But I broke her heart." He broke down and began to heave with great sobs. After a moment he struggled to continue. "I think I've destroyed my own chance for happiness. I'm so miserable and unhappy because I don't feel I'm man enough for her. Do you know what I mean?"

"Man enough? What is man enough to you?"

"I just feel inadequate in every way. I have a fear of loving women. The two women I've been involved with, I was afraid of losing. One left me for another man, and the other just played games with me. Since then, I've been so afraid of loving someone and insecure about my manhood."

"Master Jeffrey, do you measure manhood in terms of copulation? Indeed, by the length of a penis, by age, by experience?"

"Well, it's all important, isn't it?"

"Man be the spirit of his Omnipresent Self. To return back unto God the Father from which you came is to return to That Most Holy Is without the limitation of male and female energy. That which you be, be not of the entirety of gross flesh, but of the spirit of God that takes over the flesh. Flesh does not determine ones own manhood, for it be his spirit that so determines that fulfillment. The body be only the vehicle of the spirit realized; it is not the body that realizes the spirit. Man unifies and frees himself from the enslavement and duality of his flesh. Love, Master Jeffrey, does not subjugate the lover nor does love feed on the desires of flesh and, indeed, blood. Those who do in the name of human nature and, indeed, love be also the ones who have judged man by his sexual deeds and indeed by the length of his penis. They be the wretched unenlightened. It be their rules and truths that you suffer from.

"Master Jeffrey, indeed it be no love that draws a man to a woman only to breed more men and, indeed, more women for the virility of the man to call himself now a man. But man, Master Jeffrey, and woman made as one by love become inseparable, indistinguishable, and verily are they united in the prize of completeness without the duality. They be termed 'soulmate.'

"To continue to measure your manhood by the rules of delusioned sexual society is to remain segregated from the very core of eternity itself. Embrace your truth and your essence, Man-God, from within rather than the grossness of without. Then you shall embrace freedom and experience a release from the bondages of flesh. Heed not those who desire only to propagate the race from a sense of duty or those who play within their semen and blood. And listen not when they say to you that it be 'normal.' For what be normal must also be abnormal. One cannot exist without the other . . . thus then you will understand their confusion with their bodies.

"Master Jeffrey, indeed, you have intimidated yourself

by this measure into the feeling of unworthiness. The love
that burns within your soul be the love of that which unites
two to become one. Do not hide it like a child from the wind,
do not be anguished lest you position it with sexual logic.
Let it burn, Master . . . one day it shall transform you into
the phoenix."

Jeffrey sat transfixed. "Ramtha, my feelings for JZ are
not like any I have ever had. When I look at her I feel that
I'm looking at myself. It's so strange to me . . . sometimes I
see my face in hers. Is that what you're saying about this
special love?"

"Indeed. You are learning, Master."

"I heard you say something about soulmates. Is JZ my
soulmate?"

"What feel you, Master?"

"Well, I feel that she is, and if she is, I feel that I've lost
my soulmate. That's enough to make me want to kill myself.
So please, tell me!"

"Indeed, I shall tell you of a great story. It occurred in
my lifetime. A great battle ensued. I was leading my people
against a fierce enemy. A great tyrant had devastated a free
people. I marched on the tyrant and his legions. I and my
warriors slaughtered them unmercifully. I rode a great black
steed, Shamiradin. The battle completed, I sat upon my steed
at the river's edge. I looked across. In shattered ruins lay a
wretched entity. I watched him attempt to stand. The entity
watched me in hopelessness and dismay for he knew he was
looking across the water at the Great Ram. He knew his death
was imminent. He stood brave and small. I urged my great
horse across the river toward him. The fire from the eyes of
my great steed frightened him. He looked up at me with
despair in his eyes. I pulled him to my horse and held him
tightly. Then I rode with him to my encampment. He said
not a word. His frail body trembled as I held him.

"There in my encampment, I lifted him from my horse
and put him on level ground. I invited him to enter my tent.
Foodstuffs were prepared. I bade him eat, for his body was
starved. He ate warily, wondering if this was his last meal.
As he ate, I watched him. 'You are an honorable man,' I said

to him. 'Of all that I have laid down this day, you were the prize of that victory.' He uttered in dismay, 'Why should you say such a thing to me, lord? It is even.' I answered, 'You are heavy in virtue and honor. You are to be trusted.' I made the young man my robesman and the keeper of my armaments. He was given esteemed priority in my encampment. He had not the body for battle nor did he possess the desire. But he possessed a trustworthiness and a nobility which did not exist even in my greatest warriors.

"The robesman took great pride in preparing my armaments and robes, for me as well as for the warriors in the House of the Ram. There was a beautiful young woman, a daughter of mine, whom I called Ramaya. She possessed hair of raven black beauty which touched the ground gently behind her when she walked. The robesman found her beautiful. His love for Ramaya grew. In his heart burned a flame for her but he was forbidden to think or speak of it. When it was announced that Ramaya would be given in marriage to another great warrior, the robesman was charged with preparing the clothing for myself, Ramaya, and the warrior. With great pride, he sought the finest linen. He sought the smithies to construct the gold for adornments.

"When Ramaya, being boisterous of nature and rebellious as a warrior herself, was asked to be dressed by the maidens in the robes prepared by the robesman, she was indeed defiant. She did not wish the marriage. Her hair was braided into black polished knots. Her gown was draped upon her shoulders, falling loosely to the floor with a transparency that allowed one to see the shapeliness of young hips, firm breasts, and delicate legs. The robesman had done a splendid job. The robesman inspected the beautiful young woman adorned in his wedding preparation. He was proud, yet sad, for he loved her beyond all understanding. Yet she understood. Love began to spark between the two young entities. There was a blush upon their cheeks and song in their beings. It would come to pass that I would direct him to take Ramaya and flee. Thereafter, he would love and protect her for all the days of her life. You, Master Jeffrey, were that robesman. My beloved daughter was, indeed, Ramaya.

Indeed, the forsaken warrior was the beloved physician of this house. You ask is she the mate of your being? Indeed she is."

Jeffrey was crying with tears of emotional memory at Ramtha's story. At length, he found the words.

"But I have thrown her away. I hurt her so badly that I think she feels nothing for me now . . . nothing."

"Indeed. She feels nothing for you. You see, my daughteren threatened her God . . . and me. She implored him and me to remove her feelings from herself. Her plea came to pass so that she would feel no pain, no hurt, no rejection which you so cleverly bestowed upon her. Her desire was completely aligned . . . that gave it the power to manifest."

"Then you took away her feelings?"

"No, not I. You took away her feelings. She desired it so."

"How can I change that, Ramtha?"

"Tell her how you feel. Look around you at her kingdom. Was she not willing to give it up to be with you in a humble abode?"

"She said she would, but that was before she changed."

"Why feel you it is not worth communicating the truth to her? Indeed, she has laid bare her soul unto you . . . at a great price."

"But I can't give her anything. Nothing like this, Ramtha. I don't want to break up her home." Ramtha smiled as Jeff continued. "But you say I should just tell her how I feel?"

"Indeed. Be as even with her as I have been with you. You hold the key, Master Jeffrey. The adventure that waits beyond the door is far removed from the present. The woman loves your being with holy understanding. You be the mate of her being. Together the duality of male and female becomes formless back unto the One. It be a lesson for both . . . indeed, you have drawn yourselves together for this great union. This kingdom is only an illusion, Master Jeffrey. What is in your soul is real. *That* will sustain you, and even lead you unto greater kingdoms than this one. Be understanding with her in whatever she decides to do for you have been enlightened to many mysteries this day in your time.

Know that, for she is still yet to know. Know that I love you greatly. You are loyal and, indeed, trustworthy."

Within a moment I became one with the light and then felt the heaviness of my body once more. I was me again. I shook my head and rubbed my eyes and waited for the numbness to leave my lower body. "God, sometimes this is like the twilight zone for me." I focused my eyes on Jeff. "Are you all right?"

Jeff came over to sit on the floor in front of me and began massaging my numb feet. His eyes were red and his face was flushed. "JZ, so much has happened in the last few days . . . and, well, I sent the Ram a thought that I needed to talk to him. I told him how I felt about myself as a man."

"Yes?" In my fuzzy state, I realized that whatever he was trying to say, he was having difficulty expressing it.

"I told him about the two relationships I had—or almost had—and how they didn't work out for me."

I interrupted. "Who hasn't had that, Jeff? I couldn't begin to tell you all the relationships that didn't work out for me. And the reason they all failed was because I thought so little of myself." He nodded, but his mind was racing ahead of me. "But don't worry, we're all searching for that perfect someone. I think when that happens, it must unify you with God. I mean, there isn't much missing at that point. You'll find the right person, Jeff. Just be patient. Don't be so hard on yourself."

Jeff hung his head as he answered me. "But the Ram told me a story. In this story I was his 'robesman' or something like that. I can't remember exactly, but I was in charge of his robes. Then he said that I made a robe for his daughter who was to be married."

"So he told you about another lifetime? That's wonderful. And did he tell you her name? His daughter, that is?"

"Yes, he said her name was Ramaya."

I was stunned. "Ramaya? That was me."

"I know. I was the one who ended up taking care of you. We were really in love. So I've loved you for a long time, then."

I raised my eyebrows but said nothing. Jeff continued,

"And he told me to be really honest with you about everything."

"Yes, so?"

"Well, I'm your, uh, Ramtha told me that we were soulmates."

"Soulmates?" I wasn't sure exactly what he was getting at.

"He said a great adventure lies beyond that door for us—"

I interrupted. "I don't think that's true. It would all be much easier—"

He interrupted *me,* the heat of urgency in his voice. "Ramtha says that soulmates reflect everything in each other. They are the duality that represent the whole of God. I mean, everything: the securities and the insecurities, the likes and dislikes. Through mirroring, each one owns what the other lacks. Do you suppose that's what's really going on?"

I began to shift in my seat, disturbed by the possibility that what he was saying might be true. "You mean . . . you and I might be having the same problems?"

"Yes. Did you ask God to take away your feelings about me, JZ?"

I frowned. "Yes, I did, and it worked. I needed it to work, and it has."

"But it hasn't worked. You did that because you didn't want to be hurt."

"That's right," I snapped. "You have no idea what a fool I felt like. I never want to feel that dumb again. I felt like some mental tramp."

"But I'm telling you that I did it on purpose."

"What, made me feel like a mental tramp?" I huffed. "No, dear, I did that little number on myself."

"No, I mean I rejected you on purpose. JZ, please, don't let it be too late. I think both of us have some things to work out, but I really want to try."

At that moment someone knocked on the door.

"Who's there?" Jeff asked.

"It's me, man," Joe answered. "C'mon, we've got to pack."

Jeff looked back up at me. I wet my lips and said, "You'd better go, Jeff. Why don't you look up one of your old girl-friends? Maybe give yourself a chance. And Jeff, have a happy Christmas."

"I will. But will you give yourself a chance, too?" he asked.

I just stared at him vacantly. Then he bent over and sweetly kissed my cheek. After he left, I sat there caught up in a maze of thoughts, tenderly holding my cheek where he had kissed it.

Christmas Day was delightful. Jeremy, the boys, and I had a wonderful time opening up the lavishly decorated presents. I had baked lots of Christmas cookies, made fudge and divinity, and prepared trays filled with holiday food and plenty of eggnog. I realized how superficial the scene I'd created was, but I didn't want to stop laughing, eating, and playing with my family. At the end of the day we all sang Christmas carols as I picked the tunes out on the piano.

I couldn't help thinking back on all the emotional highs and lows I had experienced throughout 1980, and on the exhausting Dialogues that had taken me around the country: 152 days of channeling. Those were days spent out of my body, days that I did not live. Gone in 1980. I sighed, knowing that this festive season signaled the end of one adventure and the beginning of another. Forever I would remember with fondness this last Christmas in the great white structure.

Before bed, as I was brushing my hair, the telephone rang.

"Hello? Yes, hello, Jeff. Okay, we'll go looking when you get back. I'm glad you decided to come back. Merry Christmas to you, too. Tell Joe hello from us. See you next week." I hung up.

The day after New Year's, Jeremy went duck hunting and took the boys with him. I methodically took down all of the Christmas decorations and began to pack them up. I left the tree until Jeremy returned to help me. Then I put on my red wool coat, plaid scarf, and loafers and took a walk in the brisk January air.

I walked down the dirt road and then off into the nearby woods. Even though most of the dogwoods looked bare and stark, upon closer examination I found tiny buds forming all over them. The same was true with the pussy willows. Spring was beginning in the midst of winter. I walked farther upon the silent floor of decaying leaves, brown needles, and broken rain-soaked branches. There were small patches of snow that had frozen at the trunks of trees, and even in the frozen water spring growth was emerging.

I came upon a mossy log and sat down awhile, observing the sleeping life of this tiny forest. I remembered its lush greenery in spring, the brilliance of its wild flowers in summer, and was reminded of the miracle of nature. On the surface, all appeared dead. Stark black branches quivering in the wind. The fallen leaves of spring and summer fading from yellow, to scarlet, to ocher. Flowers long wilted by frosty mornings and icy nights. But by the soft pink buds on the trees, the endless invisible seeds fallen from the summer flowers, I knew that nature was preparing to renew itself. Nothing ever really died; it simply was born, lived, and changed for the next life cycle. Each spring the tree grows greater. That is nature, and nature is, after all, the creation of God, just as man is. And is man truly less than the trees, the flowers, and the seasons?

I wanted to grow into all that was my destiny, like the great oak tree becoming grander with each season. It seemed to me that man is like a sapling in many ways, struggling to grow in darkness, only to die because the darkness in which he lives is the darkness of superstition, ignorance, and intolerance. Too many never find the sweet warm light that engenders life. A bluejay shot like an arrow in front of me, landing on a branch nearby. It began to squawk at me, almost challenging my simple understanding. I smiled at him and soon he began to preen and groom his jewellike feathers. Ramtha had said that the Kingdom of Heaven and God was within. Jesus taught the same truth. To know the right path was to listen to the voice within. That was the power, the sap of the great oak. To deny the inner truth was to be as a sapling in utter darkness, where hideous, wretched, and vile torments lurked. I shook my head. No, I must do what feels right to me to do.

I closed my eyes and began to whisper softly, "Beloved Father that is within, I desire to be myself, to become all that I can become, in the light and love that is you. God, I love you and I love the Christ within me. I desire to live my life that that love may shine forth. Father, I ask only that you guide me, teach me truth through my life, show me the doors, and give me the strength to go through them. Teach me love and forgiveness, but most important, teach me understanding. Father, give me the courage to be courageous. Lead me away from hypocrisy to the love of God within. So be it!"

Jeff and Joe arrived back in Washington and immediately moved into a wonderful little house on the water. As their first guests, they invited the entire family to dinner, but Jeremy and the boys had already made other plans so I went by myself.

The winding country road offered a beautiful vista. The cold silver moon was already high in the sky, while the January sun, sinking in the west, appeared more like a fat harvest moon. The house was a quaint two-story that shimmered with fresh umber paint and yellow gloss trim. Jeff and his dog, Jeremiah, greeted me at the front door.

"You look beautiful . . . thanks for coming," Jeff said as he showed me into the kitchen, where he turned the pork chops. "How's Jeremy?"

I sat down at the small table, elegantly set for two with matching crockery and a vase sporting some greenery. "Oh, he's busy preparing for hunting season, and the boys are staying the night with some friends of theirs."

Jeff just nodded in his usual gentle manner.

"Smells good. What-all have you prepared, slaving over the old hot stove?"

"I'm trying pork chops and some mashed potatoes and I bought some fresh rolls. I'm not a vegetable eater, mostly meat an' potatoes. Can I offer you some milk, beer, or a Coke?"

"How about a glass of ice water?"

As he got out the ice tray and began to dislodge the cubes, he noticed I was looking around. "Joe is out with his new girlfriend."

"Oh, is it serious?"

"Who knows?" He continued to prepare the meal. "Have you talked to Ramtha lately?"

"Not really. I think he's letting me realize some things on my own." I sighed. I was becoming more nervous by the moment and didn't really know why.

Jeff turned the pork chops over, then turned the heat down to simmer, covered them, and said, "This needs another half an hour. Would you like a glass of wine?"

I quickly answered, "No, thank you . . . really, the water is fine."

Then Jeff turned on the stereo. "Maybe we'll have some music."

"Moon River" began to play, and Jeff walked over to me. "I'm as nervous as you are . . . but would you like to dance?"

I stared at him for a moment, not knowing what to say. Then I started to laugh. "Okay, why not? I haven't danced in . . . oh, I don't remember how long it's been."

Jeff slowly put out his arms. I shyly walked into them. As soon as our bodies touched, I felt the pounding of his heart in my chest. I couldn't speak. A swarm of feeling came over me. I closed my eyes as Jeff raised his hand and cupped my chin. It sent shivers through my body.

"Are you cold?" he whispered.

"Uh . . . no . . . probably just ticklish," I mumbled.

"What do you think?"

I took a deep breath and tried to focus. "I'm avoiding thinking. I just want to *be*. And that's nice."

He pulled me closer and whispered, "Me too."

The music was soothing and sweet. Silently, I thought about *my* "huckleberry friend," this beautiful simple man of elegance and grace, whose politeness and kind consideration was a natural presence within him. How different he was from anyone I had ever met. "Jeff, do you think we know too much about one another?"

He gently squeezed me. "Yes, but not enough about ourselves. Thanks again for coming, JZ."

I don't know why, but I started to cry. I gently wiped away the tears with the sides of my hands. I was feeling foolish, with a deep sorrow and a great passion at the same moment.

"Hush . . . it's all right," he whispered. I was silent, but within me a fire began to rage toward him, like hunger . . . need. I held to Jeff tightly. He pulled away and kissed me on my forehead, and then, for the first time, he very gently gave me a kiss of love. I kissed him back.

Quietly, Jeff opened the sliding glass door to the patio. The wind ruffled his black hair and the room filled with the salty scent of the sea. He led me to the couch and we sat down. The fire crackled and hissed as its light danced across his bronze face, flickering in his eyes. Shadows deepened in his cheekbones and light glistened on his lips. He caressed and kissed my neck and my mouth with the power of a gentle lover.

"I'm happy to be here in your arms. I love you, Jeffrey . . . forever and ever."

"I love you, JZ, my precious and dear soulmate."

The moments of that evening were pure in a heartfelt innocence of true love. For hours we whispered, laughed, touched, kissed, and embraced in the flood of moonlight before a dancing fire, but we did not make love. Neither of us was ready to seal this love, no matter how deep and pure our feelings for one another were. There was the honor of Jeremy and the boys to consider. But we came to an understanding . . . that we did belong together. No matter the consequences, I would go with Jeff for that was where my complete happiness lay. I could no longer live a lie.

Jeremy was sitting on the bed playing with a deck of cards when I slowly walked into the bedroom. He didn't look up as he asked, "Well, can he cook, too?"

I stared at him for a moment. "Yes, Jeremy, he can cook."

Still without looking up, he went on, "So, Zebra, is there anything you want to tell me?"

I felt a sense of calm come over me. My thoughts returned to the little forest and the great oak tree. I quietly sat
on the edge of the bed. "Jeremy, I've thought more about
you these past few days than perhaps the whole time we
have been married. I've thought about your honesty and
your even manner. I admire and respect those qualities and
think you deserve honesty from me in return. I've agonized
over what I'm going to tell you, and the best way is just to
come out with it. I'm in love with Jeff Knight."

The silence hung thickly in the room, but Jeremy didn't
look up at me or even stop playing cards. "The cowboy? The
poor cowboy?" He reached up to smoothe his mustache.
"Tell me, Zebra, how do you know you are?" His voice was
smoothed anger.

"I can't explain it. I feel something for Jeff that I have
never felt before. I only know that I love him . . . deeply."

Jeremy clenched his jaw and his face reddened, but still
he controlled his anger. "Well, Zebra, that's just fine, just
fine. I can tell you, I don't know what I did to the Ram, but
he sure pulled everything out from under me." He pursed
his lips and began to twist the corner of his mustache.

"Jeremy, it's difficult to explain all this to you, but it
seems my whole life has been suffused with a sense of guilt
and lack of self-importance. I always needed to make others
happy. Jeremy, I never loved or respected who I was. And
the most difficult thing I've had to deal with through all this
. . . this awakening . . . has been my need not to hurt you.
You have been so good to me. You have helped make my
dreams possible. But I knew it would be worse to continue,
to forget about my feelings and stay with you out of loyalty
because you were good to me. You would never be happy
like that. You don't deserve that.

"Jeremy, one thing that remains steadfast within me is
my love for you. Maybe that sounds stupid, but nonetheless
it remains. You know, I kept wishing these past months that
I could just come to you as a friend and say, 'Help me, let
us understand each other.' But I never felt I could. I was too
busy feeling guilty and hating myself, and you were always
too busy to hear me."

It was too much. Jeremy's anger and loathing for me exploded. He threw the cards across the room and sat up, clenching his fist. "I wonder if the Ram would say it's the good guys who come in last!" He raised his voice through clenched teeth. "How can this dirty clodhopper cowboy come into my house and take my whole life away from me? What the hell does he have that I don't? Does he fuck good or something?"

My face burned, but a clear peace became steadfast within me. I answered softly, "Jeremy, we have done nothing. We haven't made love. Tonight was the first time I ever kissed him. We couldn't do that behind your back. Jeremy, he loves me. *Me.* Not the Ram, *me.* He's simple, like I am."

Jeremy's face contorted in disbelief. "You're simple!"

"Yes, I'm very simple. Most of the time I felt you were disappointed by my simplicity. You intimidated me by correcting me like a schoolteacher. You never wanting me to talk at the Dialogues because you thought no one wanted to hear me, so you sat there hiding your embarrassment behind a book. But when I'm around Jeff, *I* am the important one, not Ramtha. I need to be allowed to bloom, Jeremy . . . to know who I am. So many times I felt I could have helped you, but you wouldn't listen to me, only to the Ram. You know, Jeremy, I have a lot to say because I have learned a lot. I have things to contribute. But they were never good enough for you."

"Go, Zebra. I don't need to hear anymore. Go live with him. But I'll tell you something right now—you'll be back, and I'll be waiting. You'll be back."

I know some divorced people eventually become closest friends, but somewhere within me I knew that Jeremy and I would never be close again. Yet for all the upheaval that has occurred in our lives, one feeling has remained: I will always admire, respect, and love Jeremy. Without him, none of my dreams would have been realized. I will miss him.

In the days that followed, I moved a few of my things over to Jeff's house. I explained honestly to Brandy and Chris what had happened and offered them the choice of going with me or staying. Chris elected to go, but Brandy, who had felt the greatest alienation from Jeremy, decided to stay with him. I was moved to tears when he said to me, "Jeremy doesn't have anybody. I feel sorry for him, Mom. I want to stay with him." Well, I cried for days, but Brandy showed me something about himself that I had not truly seen before. He possessed great compassion and love.

I anguished over the separation of my children and felt pangs of deep guilt. In the midst of this turmoil, my dear friend, Anne-Marie Bennstrom, insisted that Jeff and I spend a few days with her in Calabasas, California. Although I had known Anne-Marie only a year, our friendship was so immediate and close that she was more like a sister to me than a friend. Her delightful home sat on top of a mountain and was, in fact, a splendid retreat for the weary at heart. Every room was fragrant with flowers and alive with the sounds of white doves cooing, the squawking of parrots from her aviary, the ringing of phones and the voice of Anne-Marie talking Swedish peppered with exclamations of "by golly," "yah," and "baby." There I found some peace in the genuine warmth of Anne-Marie, a bubbly but wise Swede with lively sky blue eyes that could flash mischievous or pierce with electrifying thoughtfulness. With her tousled blond hair, bronze skin, and sparkling white teeth, Anne-Marie was my perfect counterpart. Silly, secretive, giggling, she gave me pointers on improving my figure while I fixed her hair. She with her intelligent wit and knowingness, me with my simplicity and naiveté. She would sleep shamelessly without any clothes, while I always dressed fully for bed. One moment Anne-Marie could be intensely discussing God's great capacity to know Himself, and the next moment, finding humor in her own words, burst into uncontrolled laughter. I loved her and felt that she utterly understood who I was.

During those days, I needed to be alone. Sorrowful emotions were surfacing that even my dear Jeff could not soothe. In the quiet times, I went off walking by myself. I wrestled with my guilt, my inadequacies, my feelings of worthlessness. Everything in my life had been a redundant melodrama of denying myself what I deserved. Even now, with the dissolution of my marriage and the supposed happiness to be found with Jeff, I would sit and look at him, seemingly my soulmate, and wonder what he really saw in me. That old feeling, "I'm not worth being the Annual Queen," came flooding back.

Then there was Ramtha. I wondered, too, why he had chosen me. Ramtha embodied all power, grace, knowing-ness, and God manifest, while I, on the other hand, was steeped in rash self-pity, uncertainty, and confusion. How could I possibly represent this truth in my own life? What was wrong? Where was the bliss I yearned for and had thought I would find with Jeff? Why still, after all the changes, did I not inherit the light that I so thirsted for?

I found that I was avoiding Jeff and Anne-Marie because I was feeling such shame and guilt. I was afraid that my presence would make them depressed. I even felt guilty for *that*. All those feelings that I had felt all my life were sticking in my throat, suffocating me, like some gentle brook clogged with pockets of decaying leaves, broken branches, and thick brown mud. Anne-Marie, in her infinite wisdom, allowed me the comfort of silence to reckon with my feelings.

Finally, one evening, unable to fall asleep, I turned over and stared at the back of my sleeping Jeff's head. Then I gazed at the curtainless window by the bed. The full silver moon was high, bathing everything below in its elfin light. It was peaceful and inviting, so I got up and crawled out the window and seated myself there on the rooftop. I gazed up to the silent silvery moon and watched a gray cloud pass in front of the great light, inheriting a silver lining. What was that cliché my mom used to say? "Behind every dark cloud there is a silver lining." I watched the flashing stars and planets that hung suspended in a midnight forever. It was so orderly, so grand, so quiet. A gentle wind caressed my face with fresh scents of sage and salt water, and nocturnal flowers. It rustled my hair in my eyes, fingering strands that locked into my lashes and into my mouth. I shivered slightly and pulled my gown down, tucking it under my feet, then wrapped my arms tighter about me. The silence was interrupted first by the far-off sound of a bird, then by a soft muffled sound behind me.

I turned around to see my dear Anne-Marie, dressed in her pink flannel gown, crawling out her window. I appreciated her keen sense of awareness, for I had not made a sound. She had just known that I was there. The moon glistened luxuriantly off her beautiful hair. She was like some wise little mouse who decided to come out and share the moon with me. We sat in complete silence together. Silence offers the hope that feeble words cannot. As I began to sob with quivering emotion—the kind that comes from a far distant place in the soul—her gentle hand softly patted my shoulder in a gesture of complete understanding.

There are those rare individuals that walk quietly upon the earth, as if they were the haunts of nature, who by their innocence possess a knowledge that with a touch heals the mangled frailties of the unenlightened. Such was Anne-Marie. Her gentle sweet voice uttered quietly the healing words, "It is all right to feel these things, for by allowing yourself to do so, they give you up forever." I turned and looked into her misty wise eyes that danced fairylike in the moonlight. As the wind blew her hair across her face, I realized that I could only find freedom from my despair by releasing it. No one in my life had ever told me it was all right to hurt, to feel guilt, pain, unworthiness, and self-hatred. Now I had that permission—to feel them and to release them.

The release came like the sudden gushing forth of a gentle stream suddenly flowing forth that had been clogged by all my inadequacies. In the clarity of the pure water that broke free, it was as if I now could flow to the ocean . . . a coming home to me. I understood for the first time all that the Ram had taught me. Now, I was free for the grand adventure called "life" that Ramtha had been talking about.

What the man in the moon saw those next few moments were two tiny figures, dwarfed by the vastness of forever, embracing in cascades of delightful and delicious laughter, then making their way back through the windows to their soft, warm beds. My Jeffrey's peaceful slumber had not been disturbed by my rooftop enlightenment. I snuggled close to him, kissed his shoulder, and felt sublime peace. As my eyes began to close, I wondered what adventures awaited us somewhere in the future. I considered this with some anxiety. Then, as I pondered, I was suddenly exhilarated and mysteriously consoled. "Do not worry," I said, and wondered at my own words. "All will be well."

SELECTED READING

Harding, Khit. *Becoming: A Master's Manual.* Adams Publishing Company, 1986.

Mahr, Douglas James. *Voyage to the New World.* Masterworks, Inc. Publishers, 1985.

Ramtha. *I Am Ramtha.* Beyond Words Publishing, 1986.

Weinberg, Steven Lee, Ph.D. *Ramtha.* Sovereignty Press Inc. 1986.